Latin American Multicultural Movements

LATIN AMERICA'S MULTICULTURAL MOVEMENTS

THE STRUGGLE BETWEEN COMMUNITARIANISM, AUTONOMY, AND HUMAN RIGHTS

Edited by
Todd A. Eisenstadt
Michael S. Danielson
Moisés Jaime Bailón Corres
and
Carlos Sorroza Polo

OXFORD
UNIVERSITY PRESS

Oxford University Press is a department of the University of Oxford.
It furthers the University's objective of excellence in research, scholarship,
and education by publishing worldwide.

Oxford   New York
Auckland   Cape Town   Dar es Salaam   Hong Kong   Karachi
Kuala Lumpur   Madrid   Melbourne   Mexico City   Nairobi
New Delhi   Shanghai   Taipei   Toronto

With offices in
Argentina   Austria   Brazil   Chile   Czech Republic   France   Greece
Guatemala   Hungary   Italy   Japan   Poland   Portugal   Singapore
South Korea   Switzerland   Thailand   Turkey   Ukraine   Vietnam

Oxford is a registered trademark of Oxford University Press
in the UK and certain other countries.

Published in the United States of America by
Oxford University Press
198 Madison Avenue, New York, NY 10016

© Oxford University Press 2013

All rights reserved. No part of this publication may be reproduced, stored in a
retrieval system, or transmitted, in any form or by any means, without the prior
permission in writing of Oxford University Press, or as expressly permitted by law,
by license, or under terms agreed with the appropriate reproduction rights organization.
Inquiries concerning reproduction outside the scope of the above should be sent to the
Rights Department, Oxford University Press, at the address above.

You must not circulate this work in any other form
and you must impose this same condition on any acquirer.

Library of Congress Cataloging-in-Publication Data
Latin America's multicultural movements : the struggle between communitarianism, autonomy,
and human rights / edited by Todd A. Eisenstadt [et al.].
  p. cm.
ISBN 978–0–19–993626–7 (hardcover : alk. paper)—ISBN 978–0–19–993628–1 (pbk. : alk. paper)
1. Social movements—Latin America.   2. Multiculturalism—Political aspects—Latin
America.   3. Communitarianism—Latin America.   4. Human rights—Latin
America.   I. Eisenstadt, Todd A.
HN110.5.A8L399 2013
323.098—dc23
2012018573

ISBN 978–0–19–993626–7
ISBN 978–0–19–993628–1

9 8 7 6 5 4 3 2 1
Printed in the United States of America
on acid-free paper

Contents

vii Acknowledgments
ix   Editors
xi   Contributors

Part One Multicultural Rights Recognition in Theory and in Practice

3   Introduction: Reconciling Liberal Pluralism and Group Rights: A Comparative Perspective on Oaxaca, Mexico's, Experiment in Multiculturalism
    Todd A. Eisenstadt

18 1. Ambivalent Multiculturalisms: Perversity, Futility, and Jeopardy in Latin America
    José Antonio Lucero

40 2. Constitutional Multiculturalism in Chiapas: Hollow Reforms That Nullify Autonomy Rights
    Araceli Burguete Cal y Mayor (translated by Andrew McKelvey)

Part Two Multicultural and Autonomy Movements in the Andes

67 3. Uses of Autonomy: The Evolution of Multicultural Discourse in Bolivian Politics
    Erik Cooke

88 4. Bolivia's New Multicultural Constitution: The 2009 Constitution in Historical and Comparative Perspective
    Miguel Centellas

111 5. The Backlash against Indigenous Rights in Ecuador's Citizen's Revolution
    Carmen Martínez Novo

Part Three Multicultural and Autonomy Movements in Oaxaca, Mexico

135 6. What We Need Are New Customs: Multiculturality, Autonomy, and Citizenship in Mexico and the Lessons of Oaxaca
    Víctor Leonel Juan Martínez (translated by Michael S. Danielson)

169   7. Political Subsystems in Oaxaca's *Usos y Costumbres* Municipalities: A Typology Based on the Civil-Religious Service Background of Mayors
      Carlos Sorroza Polo and Michael S. Danielson (translated by Andrew McKelvy)

192   8. Community Strength and Customary Law: Explaining Migrant Participation in Indigenous Oaxaca
      Michael S. Danielson

Part Four The State and Multicultural Rights: Enabler or Menace?

217   9. Multicultural Reforms for Mexico's "Tranquil" Indians in Yucatán
      Shannan Mattiace

246   Conclusion: Balancing Tensions between Communitarian and Individual Rights and the Challenges They Present for Multicultural States
      Willibald Sonnleitner and Todd A. Eisenstadt

271   Index

Acknowledgments

We have incurred many debts in writing and editing this book, and wish to at least acknowledge the most obvious ones here. Jennifer Yelle ably commented, proofread, and helped translate several of the chapters for this volume. José V. Casanova, Seda Demiralp, Sarah Fischer, Cipriano Flores Cruz, Prerna Singh, and Christopher Soper also presented papers at the 2009 American University conference, Reconciling Liberal Pluralism and Group Rights: Oaxaca, Mexico's Multicultural Experiment in Comparative Perspective, which helped launch this volume. Emilie E. Joly, Saul Newman, Diane Singerman, and Miguel Centellas (also a contributor) commented on papers at that conference, and Jenna Bramble helped organize it. Andrew McKelvy translated several chapters, and Nicole Siegel helped immensely in communications with chapter authors regarding a range of issues as the book was taking form. Data on Oaxaca, Mexico, customary law municipalities was collected with the assistance of Cipriano Flores Cruz and María de los Ángeles Morales, and the database was constructed by Martina Reyes Rámirez. Special thanks also go to Shannan Mattiace and Tony Lucero, for their comments on several chapters.

Other colleagues who have been extremely generous in reading, commenting, and otherwise encouraging this work include Diego Ayo, Max Cameron, Roderic Camp, Matthew Cleary, Federico Estévez, Marco Estrada Saavedra, David FitzGerald, Manuel Garza, Jorge Hernández-Diaz, Jonathan Hiskey, Eric Hershberg, Maria Inclán, Rene Kuppe, Jason Lakin, Ruth Lane, William LeoGrande, Carl LeVan, Soledad Loaeza, Raúl Madrid, Lourdes Morales, David Recondo, Viridiana Rios, Guillermo Trejo, the late Donna Lee Van Cott, Miguel Angel Vásquez de la Rosa, Gloria Zafra, and several anonymous reviewers. Angela Chnapko at Oxford University Press has been an outstanding editor, guiding the project capably from start to finish. We thank project manager Maureen Cirnitski of Newgen, and copy editor extraordinaire Karen Fisher. We thank Manny Sanchez and Jennifer Sisane for their patience and good humor in administering the U.S. Agency for International Development (USAID) and Higher Education in Development (HED) grant that funded the project.

Bailón Córres, Danielson, Eisenstadt, and Sorroza ran a successful USAID-HED project in Oaxaca, which, in addition to the provision of fellowships, training, and research, allowed us to learn a lot in a limited period of time. Our colleagues at UABJO, including Manuel Garza and Víctor Leonel Juan Martínez and coeditors Bailón Corres and Sorroza Polo, were exemplary partners from the moment we commenced the project, even when codirector Bailón Corres's UABJO office was inaccessible because of the 2006 teachers' protest in Oaxaca. Katya Salazar and her colleagues at the Due Process of Law Foundation also made invaluable contributions to the success of the project and this volume. In the summer of 2010, several researchers at the Latin American Faculty for the Social Sciences received Eisenstadt in Quito, Ecuador, helping him broaden his comparative horizons to encompass Andean cases also, at just the right moment. Thanks in particular to Eduardo Kingman, Santiago Basabe, Fernando García, Mark Thurber, Luis Verdesoto, and Werner Vásquez. This perspective was opened even wider at the University of Nairobi in the summer of 2011, where Eisenstadt learned about African cases with the support of several scholars including Karuti Kanyaga and Carl LeVan.

At American University, former School of Public Affairs dean William LeoGrande and associate deans Meg Weekes and Gamze Zeytinci supported this project with faculty improvement grants, as did dean of academic affairs Phyllis Peres and vice provost for research Jonathan Tubman. Rachel Pentlarge of the American University Office of Sponsored Programs provided much-needed administrative support, always coupled with her unique charm and a genuine interest in the subject matter of the project. Director Eric Hershberg of the Center for Latin American and Latino Studies offered encouragement and contacts hemisphere-wide that helped enhance our comparative perspective.

Finally, Eisenstadt thanks his wife, Mireya Solis, and his daughters Natalia and Paola Eisenstadt, who help him keep perspective. Gazing into Mireya's deep eyes, hearing Natalia's keen and caustic wit and observations, and experiencing Paola's still-innocent smiles and constant but smart questions are what make it all worthwhile. Danielson thanks his parents, Steve and Gwen Danielson, for instilling in him a love of ideas and providing him with the opportunity to pursue them, and his wife, Erica Williams, whose good humor, moral conviction, and razor-sharp intellect (and editing pen) help to make him a better scholar and person.

Todd A. Eisenstadt and Michael S. Danielson
Washington, DC, April 2012

Editors

Todd A. Eisenstadt is professor and former chair of the Government Department at American University. He is author of *Politics, Identity and Mexico's Indigenous Rights Movements* (Cambridge University Press, 2011), which received the 2012 Van Cott Prize from the Latin American Studies Association for best book in the Latin American Political Institutions category. With Moisés Jaime Bailón Corres and Michael S. Danielson, he served as principal researcher under the U.S. Agency for International Development (USAID) Higher Education and Development Program grant "Uniting Law and Society in Oaxaca, Mexico: A Research and Teaching Program," which provided for the conference leading to this book. He is also the author of *Courting Democracy in Mexico: Party Strategies and Electoral Institutions* (Cambridge University Press, 2004), and has published articles in journals including *Democratization, Party Politics*, and the *Latin American Research Review* as well as in *Comparative Political Studies* and *Latin American Politics and Society*, where he serves on the editorial boards. His research has been funded by the Ford and Mellon foundations, USAID, the Fulbright Commission, and the National Security Education Program, and he has been a visiting scholar at Harvard University, El Colegio de México, and the University of California, San Diego. A former print journalist (award-winning night police-beat reporter for the *Nashville Tennessean*) and Capitol Hill staffer, he has consulted on issues of representation and inclusion for USAID and the Organization of American States. Eisenstadt's 1998 doctorate in political science is from the University of California, San Diego.

Michael S. Danielson is a comparative politics PhD candidate at American University. He is author of "Walking Together, but in Which Direction? Gender Discrimination and Multicultural Practices in Oaxaca, Mexico" (with Todd A. Eisenstadt, *Politics and Gender*, 2009), "All Immigration Politics Is Local: The Day Labor Ordinance in Vista, California," in Monica W. Varsanyi, ed., *Taking Local Control: Immigration Policy Activism in U.S. Cities and States* (Stanford University Press, 2010), and "Uruguay and Paraguay: An Arduous Transition," with Diego Abente Brun in Jan Knippers Black, ed., *Latin America: Its Problems and Its Promise* (Westview Press, 2011). Danielson's dissertation, "Politics at Home Abroad: Mexican Migrants as Transnational Actors in Their Home Towns" has been supported by Fulbright, Gill Family Foundation, and National Science Foundation awards and by the School of Public Affairs at American University. He holds an MA in international policy studies from the Monterey Institute of International Studies and Spanish and philosophy degrees from Santa Clara University.

Moisés Jaime Bailón Corres holds a degree in sociology from the Benito Juárez Autonomous University of Oaxaca (UABJO) and received his doctorate in social sciences from the Colegio de México. He has researched and taught at UABJO, at the Mora Institute in Mexico City, and in the United States; is a member of Mexico's National System of Researchers; and collaborates with the National Center on Human Rights. Dr. Bailón is the author or coauthor of dozens of books, chapters, and articles including *Pueblos indios, élites y territorios*, 1999; *Derechos humanos y derechos indígenas en el orden jurídico federal mexicano*, 2003; *La masacre de Agua Fría, Oaxaca*, 2004; *El gobernador y los derechos de los pueblos indios: Benito Juárez en Oaxaca*, 2007; and *Derechos indígenas en las entidades federativas*, 2008. As a public servant, he has been an advisor to the controller general of Oaxaca, in the Secretariat of Government of the Republic, and a member of the Oaxaca State Congress from 1995 to 1998. As a state congressman, he served as president of the Commission on Indigenous Affairs.

Carlos Sorroza Polo holds a sociology degree from Benito Juárez Autonomous University of Oaxaca (UABJO) and a master's in political science from the Latin American Faculty of the Social Sciences in Mexico and is a doctoral candidate in economics at the National Autonomous University of Mexico. He was formerly the director and is currently a research professor at the Institute of Sociological Research of UABJO. Professor Sorroza is currently conducting field research for the project "The Region as a Space of Culture, Government, and Development in Oaxaca." His recent publications include "Gabino Cué Monteagudo: Ganó el gobierno y perdió la posibilidad del cambio social" (Raúl Hernández Reyes, ed., 2011); "La crisis política en Oaxaca: Componentes, alcances y propuestas de salida," in *El Cotidiano* (2008); "Oaxaca: ¿Conflicto Político o Crisis de Sistema?" in *Educación, Sindicalismo y Gobernabilidad en Oaxaca* (Joel Vicente Cortés, ed., 2006); *Diagnóstico y opciones de desarrollo en la región Mixe* (with Yanga Villagómez, 2006); and "La sociología en la Universidad Autónoma Benito Juárez de Oaxaca: Las tareas pendientes," in *Testimonios del cincuentenario* (UABJO, 2005).

Contributors

Araceli Burguete Cal y Mayor is a researcher at the Centro de Investigaciones en Antropologia Social (CIESAS-Sureste) in San Cristobal de las Casas Chiapas, Mexico, where she teaches political anthropology. She is author and editor of many works on the role of indigenous groups and political parties in the democratization process in Chiapas, Mexico, including *Tejiendo historias: Tierra, género, y poder en Chiapas* (with Maya Lorena Pérez Ruiz, Instituto Nacional de Antropología e Historia, 2004), "The de Facto Autonomous Process: New Jurisdictions and Parallel Governments in Rebellion," in *Mayan Lives, Mayan Utopias: The Indigenous Peoples of Chiapas and the Zapatista Rebellion* (edited by Rus, Hernandez Castillo, and Mattiace), and *Agua que nace y muere—Sistemas normativos indígenas y disputas por el agua en Chamula y Zinacantán* (UNAM, 2000). She is coeditor (with Xochitl Leyva Solano) of *La remunicipalización de Chiapas: Lo político y la política en tiempos de contrainsurgencia* (CIESAS/Miguel Angel Porrúa, 2007) and *Gobernar (en) la diversidad en tiempos de multiculturalismo: Experiencias indígenas desde América Latina* (with Leyva and Speed, CIESAS, 2008). Her current project, "Local Power and Parallel Governments: Judicial-Political Changes and Remunicipalization in the Chiapas Highlands," seeks to understand how the armed conflict of the 1990s and recent legal reforms have impacted the territorial and political structures of Chenalho and Larrainzar municipalities.

Miguel Centellas received his PhD in political science from Western Michigan University in 2007 and has been a visiting assistant professor of political science since fall 2009 at the University of Mississippi. Dr. Centellas's work focuses on the Andes, with particular emphasis on contemporary Bolivian politics. At a broader level, his research seeks to understand how democratization reshapes political imaginaries and how formal institutional mechanisms (particularly electoral and party systems) channel those processes. Dr. Centellas has conducted extensive fieldwork in Bolivia (where he was a Fulbright scholar) and is currently working on a National Science Foundation–funded collaborative project looking at the effects of electoral system reform in Latin America, Europe, and Asia. His articles on Bolivian politics have appeared in the *Latin Americanist, Latin American Perspectives, Journal of Politics in Latin America,* and *Americas Quarterly.*

Erik Cooke teaches philosophy of human rights and democracy at American University's College of Arts and Sciences (Philosophy and Religion Department).

His research focuses on the politics of indigenous social movements and parties in Bolivia and Ecuador, as well as U.S. media studies. Under the sponsorship of the School of Public Affairs, he conducted fieldwork in La Paz on Bolivia's 2006–2007 Constituent Assembly. He has long worked in international and domestic advocacy and education and service organizations, and served several years in the U.S. Senate and state and local politics.

Víctor Leonel Juan Martínez is a lawyer and journalist, holds a doctorate in sociology from the Metropolitan Autonomous University, and is a researcher at the Benito Juárez Autonomous University of Oaxaca. In 2011 Juan Martínez was elected as an ombudsman to Oaxaca's State Electoral Institute. Associate editor of Oaxaca's municipal politics magazine *En Marcha*, Juan Martínez has written dozens of academic works on customary law, local elections, and governance in Oaxaca, including *Dilemas de la Institución Municipal—Una Incursión en la Experiencia Oaxaqueña* (Miguel Ángel Porrúa Publishers, 2007, with Jorge Hernández-Díaz) and several other books.

José Antonio Lucero is an associate professor in the Henry M. Jackson School of International Studies at the University of Washington in Seattle. His research on indigenous politics, social movements, and representation in Ecuador, Bolivia, and Peru has been supported by grants from the National Science Foundation, the Fulbright Institute of International Education, the MacArthur Foundation, the Ford Foundation, and the Woodrow Wilson International Center for Scholars. His work on social movement theory and indigenous politics has been published in the *Journal of Democracy, Comparative Politics, Latin American Perspectives, Latin American Research Review, Latin American and Caribbean Ethnic Studies*, and several edited volumes. Professor Lucero's book on indigenous movements, *Struggles of Voice: The Politics of Indigenous Representation in the Andes*, was published in 2008 by the University of Pittsburgh Press. Lucero received his BA with honors in political science from Stanford University (1994), and a PhD in politics from Princeton University (2002).

Carmen Martínez Novo is associate professor of anthropology and director of the Latin American Studies Program at the University of Kentucky. Her areas of interest are indigenous identities and indigenism in Mexico and Ecuador. She is the author of *Who Defines Indigenous?* (Rutgers University Press, 2006) and the editor of *Repensando los movimientos indígenas* (FLACSO, 2009), as well as a number of articles and book chapters. She has been a visiting scholar at the Johns Hopkins University, Grinnell College, Universidad Iberoamericana in Mexico, Universidad Nacional in Colombia, and Universidad de Lleida in Spain. She has received grants from the Wenner-Gren Foundation for Anthropological Research and the Henry Luce Foundation through the Woodrow Wilson International Center for Scholars, among others.

Shannan Mattiace is an associate professor of political science at Allegheny College in Meadville, Pennsylvania, where she teaches courses in comparative and Latin American politics. She is currently working on two projects in Yucatán, Mexico:

paternalism and labor on early twentieth-century henequen haciendas in Yucatán (with Tomas Nonnenmacher) and Yucatecan migrant political organization. She has published two books on Chiapas, *To See with Two Eyes: Peasant Activism and Indian Autonomy in Chiapas, Mexico* and *Mayan Lives* and *Mayan Utopias: The Indigenous Peoples of Chiapas and the Zapatista Rebellion* (coedited with Jan Rus and Rosalva Aida Hernandez Castillo).

Willibald Sonnleitner is a professor and researcher at El Colegio de México (COLMEX), where he teaches political sociology. He served as coordinator of the French Center for Mexican and Central American Studies (CEMCA) in Guatemala and was professor and researcher at the Institute for High Studies of Latin America in Paris, France. He holds a master's degree from Sciences Po Paris and a doctorate from the University of the Sorbonne, and is an expert in processes of democratic transition in Latin America. He has published numerous articles and books, including *Democracia en tierras indígenas* (with Viqueira, COLMEX/CIESAS/IFE, 2000), *Voter dans les Amériques* (with Blanquer, Quanquin, and Zumello, Institut des Amériques/IHEAL, 2005), *Explorando los territorios del voto: Hacia un Atlas Electoral de Centroamérica* (CEMCA/BID/IHEAL, 2006), *Mutaciones de la Democracia: Tres décadas de cambio político en América Latina* (with S. Gómez-Tagle, COLMEX, 2012), and *Elecciones chiapanecas: Del antiguo régimen al desorden democrático* (COLMEX, 2012). His current research examines voting patterns and democratic participation in Mexico and Central America and is part of a broader comparative research project on Latin America's electoral geography.

PART ONE
MULTICULTURAL RIGHTS RECOGNITION IN THEORY AND IN PRACTICE

Introduction

Reconciling Liberal Pluralism and Group Rights: A Comparative Perspective on Oaxaca, Mexico's, Experiment in Multiculturalism

Todd A. Eisenstadt

Throughout the Americas, indigenous people have been arguing—with international validation—that they should be entitled, as "first peoples," to representation in local, national, and international fora in a capacity different from that of other civil society groups. In southern Mexico, calls for greater indigenous representation and participation in governance came forcefully in the 1990s at the time of the Zapatista indigenous uprising in Chiapas state and in neighboring Oaxaca. As stated by Adelfo Regino Montes (1996), an Oaxacan Mixe intellectual and collaborator in the Zapatistas' framing of their message, "It is important to recall that before the arrival of the Spanish the collectivities present in these lands were peoples, with their own culture and social, political, economic, and judicial institutions.... They believed, as some continue to affirm today, that these categories and concepts should impose themselves on the essence of things." His argument to the Foro Indígena Nacional (National Indigenous Forum), based on this strong concept of collective rights, was that "the recognition of our collective rights is necessary so that we can truly enjoy our individual rights" (Regino Montes, n.d.).

What was the result of these claims for indigenous representation at the national level, and for local indigenous participation via new forms of elections and governance? The more radical Zapatista movement in Chiapas has largely passed (although many citizens took from the rebellion renewed indigenous identities and symbolic membership in an ongoing "imaginary Zapatista" movement, and concrete results did occur—see Eisenstadt 2011, 129–156). But in more gradualist Oaxaca, where indigenous community autonomy was already de facto recognized, new forms of indigenous electoral participation and ideas of representation emerged. This introduction addresses trade-offs inherent in this new citizen involvement, which stimulates indigenous citizenship by encouraging participation on groups' own terms, but also sometimes precludes dissenters, entire minority groups, and other disenfranchised individuals from participating at all. Valuing participation by all (or at least all in the enfranchised groups) and recognizing no role for Burkean elite expertise whatsoever, customary law recognition in Oaxaca—and in other areas where it exists—has restored the institutions of native peoples to Regino's "essence of things." However, with regard to participation, they have created barriers to individuals and minority groups whom they exclude. And with regard to representation, they have implemented a philosophical position favoring loyalty and seniority at the expense of merit and technical expertise. This chapter discusses these choices and their implications, but first we consider what is meant by customary law and how these practices came about in the Mexican context.

Customary law-observing communities use a mix of Western and traditional electoral means: citizens elect federal and state authorities according to standard liberal electoral processes of secret ballot and universal suffrage, and they elect municipal authorities via indigenous customs (known in Spanish as *usos y costumbres* or UC). The definition of *usos y costumbres* practices is often debated. In Oaxaca, UC can refer to a range of practices for selecting leaders—from community-wide assemblies to appointing a council of elders to make decisions, from raising hands to support a candidate to drawing hash marks beneath a candidate's name. In general, voting under UC is done publicly and there is no guarantee of universal suffrage. Rather than rigidly defining UC practices and establishing a legal baseline for them at the moment of recognition, Mexican state authorities allowed Oaxacan legislators to designate UC municipalities and grant local citizens the right to elect leaders via the system of their choice.

Throughout indigenous Latin America, new types of representation are being adopted as several nations conduct constitutional assemblies and others create new forms of indigenous representation or finally accept old ones (see, e.g., chapters 1, 3, 4, and 5, this volume, on Bolivia and Ecuador). This trend was fueled in part by the development of indigenous movements in the region since the 1960s, the 1989 creation of the International Labor Organization's Proposition 169 (discussed extensively in chapter 2, this volume), which binds countries to international standards for recognizing indigenous rights, and in part by the 1992 quincentenary celebration of Columbus's voyage to the Western Hemisphere. Indigenous rights movements emerged across the continent, including Mexico's Zapatista Rebellion in 1994, the Pachakutik movement/party's success in Ecuador since 1996, and, most recently, the victory in 2005 of Evo Morales's Movement Toward Socialism in Bolivia. These movements have expressed themselves across a range of institutions of representation, from comprehensive recognition of local autonomy in Bolivia to judicial support for indigenous groups in Colombia, partial recognition, at least of electoral practices, in parts of Mexico, and the new UN Declaration of Rights of Indigenous Peoples approved by the General Assembly in 2008.

Hale (2002) has argued that multicultural rights recognition, even by some of Latin America's more conservative governments, has been accorded because rights recognition (without any implementing laws or commitment of resources) costs nothing and offers a gesture of solidarity to large blocks of indigenous voters. He argues that rights recognition "menaces" indigenous rights movements by driving them to complacently desist from further demands even though what they tend to receive from the states granting these rights is really nothing. Van Cott (2003), contrarily, argued that multiculturalism "from above," in the form of constitutional reforms undertaken in the 1990s in Colombia and Venezuela, did have genuine benefits for indigenous peoples, as well as offering political elites cover for neoliberal economic policies.

This issue of autonomy, and who autonomy benefits, is a central issue discussed in this volume by authors including Mattiace, Centellas, Lucero, Burguete Cal y Mayor, Cooke, and Juan Martínez in the chapters that follow. For example, Mattiace demonstrates the limits of autonomy from above in her discussion of the failures of indigenous autonomy mobilization in Yucatán, a heavily indigenous state that has failed to generate any demand "from below" for autonomy reforms (chapter 9). Centellas characterizes Bolivia's 2009 constitutional reforms, widely regarded as "from below," as from both above and below, as actual government policy remains highly centralized and hierarchical, despite the popular origins of much of the movement that President Morales has institutionalized.

In Mexico, as in Bolivia, perhaps, the inherent ambiguities surrounding the degree of autonomy of UC practices have led victims of unfavorable UC judgments to argue that customary law is so loosely defined that traditional-style chieftains are empowered to exercise a localized variant of arbitrary "top-down" rule under the guise of communitarian decision making. Moreover, UC elections have created a tension between individual and communitarian rights. A study of traditional leader selection practices in the original 412 UC municipalities (Ríos Contreras 2006, 36) revealed that 18 percent do not allow participation by women and 21 percent forbid the participation of citizens living outside of the *cabecera*, or municipal seat, where most decisions are made. The 2008 survey of Oaxaca Mexico Customary Law Municipalities (cited extensively in chapters 7 and 8) shows that discrimination remains as pervasive as it was found to be in 1995, with formal exclusion of women from voting in 18 percent of municipalities. According to María del Carmen Alanís Figueroa, president of Mexico's Electoral Tribunal of Judicial Power, however, women may face de facto exclusion from political participation in an even larger share of communities, arguing that, for all practical purposes, women do not participate in electoral community assemblies in as many as three-fourths of municipalities (Tapia 2010). And women are not the only groups excluded from meaningful local participation either, as some places exclude non-Catholics (5.6 percent), people not born in the community (25 percent), and people who live in outlying rural hamlets (22 percent).

It may be possible from a theoretical perspective to put individual rights on one side of the ledger and collective rights on the other. But one of the most basic lessons of Oaxaca's experience with UC is that these neat categories break down in practice, creating enormously messy gray areas. The case of Santa Anna del Valle, where migrants are disenfranchised from elections but must serve the community, even if from abroad, is a great example of how difficult it can be for communities to navigate this complex and fraught terrain. While the situation was clearly an affront to the individual rights of migrants in Santa Anna del Valle, credible communitarian rights claims were being made as well.

In chapter 8, Danielson focuses on the ways in which migrants continue to participate in home community institutions as well as the variety of ways in which municipal authorities in Oaxaca cajole, compel, or invite this participation. As in the case of Santa Anna del Valle, migrants who fail to fulfill required *cargo* (public service jobs) and *tequio* service (nonremunerated labor for public projects) or who fail to make financial contributions to community patron saint festivals or public works projects can lose their land or their rights to community membership, or suffer other sanctions. On the other hand, however, Danielson finds that such seemingly illiberal measures increase the likelihood that migrants will collectively contribute to public works projects and remain engaged in the public life of their hometowns after migrating, suggesting that the strength of UC institutions may help to channel remittance dollars away from private consumption and toward necessary social and infrastructure development. Danielson also finds evidence that people with migration experience are actually more likely to hold positions of local political power than nonmigrants. Framed in a certain way, then, the seemingly illiberal demands placed on migrants by some municipal governments in UC Oaxaca may function to fortify a translocal citizenship regime. Although migrants often find it difficult to escape from traditional community obligations, by continuing to participate (whether they want to or not), they often do retain their rights as members of their local community and may even be among the most powerful local political actors.

"Autonomy" as a concept contains a slew of meanings, connotations, and frames. In this case, I am referring to the degree to which groups can operate independently from the state and its dominant culture as well as the degree to which individuals are free to make conscious decisions about the institutions, parties, and practices they support. I will use the examples given throughout the book to begin to analyze the proper unit (individual, interest group, community, region) for granting of autonomy and constructing support institutions. I conclude that only a frank consideration of the trade-offs between individual and communitarian rights can yield the kind of self-aware multiculturalism that simultaneously respects the rights of groups and their individual members. Normatively, one form this could take is the adoption of "conditional multiculturalism" (Danielson and Eisenstadt 2009, 153–156), whereby institutions of autonomy are constructed that allow groups to revere and sustain whatever cultural norms they choose, but with the stipulation that they respect citizens' constitutional rights and include an "opt-out" clause so that individuals can choose not to participate without penalty or the loss of group rights. While Mexican law has scarcely taken up these normative issues, the Colombian constitutional court has found perhaps the best standards to date for mediating between individual and communitarian rights, as we elaborate in the conclusion to this volume.

WORKADAY CONFLICTS: COMMUNAL NORMS AND INDIVIDUAL RIGHTS IN OAXACA

As conveyed further in chapters 6 through 8, the Oaxacan experience with UC recognition has provided a wealth of information about how tensions between individual and communal rights are negotiated on the ground within indigenous groups and also between UC municipalities and the state, the nation, and the international community. Over the last fifteen years of UC practice, several issues have arisen time and again as major, seemingly intractable, sticking points between individualists and communitarians: women's rights, migrants' rights, and globalization.

The case of Eufrosina Cruz, who was elected and then stripped of office simply for being a woman, drew enormous attention from the national and international media and her case resonated with liberal Western elites.[1] It raised the profile of gender discrimination under UC as a serious issue, such that even national Mexican officials, including the federal electoral tribunal president, Alanís Figueroa, said that gender discrimination in indigenous communities was a problem that needed to be addressed, albeit at state and local levels (Tapia, 2010). The cases of gender discrimination in Santa Catarina Minas and Asunción Tlacolulita were somewhat more ambiguous, given that women themselves were potentially making individual rights demands to serve temporal political ends. In general, however, systematic studies of local electoral results by Vázquez García (2011) and Zafra (2009) show an epic lack of female political representation. Female municipal officials, former officials, and candidates from UC communities who were interviewed (Graciela Ángeles Carreño, former secretary and poll worker during 2001 postelectoral conflict, interview, Santa Catarina Minas, June 22, 2009; Norma Molina Maldonado, businesswoman and regent for health, interview, Juxtlahuaca, Oaxaca, June 24, 2009; and Eufrosina Cruz, mayoral candidate in Santa Maria Quiegolani, interview, Oaxaca, August 6, 2008) all independently decried "*abusos y costumbres*" (abuses and customs) of women's political rights under the UC system.

Immigration also poses persistent challenges to UC administration. As UC communities rely heavily on adult men to fill unremunerated administrative and religious service jobs (*cargos*) and labor (*tequio*) in communities, migration can put a great deal of stress on these systems. In response, many community authorities sanction migrants and other local citizens who fail to fulfill their service when called. Increasingly, local authorities in high-migration UC municipalities have altered traditional norms that required direct service by allowing migrants to make financial contributions to the community or to pay a replacement to serve in their stead. As Danielson elaborates, there has been an economic imperative to go to the United States to seek work, but migrants are often unable to escape their obligations to the community and at times suffer sanctions if they fail to serve when called. If they stay in the United States long enough to be able to send substantial remittances, they can lose their rights and land in Oaxaca. If they return to Oaxaca, they are not always well received because of the fear that migrants will bring new habits, including drug use and gang activity, back with them (Alan López Valencia, interview,

San Juan Guelavia, Oaxaca, June 24, 2009). At the same time, however, a greater share of UC mayors have migration experience than the population in general—that is, some migrants, rather than suffering disenfranchisement, have become powerful local political actors.

Furthermore, as Sorroza's rendering of the debates over *escalafón* (the practice of selecting leaders via the ladder of *cargos*) shows, economic development imperatives are presenting a whole separate set of challenges to the practice of UC (chapter 7). Traditionally, leaders have been selected based on their loyalty to the community and record of past service, regardless of their individual skills or merit. As stated by Jaime Martínez Luna (interview, Gelatao, Oaxaca, May 14, 2005), who espouses a philosophy of *comunalicracia*: "In democracy, votes are defined by rhetoric. In *comunalicracia*, your work is what defines you." The essential question for voters in *comunalicracia* is whether candidates have served the *cargos* they have been called to serve and whether they have earned respect in the community. While this approach is true to Oaxaca's communalist tradition, some people have begun to argue that merit deserves more weight. Shouldn't those people with particular skills or talents be able to use them to benefit the collective? Wouldn't it make sense to allow a college-trained accountant to run for municipal treasurer without having to first serve as an errand runner, police officer, cemetery caretaker, or church-bell ringer? In fact, Sorroza and Danielson's analysis of the 2008 Survey of Oaxaca Mexico Customary Law Municipalities shows that many UC municipalities no longer comply with the traditional *escalafón* system. Sorroza and Danielson's typology of UC Oaxaca mayors' political biographies shows that a minority of 16.1 percent have climbed the traditional ladder of leadership, with 32 percent classified as semitraditional and 52 percent classified as nontraditional.

San Miguel Tlacotepec's mayor, Cesar Esperón Angón (interview, June 24, 2009), lamented the fact that all of the talented and ambitious young people had migrated, and that no one left spoke Mixtec or observed traditional rules. His colleague, San Miguel Tlacotepec's treasury alderman, Gumesildo Bollaños Berra (interview, June 24, 2009), said that *cargos* discriminate against the poor: "For those who have the economic conditions, serving [*cargos*] offers a break. But for those who don't have the economic conditions, it is not beneficial, because your family suffers."

One of the distinctive features of Oaxaca's UC system is that it represents a very real attempt to sow group autonomy from below. In most other places in Mexico and Latin America, group autonomy has been imposed from above, generating admonitions from Hale (2002) but optimism from Van Cott (2003). This was certainly the case in Zapatista Chiapas, and that movement failed to result in greater indigenous autonomy.[2] Elsewhere in Latin America, movements to allow subnational geographical and minority group autonomy are growing. But here too, efforts to allow more local control have often been top-down, driven by governments or international development banks and other agencies. Ironically, these programs sometimes simply serve to concentrate power in the hands of those who decide how to allocate resources to decentralized bodies.

NATIONAL PARTIES AND THE QUEST FOR AUTONOMY

In order to win UC recognition, a bargain was struck: the long-governing Party of the Institutional Revolution (PRI) state would largely leave local administrations to govern their territories and, in exchange, UC winners would agree to be registered as PRI members. In other words, the PRI got rural legitimacy and the UC communities got a modicum of independence. Formal recognition of UC was meant to ensure the PRI's stranglehold in rural Oaxaca, by blocking opposition parties from making inroads. Moreover, local autonomy was constricted by the fact that authoritarian governors could send their minions to take over as administrators whenever electoral conflicts became too intense.

This willingness on the part of the government to use rights and services as leverage in order to command political support from citizens has a long history in Mexico. One recent example was President Carlos Salinas's (1988–1994) bid to decentralize welfare spending as a means of resuscitating the PRI in rural Mexico. Instead of sending out checks from the federal government, he channeled welfare spending through regional and local solidarity committees composed of PRI allies, technocrats, and cronies. The public then came to see these local PRI groups as the face of social welfare. "Hunger is tough," said one Oaxacan National Action Party (PAN) leader (PAN has traditionally opposed UC). "If you give someone food for one day, they feel beholden to raise up their hand for you in an assembly" (Leovijildo López López, secretary for doctrine and policy, Oaxaca state chapter of PAN, interview, Oaxaca City, May 12, 2005). Indeed, the power of the state to decide who eats and who doesn't is well known in rural Oaxaca, where legions of administrators have directed resources in a way that maximizes support for their political party. In this context, arguments for greater indigenous autonomy from the state carry understandable salience.

In Chiapas, the situation was even more disempowering for local populations. The state government was so authoritarian that the heavily exploited indigenous populations had no voice at all against the *latifundista* agrarian elites. Chiapas's repressive system did start to recede in 2000, however, when the state's first-ever opposition governor, Pablo Salazar, was elected by a left-right coalition of PAN and Party of the Democratic Revolution (PRD) voters. The Zapatista insurgency was able to scare the state into negotiating additional land reforms. However, the lack of local venues for dialogues between Zapatista sympathizers and detractors, especially before the 2003 declaration of the Good Government Councils, has rendered local governments easy prey for caciques and predatory interest groups. Paramilitaries representing landholders and, on occasion, some of the more belligerent squatter groups claiming to represent Zapatismo have undermined local authority.

In Mexico and other nations with long histories of patronage and repression, the advantages of devolving authority to locals must be weighed against the vulnerability of local systems to corporatist power grabs and clientelism. Patron-client relationships are easily established and manipulated under a guise of communitarianism under which political bosses paternalistically declare themselves the "authentic" voice of the movement and know what is best for their supporters. These supporters and the silent bystanders who may not even be sympathetic to the movement must simply abide by the leader's decisions without getting to express their own views or to deliberate. Apparent shows of communal decision making, even if they are theater merely to reaffirm decisions already taken in back rooms, win credibility for local movement leaders, who are then able to claim to speak for the collective and, if so inclined, translate that aggregation of interests into support for local bosses, patronage networks, and national parties.

In some cases, group solidarity has actually been manipulated by outsiders, usually interlocutors seeking to build support for a particular politician who could not otherwise access a linguistically indigenous community (Rus 1994; Hernández-Díaz and Juan Martínez 2007; Recondo 2007). Bilingual teachers are the quintessential example, but not the only ones. San Juan Chamula is dominated by alcohol distributors seeking to monopolize sales (Rus 1994), and Araceli Burguete Cal y Mayor (senior researcher at Centro de Investigaciones y Estudios Superiores en Antropología Social, interview, San Cristóbal de las Casas, Chiapas, June 6, 2008) confirmed that monopolistic commodities providers still battle for market control by taking sides in local political battles. In much of Mexico's destitute south, individuals sell votes for roof laminate, sewing machines, and canned goods (Eisenstadt 2004, 255) and receive little from the government between election seasons.[3]

Would experiments in self-governance by southern Mexico's indigenous citizens have fared better if they had included more expansive autonomy rights? Critics, like the former director of the Oaxaca electoral institute, Cipriano Flores Cruz (advisor to the PRI, interview, Oaxaca, May 17, 2005), say greater autonomy would have prompted the state to abandon autonomous areas. He argues that the more extreme groups who have sought indigenous autonomy in Mexico (e.g., the Zapatistas) do not actually wish to govern and "will not define, nor execute, nor evaluate" policies. Ultimately, this would leave the region's interests totally unrepresented at the national level, where the overwhelming amount of Mexico's public resources are doled out. Flores Cruz argues that better representation of indigenous positions within existing government and partisan structures is what's needed. In their ideological migration from revolutionary Marxists to ethnic warriors to social democrats, the Zapatistas seem to have implicitly acknowledged this.

The broader point is that autonomy must be coupled with strong local governance in order to deliver communities the independence they seek from the state. Autonomy coupled with weak local governance will be manipulated and will disenfranchise the very groups it is intended to empower. To Burguete, autonomy has four preconditions: (1) some sort of territorial definition, (2) internal self-government, (3) set jurisdiction over territory and internal governance, and (4) "specific, constitutionally established competencies and powers" (chapter 2, this volume). What the Zapatistas showed was that recognition without a share of state resources or competent governance is of limited use. Autonomy is beneficial only to communities that have the resources and capacity to effectively call their own shots.

And how can local autonomy for communitarian practices be reconciled with participation in a larger nation-state that is constitutionally committed to individual rights? According to Oaxacan anthropologist Jaime Martínez Luna, "Here and in all communities there are moments where individual preoccupations dominate, like getting a house and paying your children's school tuition. But there are also moments when the community clamps down on us and we have to serve a *cargo*, go to assemblies, do *tequio* and share our resources. The individual is diminished, but we in no way deny individual aspirations" (interview, 2005).

ETHNIC POLITICAL MOVEMENTS IN LATIN AMERICA: BOLIVIA AND PERU

Efforts to objectively study instances of subnational autonomy in Mexico have frequently demonstrated a bias on the part of researchers to be sympathetic toward the underdogs, namely, the outside agitators. Bobrow-Strain (2007, 18) confronted this issue by defying his own impulse to study the "dualism of 'good' indigenous peasants and 'bad' *ladino* landowners around which much discussion of Chiapas had revolved." Instead, he constructed a narrative from the landowners' perspective and captured their fears about the post-1994 land redistributions in Chiapas. (These reforms and the creation of hundreds of new *ejidos* coincided with a dramatic decline in the viability of the *ejido*-centric model of farming and ranching that had long dominated Mexican agriculture.)[4] In the context of this book, one way to correct for this bias is to consider a case where an autonomous government has won elections and is now in power. Bolivia's recent experiment with autonomy provides some insight into what happens when an indigenous rights movement is at least partly able to implement its agenda.[5]

In December 2005, Evo Morales was elected Bolivia's first indigenous president. This, coupled with the passage of a new constitution in early 2009, has trained intense international focus on that country as a laboratory of indigenous power and participation. Bolivia's new constitution grants multicultural rights to the Quechua, Aymara, and other indigenous groups to a degree not equaled by many countries. The interesting thing for comparative purposes is that the Aymara do not all live within Bolivia's borders. A large number of Aymara speakers also live across Lake Titicaca in Peru. But those who live in Bolivia have demonstrated a much stronger indigenous identity. I ask whether the reasons the Aymara in Bolivia are so much more communitarian than their brethren in Peru are similar to the reasons for the communitarian-individualistic split between Oaxaca's and Chiapas's indigenous groups. Although the discussion is more suggestive than conclusive, this hypothesis does appear to hold promise. That is, it seems that indigenous identity in Bolivia grew out of an organized social movement (as in Chiapas), whereas it was repressed or rechanneled in Peru via state corporatism (as in Oaxaca). If differences in agrarian institutions also prove to be explanatory variables, it would suggest that the Mexican model has some predictive power.

As in Mexico, there is much variability in how and when traditional customary law has been applied in the Andes. Examples can be found where traditional practices defy human rights norms, such as during the 2004 lynchings in Callao, Peru, and Ayo Ayo, Bolivia, which were conducted in the name of traditional law (Mulligan 2004). Examples also abound of the social capital generated by indigenous networks that was harnessed to defend villages against Shining Path terrorists in Peru (Starn 1999), and of the empowering effect of *ayllu* communitarian institutions on local democracy in Bolivia (Ticona et al. 1995; Fernández Oslo 2004; Lucero 2008; Andolina et al. 2009).[6] Such traditional practices have tended to occur in parallel with the state in Peru, while they have been integrated from the outside into Bolivia's political institutions over the last decade. At the level of the nation-state, a wide range of policies and practices fall under the broad rubric of "decentralization" and include political, economic (or functional), and administrative decentralization.

Following Willis, Garman, and Haggard (1999, 8), I define political decentralization as the establishment or reestablishment of elected autonomous subnational governments capable of making binding decisions in at least some policy areas. Economic (or functional) decentralization involves the transfer of responsibilities for expenditure and revenue-raising powers to subnational governments (Willis et al. 1999, 8). Administrative decentralization involves the transfer of management responsibilities to subnational governments but does not include the power to raise or allocate resources (Rodríguez 1997, 10). If we place decentralization policies on a continuum ranging from weak to strong, simple deconcentration would be at the weak end. Deconcentration generally involves a transfer of functions, power, and resources to the state offices of central (federal) agencies (Rodríguez 1997, 11). A strong decentralization policy involves transferring power to popularly elected local governments and providing local governments with greater political authority (e.g., to convene local elections or establish participatory processes), increased financial resources (e.g., through transfers or greater tax authority), and/or more administrative control.

During the 1990s, almost all Latin American countries experienced some political decentralization (Willis et al. 1999).[7] Decentralization initiatives were the result of two major events in the region: (1) the debt crisis, and subsequent structural adjustments and neoliberal economic policies; and (2) the transition to democracy. Great pressure was brought to bear on Latin American leaders by international financial institutions responding to the debt crisis who wanted to see greater decentralization to guard against a repeat crash. At the same time, Willis and colleagues (1999) suggest political liberalization and democratization also provided powerful motives to decentralize. They argue that democratic opposition movements and parties pushed for the decentralization of political power because they believed that they would have more success winning local offices than competing at higher levels of government. Democratic reforms during the 1980s and 1990s brought previously marginalized actors into the political process and subtly altered the terms of the decentralization debates. Blair (2000, 25) notes that decentralization reforms in the 1990s were different from the 1950s-era initiatives that sought to enhance the efficiency of public administration in the developing world. The new decentralization efforts placed more emphasis on democratic local governance and focused on citizen participation and accountability of local government for its decisions.

The effects of decentralization policies on ethnic identity in Mexico and South America have been intensely debated by scholars, in part because the policies vary significantly throughout the region, as does the strength of indigenous mobilization.

In Mexico, decentralization of administrative authority has not been met with commensurate decentralization of discretion over revenue generation or decision making with regard to governance. In Bolivia, while the new multicultural laws are still being implemented, it would appear that decentralization has contributed to indigenous mobilization.

This is not surprising when one looks more closely at the context. For one thing, communal attitudes have been more prevalent in Bolivia for generations as a result of organizing by tin worker and coca grower unions. At the same time, the state had been less effective in propagating state corporatism in the countryside. In Peru, where labor movements and collective actions have not been able to take hold nationwide, land reform has helped promote peasant rather than indigenous identities in agrarian areas. In addition, Peru has experienced extreme levels of political violence at the hands of brutal Shining Path Maoist insurgents, which effectively demobilized and silenced the indigenous population and obstructed state involvement of any kind in those victimized communities. The Peruvian case is instructive as "the dog that did not bark" in terms of multicultural identity. While we do not further consider the case in this volume, Mattiace does discuss the lack of an indigenous rights movement in Mexico's Yucatán state (chapter 9).

OUTLINE OF THE BOOK

This book started as an inquiry into subnational multicultural rights recognition in Oaxaca, Mexico, as part of an experiment ongoing since 1995. The southern Mexican state has a total population of about 3.5 million, some 50 percent of whom identify as indigenous as they speak languages other than Spanish. However, in order to broaden the debate, the book seeks to extend the discussion about multicultural rights into one about "identity-related" rights more generally, and, unlike prior works which argue at more abstract levels, to see what we could learn from case studies that might reflect back upon the broader debate. We justified comparing unitary states (Bolivia, Ecuador) with federal states with varying regimes of multicultural rights at the state level (Chiapas, Oaxaca, and Yucatán, Mexico).

While many patterns emerged from our cases, the most important contribution of this work is to compare an array of cases not normally considered together, with respect to "state collective rights recognition" and to show the true range of such policies. The combination of a broad survey of multiculturalist movements across a range of cases as well as multifaceted coverage of the Oaxaca, Mexico, case leads to the conclusion, hinted at by several chapter authors, that a solution may be to reorient the terms of the debate. First, as suggested by the first section of the book and then reiterated throughout, the multicultural rights debate needs to be resituated as a continuum between multicultural group rights from above on the one hand (as in some parts of Mexico), and multicultural autonomy rights from below (perhaps Ecuador, Bolivia, and Chiapas), as well as those which in practice acquire a more mixed (from above and from below) nature, such as in Oaxaca and in realistic renderings of other cases like Bolivia. Second, the focus on state recognition of rights may be misguided. It may be more productive to consider whether given states and societies recognize "automatic" citizenship rights, as conceived by T. H. Marshall, for example, rather than prioritizing the agency of states in recognizing rights. As authors like Burguete (chapter 2) and Lucero (chapter 1) argue, the recognition of rights is somewhat precarious, and as Cooke (chapter 3) shows us quite explicitly, sometimes rights recognition is politically driven.

This introductory section of the book (here and chapters 1 and 2) broadly assesses Latin American autonomy movements. José Antonio Lucero, in chapter 1, demonstrates a wide understanding of multicultural policies in Latin America by rating them from "strong" to "weak" and also by assessing the success of such policies in representing the views of distinctive groups. Transitioning from this Latin America–wide definition of autonomy movements, Araceli Burguete discusses the international movement for "state collective rights recognition" in the context of the 1994 revolt in southern Mexico's state of Chiapas (chapter 2). Parting from a broader discussion of the gradual definition of "autonomy" and "autonomy movements" by international organizations such as the United Nations over the last thirty years, Burguete considers the recent achievements and failures of the autonomy movement launched by the Zapatista Army of National Liberation in 1994.

Erik Cooke opens a three-chapter section on the Andean cases by explaining subnational multiculturalism in Latin America's most famous case of indigenous self-governance, Bolivia (chapter 3). Indeed, the election of indigenous president Evo Morales in 2005 has given a new impetus to indigenous rights movements around the hemisphere. However, Cooke finds that Bolivian elites too manipulated the language of multiculturalism to frame their own power struggles against Bolivia's victimized indigenous citizens as a push for the recognition of their autonomy. Miguel Centellas argues in chapter 4 that the 2009 constitution did include language about collective rights and recognized indigenous communities more explicitly, and that this was a departure from the "liberal multiculturalism" of earlier Bolivian reforms by neoliberal presidents. Much of the constitutional language is symbolic more than tangible, however, and Centellas discusses the obstacles to implementation of Bolivia's collective rights autonomy regime. Carmen Martínez Novo concludes this section with a discussion of Ecuador (chapter 5), which she classifies as a mixed autonomy case, arguing that autonomy in Ecuador started as an impulse from below with a strong indigenous movement that was able to halt neoliberal reforms and ousted two presidents.

In the 1990s, Martínez argues, autonomy in Ecuador was co-opted from above as recognition, but without redistribution. Indigenous peoples were recognized in the 1998 constitution and were given autonomy, but the state did not commit enough resources for indigenous people to carry out this autonomy effectively. Recognition without redistribution favored the indigenous leadership with some jobs and benefits, but did not clearly change the situation in indigenous communities, which resented the leadership and joined the movement of President Correa. Since 2007 and despite the 2008 constitutional commitment to plurinationalism, the Ecuadorian government, with the help of disaffected indigenous individuals, has been discontinuing autonomy and implementing instead a form of individual rights based on antidiscrimination laws. Therefore, the Ecuadorian case can be considered one of autonomy from below, co-opted as a shallow form of neoliberal multiculturalism and later at least partly dismantled under a post-neoliberal regime.

We then delve deeper into the "Oaxaca experiment" in part 3 of the book to understand the implications of Oaxaca's multiculturalism, which may be among the most rigorously studied in the world. The section commences with a piece by Victor Leonel Juan Mártinez (chapter 6), who studies different configurations of *usos y costumbres* and advocates thinking about UC participation as originating from the individual level and radiating out to the community. Next, Carlos Sorroza and Michael S. Danielson (chapter 7) discuss the trajectories of indigenous mayors and the criteria important to their elections. Finally, Michael S. Danielson (chapter 8) considers the roles played by transnational and return migrants in Oaxaca's UC communities, where individual ambitions and community aspirations can come into direct conflict.

The volume concludes with two chapters on the role of the state in defining and implementing multicultural autonomy regimes. Shannan Mattiace (chapter 9) discusses the state government's failure to implement autonomy from above in Yucatán. Next, in the conclusion, Sonnleitner and Eisenstadt consider legal cases contesting autonomy claims. This chapter addresses both the failure of the federal state to address subnational challenges in Mexico's UC elections at the national level and also the success of the Colombian state, and specifically that nation's constitutional court, in granting legal autonomy to indigenous communities and then adjudicating cases with deference to these communal norms as well as to national human rights imperatives. This conclusion circles back upon the issues of autonomy and individual/communitarian rights that form the central axes of the volume.

NOTES

1. Cruz has become a model for women's rights, receiving extensive coverage in international media like the *Los Angeles Times* (Tobar and Uribe 2008) and *El País* (Relea 2008) and visits from dignitaries like Margarita Zavala (Mexico's first lady) and Michelle Obama (the U.S. first lady).
2. This is not to diminish the accomplishments of the Zapatistas in drawing attention to the plight of Chiapas's destitute indigenous peasants, achieving land reform when no other means seemed possible, and inspiring "imaginary Zapatistas" throughout Chiapas, Mexico, and Latin America. However, as a model for sustainable development, few can argue that the movement has been a success.
3. Burguete (interview, 2008) called this "the politics of the roof laminate shingle," which is reminiscent of Africanist Jean-François Bayart's reference to "the politics of the belly."
4. For more on the decline of the *ejido* and the simultaneous rise of the *ayuntamiento* (municipal government) as the unit of governance in rural Mexico, see Torres-Manzuera (2009).
5. Shannan Mattiace coauthored portions of this section as part of a 2006 grant proposal. While I am extending the argument, Mattiace and I initially worked on this question together.
6. *Ayllus* are extended family and community structures, and their importance is rooted in pre-Conquest Andean social and political practices.

7. Eaton and Dickovick (2004) have suggested that a recentralization of political power is occurring in at least some countries that decentralized during the 1980s and early 1990s. Nevertheless, the overall trend in the region continues to favor decentralization.

REFERENCES

Andolina, Robert, Nina Laurie, and Sarah A. Radcliffe. 2009. *Indigenous Development in the Andes: Culture, Power, and Transnationalism*. Durham, NC: Duke University Press.

Blair, Harry. 2000. "Participation and Accountability at the Periphery: Democratic Local Governance in Six Countries." *World Development* 28 (1): 21–39.

Bobrow-Strain, Aaron. 2007. *Intimate Enemies: Landowners, Power, and Violence in Chiapas*. Durham, NC: Duke University Press.

Danielson, Michael S., and Todd A. Eisenstadt. 2009. "Walking Together, but in Which Direction? Gender Discrimination and Multicultural Practices in Oaxaca, Mexico." *Politics and Gender* 5 (June): 153–184.

Eaton, Kent, and J. Tyler Dickovick. 2004. "The Politics of Re-centralization in Argentina and Brazil." *Latin American Research Review* 39 (1): 90–122.

Eisenstadt, Todd A. 2004. *Courting Democracy in Mexico: Party Strategies and Electoral Institutions*. New York: Cambridge University Press.

Eisenstadt, Todd A. 2011. *Politics, Identity, and Mexico's Indigenous Rights Movements*. New York: Cambridge University Press.

Fernández Oslo, Marcelo. 2004. *La Ley del Ayllu—Práctica de jach'a justicia y jusk'a justicia (Justicia Mayor y Justicia Menor) en comunidades aymaras*. 2nd ed. La Paz: Programa de Investigación Estratégica en Bolivia.

Hale, Charles. 2002. "Does Multiculturalism Menace? Governance, Cultural Rights and the Politics of Identity in Guatemala." *Journal of Latin American Studies* 34: 485–524.

Hernández-Díaz, Jorge, and Victor Leonel Juan Martínez. 2007. *Dilemas de la institución municipal—una incursión en la experiencia Oaxaqueña*. Mexico City: Miguel Ángel Porrúa.

Lucero, José Antonio. 2008. *Struggles of Voice: The Politics of Indigenous Representation in the Andes*. Pittsburgh, PA: University of Pittsburgh Press.

Mulligan, Mark. 2004. "Bolivian Demonstration Ends in Lynching," *Financial Times*, June 16.

Recondo, David. 2007. *La politica del gatopardo: Multiculturalismo y democracia en Oaxaca*. Mexico City: Centro de Investigaciones y Estudios Superiores en Antropologia Social.

Regino Montes, Adelfo. 1996. "Los derechos indígenas, en serio." *La Jornada*, October 22. http://www.jornada.unam.mx/1996/oct96/961022/adelfo.html.

Regino Montes, Adelfo. n.d. "Taller 2: Libre Determinación de los Pueblos Indígenas." Unpublished manuscript.

Relea, Francesc. 2008. "La rebelión se llama Eufrosina Cruz." *El País*, February 10. http://www.elpais.com/articulo/internacional/rebelion/llama/Eufrosina/Cruz/elpepiint/20080210elpepiint_1/Tes.

Ríos Contreras, Viridiana. 2006. "Conflictividad postelectoral en los Usos y Costumbres de Oaxaca." Undergraduate thesis in political science, Instituto Tecnológico Autónomo de México.

Rodríguez, Victoria. 1997. *Decentralization in Mexico: From Reforma Municipal to Solidaridad to Nuevo Federalismo*. Boulder, CO: Westview Press.

Rus, Jan. 1994. "The 'Comunidad Revolucionaria Institucional': The Subversion of Native Government in Highland Chiapas, 1936–1968." In *Everyday Forms of State Formation: Revolution and the Negotiation of Rule in Modern Mexico*, edited by Gilbert M. Joseph and Daniel Nugent, 265–300. Durham, NC: Duke University Press.

Starn, Orin. 1999. *Nightwatch: The Politics of Protest in the Andes*. Durham, NC: Duke University Press.

Tapia, Alma Alejandra. 2010. "Prevalece marginación de mujeres en material electoral: Alanís Figueroa." *La Jornada-Zacatecas*, March 10, 1. http://www.trife.gob.mx/comunicacionsocial/resumen/resumen/pdf/2010/140310.pdf.

Ticona, Estéban, Gonzalo Rojas, and Xavier Albó. 1995. *Votos y Wiphalas—campesinos y pueblos originarios en democracia*. La Paz: Centro de Investigación y Promoción del Campesinado.

Tobar, Hector, and Maria Antonietta Uribe. 2008. "Refusing to Take Men for an Answer." *Los Angeles Times*, April 5, A-1. http://articles.latimes.com/2008/apr/05/world/fg-suffrage5.

Torres-Manzuera, Gabriela. 2009. "The Decline of the *Ejido* and *Ayuntamiento* Emergence Reconfiguring Local Powers: New Actors, Old Practices." Paper presented at the conference Fifteen Years after the Zapatistas: Social and Political Change in Mexico and Chiapas since 1994, David Rockefeller Center for Latin American Studies, Harvard University, April 10.

Van Cott, Donna Lee. 2003. "Institutional Change and Ethnic Parties in South America." *Latin American Politics and Society* 45 (2): 1–39.

Vázquez García, Verónica. 2011. *Usos y costumbres y ciudadanía femenina: Hablan las presidentas municipales de Oaxaca, 1996–2010*. Mexico City: Editorial Miguel Ángel Porrúa.

Willis, Eliza, Christopher Garman, and Stephan Haggard. 1999. "The Politics of Decentralization in Latin America." *Latin American Research Review* 34 (1): 7–56.

Zafra, Gloria. 2009. "Por la ley o la costumbre: Obstáculos en la participación política de las mujeres en el sureste mexicano." In *Derecho y sociedad en Oaxaca indígena*, edited by Victor Leonel Juan Martínez and Maria Clara Galvis. Washington, DC: Due Process of Law Foundation.

1 Ambivalent Multiculturalisms

Perversity, Futility, and Jeopardy in Latin America

José Antonio Lucero

Latin American societies and those who study them have long wrestled with the complex and sometimes contradictory terms of official multiculturalism. While there is widespread agreement that in the 1990s a regional model of multicultural policies emerged, important debates about the content and consequences of multicultural politics continue. Drawing from previous research in the Andes (and glimpses of Mesoamerica), this essay provides a brief overview of the varieties of multiculturalisms in Latin America and explores debates over their intended and unintended consequences. I pay special attention to the intersections between multicultural policies and debates over neoliberal governance, gender, and race. As "multiculturalism" is not one project but many, it is not surprising to find that multiculturalisms have been associated with both conservative and insurgent political projects in the Americas. After reviewing the traits of what Van Cott called the "regional model" of multiculturalism, I borrow Albert Hirschman's (1991) suggestive labels for "reactionary" arguments against ostensibly progressive policies to survey debates over official multicultural policies (MCPs).[1] In using his categories, I do not seek to cast critics of official multiculturalism as simplistic reactionaries. Rather, in moving past glowing endorsements of MCPs and their demonization, I hope to show the complexities of the empirical middle ground.

First, I explore a version of Hirschman's "futility thesis," which in this case would posit that multicultural reforms have accomplished very little, that they have been essentially symbolic and have lacked the legal and political power to be truly meaningful. Second, I present a version of his "perversity thesis," which suggests that these policies have backfired; rather than giving voice to subalterns they have actually strengthened neoliberal domination. Third, I explore a "jeopardy thesis," which holds that reforms have not only failed and backfired but have also made people worse off.

Accordingly, the following sections use Hirschman's categories to examine the alleged futility of multicultural policies, the perverse possibility that multiculturalism actually threatens vulnerable populations, and finally the claim that multicultural policies may have benefited Indigenous populations but may have jeopardized the livelihoods of women and Afro-Latin Americans.[2] While I do not endorse strong versions of these theses, these debates reveal how multiculturalism has become a complex and uneven terrain of contestation.

THE MULTICULTURAL MODEL

Before reviewing the various objections that have arisen regarding MCPs, it is important to acknowledge that these policies, in many ways, represent a sharp break with exclusionary political orders. In many Latin American states, the official ideologies of *mestizaje* (racial mixing) and the glorification of Indigenous pasts through the romantic discourses of *indigenismo* long translated into official policies of discrimination, assimilation, and/or paternalism. Even ostensible "revolutionary" efforts like that of Peruvian military leftist leader General Juan Velasco Alvarado to eliminate the colonial word *indio* from the national vocabulary and replace it with the socioeconomic category of *campesino* reflected the desire to deny Indigenous people recognition as Indigenous *peoples*, that is, as members of Quechua, Aymara, or other Indigenous collectivities. Thus, the rewriting of constitutions and the legal recognition of Indigenous and Afro-Latin American peoples is a significant development, one that came to the region as the twentieth century was coming to a close.

As Donna Lee Van Cott (2000, 2006, 2007) argues, during the late 1990s, there emerged a regional model of multiculturalism that included many features. She summarizes the various elements in the following terms:

1) rhetorical recognition of the existence of Indigenous peoples as collective entities preceding the establishment of national states; 2) recognition of customary Indigenous law as binding public law, typically limited by international human rights or higher-order constitutional rights, such as the right to life; 3) protection of collective property rights from sale, dismemberment, or confiscation; 4) official status for Indigenous languages; and 5) access to bilingual education. (2007, 132)

Of course, as Van Cott and others note, different states adopted different combinations of these elements, and not all multiculturalisms were equally intense (see table 1.1). Based on table 1.1, Van Cott (2006) suggested the following coding of MCPs:

Strong: Bolivia, Colombia, Ecuador, Panama, Venezuela
Modest: Argentina, Brazil, Costa Rica, Guatemala, Honduras, Mexico, Nicaragua, Paraguay, Peru
Weak: Belize, Chile, El Salvador, Guyana, Suriname

Table 1.1 Multicultural Policies in Latin America

Country	Date of Constitution/ Recognition	Collective Land Rights	Self-govern. Rights	Cultural Rights	Customary Law	Represent./ Consult. in Central Government	Affirmation of Distinct Status	Ratified ILO 169	Affirm. Action	Total
Argentina	1994	✓		✓	✓		✓	2000		5
Belize	1981									0
Bolivia	1995	✓	✓ For limited purposes	✓	✓		✓	1991		6
Brazil	1988	✓		✓	✓		✓	2002	✓	6
Chile	1993 by statute				✓ Limited			2008		1
Colombia	1991	✓	✓	✓	✓	✓	✓	1991	✓	8
Costa Rica	Laws passed in 1977, 1993, 1999	✓		✓	✓		✓	1993		3
Ecuador	1998	✓	✓	✓	✓	✓	✓	1998		7
El Salvador	1983/1991–1992	✓								1
Guatemala	1986	✓		✓	✓		✓	1996		6
Guyana	1980/1996	✓								1
Honduras	1982	✓		✓	✓			1995		4
Mexico	1917/1992/2001	✓	✓	✓	✓		✓	1990		6
Nicaragua	1987/1995	✓	✓	✓	✓		✓			5
Panama	1972/1983/1993–1994	✓	✓	✓	✓		✓			6
Paraguay	1992	✓	✓	✓	✓	✓	✓	1993		6
Peru	1993/2003–2004	✓ Weakened in 1993		✓	✓		✓	1994		5
Suriname	1987									0
Venezuela	1999	✓	✓	✓	✓	✓	✓	2002		7

Source: Van Cott (2006), updated by author.

While it is beyond the scope of this essay to explore in detail the various reasons that pushed states to adopt and (to varying degrees) implement MCPs, many scholars, officials, and Indigenous actors suggest a mix of forces from "above and below" that pushed, pulled, and allowed these changes. From below, Indigenous movements themselves often proved to be strong social forces that through massive marches, blockades, protests, and an updating of the tradition of *levantamientos* forced Indigenous issues onto national political agendas. With the help of allies in nongovernmental organizations and other social networks, Indigenous people were able to become serious organizational and agitational forces (Van Cott 2000; Yashar 2005). Challenging exclusionary political and economic orders, these movements exercised what James Holston (2007) has called (for the case of Brazil) "insurgent citizenship."

Yet this democratic insurgency was not always sufficient to change political conditions; it was often dependent upon the decisions of national elites who had reason to be wary of these mobilizations. While several governments (Chile and Peru are perhaps the most notable) have resorted to repression against Indigenous activism, many elites saw in these mobilizations opportunities to restore democratic legitimacy, as many states were suffering from severe political-economic crises. More self-interestedly, ruling elites advocated decentralization schemes that could give great political power to Indigenous groups on local levels because these reforms would also weaken rival regional elites (Van Cott 2001; O'Neill 2003). As many authors have noted, there is no doubt that Indigenous movements were transnational from the very beginning, from their connections to internationalist Marxist movements (Becker 2008) to their more recent alliances (and differences) with environmental movements (Andolina et al. 2009; Brysk 2000; Chapin 2004; Morin and Santana 2003).

Moreover, several international organizations helped change the international recognition of Indigenous peoples and Indigenous rights. The most significant was undoubtedly International Labour Organization (ILO) Convention No. 169 on Indigenous and Tribal Peoples, which makes various important provisions for the participation of and consultation with Indigenous people in all issues that affect Indigenous communities and livelihoods. Significantly, ILO 169 also recognizes the rights of Indigenous people to collective forms of land tenure, alternative forms of justice, and access to employment and education (ILO 1999). ILO 169 came into effect in 1991 and has been ratified by most Latin American governments, though this does not mean that governments have honored its various provisions, especially when dealing with extractive industrial activity in Indigenous territories (Brysk 2000; Bebbington 2009).

Other important international developments have included the United Nations Decade of Indigenous Peoples and the creation of a special unit within the World Bank to address issues concerning Indigenous people. These international changes have been part of a large shift in development thinking that some have called "development with identity" or "ethnodevelopment." As international multilateral organizations and nongovernmental organizations (NGOs) began to channel resources to ethnodevelopment projects, new incentives were created for Indigenous recognition.

Table 1.2 Incentives for Multiculturalism

	Domestic	International
From above	Democratic legitimacy; elite partisan calculations	ILO 169, UN declarations, World Bank ethnodevelopment policies
From below	Social movement pressures	Transnational activist networks

It is also worth pointing out that the world historical moment in which these developments emerged (the early 1990s) coincided with the global crisis of the international Left, a collapse symbolically represented by the fall of the Berlin Wall. Once traditional leftist causes seemingly entered the "dustbin of history," Indigenous peoples seemed to emerge from their own histories of oppression and neglect and found new allies in transnational activist networks (see Andolina et al. 2009; Brysk 2000; Keck and Sikkink 1998; Lucero 2008; Van Cott 2000; Yashar 2005). In 2007, after decades of debate, the United Nations approved the Declaration on the Rights of Indigenous Peoples with the support of almost every country in the hemisphere (Colombia abstained while the United States and Canada were opposed, but all subsequently endorsed the declaration). Beyond prohibiting discrimination and recognizing the "right to remain distinct," the declaration enshrines the rights of Indigenous peoples "to maintain and strengthen their own institutions, cultures and traditions, and to pursue their development in keeping with their own needs and aspirations."

To summarize, then, this striking move from exclusionary constitutional and legal orders to official recognition of the multicultural natures of Latin American states can be understood, in part, as a response to a mix of political influences from "above and below" on both national and international levels. Table 1.2 summarizes those push and pull factors that enabled the institutionalization of MCPs.

Certainly, much more can be said about the paths that different countries have taken to the multicultural present. In most countries, severe crises (brought about by forces including nightmarish political violence, severe economic problems, and/or political party meltdown) were the dark preludes to the silver linings of new reforms, though it is important to note that not all agree that these reforms were good for society or even for the Indigenous and Afro-Latin American peoples in whose name they were pursued. The rest of this chapter examines some of the controversies that have arisen regarding, in Hirschmanian terms, the alleged futility, perversity, and jeopardy of multiculturalism.

MULTICULTURAL FUTILITY?

In Hirschman's original formulation, the futility thesis suggested simply that the reforms amounted to surface change, while the structure of power remained mainly unchanged. Taking an example from Eastern Europe, he put it this way:

One of the best-known (and best) jokes to come out of Eastern Europe after the installation of Communist regimes there in the wake of World War II: "What is the difference between capitalism and socialism?" The answer: "In capitalism, man exploits man; in socialism, it's the other way round." Here was an effective way of asserting that nothing basic had changed in spite of the total transformation in property relations. (Hirschman 1991, 44)

Some critics of official multiculturalism have made essentially the same charge. These forms of recognition have been tokens to Indigenous people rather than substantive changes to the political and economic structures of Latin American societies.

One of the first objections has to do with one of the very sources of the new multiculturalism, ILO 169. While many states have ratified this convention, what it means in practice varies widely. Even when the provisions of ILO 169 are enshrined in new constitutions, without accompanying legislation and regulations these promises remain just that, promises. For example, the constitutional reform of 1998 in Ecuador included specific provisions for new "Indigenous and Afro-Ecuadorian territorial circumscriptions" (*circunscripciones territoriales indíenas*) that would be new units for the administration of Indigenous self-government. For these provisions to come into effect new legislation had to be passed, but in the course of ten years that legislation never came (Kingsman 2008; see also chapter 5, this volume). The constitution was modified again in 2008, once again including territorial units, but still depending on the political will of legislators to make that a reality.

Other states have also seen a similar dynamic. As several chapters in this volume suggest (introduction, 2, 6–9), Mexico has had its own uneven trajectory with multiculturalism. The path to reform that began with the Zapatista uprising and the San Andres Accords led to a controversial constitutional reform in 2001 that was roundly rejected by Indigenous organizations and not ratified in several states including those with the largest Indigenous populations (OACNUDH 2003, 158). The national-level legal changes, for all intents and purposes, made legislation for Indigenous autonomy and justice the responsibility of state governments, resulting in an uneven patchwork of recognition in which some states have strong provisions for the recognition of Indigenous *usos y costumbres* and others have very weak ones.

One should be careful with this skepticism, of course, as in some countries where Indigenous movements and MCPs have been strong, like Ecuador and Bolivia, politics have taken a decidedly leftward turn as the presidencies of Rafael Correa (in Ecuador) and Evo Morales (in Bolivia) have suggested. The resounding victories of Morales, the first self-identified Indigenous person to win that office, might seem to be a particularly strong refutation of the charge of futility. MCPs paved the way for an Indigenous president in one country and the rejection of "Washington consensus" neoliberal policies in both countries and beyond. Yet, in both states, these new presidents have made the remarkable decision to abolish the state agencies that were part of the new multicultural state building of the 1990s. Morales declared shortly after his inauguration in 2006 that having a single ministry simply ghettoized Indigenous people and assured people that with an Indigenous government, Indigenous people and their interests would be part of every ministry (Lucero 2008; see also chapters 3 and 4, this volume). In the case of Correa, he declared that funds had been misused by the director of the state Indigenous development agency (CODENPE), though others claimed that the decision to close CODENPE was a response to Indigenous protests against the government's continued reliance on mining and other extractive industries in Indigenous territories (Chuji 2009). Without getting too deep into the particular details of each case, these erasures of multicultural institutions suggest a kind of Penelope's cloth of reform: what was woven by one government can be (and has been) undone by the next.

The example of bilingual education offers additional reasons for pessimism. Ecuador and Bolivia during the 1990s were among the "strong" cases of intercultural bilingual education (IBE) reforms. State reforms in each country created institutions that gave Indigenous people more control over the education of their own children than ever before. Yet in both Morales's Bolivia and Correa's Ecuador, the institutions of IBE have lost the support and autonomy they once had. Morales's education policy, though it began with a radical Aymara education minister, was quickly toned down through changes in ministry leadership. Additionally, there has been greater emphasis on the literacy programs supported by educators from Cuba and Venezuela, literacy programs that may have had radical inspirations, but counted few multicultural or Indigenous teaching materials (García 2009). Reflective of his rocky relationship with Indigenous organizations, Ecuador's President Correa made the decision to take away the autonomy of the Indigenous directorate for IBE (DINEBI) and place it under the leadership of the ministry of education (Chuji 2009). For many Indigenous activists, the paradoxical words of one Aymara intellectual resonate all too clearly: "who would have thought we would have had more support [for IBE] from the neoliberals?" (quoted in García 2009). It is in fact the multicultural opening that accompanies the neoliberal years of the 1990s that encouraged the leftist suspicion that multiculturalism is simply, in Slavoj Zizek's (1997, 5) phrase, "the cultural logic of multinational capitalism." Suddenly, the critique is not simply that multiculturalism has not accomplished its goals, but that it has made things worse.

THE PERVERSITY OF NEOLIBERAL MULTICULTURALISM?

One of the more devastating rhetorical strategies against reform, Hirschman (1991,7) reminds us, is the claim that any "purposive action to improve some feature of the political, social, or economic order only serves to exacerbate the condition one wished to remedy." In debates over multiculturalism the most powerful version of this "perversity thesis" has come in the form of an argument advanced by Charles Hale (2002) under the title "the menace of multiculturalism": rather than creating more egalitarian and inclusionary political orders, multiculturalism conspires with neoliberal market reforms to weaken, divide, and ultimately thwart challenges for radical reform. In an argument that owes much to Gramsci and Foucault, Hale argues that neoliberal multiculturalism operates through a cultural logic that divides "radical" and moderate forms of indigeneity, excluding the former and co-opting the later. In a similar fashion, Elizabeth Povinelli (2002) has argued (for the case of Australia) that official multiculturalism reveals the "cunning of recognition": Indigenous identities and customs are tolerated to the extent that they are not repugnant to existing liberal understandings; thus indigeneity is framed and constrained by liberalism. We find similar sentiments in the work of Bret Gustafson (2002), Peter Wade (1997), and Andean scholars like Luis Tapia (2000). For all these authors "recognition" is hardly an innocent or innocuous act as "sometimes things are named to disarticulate them, not to articulate them, as it is in their invisibility (*clandestinidad*) or exclusion that they are dangerous" (Tapia 2000, 79).

Moreover, rather than fostering more democratic inclusion, MCPs can be part of authoritarian practices. As noted by several authors familiar with the case of Oaxaca, a Mexican state with one of the more comprehensive recognitions of *usos y costumbres* in that country, local communities have also experienced significant state repression and continuing subnational authoritarian politics despite a nationwide process of democratization. Several scholars have pointed to the Machiavellian possibility that ruling elites have used new forms of multiculturalism to preserve their own power and limit the electoral changes of their rivals (Gibson 2005; introduction, chapter 8, this volume).

Yet, as Van Cott (2006) suggests in the most comprehensive empirical review of the neoliberal multicultural thesis, no matter how cunning governing elites have been, MCPs have in several cases been the paths toward more radicalized politics, while in other cases they have led to the more limited reforms described by Hale and others. In her examination of several Latin American cases, Van Cott describes a range of outcomes:

> On one end of the spectrum are states like Chile, Argentina, Peru, and Guatemala, in which neoliberal reforms were undertaken vigorously and now coexist with a modest set of MCPs, the latter limited primarily to language, education, and limited collective land rights. We can call this "neoliberal multiculturalism," borrowing from Hale and Gustafson. On the other end of the spectrum are countries like Ecuador and Venezuela with more expansive sets of multicultural policies that include considerable political representation and autonomy rights. In these countries popular, as well as elite, resistance has delayed the imposition of neoliberal reforms, and been accompanied by political and economic instability, party system fragmentation and decomposition, and widespread social protest. We can call this "populist multiculturalism" to convey the political context in which multicultural reforms were adopted in those countries. (2006, 295)

The location of different states between these neoliberal and populist poles, Van Cott argues, depends on the relative balance in the political arena between neoliberal elites, leftists, and Indigenous organizations. A closer examination of the recent history of Bolivia and Ecuador, two states coded by Van Cott as strong examples of MCP implementation and currently (in 2009) part of South America's turn toward leftist populism, confirms and perhaps even further complicates this complex view of multiculturalism in Latin America.

Bolivia offers a particularly important test case for the neoliberal multicultural thesis. There is no question that multiculturalism and neoliberalism came together in the mid-1990s, embodied by the administration of President Gonzalo Sánchez de

Lozada, a University of Chicago–educated neoliberal technocrat, and Vice President Victor Hugo Cárdenas, an Aymara social movement leader and educator. In the mid-1990s, sweeping decentralization, bilingual education, and agrarian legislation accompanied privatization in what Goni called the Plan for All (Plan de Todos). The articulation of official multicultural and neoliberal Bolivia had the effect of creating opportunities for Indigenous actors like the lowland confederation (CIDOB, Confederation of Indigenous Peoples of Bolivia) that accepted the terms of the new laws and did not challenge the new economic agenda of the government. At the same time, the new regime of the *pluri-multi* disadvantaged (at least initially) the more radical element of Indigenous actors like *cocalero* leader Evo Morales and highland Aymara nationalist Felipe Quispe, whose anti-imperial and anti-neoliberal stance made his confederation, the CSUTCB, an unlikely partner for the government. In fact CSUTCB referred to the reforms as *leyes malditas,* evil or damned laws, and Victor Hugo Cárdenas flatly announced that the only national organization that had the capacity to carry out development programs was the lowland CIDOB (Cárdenas, interview, 1999, cited in Lucero 2008). The effect of these official multicultural policies, as many scholars argue, has been to divide Indigenous actors into pragmatic and radical categories, and thus co-opt and further divide movements.[3]

Beginning in 2000, however, a series of "wars"—over the privatization of water in Cochabamba, over taxes, over escalating militarization in the coca-growing tropics, and finally over the exportation of natural gas—have changed the dynamics in Bolivia (see figure 1.1). The cycle of protests began with the ill-considered privatization plan that resulted, in some cases, in a 400 percent increase in the cost of water in local communities.[4] Subsequent protests occurred in the valleys by the *cocaleros* led by Evo Morales, and in the altiplano led by the radical Aymara Indianista leader of the highland confederation of rural workers (CSUTCB) Felipe Quispe and subsequently by the Quechua leader of another faction of the CSUTCB, Román Loayza.[5] The waves of protest continued as Sánchez de Lozada returned to the presidency in

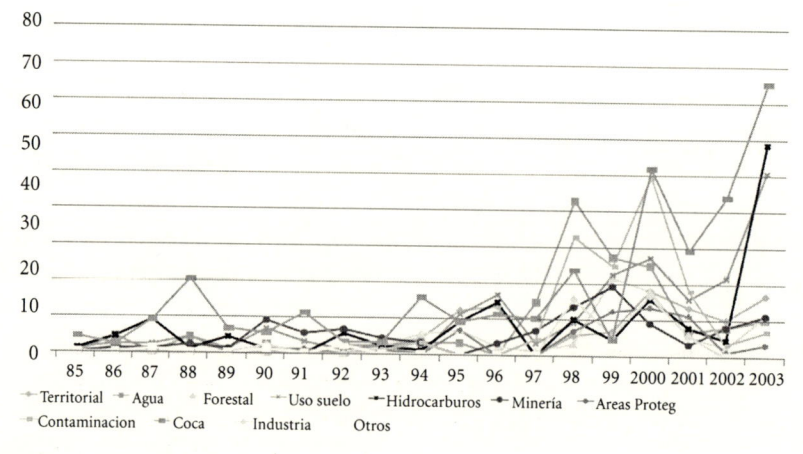

FIGURE 1.1

Frequency of Conflicts per Year (1985–2003)

Source: United Nations Development Programme (2004).

2002 and pursued unpopular tax hikes and an even less popular plan to export gas through the historic national enemy (Chile) to the contemporary imperial center (the U.S.). Hundreds of thousands of protesters took to the streets and demanded Sánchez de Lozada's resignation. Deadly violence from the state only made matters worse and the president was forced to step down from office and leave the country in October 2003. His vice president, Carlos Mesa, became the new chief executive and moved cautiously, calling for a national referendum on natural gas. Though he was able to get support for a plan to export natural gas, increasing fuel prices and greater calls for regional autonomy from lowland elites unleashed protests from both Left and Right. Indigenous leaders continued to pressure the state, though in different ways. *Cocalero* leader Morales, positioning himself as a pragmatic presidential contender, was initially willing to give Mesa time and to remain open to dialogue over how to deal with multinational natural gas corporations. Meanwhile, Quispe escalated his rhetorical assaults by calling for an independent Aymara state. Mesa was unwilling to resort to violence and instead used the threat of resignation to stoke support, especially from the middle classes who were worried about the chaos that might come in his wake. While the strategy bought Mesa some time, in June 2005 Indigenous and popular organizations came together in a united opposition that ultimately forced Mesa to tender his resignation for the last time. After a caretaker government, Evo Morales won a historic landslide victory in 2005, becoming the first Indigenous president to rule in this Indigenous-majority country.

As president, Evo Morales has provided further evidence of the complications and contradictions of the current moment of what Nancy Postero (2007) has called "post-multicultural" Bolivia. This post-multicultural moment is celebrated by some as a broad, popular project that articulates an anti-imperial and leftist politics with a stated commitment to "decolonize" Bolivia. Morales's "nationalization" of the hydrocarbon sector (which was really more of a renegotiation of contracts with foreign oil and gas companies), new land reform legislation, and a Constituent Assembly that produced a new constitution all are emblematic of that moment. Yet, in practice, there are complications and contradictions, as suggested by mixed messages in education policies (discussed above) and conflict with lowland Indigenous peoples who continue to be unhappy with a central government reluctant to consult them about extractive policies in their lands (Bebbington 2009). In 2011, conflicts reached a crisis point as the Morales government violently repressed Indigenous protesters who opposed the construction of a major road through protected Indigenous territory. Two cabinet ministers resigned and Morales declared that a referendum would decide the fate of the road. Nevertheless, the conflict showed the internal contradictions of a presidency that has sometimes governed in the name of Indigenous people and other times despite them (see chapters 3 and 4, this volume).

As Carmen Martínez Novo notes in chapter 5, Ecuador presents a similarly ambivalent tale about the consequences of MCPs. On the one hand, Ecuador was one of the strongest examples of not only Indigenous movement activity in the 1990s but also Indigenous-controlled policy making. With agencies for Indigenous development (CODENPE) and intercultural bilingual education (DINEIB) in the hands of activists from the main Indigenous confederation, CONAIE, Ecuador was hailed by many as a model to be followed by other Indigenous peoples (Alfred and Corntassel 2003). CONAIE and other Indigenous organizations proved to be powerful challengers to neoliberal policymakers including Jamil Mahuad, a Harvard-educated technocratic president, whose controversial handling of a financial crisis (which included the dollarization of the Ecuadorian economy) provoked massive discontent.

This crisis led to what was clearly a pivotal moment in the history of Indigenous politics, the dramatic events of January 21, 2000, in which CONAIE and sectors of the military led by Colonel Lucio Gutiérrez overthrew Mahuad and for a few hours held power as a "junta of national salvation." The high command of the military, under U.S. pressure, abandoned the junta and returned power to Gustavo Noboa, Mahuad's vice president. Over the following months, all those involved in the coup were granted amnesty and the negotiations with the International Monetary Fund were effectively stalled. Aside from dollarization, all the measures Mahuad had sought to implement were abandoned during the remainder of the Noboa administration. Gutiérrez, in alliance with CONAIE again, ran for president in 2002 and won, seemingly opening the doors to a renewed military-Indigenous alliance. However, Gutiérrez quickly disappointed his Indigenous partners. He signed a letter of intent with the IMF signaling his intention to pursue austerity measures, which again would be felt most sharply in the poorest sectors of society. In effect, "the economic policy of the [Gutiérrez] regime is hardly new, to the contrary, it is a more orthodox expression of the dominant thinking in Latin America over the past two decades" (Correa, quoted in Acosta 2003–2004). The Indigenous members of Gutiérrez's cabinet, Luis Macas and Nina Pacari, left the government in 2003. After less than a year in government, CONAIE returned to its role of opposition (see chapter 5, this volume).

This time, however, the constellation of forces seemed less favorable to the kind of leadership that CONAIE had exercised in the 1990s. First, Gutiérrez was more capable of dividing the Indigenous movement by reaching out to former CONIAE president Antonio Vargas, who became Gutiérrez's minister of social welfare (and was denounced as a traitor by CONAIE), as well as to other Indigenous actors, including the national Evangelical Indigenous federation (FEINE) and sectors of the Amazon still loyal to fellow Amazonian Antonio Vargas. Within the office of CONAIE and throughout Ecuador, one heard worries about a severe organizational crisis. The decline in mobilizing capacity of CONAIE was all too obvious in the noticeably small "uprising" that CONAIE convoked to protest Gutiérrez's policies, only to be called off for lack of participation. Such a thing would have been unthinkable in the 1990s.

In 2005, Gutiérrez faced more than the opposition of regrouping CONAIE, as huge protests against his closing of the Supreme Court forced him out of office. While Indigenous people were not the main actors in this case of popular insurrection, which included students, unions, and other popular sectors, in many ways Indigenous people paved the way for a broader expression of citizen outrage that took to the streets in defense of democracy. Still, there is no question that the Indigenous movement has lost some of the power that it had in the 1990s. The last spike of social mobilization in the 1990s is unlike previous ones in the decade because, as Becker (2011) notes, Indigenous organizations were notably absent (see figure 1.2).

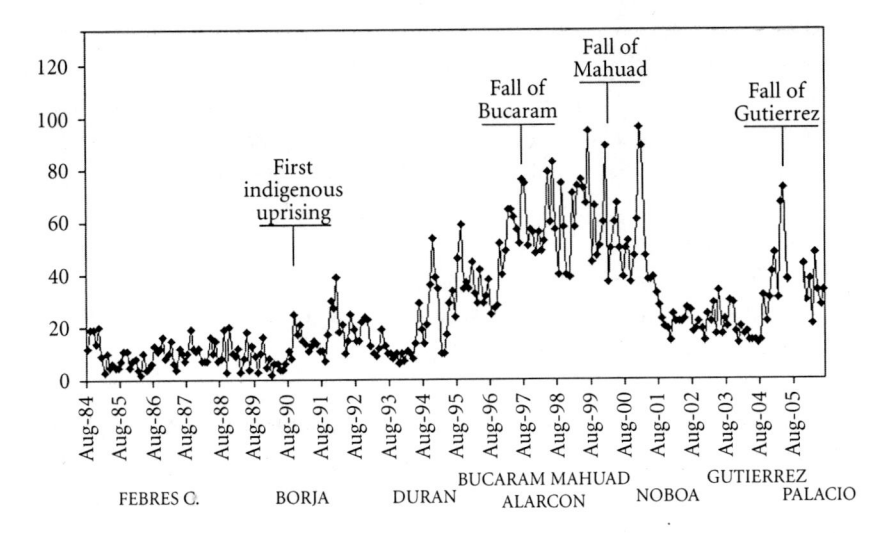

FIGURE 1.2
Number of Conflicts per Month
Source: CAAP, elaborated by León Zamosc. Reproduced with permission.

Luis Macas's decision to run for president and avoid an alliance with leftist economist Rafael Correa (the ultimate winner in the 2006 elections) has been questioned by many. Macas won just over 2 percent of the vote and fell well short of reproducing the kind of victory that Evo Morales claimed in Bolivia. He also was far behind the party of Lucio Gutiérrez, who even without Gutiérrez as a candidate placed third in the national election.

The victor at the polls, Rafael Correa, followed the lead of Chávez in Venezuela and Morales in Bolivia in speaking of nationalization and convoking elections for a Constituent Assembly that rewrote the constitution. This electoral process has been contentious, though, as fifty-seven legislators (in a congressional body of one hundred) were removed by the Electoral Tribunal for these representatives' opposition to the Constituent Assembly. The removal of the legislators was partially reversed by the Constitutional Tribunal, though that reversal too was met by the decision of Congress to remove all the members of the Constitutional Tribunal. Meanwhile, Correa declared that the "long dark night of neoliberalism" was over. However, the place of Indigenous actors and even of key political institutions in this new "post-neoliberal" morning is still an open question (*Economist* 2007). Correa rejected CONAIE's proposal for a plurinational representation in the Constituent Assembly and thus was seen as limiting Indigenous representation in that body, though it should be pointed out that Indigenous organizations in Bolivia made the same criticism of Evo Morales, who also used traditional Western criteria for electing members of the Constituent Assembly in his country (see chapters 4 and 5, this volume).

Additionally, Indigenous organizations have been divided over how much to support Correa's progressive economic initiatives. Correa's commitment to extractive mineral activities (oil and mining especially) have been the source of serious disagreement with many Indigenous organizations. The decision to close CODENPE and remove DINEIB's autonomy of the was seen by some as a reaction to the criticisms of Indigenous organizations and as further evidence of an Indigenous movement that is much weaker than it was only a few years ago. CONAIE President Marlon Santi, while endorsing the new constitution, nevertheless accused Correa of dividing and co-opting Indigenous peoples and went on to accuse him of maintaining "racist" and "neo-liberal" policies (quoted in Wood 2009). Correa has returned the favor and repeatedly accused Ecuador's social movements of being "extremist" or "infantile," going as far as saying, "I hope that the Leftist radicals who do not believe in the oil companies, the mining companies, the market or the transnationals go away" (ibid.). While the picture is complicated, it is clear that the Indigenous movement, which was weakened by its disastrous alliance with Lucio Gutiérrez, has yet to recover the cohesion and influence that it enjoyed during the 1990s.

The tensions between President Correa and Indigenous organizations raise one final possible version of the perversity thesis: that the expression of Indigenous political voice may generate a backlash from non-Indigenous actors. This backlash has been more dramatic in Bolivia as the "media luna" departments in the lowlands, especially the department of Santa Cruz, have borrowed from the vocabulary of Indigenous movements themselves and articulated their own projects for autonomy and recognition. These projects, though, have often been accompanied by thinly (if at all) veiled racist ideas and new organizations like the Unión Juvenil Cruzenista that have clashed violently with supporters of Evo Morales and his Movement toward Socialism Party. Similar clashes in the valley city of Cochabamba in January 2007 also reflected conflicts between the "civic" committees of the Right and the social movements of the Left. In this struggle between "civics" and "socials," Morales has spoken openly about assassination attempts and has expelled various U.S. officials (including the U.S. ambassador) for being on the side of what he calls "oligarchs." Opposition leaders speak of Morales's growing authoritarianism, his hatred of non-Indigenous people, and replicating the experience of Hugo Chávez in Venezuela (chapter 3, this volume; Dangl 2007; Gustafson 2009; Lucero 2012). Lost in this polarized context are the internal divisions that exist on both sides and also the popular support that Morales continues to enjoy. In December 2009, Morales won reelection by a landslide (table 1.3). What is striking about the final votes is not only the resounding national total (63 percent), but also the surprisingly strong showing in opposition strongholds like Santa Cruz and Chuquisaca.

Despite this political strength, Indigenous people remain among the poorest segments of the population in Bolivia and the region as a whole. To explain this gap between the gains of political voice and continuing economic disadvantage, a World Bank study offered this version of the perversity thesis: "Indigenous groups across Bolivia increased prominence throughout the 1990s, resulting in broad success in legislative elections and the effective overthrow of the President early in the following decade. That increased prominence may be associated with employers more frequently recognizing and penalizing Indigenous workers" (Jiménez Pozo, Landa Casazola, and Yañez Aguilar 2006, 54).

It is important to point out that the emergence of strong Indigenous movements may also have net positive effects on equity over the medium and long term. The idea that stronger voice invites stronger discrimination is troubling, not only for its

Table 1.3 2009 Bolivian Election: Vote Share Won by Evo Morales (%)

National	63
La Paz	78
Santa Cruz	46
Cochabamba	66
Chuquisaca	53
Oruro	78
Potosi	77
Tarija	49
Beni	35
Pando	46

Source: Resultados Elecciones Generales 2009, Los Tiempos.com, http://www.lostiempos.com/resultados-elecciones-bolivia-2009.php.

family resemblance to a kind of "blame the victim" logic, but also because it neglects the increased opportunities that Indigenous struggles have forged. Politically, the presence of Indigenous representatives at all levels of government is itself a substantial achievement in securing public attention to Indigenous concerns that were often invisible. Perhaps more fundamentally, the emergence of Indigenous people as political actors carries the promise of challenging what Appadurai (2004) calls the "terms of recognition," in which the dominant cultural descriptions of certain groups are themselves part of the structures of subordination and poverty. Challenging these constraints involves cultivating what Appadurai (2004) calls the poor's "capacity to aspire," which he describes as a metacapacity that enables the poor to work on increasing other capabilities by envisioning alternative political and economic horizons. Given the centuries that have gone into forging the durable and racialized inequalities in Bolivia, it is perhaps not surprising that gains in political voice and changes in the terms of recognition have not (yet?) resulted in economic improvement. That said, the increased income from the renegotiated hydrocarbon contracts has resulted in greater resources for social spending, and the economic policies in Bolivia have, even in times of global economic crisis, resulted in low inflation and surprisingly steady growth (Weisbrot and Sandoval 2007; for a different view see Webber 2011). Thus while conditions remain challenging and poverty remains very high, there are some reasons to question this and other versions of the perversity thesis.

JEOPARDY? GENDER TROUBLE AND AFRO-LATIN AMERICAN MARGINALIZATION

Beyond the possibilities of futility and perverse outcomes, Hirschman suggested that critics of reform often warn of unintended dangers for others. This line of argument is in some ways more subtle than the others in that it does not make any claims about the actual efficacy of the reform in terms of solving the problem at which it is directed. Rather, it suggests "that the proposed change, though perhaps desirable in itself, involves unacceptable costs or consequences of one sort or another" (Hirschman 1991, 81). Transposing Hirschman's description to the world of contemporary multiculturalism, there are two sectors that may find themselves in particular jeopardy. First, I consider the question made famous by Susan Moller Okin (1999): is multiculturalism bad for women? Second, I engage the argument put forth by Juliet Hooker (2005) that Latin American multiculturalisms have been designed with a bias toward Indigenous peoples and have thus worked to exclude racialized Afro-Latin Americans.

Okin (1999) was among the first to suggest that there was a crucial blind spot in the discourses and policies of multiculturalism: they neglected to ask about the gendered consequences of the recognition of certain kinds of cultural practices. Cultural recognition could be another way in which patriarchy and gender discrimination could be reproduced and even reinforced. Okin's intervention was an important one, though it was also one familiar to liberal theorists who worry that in the rush to endorse group rights, individual rights and liberties would be violated.

In the case of Indigenous politics, women continue to be less prevalent than men in leadership positions, though many Indigenous organizations insist that Occidental definitions of gender are out of place. Andean organizations, for example, suggest that their communities are characterized by gender complementarity in ways that are different from Western gender relations. In local communities, it is very common for authority to be exercised by couples, or *chachawarmi* as it is known in Bolivia. Even if men seem to be doing more of the talking, the argument goes, it is often said that the women are the "real" decision makers. This discourse, like all discourses, is itself a kind of performance and should be interrogated and investigated empirically, as many scholars have been doing throughout the region.

In Chiapas, Mexico, for example, women Zapatista leaders like Comandantas Ramona and Esther have become important figures in regional and national politics. In Ecuador, there are many high-profile women leaders in the Indigenous movement, with a celebrated tradition of strong women leaders that goes back to the 1930s, including historic figures like Dolores Cacuango (Becker 2008). Yet for many scholars these women are the exceptions that prove the rule about the enduring marginalization of women. In many communities in Mexico, for example, women have less voice in community meetings because many do not own land. In the community of Nicolas Ruís, Speed (2008) reports, community consensus still means the consensus of the men. As Comandanta Esther explains (in Speed 2008, 133), "we have to struggle more because we are triply looked down on: because we are Indigenous, because we are women, because we are poor." In many communities in Oaxaca, only men can participate in elections and in some cases women who have won local elections have not been allowed to take office (see introduction, this volume; Danielson and Eisenstadt 2009).

In the Andes, some Indigenous leaders and activists suggest that the norms of complementarity exemplified by the *chachawarmi* exercise of authority through married couples is one way in which Indigenous communities avoid the gender discrimination of Western society. Yet for women who are not married or have been widowed, it becomes quickly apparent that the *chachawarmi* solution has clear limits. Moreover, the actual workings of Indigenous organizations suggests that these spaces remain just as male dominated as non-Indigenous spaces. The intersections between gender and indigeneity are complex and even paradoxical. While women, as mothers, are often seen as the essential transmitters of culture and language, they are often confined to the domestic spaces of home and *chakra* while their husbands enter urban migratory and labor networks. Because of these and other economic realities, it is more common for women to be monolingual speakers of Indigenous languages while men acquire the linguistic skills and urban experience that often allow them to pass as mestizos or *cholos*. It is for these economic reasons that, as Marisol de la Cadena (2005) has observed for the case of Peru, women are often seen as "more Indian." Thus while women represent Indigenous authenticity, they are also relegated to secondary status, often by the men of their own communities (Speed 2006, 2008; Aillón 2006).

Critics of multicultural recognition have pointed to these patterns of discrimination as an additional reason to be concerned about the consequences of MCPs. The struggle for cultural rights becomes especially problematic, explain Deer and Leon de Leal (2002, 76, quoted in Speed 2006) "when respect for customary law of traditional customs and practices violates the individual rights of women" (see also Okin 1999). Eisenstadt (see introduction, this volume) raises similar concerns about the tensions between collective and individual rights. In challenging the exclusionary effects of liberal norms, Yashar (2005) explains, Indigenous movements have run the risk of carving out illiberal local spaces.

Nevertheless, it is important to question some of the assumptions behind this notion. First, the critique of multiculturalism as "bad for women" relies on a binary and oppositional scheme that pits "culture" against "gender." Indigenous women themselves have been among the most vocal in rejecting this false choice (Speed 2008). In local, national, and transnational spaces, many Indigenous women have carved out the room in which to forge spaces for the elaboration of projects at the intersection of indigeneity, gender, and class. In this task, they have often been aided by NGO agendas that increasingly institutionalize gender as a "transversal" component of their development work. While these spaces and collaborations are not without their own tensions and limitations, Indigenous women are not without the agency to work toward more equitable gender orders within the context of Indigenous projects of autonomy and self-governance. Additionally, it is worth pointing out that liberalism has also had a long history of being "bad for women." The liberal distinctions between private and public spaces have allowed many forms of homegrown authoritarianism to go unquestioned for much of Western history. One is reminded of Gandhi's famous response to a question about what he thought about Western civilization: it would be a good idea. Similarly, the liberal promise of equal citizenship would also be a good idea, and remains one honored in the breach in too many places. While one should avoid any romantic notions about Indigenous spaces, it is also important to avoid the opposite mistake of seeing them as the static containers of "tradition" and take a closer look to see how Indigenous men and women continue to transform what it means to be "Indigenous," "men," and "women."

Before concluding, it is important to note that in addition to the concern over gender, one other version of Hirschman's jeopardy has arisen in relation to race. Hooker (2005) argues that part of the explanation for the greater success of Indigenous people (versus Afro-descendants) in securing legal rights in Latin America lies in the ways in which they have been racialized and incorporated into the imaginary of the nation-state. She argues that Indigenous people are imagined as culturally distinct and thus deserving of special protection, while Afro-Latin Americans are seen as forming part of the mixed racial composition of national cultures. Peter Wade (1997, 36) has made a similar point and suggests that while both Afro-Latin American and Indigenous people have been seen as Other, there are important differences in the construction of these forms of alterity: "Blacks and Indians have both been characterized as Others, located in the liminal spaces of the nation, but they have fitted in different ways into what I call the structures of alterity."

The consequence of these different spaces in the "structures of alterity" is that MCPs have been designed for Indigenous people more than for Afro-descendants. Afro-Latin Americans often gain cultural rights, as Mark Anderson (2007) explains, "when Afro becomes like Indigenous." Garifuna in Honduras (Anderson 2007), and *quilombo* communities in Brazil (French 2009) are examples of Afro-descendants who have "indigenized" their claims for special recognition, usually by invoking what Greene (2007) has termed the "holy trinity of multicultural peoplehood: Culture + Language + Territory." Thus far, these cases are exceptions to the norm of MCPs that marginalize blackness that Hooker (2005) identifies. The assumptions of MCPs reflect understandings that many Indigenous activists express themselves, that Indigenous "peoplehood" is historically and culturally more valid than Afro-descendants' "peoplehood." As one Amazonian Peruvian leader put it: "We (Indigenous people of the Peruvian Amazon) are a nation, we have identity, we have culture. The Andean peoples have been a nation, have had identity, have had language and culture. The Black peoples are not a people, do not have identity, do not have language or culture" (quoted in García 2009). Multiculturalism, then, if it challenges the exclusion of Indigenous people, seems to fall into the trap of reproducing the exclusion of Afro-Latin Americans.

Nevertheless, though we should be attentive to the dangers of reifying Indigenous and black identities through state policies, we should not neglect how social actors and analysts are blurring the distinctions between "blackness" (as race) and "Indianness" (as ethnicity). Anderson's (2007) ethnographic work in Honduras reveals that the Garifuna are not becoming "like" Indigenous people; rather, they are forging an identity as an Afro-Indigenous people. "The Honduran case suggests that indigeneity and blackness need not describe mutually exclusive modes of representation or identity" (Anderson 2007, 406). Similarly, for the case of Brazil, as Jonathan Warren (2001) argues, the lines between "ethnic" and "racial" identities have been challenged by Indigenous antiracist activism. While we should explore differences in the constructions and consequences of indigeneity and blackness in Latin America,

I concur with Anderson (2007, 407) in suggesting that we "should not reify clear-cut distinctions between indigeneity and blackness, and that they should instead examine the ways they are produced as relational categories of ancestry and culture, sameness and difference, inclusion and exclusion."

CONCLUSION

Multiculturalism in Latin America has been crafted with a mix of intentions and has given rise to a host of unintended consequences. While the empirical picture is complicated and mixed, this chapter nonetheless confirms one of Donna Lee Van Cott's important contentions: the shape of contemporary cultural politics in Latin America has been largely determined by the interaction of state elites, emerging political forces, and the strength and strategy of social movements. Far from a homogenous picture of multiculturalism, the diverse configuration of state and social forces should alert us to a range of causes and consequences of MCPs in the region.

In borrowing from Albert Hirschman's suggestive theses against reform, I have also borrowed his intention of using these critiques not to make the case for reaction but to suggest the importance of avoiding rhetorical standoffs produced by the claims of both progressives and conservatives, each side claiming that action (or inaction) will not solve the problem, will make things worse, or will jeopardize other things we should treasure. While the truth claims of each position (for or against reform) should be the subject of serious and sustained debate, it is the debate and not the resolution of it that for Hirschman (1991, 168), ever the optimist, holds the promise of a more "democracy friendly" kind of dialogue. In a similar vein, I would like to suggest that examining the mixed legacy of multicultural reforms in Latin America suggests two debates that can usefully improve our understanding of those reforms and also hopefully contribute to more democracy-friendly futures.

First, there is the debate over opportunities and dangers in an age of multicultural neoliberalism. As Charles Hale (2002), Bret Gustafson (2002), Peter Wade (1997), and many others have warned, there is the danger that the official recognition of Indigenous identities and projects becomes one more tool of dominant power, authorizing certain kinds of Indigenous subjects (*el indio permitido*) while ruling others out. Yet it is important not to give too much power to either neoliberalism or multiculturalism as neither of these large labels (alone or together) sets hard limits on the fluidity of social subjectivities. Suzana Sawyer (2004) and Donna Lee Van Cott (2006) in different ways have shown that neoliberal and multicultural projects have generated both transgressive and compliant forms of Indigenous subjectivities. Though Van Cott saw much to criticize in Hale's arguments about neoliberal multiculturalism and the *indio permitido*, Hale himself noted that "a crucial facet of resistance...is rearticulation, which creates bridges between authorized and condemned ways of being Indian" (2004, 20). In these large and complex cultural politics of resistance and accommodation, there are no unbridgeable divides between *indios permitidos* and *indios rebeldes*.

Second, and along the same lines, there is a debate about the scale of multiculturalism. In order to understand the politics of actually existing multiculturalisms, we may take a lesson from the trajectory of the work of Van Cott. Like many other students of constitutional multiculturalism, her early work was on national-level actors and processes. Her comparison of constitutional change in Colombia and Bolivia reflected some of the optimism around MCPs of the 1990s and even carried the perhaps overly cheerful title *The Friendly Liquidation of the Past* (2000). Her last book, *Radical Democracy in the Andes* (2008), was no less ambitious but it turned to the level of Indigenous municipalities and explained a checkered set of outcomes. In some municipalities, Indigenous mayors and councils had created a remarkably vibrant and effective style of participatory democracy, while in others their efforts had been thwarted. Much can be learned from both books, but there is no question that the change in scale, moving from national to local dynamics, allowed Van Cott to explore carefully the peaks and valleys of Indigenous politics. As many anthropologists and, increasingly, political scientists have found, indigeneity and blackness, along with the policies that seek to manage them, are multiscalar phenomena; they are connected to global histories and processes but are constantly (re)constructed and negotiated through interactions in concrete local settings (see, e.g., Warren and Jackson 2002). Only by comprehending these processes at their various scales can we approach an accurate picture of the challenges they pose for democracy.

ACKNOWLEDGMENTS

If chapters could have dedications, this one would be dedicated to the memory of our colleague Donna Lee Van Cott. It can be read as part of the ongoing conversation to which her work contributed so much. I also thank Todd Eisenstadt, Shannan Mattiace, and María Elena García for their help with the ideas presented here.

NOTES

1. These are, of course, taken from Hirschman's (1991) classic *The Rhetoric of Reaction*. In using his categories, I do not seek to cast critics of official multiculturalism (among which I count myself) as simplistic reactionaries. Rather, in moving past glowing endorsements of MCPs and their demonization I hope to show the complexities of the empirical middle ground.
2. In solidarity with Native intellectuals and activists and in emphasizing the politics of peoplehood that comes with other terms (Afro-Latino, Asian-American, etc.) and peoples, I capitalize the term "Indigenous" in this chapter.
3. See, for example, Hale (2001) and Wade (1997).
4. Even officials from the World Bank called the privatization scheme a "fiasco" in terms of design and implementation, and formally withdrew support for the plan (see Walton 2004).
5. In 2003, the CSUTCB splintered into two groups: one led by Quispe, the other by Loayza. Quispe was the main figure in the Aymara altiplano while Loayza commands a greater following in the Quechua valleys. The Confederación Unica was anything but *única* (Lucero 2008). After that, the CSUTCB became one organization again, led, for the first time, by a Guaraní from the eastern lowlands, Isaac Avalos. As is often the case in social movement organization, however, internal tension continues to exist within the CSUTCB.

REFERENCES

Acosta, Alberto. 2003–2004. "Ecuador: El coronel mató pronto a la esperanza." *Ecuador Debate* 61 (November 2003–February 2004).

Aillón, Virginia, ed. 2006. *Género, etnicidad y participación política*. La Paz: Diakonia.

Alfred, Taiaiake, and Jeff Corntassel. 2003. "A Decade of Rhetoric for Indigenous Peoples." *Indian Country Today*, May 11.

Anderson, Mark. 2007. "When Afro Becomes (Like) Indigenous: Garifuna and Afro-Indigenous Politics in Honduras." *Journal of Latin American and Caribbean Anthropology* 12 (2): 384–413.

Andolina, Robert, et al. 2009. *Indigenous Development in the Andes: Culture, Power, and Transnationalism*. Durham, NC: Duke University Press.

Appadurai, Arjun. 2001. "The Capacity to Aspire." In *Culture and Public Action*, edited by V. Rao and M. Walton, 59–84. Stanford, CA: Stanford University Press.

Bebbington, Anthony. 2009. "The New Extraction: Rewriting the Political Ecology of the Andes." *NACLA Report on the Americas* 42 (5): 12–19.

Brysk, Alison. 2000. *From Global Village to Tribal Village: Indian Rights and International Relations in Latin America*. Stanford, CA: Stanford University Press.

Chapin, Mac. 2004. "A Challenge to Conservationists." *World Watch Magazine* 17 (6). http://www.worldwatch.org/node/565.

Chuji, Mónica. 2009. "El cierre del CODENPE: Otro ejemplo del racismo y autoritarismo del presidente Correa." January 27. http://www.llacta.org/notic/2009/not0127a.htm.

Dangl, Benjamin. 2007. *The Price of Fire: Resource Wars and Social Movements in Bolivia*. Oakland, CA: AK Press.

Danielson, Michael S., and Todd A. Eisenstadt. 2009. "Walking Together, but in Which Direction? Gender Discrimination and Multicultural Practices in Oaxaca, Mexico." *Politics and Gender* 5 (2): 153–184.

De la Cadena, Marisol. 1995. "Women are More Indian: Ethnicity and Gender in a Community near Cuzco." In *Ethnicity, Markets and Migration in the Andes: At the Crossroads of History and Anthropology*, edited by Brooke Larson and Olivia Harris, 329–348. Durham, NC: Duke University Press.

Economist. 2007. "Ecuador's Rafael Correa: Tightening His Grip." April 19. http://www.economist.com/node/9040321

French, Jan Hoffman. 2009. "Ethnoracial Land Restitution: Finding Indians and Fugitive Slave Descendants in Northeastern Brazil." In *The Rights and Wrongs of Land Restitution: "Restoring What Was Ours,"* edited by Derick Fay and Deborah James, 123–140. New York: Routledge-Cavendish.

García, María Elena. 2009. "Lessons from the Andes: The PROEIB Andes and the Challenges of Indigenous Higher Education in Latin America." Paper Presented at the Meetings of the Native American and Indigenous Studies Association, Minneapolis, May 20–23.

Gibson, Edward L. 2005. "Boundary Control: Subnational Authoritarianism in Democratic Countries." *World Politics* 58 (1): 101–132.

Greene, Shane. 2006. "Getting over the Andes: The Geo-Eco-Politics of Indigenous Movements in Peru's Twenty-First-Century Inca Empire." *Journal of Latin American Studies* 38 (2): 1–28.

Gustafson, Bret. 2002. "Paradoxes of Liberal Indigenism: Indigenous Movements, State Process, and Intercultural Reform in Bolivia." In *The Politics of Ethnicity: Indigenous Peoples in Latin American States*, edited by David Maybury-Lewis, 267–306. Cambridge, MA: Harvard University Press.

Gustafson, Bret. 2009. *New Languages of the State: Indigenous Resurgence and the Politics of Knowledge in Bolivia*. Durham, NC: Duke University Press.

Hale, Charles. 2002. "Does Multiculturalism Menace? Governance, Cultural Rights, and the Politics of Identity in Guatemala." *Journal of Latin American Studies* 34: 485–524.

Hale, Charles. 2004. "Rethinking Indigenous Politics in the Era of the 'Indio Permitido.'" *NACLA Report on the Americas* 38 (2): 16–21.

Hirschman, Albert. 1991. *The Rhetoric of Reaction*. Cambridge, MA: Harvard University Press.

Holston, James. 2007. *Insurgent Citizenship: Disjunctions of Democracy and Modernity in Brazil*. Princeton, NJ: Princeton University Press.

Hooker, Juliet. "Indigenous Inclusion/Black Exclusion: Race, Ethnicity and Multicultural Citizenship in Latin America." *Journal of Latin American Studies* 37 (2): 285–310.

ILO. 1999. "Introduction to ILO Convention No.169." http://www.ilo.org/public/english/region/ampro/mdtsanjose/indigenous/intro169.htm

Jiménez Pozo, Wilson, Fernando Landa Casazola, and Ernesto Yañez Aguilar. 2006. "Bolivia." In *Indigenous People, Poverty and Human Development in Latin America: 1994–2004*, edited by Gilette Hall and Harry Patrinos, 40–65. New York: Palgrave.

Keck, Margaret, and Kathryn Sikkink. 1998. *Activists beyond Borders: Advocacy Networks in International Politics*. Ithaca, NY: Cornell University Press.

Kingsman, Santiago. 2008. "Entre la asimilación y la diferencia: la Asamblea Constituyente y los territorios indígenas." *Iconos: Revista de Ciencias Sociales* 32: 25–29.

Lucero, José Antonio. 2008. *Struggles of Voice: The Politics of Indigenous Representation in the Andes*. Pittsburgh, PA: University of Pittsburgh Press.

Lucero, José Antonio. 2012. "'El encuentro entre campesinos y ciudadanos no se pudo evitar': Violence, Democracy, and Contention in Bolivia." In *Interrogating the Civil Society Agenda*, edited by Sonia Alvarez et al. Manuscript in preparation.

Morin, Françoise, and Roberto Santana, eds. 2003. *Lo Transnacional: instrumento y desafío para los pueblos indígenas*. Quito: Abya Yala.

OACNUDH. 2003. *Diagnóstico sobre la Situación de los Derechos Humanos en México*. Mexico City: Oficina del Alto Comisionado de las Naciones Unidas para los Derechos Humanos en México.

Okin, Susan Moller. 1999. *Is Multiculturalism Bad for Women?* Princeton, NJ: Princeton University Press.

O'Neill, Kathleen. 2003. "Decentralization as an Electoral Strategy." *Comparative Political Studies* 36 (9): 1068–1091.

Postero, Nancy. 2007. *Now We Are Citizens: Indigenous Politics in Post-Multicultural Bolivia*. Stanford, CA: Stanford University Press.

Povinelli, Elizabeth. 2002. *The Cunning of Recognition: Indigenous Alterities and the Making of Australian Multiculturalism*. Durham, NC: Duke University Press.

Sawyer, Suzana. 2004. *Crude Chronicles: Indigenous Politics, Multinational Oil, and Neoliberalism in Ecuador*. Durham, NC: Duke University Press,.

Speed, Shannon. 2006. "Rights at the Intersection: Gender and Ethnicity in Neoliberal Mexico." In *Dissident Women: Gender and Cultural Politics in Chiapas*, edited by Shannon Speed, R. Aida Hernández Castillo, and Lynn M. Stephen. Austin: University of Texas Press.

Speed, Shannon. 2008. *Rights in Rebellion: Indigenous Struggles and Human Rights in Chiapas*. Stanford, CA: Stanford University Press.

Tapia, Luis. 2000. "La densidad de la síntesis." In *El retorno de la Bolivia plebeya*, edited by Luis Tapia et al. La Paz: Muela del Diablo Editores.

United Nations Development Programme. 2004. *Human Development Report 2004: Cultural Liberty in Today's Diverse World*. New York: UNDP.

Van Cott, Donna Lee. 2000. *The Friendly Liquidation of the Past: The Politics of Diversity in Latin America*. Pittsburgh: University of Pittsburgh Press.

Van Cott, Donna Lee. 2001. "Explaining Ethnic Autonomy Regimes in Latin America." *Studies in Comparative International Development* 35 (4): 30–58.

Van Cott, Donna Lee. 2006. "Multiculturalism against Neoliberalism in Latin America." In *Multiculturalism and the Welfare State*, edited by Keith Banting and Will Kymlicka, 272–296. London: Oxford University Press.

Van Cott, Donna Lee. 2008. *Radical Democracy in the Andes*. Cambridge: Cambridge University Press.

Wade, Peter. 1997. *Race and Ethnicity in Latin America*. London: Pluto Press.

Walton, Michael. 2004. "Neoliberalism in Latin America: Good, Bad, or Incomplete?" *Latin American Research Review* 29 (3): 181–196.

Warren, Jonathan W. 2001. *Racial Revolutions: Antiracism and Indian Resurgence in Brazil*. Durham, NC: Duke University Press.

Warren, Kay, and Jean Jackson, eds. 2002. *Indigenous Movements, Self-Representation, and the State in Latin America*. Austin: University of Texas Press.

Webber, Jeffrey. 2011. *From Rebellion to Reform in Bolivia: Class Struggle, Indigenous Liberation, and the Politics of Evo Morales*. Chicago: Haymarket Books.

Weisbrot, Marc, and Luis Sandoval. 2007. Bolivia's Economy—An Update. CEPR Issue Brief. August. http://www.cepr.net/documents/publications/bolivia_update_2007_08.pdf.

Wood, Rachel. 2009. "What does Ecuador's '21st Century Socialism' Mean for the Amazon's Indigenous?" Council on Hemispheric Affairs, January 28. http://www.coha.org/2009/01/what-does-ecuador's-"21st-century-socialism"-mean-for-the-amazon's-Indigenous.

Yashar, Deborah. 2005. *Contesting Citizenship in Latin America: The Rise of Indigenous Movements and the Post-Liberal Challenge*. Cambridge: Cambridge University Press.

Zizek, Slavoj. 1997. "Multiculturalism, or, the Cultural Logic of Multinational Capitalism." *New Left Review* 225 (September–October): 28–51.

2 Constitutional Multiculturalism in Chiapas

Hollow Reforms That Nullify Autonomy Rights

Araceli Burguete Cal y Mayor
(translated by Andrew McKelvey)

Multiculturalism has expanded in Mexico through constitutional reforms and government policies relating to indigenous rights and cultures. This advance in implementation has not, however, been accompanied by a theoretical-political debate on what such a concept and its related policies mean. Moreover, its application has been without prior consultation. Discussion of the concept of multiculturalism has hardly gotten underway in the last few years because one of the traits of the term's use in Mexico is its imprecision. The same term is used to denote the social fact of cultural diversity and the emergence of the indigenous movement. In some cases, struggles for autonomy are labeled "multicultural," while in others multiculturalism is identified as synonymous with indigenous autonomy, among other errors in its usage.

This work tries to contribute to the clarification of the concept. The first part explores the theoretical and political differences between the paradigms of indigenous autonomy and multiculturalism. The second and third sections present an anthropology-driven approach to the debates surrounding the concept of multiculturalism. Specifically of interest is the so-called constitutional multiculturalism, which, due to the emphasis on constitutional reforms of the politics of recognition, is the way that multiculturalism has been defined in Latin America. In order to clarify the use of the term "multiculturalism" in Mexico, and particularly in Chiapas, texts of recent constitutional reforms are analyzed. In these, it can clearly be seen how, through the legislative technique, recognized rights are emptied and turned into "hollow rights" that are useless in bringing about change in the order of things.

INDIGENOUS AUTONOMY AND MULTICULTURALISM: A CONCEPTUAL BOUNDARY

Rights for the protection of minorities and rights of indigenous peoples are both drawn from a single theoretical concept: human rights. The new configuration of postwar Europe placed cultural groups that differed from the national majority in the position of being "minorities." A few years after its creation in 1945, the United Nations (UN) approved two instruments of protection. First came the proclamation of the Convention against Genocide on December 9, 1948. A day later, the Universal Declaration of Human Rights (UDHR) was adopted. The convention had as its purpose the avoidance of discrimination against cultural groups. At the same time, it committed states to guaranteeing the rights of those groups' members. The matters of minorities, nations, and nationalisms were themes of great interest in Cold War Europe (Lerner 1991).

Additionally, during those same years, other concerns erupted in the field of human rights. Until the 1960s, collective rights had no recognition at the UN, but little by little they were incorporated as a concern of the UN system. The change had its origin in the doctrine of decolonization. The UDHR established equal rights and the principle of nondiscrimination. This doctrine called into question the colonial paradigm that legitimized social hierarchies built on racial and ethnic bases. The colonial paradigm had enjoyed acceptance from the sixteenth century through the first half of the twentieth. In the imagination of European society, colonial relationships were accepted as legitimate,[1] but by the second half of the twentieth century, these ideas were losing legitimacy. Also at that time, nationalist struggles sprang up in some of the imperial colonies, placing the problem of colonialism directly on the table.

These struggles put in motion ideas that, while not new, had never before received such attention. The most novel proposal was to establish as a universal principle the right of all the world's peoples to determine their own destiny. This was brought into the Atlantic Charter and then into the United Nations Charter, and it would serve as a cornerstone for the paradigm of the right of self-determination of peoples. In the second half of the twentieth century, in the midst of the Cold War, the UN took on the challenge of contributing to decolonization around the world and of monitoring the right of self-determination. For this purpose, it created the Special Committee on Decolonization, known as the Committee of 24, in 1961. The committee's purpose was to motivate and mobilize public opinion in support of the decolonization process, battling for the implementation of the Declaration on the Granting of Independence to Colonial Countries and Peoples (Falk 2002).[2]

To ratify this commitment, the UN proclaimed the so-called twin covenants: the International Covenant on Civil and Political Rights and the International Covenant on Economic, Social and Cultural Rights, which were adopted and made available for signature, ratification, and accession on December 16, 1966. The first article of both covenants reads: "All peoples have the right of self-determination. By virtue of that right they freely determine their political status and freely pursue their economic, social and cultural development." From 1961 to 1977, dozens of countries on several continents (principally Asia and Africa) gained their independence, inspired by the doctrine of decolonization (Stavenhagen 1986).

While struggles for decolonization were taking place in those areas, indigenous societies in Latin America were facing situations that they described as "internal colonialism" and invoked the right of self-determination. Emerging indigenous organizations, together with groups of academic and nascent international NGOs such as the International Work Group for Indigenous Affairs (IWGIA), went to the Committee of 24 to demand the right of decolonization. The committee showed reservations about the petition. The idea of "colonized peoples" had not originally included indigenous groups, and so it turned the matter over to the Subcommission on the Prevention of Discrimination and Protection of Minorities (Rouland et al. 1999).

The indigenous actors and the NGOs supporting them disagreed with this redirection. They rejected being considered minorities within their own territories. They had been the first nations, with an existence that predated the formation of the national states, and their autonomous development had been stunted by the actions of the colonization under which they had suffered since the sixteenth century (Burguete and Ruiz 1994). To bring together the elements in this debate, in 1970, the Subcommission on Prevention of Discrimination and Protection of Minorities asked José R. Martínez Cobo to conduct a study to clarify the issues at hand. The results of the study, presented in 1983, were unequivocal. Martínez Cobo concluded that these groups maintained a historical continuity with the societies that had existed prior to the European invasion. They were assumed to be different from the societies that had become prevalent in their lands (or part of their lands), allowing them to affirm that colonial and postcolonial integration had not been achieved. Agreeing with Martínez Cobo, the indigenous groups consulted during the study showed their determination to continue as distinct societies, along with the will to preserve, develop, and pass on to future generations their ancestral lands and their ethnic identity as a basis for continued existence as a people. This identity was based in their own particular cultural patterns, social institutions, and legal systems. In his conclusions, Martínez Cobo accepted these groups as "peoples," and recommended that the UN take steps toward recognizing them as such. He also proposed an agenda that included recognizing their right to self-determination.

In rejecting treatment as minorities, the nascent indigenous movement in Latin America took the Martínez Cobo report as its own and began to build its own theoretical-political proposal. Thus emerged the indigenous autonomy paradigm. Under this approach, the indigenous groups were seen as peoples and claimed the right to decolonization through autonomy arrangements, including: (1) control of territory; (2) administering the natural resources found within their lands; (3) governing themselves using their own authorities and their own institutional structure; (4) exercising the powers belonging to them within the framework of the nation-states in which they lived; and (5) other arrangements deriving from the same approach.

Various ethnic groups around the world, who claimed that their separate cultural development had been halted by their colonial status, also took on the name "indigenous." This occurred in northern Europe, and also in Asia, Africa, Oceania, the United States, and Canada. The majority of these groups clung to the principle of self-determination, and they sought its realization in most cases by (but not limited to) autonomy arrangements. These claims crystallized a global indigenous movement that could be found at the UN year after year building an agenda for autonomous rights (Burguete and Ruiz 1994). Today, more than 200 million people worldwide identify themselves as belonging to indigenous peoples, sharing the status of a people under a relationship of internal colonialism to the nation-state in which they live.[3] This political self-identification produced what Castro (2008) has called the "universalization of the indigenous condition."

On another front, while this was occurring in Latin America, the theory of the rights of "national minorities" was also opening up new theoretical-political routes of inquiry and changing the points of focus that were dominant in postwar Europe. The fall of communist regimes in Eastern Europe unleashed a wave of nationalisms, shifting the ethnic map in that part of the world and giving rise to nationalist conflicts that had been thought to have ended. In addition, other ethnic groups that sprang up as a result of massive transnational migrations had to be added. The countries of the Northern Hemisphere, in Europe, the United States, and Canada, saw the ethnic composition of their societies change, taking on a multiethnic appearance (Rex 2002). In response to the issues raised by the emergence of ethnicity, states have had to put forward policies aimed at accommodating the multicultural challenge. In this way, the multiculturalism paradigm arose as a public policy strategy for confronting, from a liberal perspective, the challenges of governing cultural diversity (Kymlicka 1996). These policies have been referred to as the "politics of recognition" (Taylor 2001).

In spite of the growing expansion of the concept of multiculturalism in various regions of the world, it has not been accepted in Mexico. It is not a point of rhetoric on which political and government actors draw, and it is absent from the public discourse of the country's indigenous organizations. It is instructive that this concept is not included anywhere in the more than forty pages of the Accords on Indigenous Rights and Culture (also called the San Andrés Accords), signed in February 1996 between the Zapatista National Liberation Army (EZLN) and the government of Mexico (Hernández and Vera 1998), nor is it mentioned in the documents on indigenous policies that have grown out of them.

However, such rhetorical silence does not hide the fact that the policies of multiculturalism have in fact been implemented in Mexico since the 1990s, especially after 1994. The result is a paradox. The word "autonomy" is repeated frequently throughout the San Andrés Accords, since that was the right that the federal and state governments promised the Zapatistas they would recognize. But the Accords' actual interpretation, both in their legal dimension and in the government's policies, has thrown out the multiculturalism paradigm. This fact should be evident as one reflects on the politics of recognition in Chiapas and the constitutional reforms regarding indigenous rights and culture (constitutional multiculturalism, as it is called).

CONSTITUTIONAL MULTICULTURALISM IN LATIN AMERICA

After 1994, the concept of multiculturalism began to be used in Mexico, mostly in academia, but its usage is confused. The same word serves to represent the social fact of cultural diversity (Carbonell 2004),[4] as well as to describe the political strategies of indigenous organizations (Arias 2008).[5] Various authors have turned to the conceptual corpus created by Kymlicka to explain the questions that pertain to indigenous peoples, but they have done so uncritically. Thus, inspired by that author's liberal thought, they frequently call indigenous peoples "national minorities," and they concern themselves with how to "accommodate" them as such within the organization of the Mexican state. These interpretations ignore the dividing line that the indigenous movement has drawn for over two decades between itself and the concept of minorities, with the result that they do not distinguish "indigenous peoples" and "minorities" as nonequivalent concepts.

Within anthropology the concept has been met with reservations and a critical eye. In Latin America, the notion of multiculturalism has been associated with the politics of recognition, specifically those that have developed out of the constitutional reforms that recognize the rights of indigenous peoples (Sieder 2002; Toranzo 1993; Yashar 2005; Assies et al. 1999; Pineda 1997; Verdum 2008). By this perspective, the concept has been redefined as Latin American multiculturalism or constitutional multiculturalism (Clavero 2002; Van Cott 2000).

A second group of authors identifies it as a synonym of indigenism, which has allowed multiculturalism to be made equivalent to neoindigenism (Hernández et al. 2004). From this perspective, multiculturalism is the new indigenism in a time of globalization. In the case of Mexico, the constitutional reforms of 1992 and 2001 established new rules for state intervention in indigenous regions, inspired by the multiculturalism paradigm. They spotlighted the fact that multiculturalism does not mean a break with the old indigenism, but rather its contemporization through policies now referred to as multicultural. Critics have pointed out that even if such policies do recognize diversity, they ignore the inequity and the hierarchical relationships between ethnic groups that coexist within the multicultural context (Barabas 2006).

Fed by the multiculturalism paradigm, old-style indigenism has been rejuvenated, and openly assimilationist policies have been modified. In the interests of constructing new forms of governance within the framework of policies calling for structural adjustment and state downsizing, as prescribed by international agencies, the new multiculturalism fits into the process of dismantling the state in developing nations. Policies based on a stakeholder model have been integrated into multiculturalism, displacing the core autonomy rights claimed by indigenous peoples (Assies 2005). Under this value system, it may be said, generally speaking, that three decades of constitutional multiculturalism reforms have failed to improve conditions for indigenous peoples. On the contrary, these reforms have been used by the state as a tool in legitimizing and reasserting its hegemony.

There is a wealth of literature evaluating Latin American multiculturalism. Assies and Gundermann (2007) inquired into whether the language of ethnic identity served only as a rhetorical device, used by those in power as a smoke screen to put into effect other, deeper policies in favor of capital and international organizations (such as the World Bank or the Inter-American Development Bank). For their part, Bastos and Camus (2004) notice the rise of a "cosmetic multiculturalism" in post–civil war Guatemala as a new strategy for political regulation of ethnic difference in that country. For Recondo (2007), the recognition of *usos y costumbres* for election of authorities in Oaxaca forms part of the political strategy of multiculturalism in Mexico, a strategy that the author calls "the politics of the leopard."[6] Other approaches go further, referring to multiculturalism as "the cultural logic of multinational capitalism," leading to "neoliberal multiculturalism," which accepts some cultural demands but at the same time rejects any redistribution of power to indigenous peoples, favoring instead the penetration of capital into indigenous regions (Hale 2007).

It is worth pointing out that these results do not seem to be accidents, but rather part of the multiculturalism paradigm. Díaz-Polanco (2006, 176) offers a reminder that Kymlicka (1996) places limits on the recognition of cultural groups, clearly specifying which recognitions are acceptable within the perspective of liberal theory and which should not be allowed. Kymlicka distinguishes between "external protections" and "internal restrictions." His recommendation is that public policies should work for protections that safeguard minorities against outside threats, which they could suffer at the hands of a majority culture holding the reins of power. From his perspective, it is the state's responsibility to guard this diversity and to put out cultural protection policies that allow ethnic and national minorities to enjoy their rights without being threatened. Doing so would guarantee this form of cultural equality.

Indeed, Kymlicka thinks that external protections do not conflict with liberal principles that protect individual liberty. The protections are legitimate to the extent that they promote equality between groups and correct the prejudicial or vulnerable status to which members of a particular cultural group are subject. But the same is not acceptable with internal restrictions. As examples, he mentions cases where some indigenous tribal governments discriminate against members of the tribe who abandon the group's traditional religion, or where some minority cultures discriminate against girls with respect to education. "Must we give approval to these decisions in the name of respect for a community's internal structure?" he asks. Being a liberal, he responds: "we cannot accept the violation of individual liberty for the sake of safeguarding the group's cultural identity" (Kymlicka 1996, 212).

It is quite easy to see that the multiculturalism paradigm does not accept allowing ethnic groups themselves to make decisions, to exercise control over their own members, or to decide about their cultural, economic, religious, social, and political life, since doing so could put the individual rights of the group's members at risk. Kymlicka does admit that national minorities constitute distinct political communities, and therefore their right to self-government should be recognized. He recommends their accommodation within the state structure, perhaps in a federal relationship. But, he warns, if those national minorities have some customs that would put individual rights at risk, they should make efforts to "liberalize their culture," bringing in the basic principles of liberalism. He is emphatic on this point: "Liberals can only approve of the rights of minorities to the extent that they are consistent with respect for the liberty or autonomy of individuals" (Kymlicka 2006, 19).

Such limits end up being restrictions on the right of self-determination, since they limit the right of groups to decide their own affairs. The result is that the components of indigenous autonomy are precisely those which fall into the category that Kymlicka calls internal restrictions.

To draw the contrast more clearly, it is useful to remember that an autonomy arrangement has four elements. First, there is the definition of a legal-political entity (or several such entities at different levels). This implies territory. Such definition and recognition ought to be incorporated as an integral part of the state structure itself. Second, such an arrangement supposes the existence of a group's own government, either self-government or an autonomous government. Third, a government of this kind must possess its own jurisdiction, with the ability to make decisions and to regulate and organize society, both within the group and with respect to the group's links with outside entities. Given that all of this takes place within the framework of a particular nation-state, a fourth component is needed: specific, constitutionally established competences and powers (Díaz-Polanco 2008, 249). As can be seen, all of these components lie squarely within the area forbidden by the multiculturalism paradigm: internal restrictions

In this respect, it is important to note that insofar as rights of self-determination and indigenous autonomy are regulated by the UN, indigenous peoples are obligated to integrate values of human rights into indigenous life. The principle has thus been established in several instruments of international law that indigenous peoples have accepted.[7] However, it belongs to them alone to decide the forms, processes, and procedures by which they should do this. It should not be the states that intervene to set the definitions.

In sum, as I have tried to argue to this point, autonomy and multiculturalism are not twin concepts. As will be seen below in the Mexican examples, with the case of Chiapas, the multiculturalism paradigm in Latin America (in its constitutional multiculturalism version) has been used by the state to depoliticize indigenous demands for autonomy, making them out to be equivalent to their efforts to gain legitimacy. It can be concluded that, more than thirty years after the indigenous emergence in Latin America, in the struggle for territory, self-government, and decolonization, the state's responses have been policies of recognition that use multicultural language, but without seeking to question ethnic hierarchies. However, the policies have hardly tried to make accommodation for indigenous peoples, treating them as minorities so that they in turn can serve the purposes of capital and the existing order (Burguete 2008).

When the indigenous peoples mobilized in Latin America in the 1980s and 1990s, and when the EZLN signed the San Andrés Accords, they did so deploying arguments that used the language of autonomy. They were answered with policies that were constructed using the language of multiculturalism, as I show next.

CONSTITUTIONAL MULTICULTURALISM IN CHIAPAS

In Mexico, constitutional multiculturalism as a policy of recognition neither contradicts nor is in competition with neoliberal policies, and it can be said that they arrived on the scene together. Both were born in the decades of the 1980s and 1990s. In 1990 President Carlos Salinas de Gortari (1988–1994) sent a proposed reform of Article 4 of the federal constitution to the Chamber of Deputies.[8] The reform promoted the recognition of cultural diversity in Mexico. But it was not put into effect, and concrete benefits failed to reach the indigenous population, because no regulatory law was written to accompany it. Despite this limitation, the importance of the reform is rooted in the fact that, with its approval, the multiculturalist perspective was integrated into the policies of the Mexican state. The text of the constitution served to bring governmental discourse up to date, transitioning it away from an integrationist to a multicultural indigenism (Aragón 2007).[9]

Other changes were taking place at the same time. President Salinas proposed a constitutional reform that amended Article 27,[10] ending land redistribution. With this, new legal avenues were opened to privatization of land and water. This reform was a response to the economic interests that favored opening Mexico to neoliberal policies. Unlike the reform on indigenous culture and rights, which did not have a regulatory law to accompany it, the regulatory law for Article 27 was prepared quickly[11]—except for the sections that contained rights related to indigenous groups. Thus, for example, although the second paragraph of Section VII of Article 27 established that "the Law shall protect the integrity of the lands of indigenous groups," this section was not implemented in the regulatory law. Partly this was because no regulatory law was produced for Article 4, but it was also because the legal term "indigenous groups" does not exist in the constitution (nor was it included as a category under agrarian rights). The result was that the second paragraph of Section VII was useless.

This practice of approving reforms in the area of indigenous culture and rights that turn out to be mere rhetoric, because they do not attain legal standing, has the marks of a pattern in Mexico. As will be seen, this is the path that other reforms on the same subject always take. The principle has also been applied to international legislation. During Salinas's presidency, Mexico acceded to International Labour Organization (ILO) Convention 169 and signed the North American Free Trade Agreement (NAFTA). Both the convention and NAFTA (which were approved at almost the same time) have the status of law in the Mexican constitution.[12] But ILO Convention 169 (which recognizes, among other things, the collective nature of rights: the indigenous people and their territorial rights, right to informed consent, and right to autonomy, as well as other rights of equal importance) has not been implemented because there were no regulatory laws to make it binding. NAFTA, meanwhile, has been applied with greater consistency and effort.

It was in this way that multiculturalism and neoliberalism entered the constitution of Mexico together. They arrived at the same time and entered through the same door, and each reform was signed by the hand of President Carlos Salinas de Gortari. But the reforms touching on indigenous rights were reduced to rhetoric, without being implemented for the benefit of indigenous peoples. Doubt remains over whether indigenous reforms were not in fact intended as distractions, making it easier for the president to sign major reforms on the side—reforms that would have a strong impact on indigenous peoples, just like the agrarian reform that was favorable to privatization of their lands and the opening to international capital that invited unrestricted investment.

The modernization perspective that drove the government of President Salinas was matched by that of Patrocinio González Garrido, governor of Chiapas during the same period, 1988–1994. Before the multicultural focus was added to the constitution, in Chiapas, as in the rest of the country, an assimilationist focus prevailed. But the change in indigenous policy at the national level that came with the reform of Article 4 had repercussions in Chiapas. The state constitution was reformed and modifications were made in the state indigenous affairs agency, which was raised from the level of a mere coordination (*coordinación*) to a full Office of Indigenous Affairs (Dirección de Asuntos Indígenas).[13] At the same time, a new position was created, defender of ethnic groups (Government of Chiapas 1991, 15). With this reform, indigenous policy became protective, with the state assuming responsibility for "defending" its ethnic groups. Conceptually, this seemed consistent with Kymlicka's idea of external protections for ethnic minorities.

Reform on the matter of indigenous rights and culture had an impact on Chiapas. Starting in 1990, when the process of reforming Article 4 began in Mexico, there were legislative and policy changes at the state level. That year, Chiapas reformed Article 4 of its state constitution to read as follows: "This Constitution protects the culture, languages, and dialects used for communication by the different ethnic and mestizo groups in Chiapas. For the purpose of guaranteeing said protection, the State Indigenous Council is created."[14] The constitutional text is ambiguous, bordering on confusion. There is also a predominant emphasis on protection in this recognition. Thus, on one hand it admits cultural diversity. However, it does so not to recognize the rights of indigenous persons, but to establish a new political control apparatus: the State Indigenous Council (CIE). This organization for indigenous representation was integrated into the Central Nacional Campesina (CNC), a component of the Party of the Institutional Revolution (Alfaro 1996). It is significant that the CIE's elimination was an outcome of the negotiations between the state government and the EZLN and was included as a part of the San Andrés Accords.

In addition to their rhetoric, the reforms of 1990 included the recognition of some aspects of indigenous institutions, but with the purpose of administering them rather than actually recognizing them. This required the institutions to become uniform and to take a subordinate place within the governmental system, making bureaucratic control of them easier. That is what happened with the recognition of indigenous traditional medicine. Indeed, the state Health Act was amended in October 1990, with the goal of regulating the practice of indigenous traditional healers, situating them as "assistants [*auxiliares*] in the promotion of health" through both intensive training and registration and authorization. At the same time, it penalized those who would not submit to the state's control. It was a reform that, it must be said, was brought about unilaterally by the government, and not due to any express request on the part of indigenous traditional healers. The legislation laid down the following:

Article 81. The purpose of the present article is the control of the exercise of traditional medicine...indigenous medicine, and herbal medicine.

Article 82. For the purposes of the previous article, the following definitions shall apply.... II. Traditional healers: referring principally to those persons of indigenous extraction who participate, by tradition and custom, in the exercise of health promotion in the heart of their communities....

Article 84. Traditional *empíricos* and healers shall be considered auxiliaries in the promotion of health when offering their services under terms of the preceding article....

Article 91. Every person who engages regularly in activities for the promotion of health in the manner of an *empírico*, and who does not conform to the provisions of the present chapter, shall not be recognized as assistants in the promotion of health by the health authorities of the State and shall be subject to penalties as determined by law. (Government of Chiapas, 1991, 59–60)

These articles allow one to see a pattern of behavior in the policies of multiculturalism as they are applied in Chiapas, and possibly other parts of Mexico as well. They show a limited recognition of indigenous institutions and practices, a recognition conditioned on liberalization of their cultural practices and acceptance of the hegemonic cultural logic of the state that regulates them. Thus, cultural diversity is recognized, in this case so-called traditional medicine, but in a bounded manner. That is to say, not even the institutional setting of these practices (Mayan medicine, strictly speaking) is recognized. Rather, what is sought is their uniformity as "assistants" who can be trained and regulated by the state itself. Such requirements quite obviously strip away the elements that make them unique. With the reform, the Health Act lays down on one hand a type of traditional medicine that is permissible, while on the other hand it penalizes medical practices that do not conform to its regulations. In this sense, it penalizes difference within the diversity that it recognizes.

It is important to point out that, in contrast, the autonomy proposal calls for the recognition of Mayan medicine, along with its medical practices, its worldview, and its explanation of the world, all to be exercised in its own institutional setting. The opportunity for training would depend on the desires of the doctors themselves and what they thought necessary, but it would not be a condition required by law, still less one that they would be coerced into through penalties.

This particular method of legislating on indigenous rights and culture, which creates reforms in order to marginalize and depoliticize indigenous autonomy demands, was used in Chiapas even after 1994. It is what occurred with the constitutional reforms that arose out of the San Andrés Accords, reaffirming the idea of a legislative pattern. In 1998 and 1999, the state government brought forward constitutional and institutional reforms regarding indigenous rights and culture. These reforms, as stated in the documents, were part of the government's strategy to comply with the San Andrés Accords that it had signed with the EZLN. However, upon closer analysis, one can see that the reach of these reforms is limited, and also that they fall far short of the commitments that had been made (Hernández and Vera 1998). For example, the reformed Article 13 (1999), which recognizes cultural diversity in Chiapas, states:

> Article 13. The State of Chiapas possesses a population of many cultures, supported in its indigenous peoples. This Constitution recognizes and protects the following peoples: Tzeltal, Tzotzil, Ch'ol, Zoque, Tojolabal, Mam, Kaqchikel, Lacandon and Mocho'....
>
> The State shall protect and promote the development of the culture, languages, *usos y costumbres*, traditions, and forms of social, political, and economic organization of indigenous communities. It shall also guarantee to their members full access to the courts, to health services, and to a bilingual education that preserves and enriches their culture. It shall, in addition, encourage the full enjoyment of the rights of the indigenous to decide in a free, responsible, and informed manner the number of and spacing between their children, to a decent and respectable house, as with the rights of women and children.
>
> The right of indigenous communities to elect their traditional authorities in accordance with their *usos y costumbres* and traditions is recognized and protected....
>
> In municipalities with a majority indigenous population, procedures for and resolution of disputes between persons belonging to indigenous communities shall conform to their *usos y costumbres*, traditions, and cultural values, with participation of their traditional authorities, and shall be required to safeguard both the fundamental rights confirmed in the Constitution of the Republic and respect for human rights.[15]

Taking a careful look at the article, one finds that the first paragraph recognizes cultural diversity as a social fact, and the state assumes responsibility for guarding diversity. In the second paragraph, no rights of the people are recognized. Indeed, the state is given the power to assume the responsibility for guarding ("[it] shall protect and promote") the development of their cultures, languages, *usos y costumbres*, and so on. In the third paragraph, the right of indigenous communities to elect their traditional authorities according to their traditions and *usos y costumbres* is recognized and protected. This recognition, which could be considered the most salient because it supposes the right of self-government, is reduced to a rhetorical statement. Neither in Mexico nor in Chiapas is the community a level of government. As a result, the "traditional community authorities," when they exist (in a very few of the state's municipalities), have only moral authority and lack any legal power.

Furthermore, in the case of Chiapas, the traditional authorities, as they are called, lack power and have no special influence in the social and political life of the indigenous municipalities (because there is no competition to hold those positions). Thus, the external protection that the state commits to provide for these authorities is rendered ineffective. Because of this, and because the traditional authorities in the indigenous communities are the figures that the constitution recognizes for purposes of self-government, this right (which had been promised in the San Andrés Accords) has been reduced to a dead letter.

The rhetoric is not troublesome for the state: it contains a political communication strategy that serves to deepen its intervention in the lives of indigenous peoples. The fourth paragraph states that "procedures for and resolution of disputes between persons belonging to indigenous communities shall conform to their *usos y costumbres*, traditions, and cultural values, with participation of their traditional authorities," so long as constitutional and human rights are guaranteed. Stated in the words of multiculturalism, it recognizes the rights of national minorities, so long as they integrate liberal values into their own internal structure (that is, so long as they "liberalize their culture").

This constitutional text reinforces other legislative and administrative measures that the state government had implemented a couple of years before the 1999 reform. On March 12, 1998, a reform altered the structure of the state's Supreme Court of Justice.[16] It recognized traditional indigenous authorities as playing an auxiliary role in the justice system, through an Indigenous Peace and Conciliation Court that would be created for that purpose. As ordered by the reform, these courts were established in each one of the municipalities that were described as "majority indigenous."[17] To this end, the Indigenous Rights and Culture Act of the State of Chiapas, which served as the regulatory law for the reform of Article 13 of the state constitution,[18] and other legislation[19] both included the following:

Article 6. This act recognizes and protects the traditional authorities of indigenous communities, named by the consensus of their members and in conformity with their own customs.

The traditional authorities, who have historically applied the *usos y costumbres* and traditions of their communities in resolving internal conflicts, shall be assistants in the justice system. Their opinions shall be taken into account, under the terms of the respective procedural legislation, when resolving disputes that come under the jurisdiction of the Indigenous Peace and Conciliation Courts.

In order to implement this external protection, the Organic Law of the State Judicial Power was amended to add Indigenous Peace and Conciliation Courts to the structure of the state judiciary, making them a part of it. Between 1998 and 2000, buildings were constructed to house the courts in twenty-one municipal seats in the indigenous regions of Altos, Norte, Selva, and Centro.[20] The staff attached to the judiciary who are charged with administering justice are an indigenous peace and conciliation judge and a clerk of the court. The judge and his substitute are persons named by the residents of the municipality, usually through its community assembly. The clerk is paid using funds from the state Supreme Court of Justice, while the judge is paid out of the resources of the municipal government and is not part of the judiciary's structure.

Article 56 provides that "Peace and Conciliation Judges...shall be named by the Supreme Court of Justice of the State, which shall take into consideration the names proposed by the respective municipal governments, which shall have previously consulted with the community, when the proposed candidates satisfy the requirements of integrity and ability as established by the Court in plenary session." Although they are not mentioned explicitly, the requirements established by the judiciary are that a judge must be educated and neither very young nor very old. The judge must also be open to accepting the national legal framework as legitimate and valid, and must regularly attend training courses on human rights and instruction in the various civil and criminal codes.

In his or her administrative tasks, the judge is assisted by a clerk of records who is appointed by the judiciary. The clerk is charged with advising the judge to ensure that the resolutions do not conflict with the constitution. The clerk also prepares the court record and the agreements that the parties have reached. The most common cases involve petty theft, abuse of women, and altercations, among others. In criminal matters, peace and conciliation judges handle, within the conciliation process, all crimes open to private prosecution that the parties decide to settle through conciliation. The code itself prescribes this, so long as they do not include crimes that the law defines as felonies or in which society is noticeably affected, such as homicide, kidnapping, trafficking in minors, and assault, among others (Gómez 2004). Alongside this structure, traditional authorities are recognized as assistants. Inside the court buildings (all of which have the same uniform design), benches are placed along the right side of the courtroom. This is where the traditional authorities, named to their positions by the assembly, are seated. For their presence and involvement, they receive nominal compensation from the municipal government.

All records ordinarily follow a format that is acceptable to the state judiciary. In their preparation, the arguments put forward by the parties are not included, since the cultural elements of the dispute are not important. Instead, only the agreements reached, and the legal points on which they are based, are registered. Almost all records conclude by saying more or less the following:

Finally, the judge declares that, in view of the parties having come to an amicable agreement, he only requests and urges that the parties fulfill the commitments that they have contracted today, and proceeds to approve the agreement as being according to law and based upon the *usos y costumbres* governing this municipality...by reason of which the present proceedings are adjourned....[Signatures]. [Date]....[The parties] agree that this amicable agreement has the authority of *res judicata* to the fullest extent provided by law.

It should be noted that the text of this paragraph was obtained from the record of a family court trial in the Indigenous Peace and Conciliation Court in the municipality of San Juan Cancuc.[21] It is notable that in this municipality the traditional authorities were not brought in as part of the court. Ever since the court building in San Juan Cancuc was built in 1998, the benches that they are supposed to occupy have remained empty. This is because there is no consensus among the municipality's residents over who should serve as the traditional authorities. The lack of consensus, in turn, arises because the category of traditional authorities is not recognized as legitimate in that municipality (Burguete and Gómez 2008). Thus, including recognition of indigenous *usos y costumbres* as part of the trial cited above is nothing more than rhetoric.

Among laws passed between 1998 and 2000, in the context of the conflict with the EZLN, the creation of the Indigenous Peace and Conciliation Courts has been the reform with the greatest impact in the indigenous regions of Chiapas. It has created a new institutional structure, which was, in fulfillment of the signed commitments, an expected part of the recognition of the right of indigenous self-determination and autonomy. Moreover, these courts are living institutions, actually used by indigenous peoples, regulating indigenous local life from a liberal perspective, a perspective that was not present before the reforms of 1998–1999.

On balance, one can affirm that, more than ten years after the commitments made at San Andrés, indigenous autonomy rights have not advanced. On the contrary, they have diminished. The purpose of the legislation enacted within the framework of constitutional multiculturalism has not been to recognize autonomy rights for indigenous peoples, but rather to expand the powers of the state to intervene in matters where before it did not have a presence. Whether due to omission on the state's part or simply because it considered them unimportant, the state had let indigenous communities and municipalities operate through *usos y costumbres*, a rhetorical tool that served to allow for social practices that worked in the communities and that filled in the empty indigenous social spaces or spheres where the state had no interest. Those vacuums were claimed and ethnicized by the indigenous groups, making them into spaces of their own where they could maintain and reproduce their ethnicity. These spaces became political, and the groups asked the state to grant them as arenas for self-government (Burguete 2008).

In the case being considered here, a reform was passed that affirmed its recognition of the legality of *usos y costumbres* in administration of justice for indigenous peoples, but within limits and under the control of state institutions. In contrast to what was supposed to have occurred, the creation of these courts has had the effect not of recognizing cultural diversity in the practice of administering justice for indigenous peoples, but of suppressing it through a single, unified format that is applied to all. In establishing a single method of functioning and in putting everyone together under a single set of procedures, it denies cultural diversity, the very thing that it was, paradoxically, attempting to recognize. Generally speaking, one can say that, with Indigenous Peace and Conciliation Courts, the state, and the liberal viewpoint it represents, expanded its presence toward the Indian regions. The result has been a success for effecting multicultural policies, but far from it for autonomy policies, the implementation of which would have been expected to be required after the signing of the San Andrés Accords.

Thus, just as the constitutional reform in 1990 used recognition of traditional healers as assistants in the health system as a strategy for regulating the practice of indigenous medicine, it did so again with traditional authorities eight years later, placing them in the position of assistants to the state judicial system. Before this reform, justice in indigenous municipalities was administered according to their own rules and their own mediators, using a loose interpretation of state standards (interlegality). On the basis of its own reforms in constitutional multiculturalism, the state judiciary had a legal foundation with which to expand into indigenous territory and to occupy those spaces that had remained, for various reasons, subject to the decisions of the people and outside direct state control. In sum, everything seems to indicate that, with the reforms that recognized *usos y costumbres* for indigenous medicine and justice, the state institutions ended up being strengthened, with new powers to weave their way more intricately into indigenous life. The cost of this has been the weakening, subsuming, and in a certain measure, nullification of the indigenous groups' own institutional systems. That is to say, it has been a detriment to their de facto autonomy.

However, as occurred in the past, indigenous resistance and the logics of cultural control (Bonfil 1987) created struggles to try to (re)create an important place for culture in the state institutions that came into the indigenous regions. This resistance is what allowed them to fight for preservation of their differences in spite of state attempts to homogenize the indigenous institutions (Burguete 2008).

CONSTITUTIONAL MULTICULTURALISM, AUTONOMY, AND INDIGENOUS SELF-GOVERNMENT

The Agreement of the Federal Government and the Zapatista National Liberation Army on Indigenous Rights and Culture was signed on February 16, 1996, during the first phase of the San Andrés peace talks. Its first chapter, "Commitments between the Federal Government and the Indigenous Peoples," states:

1. Recognition of indigenous peoples in the federal Constitution. The state must promote, as a constitutional guarantee, recognition of the right of self-determination for indigenous peoples who are descended from the populations that inhabited the country in the time of the Conquest or colonization and of the establishment of current state boundaries and who, regardless of their legal status, preserve in whole or in part their own social, economic, cultural, and political institutions. Consciousness of group identity shall be considered a fundamental criterion for determining the groups to whom the provisions concerning indigenous peoples shall apply. The right of self-determination shall be exercised in a constitutional framework of autonomy that ensures national unity. They shall, in consequence, have the power to decide their form of internal government and their manner of organizing themselves politically, socially, economically, and culturally. The constitutional framework shall allow for the full effectiveness of social, economic, cultural, and political rights with respect to their identity. (Hernández and Vera 1998)

For its part, Document 3.1 ("Commitments to Chiapas by the State Government, the Federal Government, and the EZLN, pursuant to Section 1.3 of the Rules of Procedure") mentions the government's commitment to establish a "constitutional framework of autonomy." It takes as its starting point the federal recognition of the right to self-determination and autonomy for indigenous peoples, in their position of being collective groups with a differing culture that have the ability to decide on fundamental matters themselves within the framework of the nation-state. On this basis, in the state of Chiapas:

The recognition of the autonomy of indigenous peoples shall be promoted.... In formulating the constitutional framework of autonomy, the characteristics of self-determination and autonomy that shall be established shall be those that best express the varied and legitimate conditions and aspirations of the indigenous peoples.

The commitments established recognition of:

b. The right to practice, exercise, and develop their specific forms of political, economic, and social organization.

c. The right to have their own autonomous forms of government, in the communities and municipalities where they meet, respected. Elections of indigenous authorities shall be conducted in conformity to the respective traditions of each people.

In spite of these commitments, the constitutional reforms of June 17, 1999, specifically Article 13 mentioned above, failed to incorporate the promised recognition of the right of self-determination and autonomy into the constitution of Chiapas. The state legislature, however, understood the political value of such an omission and placed these precepts in the regulatory law for Article 13, which was published one month later on July 29. Article 5 of the Indigenous Rights and Culture Act of the State of Chiapas states the following:

In the context of the state's competences, the right of self-determination and autonomy for the indigenous peoples and communities of Chiapas is recognized to the fullest extent politically, economically, socially, and culturally, and the sovereignty, democracy, and three levels of government set out in the Political Constitution of the United Mexican States and that of the State of Chiapas are strengthened.

This deserves some comment. In the first place, it is important to highlight the role that the previously mentioned legislative technique plays as a resource for the state to empty autonomy rights, which they supposedly recognize, of all their meaning. Through rhetorical devices in the legislation, the rights are left hollow, devoid of their autonomous content. Legal speech on the subject of indigenous rights is characterized by a logic of double standards and deceit. To illustrate this, consider the way in which the paragraph is put together. The authors recognized the right but immediately put a legislative lock on it, preventing it from having any effect. For example, the paragraph that recognizes "the right of self-determination and autonomy for the indigenous...communities" then continues immediately with a phrase that nullifies it: "the sovereignty, democracy, and three levels of government set out in the Political Constitution of the United Mexican States and that of the State of Chiapas are strengthened."

The empty rhetoric, even bad faith with which the government and legislators acted, is also manifested in the fact that the rights of self-determination and autonomy are recognized only in the regulatory law, without having been previously included as rights within the state constitution. This difference sows the seeds of problems with constitutional validity. The result is exactly what the legislators expected: the rights of self-determination and autonomy, though recognized, are worthless and stillborn, given the bad faith with which they were written. The seriousness of the situation, with the perverse actions of the Chiapas government and legislators in legislating on indigenous rights and culture in 1999, did not end there. The same legislative technique was also used at the national level in the reform of Article 2 of the federal constitution in 2001.

After the EZLN's "March of the Color of the Earth" in 2000, the federal congress reformed the nation's constitution. The first paragraph of Article 2 states: "A. This Constitution recognizes and guarantees the right of indigenous peoples and communities to self-determination and, in consequence, to autonomy for:…" The constitution goes on to list seven sections defining the specific rights that all of Mexico's indigenous peoples would have:

1. "deciding their internal forms of community life and social, economic, political, and cultural organization"
2. "applying their own laws and standards for regulating and resolving internal conflicts"
3. "electing, in conformity with their traditional norms and procedures, authorities and representatives to serve according to their forms of internal government"
4. "preserving and enhancing their languages, understandings, and other elements that constitute their culture and identity"
5. "preserving and improving their surroundings"
6. "the special use and enjoyment of natural resources in the places that their communities occupy and inhabit, respecting the forms and modes of property and land tenancy established by this Constitution and the relevant laws"
7. "electing, in municipalities with an indigenous population, representatives to the municipal government."

However, after spelling out the autonomy rights, it immediately limits them in the succeeding paragraph, declaring that they can be recognized and legislated on only by the states, and can take effect only at the municipal level: "The constitutions and laws of the states and the Federal District shall recognize and regulate these rights in the municipalities, for the purpose of strengthening political participation and representation in conformity with their traditions and internal standards."

It is up to that point that recognized rights are spelled out. The range that the legislators marked out for autonomy rights is made clear in the section "Evaluation of the Proposal" that precedes the text of the reform. A part of that section reads:

Social variations [among indigenous peoples] are complex and vary by culture and religion.... For this reason, it is the constitutions and laws of the states that, naturally, should give recognition of one and another group according to their particular circumstances. Such recognition may only be given within the order established by the Constitution, respecting the existing political forms, especially in free municipalities. The free municipality is a flexible institution, the organization of which permits a wide array of variation. The natural political expression of the communities takes place in municipalities. Municipal governments [*ayuntamientos*] are accessible to indigenous populations by integrating their representatives into them. Through them, the populations act in accordance with their *usos y costumbres* that acquire full constitutional and legal recognition.... The basic obligation is to be subject to and to abide by the constitutional framework.

And in the text of the constitution, by which autonomy rights must "abide," one finds:

Article 115. The States shall adopt, as their internal regime, a form of government that is republican, representative, popular, having the free municipality as its basis of territorial division and political and administrative organization, in conformity with the following:

I. Each municipality shall be governed by a municipal council elected by direct popular vote, consisting of a mayor [*presidente municipal*] and a number of aldermen [*regidores*] and judicial regents [*síndicos*], as provided by law. The powers that this Constitution grants to the municipal government shall be exercised exclusively by the municipal council and there shall be no intermediate authority between it and the government of the State.

Thus speak the legislative texts. In reading them, four matters immediately call for attention to themselves:

1. The only forms of social, political, and cultural organization that the Article 2 reform permits indigenous peoples to have are those that are protected by the free municipality.
2. The only form of local government that the constitution recognizes for all indigenous peoples in the country is that of the municipal councils.
3. The only offices that the constitution recognizes are mayor, *síndico*, and *regidor*.
4. The only method of election for local authorities is through the machinery of party competition, with free and secret ballots (except in Oaxaca, where the state constitution has established an *usos y costumbres* electoral regime; see introduction and chapters 6–8, this volume).

In the face of such boundaries, one is led to seek an answer to the question, to what extent does the institution of the free municipality in Mexico allow indigenous peoples to effectively exercise their right to decide on their forms of government, social organization, and representation, among others (which is, in the end, one of the principal autonomy rights), as recognized in Article 2 of the constitution? The answer is that the free municipality, under its current design, does not permit the exercise of indigenous autonomy rights because it ignores the diversity of the forms that sociopolitical organization takes. For example, through its condition of a single form of local government (which matches the form of the national government), it prevents the exercise of the right of indigenous self-government. In this way, in limiting the effectiveness of the autonomy rights recognized through the institution of the free municipality, the legislators ignored the complex cultural diversity that is characteristic of forms of indigenous government and the diverse possibilities for integrating the municipal government with these societies. Sánchez (2008) has called this type of fragmented autonomy "heteronomous autonomy."

As one can see, by requiring recognized rights to be brought into force through the free municipality, indigenous autonomy rights were obviously stillborn, since the design of Mexico as a nation-state—and within it, the institution of the free municipality—does not leave room for multiethnicity at the local government level. It also does not leave room to uphold other forms of organization, integration, and appointment of authorities as legal. In limiting the rights of self-determination and autonomy and subordinating them to the grip of the free municipality, the state of affairs remained the same as before: indigenous peoples' social organization and governance practices were once again outside the constitution, because the constitution had not really been modified. Thus, when they try, based on their own sociocultural practices, to exercise some of the supposed autonomy rights recognized in Article 2, they are in fact acting outside the bounds of the constitution.

This is where things stand. Numerous legislative barriers have made constitutionally recognized autonomy rights inapplicable in practice, causing their application in the states and in supplementary legislation to be of very limited reach. Most of the time recognition has been symbolic for indigenous peoples, but not for the neoliberal state. The state is the entity that has benefited most from constitutional multiculturalism, since it has served as a way of reasserting its hegemony. It has also served as a legal instrument for regulating its intervention and, possibly, to ease the penetration of capital into indigenous regions.

FINAL REFLECTIONS

Beginning in the 1970s, Latin America witnessed an indigenous emergence. The emergence was characterized by struggles and movements on the part of communities, peoples, and organizations that demanded a new relationship with and new treatment from the Latin American states, both at the UN and within their own domestic contexts. The people saw in autonomy the paradigm that would allow them to overcome the condition of internal colonialism to which they had been subjected for over five centuries. In an effort to maintain national unity and avoid separatist or sovereignty movements, the indigenous peoples bet on modifying the nation-states where they lived as the way to achieve integration into the states on the basis of recognition. Causing constitutional reforms that would establish autonomy regimes was the political strategy on which they banked during the 1980s and 1990s. The Mexican indigenous movement signed on as part of the same fight.

Taking stock of two decades of the politics of recognition in Mexico and Chiapas, the results are disappointing. In spite of the constitutional reforms attained, the executive and legislative branches (and, since the matter was not declared to be outside its jurisdiction, the judicial branch as well) developed an ad hoc legislative technique that recognizes rights in order to nullify them at the same time. Under this strategy, constitutional multiculturalism has served as a new indigenous policy to recognize some aspects of cultural diversity, with the goal of achieving political control and governability through homogenizing and bureaucratizing cultural diversity.

Things standing as they are, uncertainty remains over whether it makes any sense for the indigenous peoples of Mexico and Chiapas to continue betting on constitutional reforms as the best way to alter the state's organization and to complete the advances in the decolonization process that started at the UN in the 1970s, when they began building the autonomy paradigm. When the EZLN rose out of the jungle and put armed resistance on the table, Mexicans, both men and women, took to the streets to demand that both the state and the EZLN seek out negotiated political options, within the framework of what was legal, that could lead to a mutual understanding. The hope of reaching a just and honorable set of agreements fed the desire to move forward toward dialogue. Unfortunately, that past, so recent, has already turned out to be very far away. The Mexican state made commitments to some accords, but it did not fulfill them. Thus, the conclusion of the conflict, and the future of indigenous political strategies, remains uncertain.

NOTES

1. Henri Grimal (1989, 8) cites an intellectual of the era, who wrote in 1912: "Colonizing consists of establishing a relationship with new countries in order to take advantage of their resources, whatever they are, to increase their value to serve the interests of the nation, and at the same time to bring to the primitive populations that have lacked them the advantages of the intellectual, social, scientific, moral, artistic, literary, commercial and industrial culture that are the heritage of superior races. Therefore, colonization is an establishment that is founded in new countries by a race with an advanced civilization in order to achieve the dual purpose that we have just explained."
2. Resolution 1514 (XV) of December 14, 1960.
3. Many peoples of the world share the status of indigenous due to being colonized peoples. The indigenous population of the world is estimated at more than 200 million. According to IWGIA, the indigenous population is distributed in approximately the following manner: in North America, 1.5 million; in Greenland, 100,000; in Mexico and Central America, 13 million; in South America, in the lowlands, 1 million, and in the mountainous regions, 17.5 million; the Sami of northern Europe (Scandinavia), 80,000; nomads in West Africa, 8 million; Pygmies, 250,000; the San and Basarwa, 100,000; nomads in East Africa, 6 million; aborigines in Australia, 250,000; the Maori, 350,000; indigenous Pacific Islanders, 1.5 million; in Southeast Asia, 30 million; in South Asia, 51 million; in East Asia, 67 million; in Western Asia, 7 million; in Russia, 1 million. If all of these numbers are added together, they confirm that around the world there are 205,630,000 people who are viewed, and who self-identify, as indigenous (IWGIA 1999, 4–5)."
4. Carbonell (2004, 23) says: "In recent years, nationalist and culturalist passions have been excited as never before, generating major conflicts that derive in part from the challenges that multiculturalism poses for co-existence and state organization."
5. In Arias's opinion (2008, 142): "The EZLN was late in incorporating multiculturalism. It did so at the wrong time, in indirect ways, and without fully formulating its discourse on the subject.... To a large degree, the EZLN has done the right thing in using multiculturalism politically and in its communications, thanks to its conceptual matrix being definable as extra-theoretical. The assimilation of multiculturalism complemented but did not replace the EZLN's revolutionary ideology, which was rooted in Marxism-Leninism."

6. In Chiapas, Renard (2003) observed this phenomenon in studying *usos y costumbres* elections in the municipality of Amatenango del Valle.
7. For example, the "Nuuk Conclusions and Recommendations on Indigenous Autonomy and Self-Government" produced by the United Nations Meeting of Experts at Nuuk, Greenland (September 24–28, 1991), states: "7.- Indigenous autonomies and self-governments must, within their jurisdiction, assure the full respect of all human rights and fundamental freedoms and popular participation in the conduct of public affairs" (UN Commission on Human Rights 1991, 12). For its part, the United Nations Declaration on the Rights of Indigenous Peoples (adopted as a resolution of the General Assembly on September 13, 2007) sets out the following in Article 46: "2. In the exercise of the rights enunciated in the present Declaration, human rights and fundamental freedoms of all shall be respected. The exercise of the rights set forth in this Declaration shall be subject only to such limitations as are determined by law and in accordance with international human rights obligations. Any such limitations shall be non-discriminatory and strictly necessary solely for the purpose of securing due recognition and respect for the rights and freedoms of others and for meeting the just and most compelling requirements of a democratic society. 3. The provisions set forth in this Declaration shall be interpreted in accordance with the principles of justice, democracy, respect for human rights, equality, non-discrimination, good governance and good faith" (UN General Assembly 2007).
8. "Decreto por el que se reforma el Artículo 4o. de la Constitución Política de los Estados Unidos Mexicanos." *Diario Oficial de la Federación*, January 28, 1992.
9. Article 2 of the constitution stipulates: "The Mexican nation is composed of many cultures, supported in its origins in its indigenous peoples. The Law shall protect and promote the development of their languages, cultures, usages, customs, resources, and specific forms of social organization, and shall guarantee to their members effective access to the courts of justice of the State."
10. "Decreto por el que se reforma el artículo 27 de la Constitución Política de los Estados Unidos Mexicanos." *Diario Oficial de la Federación*, January 6, 1992.
11. The new Agrarian Act was published on January 6, 1992, several days before the reform of Article 4 was approved.
12. Article 133 of the constitution states that international treaties and conventions that do not violate the constitution, when they have been signed by the president and approved by the Senate, are the supreme law of the land.
13. The name of the state government agency by which indigenous policies have been made says a good deal about the focus of those agencies. In the twentieth century, the Department of Social Action, Culture, and Indigenous Protection was born. It lasted from 1934 to 1944. In 1945 it became the Department of Indigenous Protection, a name evoking governmental policies that had a protective focus. In the 1950s, integrationist policy arose, which was implemented by the General Office of Indigenous Affairs (1954–1982). In 1982 the office moved up to become the Secretariat of Indigenous Affairs, but was then demoted to the Subsecretariat of Indigenous Affairs from 1983 to 1988. In 1988 it was further reduced to the level of Coordination of Indigenous Affairs (1988–1991). Then, as a result of the change from an integrationist to a multicultural paradigm, the name was changed again and it was moved back up the administrative hierarchy. Before the armed rebellion, all of the directors of these various agencies were nonindigenous. But in 1994, the state government agency in charge of indigenous people's affairs moved further up the public administration hierarchy, becoming the Secretariat for the Assistance of Indigenous Peoples (1994–2000). From that point on the secretary would be a member of one of the state's indigenous groups, usually

Mayan (Tzotzil or Tzeltal). Between 2000 and 2006, the name changed to Secretariat of Indian Peoples, a name and rank the office continues to hold.
14. "Decreto Número 60." *Periódico Oficial del Estado de Chiapas* (hereafter *Periódico Oficial*) No. 95, October 9, 1990.
15. "Decreto Número 191, que reforma los artículos 4, 10, 12, 13, 29 y 42, de la Constitución Política del Estado de Chiapas, en materia de derechos y cultura indígenas." *Periódico Oficial*, June 17, 1999.
16. "Decreto Número 247." *Periódico Oficial* No. 15, March 12, 1998.
17. The creation of Indigenous Peace and Conciliation Courts dates back to 1997. News of their creation was announced in June of that year by then-governor Julio César Ruiz Ferro. He reported the creation of courts in the municipalities of Mitontic, Zinacantán, Tenejapa, Huixtán, Oxchuc, Altamirano, and in Chilón in the community of Bachajón ("Edifican Juzgados" 1997).
18. "Decreto número 207, Ley de Derechos y Cultura Indígena del Estado de Chiapas." *Periódico Oficial*, July 29, 1999.
19. "Decreto número 247." *Periódico Oficial* No. 15, March 12, 1998.
20. Courts were established in Amatenango del Valle, Aldama (a new municipality), San Juan Cancuc, Chamula, Chenalhó, Chanal, Chalchihuitán, Huixtán, Larráinzar, Mitontic, Oxchuc, Pantelhó, Santiago El Pinar (a new municipality), Tenejapa, Zinacantán, Altamirano, Ángel Albino Corzo, Maravilla Tenejapa (a new municipality), Marqués de Comillas (a new municipality), Montecristo de Guerrero (a new municipality), and San Andrés Duraznal (a new municipality).
21. Expediente No. 20/JPCI/2002. Plaintiff: María Hernández Santiz. Defendant: Jorge Santiz Gómez.

REFERENCES

Alfaro Camacho, Carlos Fernando. 1996. "Gestiones del consejo indígena en el municipio de San Cristóbal de Las Casas, Chiapas." Master's thesis, Universidad Autónoma de Chiapas, San Cristóbal de Las Casas.

Aragón Andrade, Orlando. 2007. *Indigenismo, movimientos y derechos indígenas en México: la reforma del artículo cuarto constitucional de 1992*. Morelia, Michoacán: División de Estudios de Posgrado de la Facultad de Derecho y Ciencias Sociales, Instituto de Investigaciones Históricas, Universidad Michoacana de San Nicolás de Hidalgo.

Arias, Alán. 2008. "El giro multicultural del EZLN." In *Multiculturalismo y derechos indígenas: El caso mexicano*, coordinated by Alan Arias, 127–142. Mexico City: Comisión Nacional de los Derechos Humanos.

Assies, Willem. 2005. "Reforma estatal y multiculturalismo latinoamericano al inicio del siglo XXI." Paper presented at Jornadas Pueblos Indígenas en América Latina Conference, April 27–28, Barcelona.

Assies, Willem, and Hans Gundermann. 2007. "Introducción." In *Movimientos indígenas y gobiernos locales en América Latina*, edited by Willem Assies and Hans Gundermann, 11–25. Mexico: IIAM, Colegio de Michoacán, International Work Group for Indigenous Affairs.

Assies, Willem, Gemma van der Haar, and André Hoekema, eds. 1999. *El reto de la diversidad*. Zamora, Michoacán: El Colegio de Michoacán, A.C.

Barabas, Alicia. 2006. "Notas sobre multiculturalismo e interculturalidad." *Diario de Campo*, Supplement 39 (October): 13–19.

Bastos, Santiago, and Manuela Camus. 2004. "Multiculturalismo y pueblos indígenas: Reflexiones a partir del caso de Guatemala." *Encuentros, Revista Centroamericana de Ciencias Sociales* 1 (1): 87–112.

Bonfil Batalla, Guillermo. 1987. "La teoría del control cultural en el estudio de los procesos étnicos." *Papeles de la Casa Chata* 2 (3): 23–43.

Burguete Cal y Mayor, Araceli. 2008. "Gobernar en la diversidad en tiempos de multiculturalismo en América Latina." In *Gobernar (en) la diversidad: Experiencias indígenas desde América Latina. Hacia la investigación de co-labor*, coordinted by Xochitl Leyva, Araceli Burguete, and Shannon Speed, 15–64. Mexico City: CIESAS, FLACSO-Ecuador, FLACSO-Guatemala.

Burguete Cal y Mayor, Araceli, and Miguel Gómez. 2008. "Multiculturalismo y gobierno permitido en San Juan Cancuc, Chiapas: Tensiones intracomunitarias por el reconocimiento de 'autoridades tradicionales.'" In *Gobernar (en) la diversidad: Experiencias indígenas desde América Latina. Hacia la investigación de co-labor*, coordinated by Xochitl Leyva, Araceli Burguete, and Shannon Speed, 343–390. Mexico City: CIESAS, FLACSO-Ecuador, FLACSO-Guatemala.

Burguete Cal y Mayor, Araceli, and X. Margarito Ruiz Hernández. 1994. "Hacia una carta universal de derechos de los pueblos indígenas." In *Derechos indígenas en la actualidad*, edited by Instituto de Investigaciones Jurídicas, 117–138. Mexico City: Universidad Nacional Autónoma de México.

Carbonell, Miguel. 2004. "Constitucionalismo y multiculturalismo." *Revista Derecho y Cultura* 13: 21–80.

Castro, Milka. 2008. "La universalización de la condición indígena." *Alteridades* 18 (35): 21–32.

Clavero, Bartolomé. 2002. "Multiculturalismo constitucional, con perdón, de veras y en frío." *Revista Internacional de los Estudios Vascos* 47 (1): 35–62.

Díaz-Polanco, Héctor. 2006. *Elogio de la diversidad: Globalización, multiculturalismo y etnofagia*. Mexico City: Siglo XXI.

Díaz-Polanco, Héctor. 2008. "La insoportable levedad de la autonomía: La experiencia Mexicana." In *Estados y autonomías en democracias contemporáneas: Bolivia, Ecuador, España y México*, coordinated by Natividad Gutiérrez Chong, 245–271. Mexico City: IIS, Universidad Nacional Autónoma de México, Plaza y Valdés Editores.

"Edifican Juzgados de Paz y Conciliación en siete municipios indígenas de Chiapas." 1997. *La Crónica*. June 2. http://www.cronica.com.mx/cronica/1997/jun/02/nac05.html.

Falk, Richard. 2002. "Self-Determination under International Law: The Coherence of Doctrine versus the Incoherence of Experience." In *The Self-Determination of Peoples: Community, Nation, and State in an Interdependent World*, edited by Wolfgang Danspeckgruber, 31–66. Princeton, NJ: Princeton University Press.

Gómez Mayorga, Francisco. 2004. "Chiapas: La impartición de justicia por Juzgados de Paz y Conciliación." In *Memoria del Taller Interestatal: Formas de integración del gobierno en municipios con población indígena y ciudadanía multicultural: Oaxaca-Chiapas*, coordinated by Leticia Santín del Río, Araceli Burguete, and Fausto Díaz Montes, 89–96. Mexico City: FLACSO.

Government of Chiapas. 1991. *Legislación en materia de indigenismo*. Tuxtla Gutiérrez, Chiapas: Instituto Chiapaneco de Cultura.

Grimal, Henri. 1989. *Historia de las descolonizaciones del siglo XX*. Madrid: IEPALA Editorial.

Hernández, Rosalva Aída, Sarela Paz, and María Teresa Sierra, coords. 2004. *El Estado y los indígenas en tiempos del PAN: Neoindigenismo, legalidad e identidad*. Mexico City: Centro de Investigaciones y Estudios Superiores en Antropología Social.

Hernández Navarro, Luís, and Ramón Vera Herrera, comp. 1998. *Acuerdos de San Andrés*. Mexico City: Era.

IWGIA (International Work Group for Indigenous Affairs). 1999. *El mundo indígena, 1998–1999*. Copenhagen: IWGIA.

Kymlicka, Will. 1996. *Ciudadanía Multicultural: Una teoría liberal de los derechos de las minorías*, translated by Carme Castells Auleda. Barcelona: Paidós.

Lerner, Natán. 1991. *Minorías y grupos en el derecho internacional: Derechos y discriminación*. Mexico City: Comisión Nacional de Derechos Humanos.

Martínez Cobo, José R. 1983. "Conclusions, Proposals, and Recommendations." In *Study of the Problem of Discrimination against Indigenous Populations*. UN Commission on Human Rights. UN Document Symbol E/CN.4/Sub.2/1983/21/Add.8. http://www.un.org/esa/socdev/unpfii/documents/MCS_xxi_xxii_e.pdf.

Pineda Camacho, Roberto. 1997. "La constitución de 1991 y la perspectiva del multiculturalismo en Colombia." *Alteridades* 7 (14): 107–129.

Recondo, David. 2007. *La política del gatopardo: Multiculturalismo y democracia en Oaxaca*. Mexico City: Centro de Investigaciones y Estudios Superiores en Antropología Social.

Renard, María Cristina. 2003. "Gatopardismo en una comunidad de los Altos de Chiapas." Paper presented at the fourth meeting of the Asociación Mexicana de Estudios Rurales, Morelia, Michoacán.

Rex, John. 2002. "Multiculturalismo e integración política en el Estado nacional moderno." *Isegoría, Revista de Filosofía, Moral y Política* (26): 29–43.

Rouland, Norbert, Stéphane Pierré-Caps, and Jacques Poumarède. 1999. *Derecho de minorías y de pueblos autóctonos*. Mexico City: Siglo XXI.

Sánchez, Consuelo. 2008. "La autonomía en los senderos que se bifurcan: El proyecto político y la autonomía de hecho." In *Estados y autonomías en democracias contemporáneas: Bolivia, Ecuador, España y México*, coordinated by Natividad Gutiérrez Chong, 273–295. Mexico City: IIS, Universidad Nacional Autónoma de México, Plaza y Valdés Editores.

Sieder, Rachel, ed. 2002. *Multiculturalism in Latin America: Indigenous Rights, Diversity and Democracy*. London: Palgrave Macmillan.

Stavenhagen, Rodolfo. 1986. "Derechos humanos y derechos de los pueblos: La cuestión de las minorías." In *Revista del Instituto Interamericano de Derechos Humanos* (4): 43–62.

Taylor, Charles. 2001. *El multiculturalismo y "la política de reconocimiento."* Mexico City: Fondo de Cultura Económica.

Toranzo Roca, Carlos F., comp. 1993. *Lo pluri-multi o el reino de la diversidad*. La Paz: Instituto Latinoamericano de Investigaciones Sociales.

UN Commission on Human Rights. 1991. "Report of the Meeting of Experts to Review the Experience of Countries in the Operation of Schemes of Internal Self-Government for Indigenous Peoples, Nuuk, Greenland, 24–28 September 1991." UN Document Symbol E/Cn.4/1992/42.

UN General Assembly. 2007. "United Nations Declaration on the Rights of Indigenous Peoples." General Assembly Resolution 61/295 of September 13, 1995. UN Document Symbol A/Res/61/295. http://www.un.org/esa/socdev/unpfii/en/drip.html.

Van Cott, Donna. 2000. *The Friendly Liquidation of the Past: The Politics of Diversity in Latin America*. Pittsburgh: University of Pittsburgh Press.

Verdum, Ricardo. 2008. "El indigenismo brasileño en tiempos de multiculturalismo." *Alteridades* 18 (35): 33–46.

Yashar, Deborah J. 2005. *Contesting Citizenship in Latin America: The Rise of Indigenous Movements and the Postliberal Challenge*. New York: Cambridge University Press.

PART TWO
MULTICULTURAL AND AUTONOMY MOVEMENTS IN THE ANDES

3 Uses of Autonomy
The Evolution of Multicultural Discourse in Bolivian Politics

Erik Cooke

INTRODUCTION

The drawn-out volatility in Bolivia's Constituent Assembly (Constituyente) process in 2006 and 2007, including the postassembly redrafting of the new constitution through 2008, highlights the tension in the country's multicultural politics. One of the main fights in that process, which was always confrontational and sometimes violent, revolved around the demands of departments (states) in the eastern Media Luna region to obtain departmental autonomy from the central government. The movement that coalesced around these demands is considered by many to be an elite mestizo backlash against the government of Evo Morales, an Aymara and longtime social movement leader. The Media Luna fight for autonomy began in the aftermath of the 2003 water and gas wars that forced the ouster of President Gonzalo Sánchez de Lozada. During this period, indigenous and other social movements were at the height of intense mobilization and the central government was incredibly unstable. This period of intense mobilization set the stage for the historic 2005 electoral victory of Morales and his Movimiento al Socialismo (MAS) party.

The indigenous movement in Bolivia slowly emerged from the 1970s to the present, and reached its peak in the years leading up to the election of Evo Morales in 2005. It came to embody two movements for the poor majority: a banner for social and economic justice, and a public return to the indigenous roots (more than thirty distinct ethnic groups) of Bolivia. It emerged from networks and confederations of peasant organizations established in the 1950s that were instituted by the government to assimilate indigenous peoples into the modern state. One of the primary goals of these peasant organizations was to redefine the identity of the rural indigenous as peasant or campesino, thus negating the ethnic cleavage. However, following the collapse of the tin mining industry in the early 1980s, the resulting massive internal displacement, and the subsequent entrenchment of neoliberal economics, many campesinos rejected the official concealment of indigenous ethnicity. Many turned to *katarismo*, which was inspired by the indigenous rebellion led in the 1780s by Tupac Katari, and became a banner of indigenous (particularly Aymara) solidarity and autonomy (Albó 2002). Thus, indigenous autonomy was wrapped up not only in ethnic solidarity, but in historical grievances of the marginalized majority of Bolivia.

The emergence of the Media Luna autonomist movement is readily understood as an ethnic- and class-based backlash, even though this oversimplifies the phenomenon (Eaton 2007). However, what remains perplexing about the calls of "Iyambae!" ("Freedom" in Guaraní) by Media Luna leaders is how they appear to have co-opted the long-held indigenous discourse of autonomy and self-determination. This discourse emerged in the *katarista* movement of the 1970s and was frequently used during the *pluri-multi* period of the 1990s.[1] During these periods of indigenous activism, autonomy was invoked as a protest against the social and political elites (of which the Media Luna leaders were part) that had historically subjected them. Had the indigenous discourse outlived its utility? Did the Media Luna activists steal the indigenous discourse and, if so, how?

This chapter's argument is that the discourse of autonomy, though originally grounded in indigenous grievances against the state, has been infused with political potency so that its utility redounds to the challengers to state power. Thus, though social movements (cast as indigenous) originated the autonomy discourse, they do not own it. Social movements developed the discourse of autonomy as part of the core articulation of "indigenous" grievances against the state in the 1970s. These grievances were at the heart of the multicultural political context in the 1990s. During this time period, multiculturalism became a powerful political discourse through which indigenous movements secured constitutional and legal recognitions of language, culture, and political participation. Though outright autonomy—a legal structure parallel and separate from the central and regional governments—remained unrealized, it figured as a powerful symbol of popular and local social movements.

The autonomy discourse remained useful to the indigenous movement throughout the 1990s and into the 2000s, when popular movements were still challengers to state authority. These indigenous challengers were diverse and far from unified. On one end of the spectrum were hard-liners like Felipe Quispe, who is notorious for his role in a failed 1980s guerrilla uprising that sought the establishment of an indigenous breakaway government (Hylton 2003). Others, like former coca grower Evo Morales, emerged through the national union confederations and worked to forge strong alliances built on class (not ethnic) solidarity. To many indigenous Bolivians, Quispe represents an important and more authentic indigenist alternative to Evo Morales's leftist, but mainstream, majority. But once the movement challengers gained direct access to state power following Morales's huge 2005 electoral victory, the maturing Media Luna movement appropriated the discourse of autonomy as the new challengers to state power. However, the vision of autonomy articulated by Media Luna regional activists, an attempt to protect material and social advantage, is distinct from the popular movement vision, which attempts to redress historic grievances and to protect culture.

As in Demiralp's (2009) Turkish example, framing theory is critical to my hypothesis. This chapter proceeds first by establishing Bolivia as a distinct and useful case study. Then, I examine the origins of modern citizenship as a backdrop for the emergence of autonomy rhetoric in the 1970s. This allows the chapter to next explore the early usage of the autonomy discourse from the 1970s into the 1990s, as part of a larger repertoire of indigenous rights and in the context of national and international multiculturalism. During this period, autonomy came to be used as a general rallying cry against historic injustice, ethnic homogenization, neoliberal economics, and entrenched poverty, even though the demand originated from divergent indigenous sectors. This period was marked by an explosion of activism around the International Labour Organization's Convention 169 (ILO 169) on the rights of indigenous peoples, constitutional reforms, and many legal changes that restructured the participation of indigenous people at all levels of government. The next section explores the use of autonomy from 2002 to 2005, when the MAS had significant electoral gains but was still in a challenger position. In this short but explosive period, many of the social movement and MAS challenges were focused on liberal economic policy and the state's role in the exploitation of natural resources.

In these years, the autonomy demand was less frequently invoked but was still primarily part of the indigenous repertoire in national politics, and was often connected to the long-standing demand for a new constitution. It was also during these years that the calls for departmental autonomy in the Media Luna emerged, establishing contours of conflict under the Morales government. Then, the chapter turns to the phase from 2006 to 2009, during which the MAS was the governing party. Following this reversal of power, ownership of the autonomy frame also reversed. Initiated following the ouster of Sánchez de Lozada in 2003, the Media Luna autonomy movement became the primary challenge to Morales's government and the Constituent Assembly. I conclude with considerations of how autonomy is used and suggest that although the Media Luna movement has vigorously appropriated it, autonomy may only end up mobilizing its partisans rather than successfully challenging the Morales government.

The use of Media Luna autonomist discourse reached its peak during the constitutional rewriting process. The long-standing demand for a Constituent Assembly to rewrite the constitution forced the confrontation of the opposing visions of the Bolivian state. This chapter relates how the old liberal conception of civic-national citizenship and free-market economic policy collided with the indigenous conceptions of communal citizenship, ethnic pluralism, and participatory governance and economics. This struggle was acute, especially because as long as Morales was operating under the old constitution, the essence of the old state remained intact. However, the potential success of Morales's coalition threatened the institutionalization of a new state more closely aligned with the social movement vision.

The evolution of this autonomy frame is significant for several reasons. The autonomy frame demonstrates that the life that political ideas assume often becomes independent of the actors that develop and initially utilize them. It also illustrates the political potency of multiculturalism in Bolivia, where calls for ethnic tolerance and accommodation can cut both ways politically. That a primarily wealthy, mestizo elite can successfully claim ethnic disadvantage against an indigenous majority that it traditionally dominated demonstrates that the multicultural discourse belongs to no one sector and can potentially be utilized by any mobilized minority. The many appropriations of the concept of autonomy in contemporary Bolivian politics also suggests that a general indigenous identity—as distinct from more specific Guaraní or Quechua identities—is itself a strategic discourse, perhaps a master discourse, that the rhetoric of autonomy buttresses. This instrumentality resonates with Tilly's contention that "identities become political identities when governments become parties to them," and Yashar's poststructuralist view of identity (Tilly 2003; Yashar 1998). Finally, the current appropriation of "autonomy" illustrates that certain frames are only accessible to political challengers, but challengers who obtain power will often attempt to redefine these frames to maintain ownership and to continue to access the political advantage of the frames. Once the state was appropriated to channel popular demands and grievances, autonomy from the state lost much of its utility, and Morales has attempted to conflate indigenous and popular autonomy with state autonomy.

BOLIVIA AS A DISTINCT CASE

Although the indigenous movements in Latin America since the 1980s share many common features, including assertions of ethnic identity, rights, and redress of historical oppression, it is important to be on guard against reductionism in examining specific cases. As is often true of advocates of social movements, narratives frequently refer to cases as components of the regional and global wave of indigenous movement and cast indigenous rights in the context of five hundred years of oppression. While these assertions are arguably true, more useful are analyses of the distinct movement politics within countries. The politics of Bolivia's indigenous movements are compelling specifically because of how its national movement dynamics differ so greatly from those of other countries, and because of the substantial variation between movements.

Bolivia shares with other countries in the region the trends of Third Wave democratization, implementation of neoliberal economic policies, and the rising international focus on indigenous rights (Yashar 1999). These trends seemed to peak in the early to mid 1990s, as seen in the adoption of ILO 169, the awarding of the Nobel Peace Prize to Guatemalan indigenous rights activist Rigoberta Menchú, the rise of the Confederation of Indigenous Nationalities of Ecuador (CONAIE) in Ecuador, and the adoption of several multicultural recognitions and protections in regional laws and constitutions (Van Cott 2000a, 200b). However, Bolivia differs greatly from other countries with active indigenous movements. Bolivia is one of only two majority-indigenous countries in the hemisphere, and is home to more than thirty distinct native ethnicities.[2] None of these groups have the majority in the population. It has also been relatively free of violence compared to other significantly indigenous countries, such as Guatemala and Peru. Also, although Bolivia is far from the only country to implement market-oriented reforms and austerity measures, it did so before almost every other country (save Chile) and to a much greater degree. Today, Bolivia is the poorest country in South America and the second-most unequal country in the entire hemisphere (Wanderley 2008). As such, class-based demands are intertwined with indigenous demands in Bolivian popular movements. Though it shares similarities with other countries, the Bolivian case is indeed distinct.

EMERGENCE OF INDIGENOUS POLITICS IN BOLIVIA

The Bolivian sociologist Xavier Albó (1991) has argued that it is nonsensical to distinguish between ethnicity and class in Bolivian politics. Indeed, more than 60 percent of the population identifies as indigenous (Deruyttere 2006). As mentioned earlier, there are more than thirty indigenous people groups in Bolivia, with no one group holding a majority. What does it mean, then, to be indigenous? Bolivians individually and collectively have not always referred to themselves as indigenous. For much of Bolivia's history, the term *indio* was a pejorative meant to degrade and oppress people of native descent. It also distinguished between citizens and noncitizens. Thus, the old notion of citizenship was distinctly conflated with ethnicity.

Following the 1952 Revolution, the Nationalist Revolutionary Movement (MNR) government worked to cleanse citizenship of its ethnic character, casting Bolivian citizenship as an inclusive, civic-national project (Albó 2004). Indigenous identity and organization were folded into the state: the *indio* emerged as the *campesino*, the *ayllu* and the *marka* became *sindicatos*, and everyone could vote (Postero 2004). However, the corporatizing of citizenship and the relationship of campesinos to the central government was conditional on a certain level of economic security. When the state-led economy faltered and dictatorship gave way to elected civilian leadership, campesinos lost their incentive to accede to, and the government lost its ability to enforce, the agreement (Grindle 2003). Alternative visions of identity and organization had been planted by the Aymara *katarista* movement in the 1970s, and many campesinos in the 1980s and 1990s invoked this vision to articulate their demands of the state.

In the absence of state legitimacy and enforcement of a specific vision of citizenship, people began to voice their own. And, because the different ethnic groups throughout Bolivia had different realities of territory, livelihood, migration, language, and relations to the central and regional governments, their visions were distinct, even if they bore similarities. What did citizenship mean in the wake of the new national project? An important factor, even if contested, is the way in which the state defines citizenship and ethnicity (Wade 1997, 30–35). Prior to the 1952 Revolution, ethnic supremacy was the standard, and afterward citizenship was officially color-blind. In the early 1990s, the *pluri-multi* period was marked by the recognition of the multicultural, plurinational nature of the state. Aymara, Quechua, and Guaraní were adopted as official languages alongside Spanish. But, far from settling the ethnicity-citizenship question, indigenous groups now had another foundation on which to press for further distinctions of citizenship.

Because the state created a *pluri-multi* citizenship, it legitimized further demands for protections that would uphold the right to be Guaraní or Aymara, now co-equal with being Bolivian. The indigenous movements now had the "right to have rights," which were multiple and mostly distinct between the groups (Dagnino 1998, 50). I attempt to demonstrate that autonomy discourse had multiple distinct origins by examining the paths that different indigenous groups took towards articulating their own demands up to and during the *pluri-multi* period. Over time, the fragmentation between indigenous movements eased on some fronts, and autonomy was integrated into a more general popular discourse by the MAS. This reflects the multiple challenges to the state's terms of citizenship in the 1990s, and the trend toward a new popular form of citizenship as promoted by the MAS government since 2006 (Albro 2005). Although the Media Luna autonomist movement has managed to mobilize support regionally, its attempts to replicate the indigenous-popular approach have failed to succeed because of the movement's tone deafness to the drastically altered political context.

CONCEPTIONS OF AUTONOMY

Autonomy implies moral responsibility and self-determination on one level, suggesting that actors should be the arbiters and agents of their behavior (Hill 1989). A liberal conception of autonomy ascribes this agency and responsibility to the individual, who then operates within a society and system of laws. Accountability and liberty are conceived in terms of the person. While this conception dominates, almost exclusively, in the West, other communitarian visions, including many indigenous ones, ascribe autonomy to a group (Forst 2002; Kymlicka 1989; Taylor 1992). Moral failings are not exclusively those of individuals, but also of communities. The arbiter and the agent is often the family, the village, and the extended community.

Under colonial rule, many forms of communal autonomy were tolerated, or at least not eliminated entirely. However, as states were formed out of former colonies, and especially as those states modernized, communal autonomy was challenged, subordinated, and replaced when possible. The modern conception of citizenship in many countries, including Bolivia, was civic-national and attempted to homogenize the individuals within the state's sphere. While indigenous peoples were no longer less than citizens, they were forced to adopt a citizenship that made them members in a state they perhaps did not recognize and often considered illegitimate. In terms of the popular movements that invoked indigeneity, an identity based in indigenous roots but not necessarily within a specific ethnicity, what did autonomy mean?

As Burguete (chapter 2) also shows in her discussion of social movements in Chiapas, Mexico, autonomy itself is an ambiguous term, ranging from individual agency to self-governance by a group, such as San Andrés y Providencia in Colombia or the Regiónes Autónomas del Atlántico Sur y Norte in Nicaragua. The autonomy articulated by Bolivian social movements generally refers to the self-aware *ethnie*—the Quechua, the Aymara, the Guaraní—and its self-determination. It implies the validity of culture and language, a level of independence from central government interference, acceptance of *usos y costumbres* as legally valid, and rights to economic independence. There is also a strong territorial component. The integrity of communities, homes, and agricultural land is important in this discourse. The fact that autonomy is central to such a wide array of group demands reflects Diaz Polanco's conception of autonomy as the "articulating demand" through which other demands are advanced (Van Cott 2001). While imperfect, the treatment of autonomy here includes demands for territory, self-determination, legal pluralism, and other essential components in the construction of group autonomy.

This chapter sticks close to more explicit calls for autonomy, however, I will argue that the Media Luna movement missed the mark in appropriating this discourse. The essential difference between the autonomy demands of indigenous and popular movements and the Media Luna autonomists is that the indigenous discourse is grounded in actual dispossession and deprivation of autonomy and served to unify most of the country. However, the Media Luna discourse attempts to protect the spoils of old privilege and to divide the country. Furthermore, the movement discourse of autonomy was grounded in a specific political opportunity context, in which the state was devoid of legitimacy. Media Luna autonomist discourse may mobilize its movement participants, but this discourse resonates differently vis-à-vis the Morales government, and its widespread popular support sustained with landslide national votes.

EMERGENCE OF INDIGENOUS AUTONOMY DISCOURSE, 1970S–1990S

Though the historic grievances of Latin America's indigenous peoples extend back more than five hundred years, it has only been since the Third Wave of democratization that a meaningful negotiation of the state's relation to indigenous peoples has occurred. In the indigenous social movements that have emerged since the mid-1980s, the issue of autonomy has figured prominently. The articulation of autonomy demands are politically potent throughout the region due to the convergence of several factors: the transition to democracy, the development of international fora and conventions on self-determination, the weakness and fragmentation of party systems in Latin America, and crises of legitimacy of these young democracies (Yashar 1999; Stavenhagen 1992). In Bolivia, all of these factors were relevant, in addition to the significant fact that a majority of Bolivia's population identifies as indigenous. Further, that Bolivia is the most unequal country in the region, and that its poorest are also its indigenous majority, adds significant fuel to indigenous demands for equity, inclusion, and redress.

In Bolivia, the 1952 Revolution instituted its version of modern citizenship. To government leaders, this solved the "Indian problem."[3] By fully and formally including all of Bolivia's people, the state attempted to channel attention, loyalty, and commonality through the central government rather than through the country's more than thirty indigenous groups and their community leaders (Albó 1987). To this end, the government created *campesino sindicatos* throughout the countryside, which further organized indigenous people and intermediated their interests to the state (Gill 2000; Healey 1991). This network of peasant *sindicatos* reached its breaking point under the peasant-military alliance, and in the early 1970s an Aymara indigenous movement called *katarismo* (drawing on the 1781 siege of La Paz by Tupac Katari) challenged the civic-nationalist citizenship imposed by the state. The opening salvo was the 1973 Tiwanaku Manifesto, organized by the Aymara activist Fausto Reinaga (Rivera 1987). The Tiwanaku Manifesto rebuked the modern state project initiated by the 1952 Revolution, calling for an indigenous awakening and an "autonomous campesino movement." The manifesto and military violence against campesinos eventually caused the replacement of the state-organized campesino network with the *katarista*-inspired Unitary Trade Union Confederation of Bolivian Peasant Workers (Confederación Sindical Única de Trabajadores Campesinos de Bolivia, or CSUTCB). The *katarista* movement quickly grew and inspired a flood of indigenous activism and scholarship.

The influence of *katarismo* is apparent in the many highland organizations formed in the 1970s, including the CSUTCB, the Revolutionary Tupac Katari Movement (Movimiento Revolucionario Tupac Katari, or MRTK), and the militant Indigenous Tupac Katari Movement (Movimiento Indígena Tupac Katari, or MITKA). Many of these intellectuals became active and influential in politics. Those affiliated with MRTK, such as former vice president Victor Hugo Cardenas, advocated a platform of indigenous rights that involved collaboration with traditional political leaders. Those involved with MITKA, such as Felipe Quispe, adopted a less conciliatory position vis-à-vis mestizo leaders.

In the early 1990s, several factors converged to catalyze the growth of indigenous collective action in Bolivia. The collapse of mining and the "shock therapy" imposed by governments beginning in the 1980s forced a major migration of tens of thousands of miners throughout Bolivia. Many of these displaced miners relocated in coca-growing areas in the highland valleys, and many more migrated to the growing slum of El Alto that surrounds La Paz (Gill 2000). These displaced miners were part of what was widely considered to be the most militant labor movement in South America (Sanabria 2000). This organizing tradition, along with the peasant syndicates long in place throughout the countryside, was now dispersed in communities across Bolivia (Albro 2005). The steady emphasis on liberal economic policies, such as privatization, decreased social spending, deregulation, and lower tariffs, extended economic insecurity to increasingly wider swaths of society in the 1990s. The campesino federations, infused by the displaced labor militancy of the former miners, provided a ready organizing network, and the growing threat of economic austerity that disproportionately impacted indigenous people provided the incentive for massive popular mobilization in the 1990s.

Social movements in the 1990s, prior to the viability of the MAS and indigenous parties in the 2000s, served as the primary vehicle for indigenous representation, promoting and advancing calls for indigenous rights. In the milieu of a party system shattered by the dual processes of economic and political liberalization since the 1980s, social movements became far more effective political mechanisms than the previous alliances with traditional parties (Van Cott 2005). These social movements rallied for the advancement of indigenous interests that the traditional parties either did not or could not provide, in particular demands for indigenous autonomy, cultural and language rights, and territory. Most notably, indigenous movements through the hemisphere have mobilized to pressure governments to ratify Convention 169 of the International Labor Organization (ILO 169), which establishes specific rights of indigenous peoples and the obligations of the state toward them (Assies 2000; ILO 1989). Bolivia, along with other highly indigenous countries, ratified ILO 169 in 1990, and a major thrust of indigenous movements was to push governments to codify and fulfill the terms of the convention.

ILO 169 established the legal recognition of indigenous rights to some unspecified form of autonomy and the recognition of indigenous cultures by the state. Bolivia ratified ILO 169 in 1991 and, under social movement pressure, reformed its constitution to include various recognitions of indigenous language, of the multicultural and plurinational nature of the country, and of indigenous peoples as "originary" and as constituted prior to the establishment of the modern state (Assies 2000; Van Cott 2007). Some of the most notable early accomplishments awere constitutional reforms that recognize indigenous customary law, indigenous languages as official state languages, and the right to collective land titling (Van Cott 2000a, 2005). Van Cott (2007, 132) contends that by 2000, a "multicultural regional model of constitutionalism" advanced indigenous rights through recognition of indigenous peoples as first peoples, the establishment of customary laws as authoritative, strong collective land rights, official recognition of indigenous languages, and provision of bilingual education.

In 1990, a significant advancement for indigenous rights was the March for Territory and Dignity, organized by the lowland Confederation of Indigenous Peoples of Eastern Bolivia (Confederación de Indígenas del Oriente de Bolivia, or CIDOB). This thirty-five-day march, which began in the lowlands and culminated at La Paz, highlighted the lowland indigenous proposal for a parallel and separate indigenous legal authority that would codify indigenous forms of governance. This march was followed by another in 1996, which was coordinated between the main highland and lowland groups. It had many of the same goals as the first, but expanded its scope to include demands important to highland groups. However, the law that eventually passed, the Law of National Institution of Agrarian Reform (Ley Instituto Nacional de Reforma Agraria, or Ley INRA), was a compromise between indigenous communalism and full privatization and did not set aside a separate indigenous legal authority parallel to the state. The Ley INRA conspicuously omits mention of "territory," a term that has connotations of governance and autonomy (Assies 2006). Rather than recognizing the indigenous conception of communal land titles, the Ley INRA instituted a complicated process that resulted in few collective land titles. However, the early calls for autonomy gained wide attention, forced the central government to acknowledge indigenous demands, and set the stage for future collective action.

Coordination in the 1990s between the movements of the highlands and the lowlands helped to create a common understanding of the broader indigenous discourse. Highland organizations have assented to a broader notion of autonomy and territory, which has always been important to CIDOB and its allies. Likewise, lowland groups adjusted to the legal demands for territory imposed by the Ley INRA.

Advances in understanding helped to synthesize discourses about indigeneity and the common struggle of originary peoples, which transcended ethnic difference. During the 1990s, this trend helped to produce useful spectacles, such as marches and public demonstrations, although it had not yet overcome the hard problems of coordination. The incorporation of ethnic imagery into political party agendas was also a signal of a heightened indigenous awareness. However, the *wiphalas* waved at Conference of the Fatherland (CONDEPA) rallies, and even the election of Cardénas as vice president in 1993 did little to seriously advance indigenous rights. The advances in discourse were important in establishing common space and rhetorical tools for movements, but without a real catalyst, movements remained mostly splintered.

INDIGENOUS TRANSITION TO POWER, 2000–2005

This section highlights the first half of the present decade, which was a transitory period in multiple ways. It marked the collapse of *partidocracia*, in which traditional political parties were essentially delegitimized, at least at the national level. This period also marked the ascendance of a unified popular movement, which culminated in the 2005 election of Morales. The electoral unity of social movements marked an advance in movement coordination, as movements still have quarrels and different objectives. However, they have managed to transcend those differences for large common purposes. This period, then, is in one sense a reversal. Power has been reversed from the traditional political establishment to its challengers. The new opposition is far from coordinated or monolithic, and it has manifested most vociferously in the Media Luna autonomy movement, which now invokes many themes from 1990s movement discourse. Prior to the emergence of autonomy calls in the Media Luna, the indigenous autonomy discourse evolved by becoming more generalized and serving as a proxy for many other claims. Also, during this time, Morales and the MAS initiated a popular and plural articulation of sovereignty that helped to build coalitional discourse and further bind movements in solidarity (Albro 2005).

By the end of 2005, autonomy no longer made sense in the ways that it had been previously invoked. Not only had Morales been elected, but also his popular sovereignty project was also legitimized on the basis of robust civic multiculturalism. In a sense, the calls for autonomy had been met, or at least had begun to be fulfilled. The fears in Santa Cruz of nationalization of natural gas reserves, which must have seemed threatening at least since the ouster of Sánchez de Lozada, were now imminent. And although the old autonomy claims for popular movements were muted, the mestizo leaders and businessmen in Santa Cruz must have seen a connection between their new position in the political minority and the campesino invocations of autonomy when they launched their autonomy movement.

The 1990s were full of false starts for social movement unity, and most movements remained tied to particular regions, occupations, or ethnicities. This was not simply attributable to power struggles among movement leaders. The interests of each group, their distinct collective action repertoires, and their relations to the state presented serious differences that were not easily bridged. In some situations, groups held not only divergent interests but contrary ones, such as in the implementation of the Ley INRA. Thus, many of the collective action discourses like autonomy could not transcend intergroup difference among indigenous groups. Autonomy remained part of a specific indigenous discourse, primarily that of lowland groups. The discourse of autonomy was indeed part of an ethnic repertoire against the state, but it was not yet panindigenous. It was still the domain of CIDOB and lowland organizers.

It was the battles over natural resources in the 2000s that finally transcended the movement fragmentation of the 1990s, at least at the national level. The events that would help to unify the disparate groups from across the country began in 2000, with the Cochabamba water war. Although a primarily local struggle, the move by the government to privatize the city's water system through a contract to a foreign (U.S.-based) corporation provoked a widespread outcry. The 2000 water war was succeeded by 2003 wars for natural gas and water, and each successive episode seemed to encompass larger circles of society. Perhaps it is because the impacts of natural resource policies are both basic and central to the Bolivian commons that it bound movements together in solidarity. However, that social movements were joined finally by struggles for natural resources is no small fact, as the role of natural gas figures centrally in the Media Luna autonomy discourse (Weisbrot and Sandoval 2008).

As movements began to unite and coordinate against the Sánchez de Lozada government and its successors, the discourse shifted. Also, the CIDOB's calls for autonomy were now being made by Morales and Quispe, charging that the central government had dispossessed all indigenous peoples, and that the neoliberal citizenship regimes imposed since the mid-1980s were affronts to the national patrimony. Autonomy was now important not just as a territorial issue for a specific group as a protection against the state; now the state was being accused of asserting autonomy from its people. The only way to correct the imbalance was a new popular nationalism that truly embodied the *pluri-multi* rhetoric and laws of the 1990s. Because the state was officially multinational and pluricultural, the only way for the state to have legitimacy was for each of these nations and cultures to assert their autonomy in the Bolivian project. In other words, a new citizenship and vision of the state was being constructed that did not simply accommodate the array of ethnicities within it. Rather, the new state would be contingent on those ethnicities, requiring each to have real autonomy.

The parallel liberalization of the economy and politics since the 1980s provided both the motivation and the means for massive social mobilization over the past fifteen to twenty years. These mobilizations came to a head in the resource wars of the early 2000s, in which a wide cross-section of Bolivian society challenged the privatization of natural resources, particularly water and natural gas. Although the struggle over natural resources was initially a competition between the unpopular structural adjustment agenda and the popular nationalization agenda, it has become more expansive and volatile in recent years.

In the fall of 1999, the Bolivian government was under pressure from the World Bank, which refused to finance water service in Cochabamba unless the water system was privatized. The government awarded a noncompetitive, forty-year contract to a subsidiary of the U.S. corporation Bechtel. The deal transferred rights to all water in the area, from the municipal water structure, to aquifer holdings, to even the wells created without government funds or labor, but installed by campesinos with aid worker assistance.

The 1994 Capitalization Law and 1996 Hydrocarbons Law privatized the hydrocarbon (petroleum and natural gas) industry, which had been a state-owned resource for more than sixty years. During that earlier time, the government's share of oil and other hydrocarbon revenues was 50 percent, with the other half going to foreign partners. After privatization, the state's share fell to about 18 percent, which forced massive government borrowing and deficits. After years of debate about new plans to export gas, the Sánchez de Lozada government in 2003 announced a plan that would both export the gas through Chile, a long-standing national rival, and would sell it at a price that was seen as far less than it was worth. While national polls showed that half the country supported some form of gas exportation, the public was strongly opposed to the specific plan. Social movements and other popular sectors loudly rallied against the sale, and further demanded the nationalization of gas.

Civil society and social movement groups, led by Quispe, Olivera, and Morales, quickly coordinated the response. Beginning with hunger strikes led by Quispe in September 2003, the confrontations quickly intensified. In mid-September, Olivera coordinated protests of 50,000 in Cochabamba and 25,000 in La Paz against the government plan. The government instructed the military to respond to regain control, resulting in several repressive confrontations. The most notorious incident was the ambush and apparent assassination of seven campesinos in Warisata, a small town near Cochabamba, by the military. The incident spurred widespread anger and resistance to the Sánchez de Lozada government. Almost half a million demonstrators mobilized in La Paz in October 2003, demanding the immediate and full attention of the government to their demands. Road blockades were set up on routes between major cities and campesino demonstrators surrounded La Paz, creating an effective state of siege. In all, the clashes resulted in the deaths of at least sixty civilians.

Sánchez de Lozada quickly lost whatever public backing he had, which was soon followed by the withdrawal of support by his own government and vice president. He was forced to resign on October 23, 2003, and his successor, Carlos Mesa, quickly responded to the crisis by withdrawing the export plan, ordering an investigation of military violence, and announcing a public referendum on the gas plan. Mesa's referendum in May 2004 offered a clear repudiation of privatized natural gas: 89 percent of Bolivians demanded that the gas be nationalized. Mesa, however, was unable to produce a plan that satisfied the demands of both international investors and lending institutions, and the Bolivian public. His government faced massive mobilizations and roadblocks throughout 2004 and 2005. The massive mobilizations since 2003 had already ousted one president, stymied another, and now posed a credible threat to redistribute the private wealth of Media Luna–based natural gas industrialists to the rest of the country.

AUTONOMY RISES IN THE MEDIA LUNA

The consolidation of democratic norms, the multicultural decentralization in 1990s legal reforms, and the subsequent mobilization of indigenous peoples shifted the context in which Santa Cruz elites could defend enclaves of political and economic power. Added to this, the indigenous demands for nationalization of natural resources and the inability of traditional parties to defend liberal economic policies in the 2000s forced Santa Cruz economic interests into a discourse of departmental autonomy to guard against MAS incursions from the municipal level (aided by Popular Participation) and from the central government (now controlled by MAS without coalition partners). As Eaton (2007) argues, the emergence of the Santa Cruz–led movement for regional autonomy is a more viable option, in the current democratic context in Latin America, for elite backlash than the traditional resort to authoritarianism. The regional autonomy articulated by Santa Cruz *autonomistas* is broadly conceived. The *cruceños* argue that autonomy should include departmental control over tax revenues, over natural resources, police, and other policies, except for national defense and trade (Eaton 2007).

Santa Cruz has long retained a distinct territorial identity. The 1952 Revolution's land redistribution, which broke up *latifundios*, occurred primarily in the western part of the country (Klein 2003). The ownership of most Santa Cruz landholdings has remained in the possession of a tiny elite, which has managed to diversify into agricultural, natural gas, and other extractive industries. As Weisbrot and Sandoval (2008) demonstrate, land tenure in Bolivia is among the most highly concentrated in the world (0.63 percent own more than 66 percent of the land) and land tenure in Santa Cruz is far more concentrated than elsewhere in Bolivia. The implication is that land ownership in Santa Cruz is among the most concentrated globally.

In response to the centralization of the 1952 Revolution, which challenged the local authorities in departments, civic committees emerged in each department. These civic committees, formed by conservative business leaders and landowners, emerged in almost every department in the country to counter the MNR government's authority at the local levels. The elites in the region were wary of the new promises to break up the old oligarchies, redistribute land, and shift power within the country. The earliest and most influential of these committees, both within its department and vis-à-vis the central government, was the Pro–Santa Cruz Committee (Comité Pro–Santa Cruz, or CPSC). The CPSC effectively challenged the MNR for authority in the department, becoming the de facto local authority.

During the period of military rule, the generals recognized that the civic committees were often the most effective channels of regional influence. These regimes supported the civic committees and granted prominent government positions to civic committee leadership. Several military leaders during this period, most notably Hugo Banzer, were either from or had close ties to Santa Cruz, providing the department with a special relationship to the central government. However, the CPSC also challenged the military rule, as in the case of General Torres and the ouster of General García Meza that returned the country to civilian rule in 1982. Upon the return to democratic governance, the civic committees had become important and entrenched mechanisms of local authority and were perceived as protectors of local identity and culture. Further, because the new democratic leadership was addressing the pressing issues of stabilizing the economy, the civic committees remained unchallenged. The preeminence of Santa Cruz and the CPSC is reflected in the ability of departmental leaders to maintain political strength in support and opposition to the central government, as well as in the ability to cultivate a distinctly *cruceño* identity.

The story of why Santa Cruz has remained distinct politically and economically is contested, however, between those in the east and in the west. *Cruceños* claim that their traditional alienation from La Paz fostered a separate and more liberal departmental economy than the national one centrally planned by the government. However, *altiplano* leaders contend that the central government funded the infrastructure that now supports *cruceño* industries, in particular natural gas. Further, the central government's "March toward the East" generated a significant national debt in the 1940s and 1950s that almost exclusively funded infrastructure development in Santa Cruz, such as highways and railways (Gill 1987). Business interests in Santa Cruz also found allies in the Banzer government, which generously and prejudiciously funded agricultural development and fixed commodity prices so that producers never recorded losses on production (Conaghan and Malloy 1994). From this starting point, the nationwide shift to Washington consensus–style economic liberalism in 1985 highly advantaged Santa Cruz and other eastern departments, where the majority of the country's exports are produced (Weisbrot and Sandoval 2008).

The *pluri-multi* period helped to set the stage for the autonomy calls in the 2000s, particularly through several key legal reforms. In line with the regional decentralizing trend and the efforts to include more local and indigenous participation, the 1994 Popular Participation law created 311 municipalities across Bolivia. While this increased local and indigenous participation, it was a challenge to Santa Cruz departmental leadership due to the focus on the municipal level. While Santa Cruz had always successfully navigated its relationship to La Paz during the peak of centralization, Popular Participation created local authority that was legally and financially independent of the departmental level (Molina 2002). The empowerment of municipalities diverted revenue to municipalities, and simultaneously empowered a new wave of indigenous leadership. It did so not only by raising indigenous leaders to mayoral posts, but also by consultative oversight of mayoralties by oversight committees composed primarily of indigenous leaders (Hiskey and Seligson 2003). It was from the growth of indigenous leadership at the municipal level that indigenous parties developed their bases of support, which translated into growing national-level support in 1997, 2002, and 2005. Thus, there is a direct correlation between the rise of indigenous mobilization and Media Luna autonomy movement.

Though historically Bolivia relied on mining as its primary extractive industry, since the 1990s the exploitation of hydrocarbons (natural gas, petroleum, and liquefied petroleum gas) has emerged as not only the primary extractive industry but also one of the primary sources of government revenues. With the second-largest reserves in South America, natural gas represents one of the most significant sources of national revenue. In recent years the potential of natural gas has become even more evident, with proven reserves increasing by a factor of seven between 1996 and 2002. In 2007, natural gas accounted for slightly more than 10 percent of Bolivia's GDP and is one of the primary export sectors. However, natural gas is heavily concentrated in the Media Luna. Almost no natural gas reserves exist in the *altiplano*.

Traditionally, the imbalance of resource wealth was weighted toward the west, where the silver and tin mines are located. Throughout most of the twentieth century the revenues generated by the west were used to develop infrastructure and finance government operations around the country, including the then-primarily agricultural Media Luna. In fact, in the 1980s when natural gas reserves were discovered in the Media Luna, it was largely mining wealth that was redistributed to build the infrastructure to exploit the reserves. In the mid-1980s mining completely collapsed, undercutting the funding of the east by the west. However, the natural gas infrastructure remained, and by the mid-1990s the real value of the gas reserves became apparent.

Beyond the growth of natural gas development, the 1990s were notable for the eastern departmental elites because of the explosion in indigenous political mobilization. As discussed earlier, Popular Participation ushered in a new generation of leaders from the local level upward, and they were largely indigenous. Economic liberalization had provided a strong, salient mobilizing incentive for these leaders and their movements. These movements strongly contested the economic privilege of traditional elites across Bolivian society. The leaders of the Media Luna departments and civic committees were shocked by the sheer numbers of mobilized and angry indigenous people, and determined to dig their heels in and resist. This dynamic escalated during the second Sánchez de Lozada presidency, when natural resource issues were at their peak in the gas war. The indigenous and popular sector calls to nationalize the gas ("El gas no se vende—¡carrajo!"[4]) were a direct threat to the economic base of the civic committees. They were also viewed as government encroachment on the self-sufficiency of the departments. The rise of indigenous movements also exacerbated a long-standing ethnic rivalry between the eastern lowlands, whose residents often refer to themselves as *cambas*, and those in the western *altiplano*, who are referred to as *kollas*. This rivalry has always had implications of regional pride and disdain for the other, but the racial overtones have become more charged and have often manifested in outright racism.

The calls for departmental autonomy accelerated following the ouster of Sánchez de Lozada in 2003. Led by the CPSC, in June 2004 and January 2005, hundreds of thousands of residents turned out in the streets of Santa Cruz to demand autonomy and held a general strike in November 2004 to force the Mesa government to call a referendum on departmental autonomy (Buitrago 2005; Eaton 2006). By 2005, the CPSC had exerted enough pressure on Mesa to force him to allow the first-ever prefectural elections, resulting in the ascension of former CPSC president, Rubén Costas to the office of prefect in Santa Cruz. Led by Costas, the autonomy movement also gained enough momentum to pressure the government into holding the national referendum on departmental autonomy in July 2006. This referendum was indicative of the divisions to emerge. While each of the autonomist departments voted for autonomy, a majority of Bolivians did not (Crabtree 2008).

Ironically, the implementation of decentralization reforms has disempowered the departments at the national level, and empowered indigenous groups. This is due to the emphasis on municipal-level authority, where indigenous forms of organization are traditionally organized, and the bypassing of departmental authority, which has long been advanced by CPSC leaders. This coincides with increasing indigenous unity at the national level, strong mobilizations for nationalization of natural resources, the collapse of *partidocracia*, and the inability of Santa Cruz leaders to maintain their favored position with La Paz. CPSC leaders bundled these many cleavages—class, region, and industry—into calls for autonomy. The autonomy discourse provided a powerful mobilization strategy among its participants, but it risked accusations of disingenuous framing of elite concerns into a regionally popular discourse.

MAS AT THE HELM OF STATE, 2006–PRESENT

Since the 2006 autonomy referendum, *autonomistas* have accelerated their movement. Throughout 2007, the CPSC and Santa Cruz Prefect Costas rallied the civic committees in the departments of Beni, Pando, Chuquisaca, Cochabamba, and Tarija, in a series of strikes and actions against the central government, all the while building momentum for departmental autonomy votes. In May and June 2008, departmental autonomy referenda were held in Santa Cruz, Beni, Pando, and Tarija, which passed by large majorities. Following these referenda, the departments began establishing councils and legal frameworks to implement autonomy. The referenda, councils, and legal structures were denounced as illegal by the Morales government, as well as by regional governments and international organizations.

Especially since August 2008, the calls and actions of the autonomy movement have accelerated into a violent struggle for power in the departments. The August 2008 recall referendum (*revocatorio*), called by Morales following the opposition boycott of the constitution, renewed the mandates of Morales and six out of eight prefects. Each side has interpreted the *revocatorio* results as affirmations of their diametrically opposed agendas. The entrenchment of these agendas exploded in violence throughout the Media Luna. Several youth militias, particularly the Santa Cruz Youth Union (UJC), have seized central government buildings and raided the offices of indigenous organizations. In Pando, autonomy-aligned militias killed between seventeen and thirty indigenous residents, with more than one hundred others missing.

The bottom line is that all sides want to push forward the various autonomies in the constitution, from departmental to municipal to indigenous. This is a commonality between the autonomy statutes and the draft constitution. In fact, some observers contend that on paper there is little difference between the assortment of autonomies proposed by the statutes and the Constituyente (Centellas 2008). Beginning with Popular Participation in 1994, decentralization of central state power has been a popular agenda. Popular Participation was seen by many as an attempt to subvert the authority of departments by devolving directly from the state to the municipality. Indeed, Sánchez de Lozada, who is a mining magnate from Cochabamba, always had a tense relationship with the eastern gas and petroleum interests. Add to the mix the indigenous sector demands since the 1990s, and the resulting consensus is not whether to have autonomy, but rather what kinds and to what extent.

Bolivia's government was one of the most centralized in the region after years of state-led development and strong military rule. Both the autonomy statutes and the draft constitution contained major and detailed provisions for decentralizing authority to departmental and indigenous autonomies. The difference is really the hierarchy of powers. The autonomy statutes would structure subnational and national autonomies in such a way that the departmental level would mediate all other autonomies with the central government, whereas the constitutional vision is for a set of roughly equal subnational autonomies that are each directly accountable to the central government (Böhrt et al. 2008).

The strident rhetoric of the autonomists belies the widespread agreement on autonomy and decentralization, which has been developing for years from a number of sectors. However, the invocation of autonomy appears to signal a project that is distinct from, and perhaps incompatible with, the *pluri-multi* advocacy of popular and indigenous sectors. Should something deeper be interpreted from the fervor of the autonomist movement? Is the effort to undermine the constitution and Morales less about autonomy and more a counterreaction to indigenous ascendancy? Is it an effort to retain traditional domains of economic power? Perhaps, and most likely, the autonomy movement encapsulates all of these reasons. The irony of this political moment is that the militancy of the autonomist camps may derail their signature issue if the political violence and stalemate prevents the ratification of the new constitution.

CONCLUSION: WHITHER MEDIA LUNA AUTONOMY?

There was no question in August 2007 that Bolivia's leaders had been charged with the creation of a new constitution. Bolivians had ousted the two most recent governments based on a core of demands that included the convening of a Constituent Assembly—the Constituyente—to draft a new constitution to be voted on in a national referendum. Social movement leader Evo Morales had based a substantial portion of his successful 2005 presidential campaign on a pledge to convene the Constituyente and "refound" Bolivia. Morales won the election with the first outright majority in the country's history, and his MAS party won a majority in the lower chamber of Congress and barely missed a Senate majority.[5] Morales's victory unquestionably represented a break with traditional party rule, a new ascendance of indigenous political leaders to the national stage, and an unprecedented mandate to lead the country. However, the many cleavages in Bolivian politics and society were not eased by the ascendance of Bolivia's first indigenous leader to the majority-indigenous country. Rather, most of these cleavages appear to have been reconfigured, as well as reinforced.

Indeed, the Media Luna autonomy movement appears to be based on a melding of several cleavages. The attempt to reframe autonomy, which had been made salient by the indigenous discourse of popular movements, as a regional, nonethnic demand was successful in mobilizing many in Media Luna departments who were unsure of their economic and political positions in the Morales era. Its mobilizational power is evident: crowds of hundreds of thousands turned out for the Gran Cabildos in Santa Cruz in 2004 and 2005 (Eaton 2006). However, the Media Luna autonomists appear not to have appropriated the larger political success of indigenous movements, who successfully challenged the nature of the Bolivian state. The current autonomy movement remains a regional phenomenon and, though a serious force to be reckoned with in La Paz, lacks the broad authority of indigenous movements that articulated autonomy demands.

Why did indigenous and popular movements enjoy greater benefits from their demands of autonomy? I submit that the political context in which social movements made their claims was fundamentally different than that in which the Media Luna movement makes its claims. First, the decentralization agenda of the central government in the 1990s was focused on the municipal rather than the departmental level. This advantaged indigenous and campesino forms of organization, particularly *ayllus* and *sindicatos*. Second, the multicultural zeitgeist of the 1990s was centered on ethnic diversity and protection, not regionalism. The Media Luna autonomy appeals are grounded in a territorial conception of autonomy. Though territorial autonomy is common in other places, it is usually a component of an ethnic autonomy. The Media Luna rhetoric is marked by regional distinctions (*cambas* versus *kollas*), not ethnic ones. Third, the popular movements of the 1990s and 2000s were possible due to, and directed toward, the erosion of state legitimacy. The demands particularly to break with the state liberal economic agenda peaked in 2003–2005, when mobilizations against the state were at their height. The lack of perceived legitimacy of the central government helped to unify movements from across the country. In contrast, the Media Luna movement seeks to fragment the country, and challenges a state that is now endowed with unprecedented legitimacy. Finally, the international context is vastly different. The international wave of indigenous rights mobilization in the 1990s buoyed Bolivian social movements, which increasingly adopted indigenous discourses. However, the current Media Luna autonomy campaign lacks the support of even a single country, and has been repeatedly condemned by intergovernmental organizations and human rights organizations.

While indigenous social movements may no longer control the rhetoric of autonomy in Bolivia, their record in utilizing it as an effective mechanism to achieve political success far outshines the Media Luna attempts. Indigenous movements used broad appeals to generate new leadership at all levels, especially within the central government, began to alter the country's legal structure, and articulated and began to execute a new vision of the Bolivian state. Media Luna leaders, on the other hand, articulated a parochial vision that sought to retain the repudiated status quo. Even though the indigenous challengers were now wielders of state power and could no longer use the rhetoric of autonomy, their success is not likely to be replicated by the Media Luna autonomy movement. The new autonomists have neglected that the weight of oppression animated the urgency and broad acceptance of the indigenous use of autonomy.

Furthermore, autonomy was not the only demand used by the indigenous movements—far from it. Autonomy was used as a means to achieve other, perhaps more important, demands, such as rights to language, education, religion, cultural customs, and economic fairness. Because autonomy stood for tackling systemic poverty, overturning the political system, and reclaiming power, social movements were able to use it as a prism to focus grievances with which most Bolivians could identify. Though a strong regional identity is rightly claimed by the Media Luna—it is a fiercely independent, beautiful, and unique place—its autonomy demands appear to have far less historic weight than those of the indigenous social movements that originated them.

ACKNOWLEDGMENTS

I extend my gratitude to Todd Eisenstadt for sponsorship of my studies and invaluable guidance, to my colleagues in the School of Public Affairs doctoral program, and to participants at the conference, "Reconciling Customary Law Norms, Identity-Related Conflicts, and State Political Institutions: Mexico's Multicultural Experiment in Comparative Perspective," American University, Washington, DC, February 19–20, 2009.

NOTES

1. *Pluri-multi* refers to the zeitgeist of the 1990s that advocated the plurinational and multicultural nature of the country, focusing particularly on the recognition of indigenous peoples as originary that preceded the establishment of the modern state (Assies 2000; Van Cott 2007).
2. Recent data indicate that 71 percent of Bolivia's population identifies as indigenous, and the other majority-indigenous country, Guatemala, is comprised of 66 percent indigenous peoples (Deruyttere 2006; Rice 2006).
3. "Indian problem" refers to government policies that attempted to integrate indigenous peoples into the modern state and society. The term was used in many Latin American countries with significant indigenous populations, such as Bolivia and other Andean countries (see Stavenhagen 2002; Lucero 2003).
4. "The gas is not for sale, damn it!" The phrase is representative of antiprivatization graffiti scrawled on public buildings.
5. Morales was also reelected in 2009 with an even larger (64.2 percent) mandate.

REFERENCES

Albó, Xavier. 1987. "From MNRistas to Kataristas to Katari." In *Resistance, Rebellion, and Consciousness in the Andean Peasant World, 18th to 20th Centuries*, edited by S. Stern, 382–384. Madison: University of Wisconsin Press.
Albó, Xavier. 1991. "El Retorno del Indio." *Revista Andina* 9 (2): 299–366.

Albó, Xavier. 2002. "Bolivia: From Indian and *Campesino* Leaders to Councilors and Parliamentary Deputies." In *Multiculturalism in Latin America*, edited by R. Sieder, 76–77. New York: Palgrave Macmillan.

Albó, Xavier. 2004. "Ethnic Identity and Politics in the Central Andes: The Cases of Bolivia, Ecuador, and Peru." In *Politics in the Andes: Identity, Conflict, Reform*, edited by J. Burt and P. Mauceri. Pittsburgh: University of Pittsburgh Press.

Albro, Robert. 2005. "The Indigenous in the Plural in Bolivian Oppositional Politics." *Bulletin of Latin American Research* 24 (4): 445–448.

Assies, Willem. 2000. "Indigenous Peoples and Reform of the State in Latin America." In *The Challenge of Diversity: Indigenous Peoples and Reform of the State in Latin America*, edited by W. Assies, G. van der Haar, and A. Hoekema, 3. Amsterdam: Thela Thesis.

Assies, Willem. 2006. "Land Tenure Legalization, Pluriculturalism, and Multiethnicity in Bolivia." Paper prepared for the symposium At the Frontier of Land Issues: Social Embeddedness of Rights and Public Policy, May 17–19, Montpellier, France.

Böhrt, Carlos, Carlos Alarcón, and Carlos Romero. 2008. *Hacia una Constitución Democrática, Viable y Plural*. La Paz: Fundación Boliviana para la Democracia Multipartidaria.

Buitrago, Miguel A. 2005. "Santa Cruz's Town Hall." *MABBlog*, January 28, http://mabb.blogspot.com/2005/01/santa-cruzs-town-hall.html.

Centellas, Miguel. 2008. "Comparing Autonomy Models (Proposed CPE v. Santa Cruz Autonomy Statute)." *Pronto** (blog), August 16, http://www.mcentellas.com/archives/2008/08/comparing-autonomy-models.html.

Conaghan, Catherine, and James Malloy. 1994. *Unsettling Statecraft: Democracy and Neoliberalism in the Central Andes*. Pittsburgh: University of Pittsburgh Press.

Crabtree, John. 2007. "Bolivia: A Tale of Two (or Rather Three) Cities." *Open Democracy*, September 18, http://www.opendemocracy.net/article/democracy_power/politics_protest/bolivia_three_cities.

Dagnino, Evelina. 1998. "Culture, Citizenship, and Democracy." In *Cultures of Politics, Politics of Culture*, edited by S. Alvarez, E. Dagnino, and A. Escobar. Boulder, CO: Westview Press.

Demiralp, Seda. 2009. "Beyond Pluralism and Multiculturalism: Religion, Culture, and Class in Turkey." Paper presented at "Reconciling Customary Law Norms, Identity-Related Conflicts, and State Political Institutions: Mexico's Multicultural Experiment in Comparative Perspective." American University, Washington, DC, February 19–20.

Deruyttere, Anne. 2006. "Operational Policy on Indigenous Peoples and Strategy for Indigenous Development." Washington, DC: Inter-American Development Bank. http://idbdocs.iadb.org/wsdocs/getdocument.aspx?docnum=691246.

Eaton, Kent. 2006. "Bolivia's Conservative Autonomy Movement." *Berkeley Review of Latin American Studies* (Winter/Spring): 18–21.

Eaton, Kent. 2007. "Backlash in Bolivia: Regional Autonomy as a Reaction against Indigenous Mobilization." *Politics and Society* 35 (2007): 71–102.

Forst, Rainer. 2002. *Contexts of Justice: Political Philosophy beyond Liberalism and Communitarianism*. Berkeley: University of California Press.

Gill, Lesley. 1987. *Peasants, Farmers, Entrepreneurs, and Social Change: Frontier Development and Lowland Bolivia*. Boulder, CO: Westview Press.

Gill, Lesley. 2000. *Teetering on the Rim*. New York: Columbia University Press.

Grindle, Merilee S. 2003. "Shadowing the Past? Policy Reform in Bolivia, 1985–2002." In *Proclaiming Revolution: Bolivia in Comparative Perspective*, edited by M. Grindle and P. Domingo, 318–343. Cambridge, MA: Harvard University Press.

Healey, Kevin. 1991. "Political Ascent of Bolivia's Peasant Coca Leaf Producers." *Journal of Interamerican Studies and World Affairs* 33: 88–89.

Hill, Thomas. 1989. "The Kantian Conception of Autonomy." In *The Inner Citadel*, edited by J. Christman, 91–105. New York: Oxford University Press.

Hiskey, Jonathan T., and Mitchell A. Seligson. 2003. "Pitfalls of Power to the People: Decentralization, Local Government Performance, and System Support in Bolivia." *Studies in International Comparative Development* 37: 64–88.

Hylton, Forrest. 2003. "Left Turns in South America: United Opposition to Neoliberalism in Bolivia?" *CounterPunch*, January 25. http://www.counterpunch.org/hylton01252003.html.

International Labor Organization. 1989. "Convention 169, Indigenous and Tribal Peoples Convention." http://www.ilo.org/ilolex/cgi-lex/convde.pl?C169.

Kymlicka, Will. 1989. *Liberalism, Community and Culture*. New York: Oxford University Press.

Molina, George Gray. 2002. "Popular Participation, Social Service Delivery, and Poverty Reduction 1994–2000." Paper presented at the conference Citizen Participation in the Context of Fiscal Decentralization: Best Practices in Municipal Management in Latin America and Asia, September 2–6, Tokyo, Japan.

Postero, Nancy Gray. 2004. "Articulation and Fragmentation: Indigenous Politics in Bolivia." In *The Struggle for Indigenous Rights in Latin America*, edited by N. Postero and L. Zamosc, 194. Portland: Sussex Academic Press.

Rivera Cusicanqui, Silvia. 1987. *Oppressed but Not Defeated: Peasant Struggles among the Aymara and the Qhechwa in Bolivia, 1900–1980*. Geneva: United Nations Research Institute for Social Development.

Sanabria, Harry. 2000. "Resistance and the Arts of Domination: Miners and the Bolivian State." *Latin American Perspectives* 27: 56–81.

Stavenhagen, Rodolfo. 1992. "Challenging the Nation-State in Latin America." *Journal of International Affairs* 45: 421–440.

Taylor, Charles. 1992. *The Ethics of Authenticity*. Cambridge, MA: Harvard University Press.

Tilly, Charles. 2003. "Political Identities in Changing Polities." *Social Research* 70: 605–620.

Van Cott, Donna Lee. 2000a. "Latin America: Constitutional Reform and Ethnic Right." *Parliamentary Affairs* 53: 41–55.

Van Cott, Donna Lee. 2000b. "A Political Analysis of Legal Pluralism in Bolivia and Colombia." *Journal of Latin American Studies* 32: 207–234.

Van Cott, Donna Lee. 2005. *From Movements to Parties in Latin America: The Evolution of Ethnic Politics*. New York: Cambridge University Press.

Van Cott, Donna Lee. 2007. "Latin America's Indigenous Peoples." *Journal of Democracy* 18: 127–141.

Wade, Peter. 1997. *Race and Ethnicity in Latin America*. London: Pluto Press.

Wanderley, Fernanda. 2008. "Beyond Gas: Between the Narrow-Based and the Broad-Based Economy." In *Unresolved Tensions: Bolivia Past and Present*, edited by J. Crabtree and L. Whitehead, 194–211. Pittsburgh: University of Pittsburgh Press.

Weisbrot, Mark, and Luis Sandoval. 2008. "The Distribution of Bolivia's Most Important Natural Resources and the Autonomy Conflicts." Washington, DC: Center for Economic and Policy Research. http://www.cepr.net.

Yashar, Deborah J. 1998. "Contesting Citizenship: Indigenous Movements and Democracy in Latin America." *Comparative Politics* 31: 23–42.

Yashar, Deborah J. 1999. "Democracy, Indigenous Movements, and the Post-Liberal Challenge in Latin America." *World Politics* 52: 76–104.

4 Bolivia's New Multicultural Constitution
The 2009 Constitution in Historical and Comparative Perspective

Miguel Centellas

On January 25, 2009, Bolivian voters approved a new constitution in a national referendum—the first time in the country's storied constitutional history that such a document was subjected to a popular mandate—with a comfortable margin of victory (61.43 percent).[1] The vote followed a tumultuous and divisive political process that began in earnest in 2006, with the election of a Constituent Assembly, but with roots in the political crisis that had forced then-president Gonzalo Sánchez de Lozada to resign on October 17, 2003, in the midst of a broad popular uprising. The period from October 2003 through January 2009 was one of the most polarized in Bolivia's political history; many observers worried about the ability of the Bolivian state to survive the tensions tearing the country's social fabric apart. In fact, the constitutional reform process itself stalled repeatedly—including violent political confrontations in the city of Sucre (the site of the assembly's deliberations) that left three dead in November 2007 and threatened to derail the entire process. Thus, the sheer fact that a constitutional document was put before voters, approved by them in a free and fair election, and accepted as legitimate by all relevant political actors is a remarkable achievement.

The new constitution has been celebrated—within Bolivia, but especially around the world—as a significant advance for indigenous rights in a country where, despite being a significant majority, indigenous peoples have long been marginalized. The new constitution contains elements that address indigenous groups' aspirations for collective rights and liberal concerns over the protection of individual rights. However, Bolivia's new constitution is often presented as a radical, far-reaching departure from the country's past political tradition. Such praises tend to focus on the document's broad recognition of indigenous autonomy and the multicultural language that recognizes thirty-two indigenous "nations" and even incorporates many indigenous cultural symbols and norms—as well as the recognition of collective cultural rights—into what is truly a multicultural constitutional text. Of course, the government of Evo Morales—Bolivia's first indigenous president—has actively promoted this view both at home and abroad. Therefore, one must look very carefully beyond the rhetoric and symbolism of the new Bolivian politics to assess the actual scope and impact of multicultural reforms on the day-to-day politics of ordinary Bolivians.

This chapter makes an attempt to do just that in three ways: first, by looking at the Constituent Assembly itself and offering a historical context and an institutional analysis of the body's formation, deliberations, and dissolution. The historical context begins with three moments: the 1938 Constituent Assembly, the 1945 Indian Congress and Constitutional Convention, and the 1971 Popular Assembly. Each was an important milestone in Bolivia's political history and provided both inspiration and benchmarks for the 2006–2008 constitutional reform process. But another important context—particularly for the multicultural dimension relevant to this volume—is the broad range of reforms during Sánchez de Lozada's first presidency (1993–1997), which included changes to constitution that made it explicitly more multicultural than previous documents—but maintaining a liberal-pluralist emphasis on individual (rather than collective) rights. The institutional analysis focuses on the Constituent Assembly's formation and deliberative process. That process was highly polarized and quickly broke down—threatening the entire constitutional reform project. The process was rescued by an eleventh-hour political compromise forged within the Senate (rather than the Constituent Assembly) in October 2008 that modified nearly a quarter of the 412 articles in the text approved by the Constituent Assembly, nearly a year earlier, in December 2007. The result is an image of a fragile, chaotic, and deeply polarizing process that very nearly failed.

Next, this chapter turns to a discussion of the relative gains and losses for indigenous and multicultural rights in the final constitutional text that went before voters in January 2009. Gains are relative to previous constitutional reforms, which had progressively included greater multicultural language—particularly in the constitutional reforms of 1995. Losses are understood in two ways: first, starting with the draft approved by the Constituent Assembly in December 2007—but especially after the compromise of October 2008—the scope of the reforms fell below the expectations of many indigenous actors. Second, many of the gains made were in practice limited in various ways: by the extended reach of the state (as interpreted by the new MAS [Movement toward Socialism] regime), because they were contingent on special enabling laws, or through the introduction of other reforms (not approved by the Constituent Assembly but incorporated in the final text) that had been opposed by indigenous activists. The result is an image of a new constitution that is not quite as radical a departure from previous political traditions as is often imagined.

Finally, the chapter analyzes the Bolivian case within the framework of Arend Lijphart's "power-sharing" model. Beginning in the 1990s, the "constitutional engineering" scholarship actively debated different institutional solutions to "divided societies." While Bolivia clearly meets the criteria for a "divided society" (whether defined by its ethnic diversity, its regional cleavages, or its deep political polarization), the new constitution does not easily fit within the framework of a power-sharing model of democracy. True, many of the constitutional reforms—particularly the different kinds of autonomy granted to municipalities, departments, and "regions" (a new, intermediate political unit)—suggest a new "devolved" political structure that radically departs from Bolivia's long-standing unitary state tradition. Likewise, the eleventh-hour compromise between rival political leaders that amended the constitutional text suggests the kind of extrainstitutional consociational approach long advocated by Arend Lijphart (see Lijphart 1977). Yet a closer look—both at the constitutional text itself and its current application—suggests that Bolivia has not moved as neatly toward a power-sharing model as some imagine. In fact, many elements of the new constitution harken back to the corporatist tradition of the 1950s, emphasizing a strong state role in national development—a role that often puts the state in direct conflict with indigenous communities.

One key example is the conflict involving indigenous communities in the Isiboro Sécure National Park and Indigenous Territory (TIPNIS) and the central government over a highway construction project (see BIF 2011). The TIPNIS territory was originally established as a national park in 1965 before becoming recognized as one of the first "native indigenous territories" (Tierra Comunitaria de Origen, TCO) in 1990. Like the other three TCOs established in 1990 and the seven created in 1992, the TIPNIS territory was created by an executive decree in response to the 1990 March for Dignity spearheaded by the Confederación de Pueblos Indígenas del Oriente de Bolivia. It is significant that the first recognition of indigenous autonomy was the product of demands "from below"—but it is also important to note that these were narrowly circumscribed to small indigenous groups located in Bolivia's interior. In August 2010, the three indigenous peoples who live in TIPNIS (the Chimán, Yuracaré, and Trinitario-Mojeño) began a 260-mile march to La Paz to protest the construction of a highway through TIPNIS, primarily by arguing that the decision by Morales's government to build a highway without prior consultation violated their rights established in the creation of their TCO in 1990, as well as the new 2009 constitution. After a confrontation that lasted two months—during which Morales and his government officials insisted that the highway was essential for national development goals—the government agreed to halt construction. The incident generated a serious political (and moral) crisis for Morales's government, as public outcry over a harsh police crackdown on the marchers on September 25, 2010, galvanized public support for the indigenous people's demands. Overall, the evidence suggests that despite indigenous autonomy originating as a grassroots demand, the application of indigenous autonomy is still primarily understood as structured and applied "from above" in ways that privilege the central state. Despite legal and constitutional assurances, indigenous autonomy is still very fragile in Bolivia.

None of this suggests that the Bolivian model is a failure. Instead, the purpose of this chapter is to point out the limitations facing multicultural reforms in a country with a significant indigenous majority—even when the dominant political actor (in this case, MAS)—has made such reforms a cornerstone of its political campaigns.

It is critical to understand that these limitations come not merely from entrenched elites but from the difficult reality facing an underdeveloped country like Bolivia. In the end, one sees a clear trajectory in the policy orientation of Evo Morales's government: Although it has made multiculturalism and indigenous rights a high priority, this has been repeatedly subservient to the goal of strengthening the central state—seen as crucial for the country's economic development. Yet, despite these limitations, the advances in the 2009 Constitution do signal a shift in Bolivian politics that will have long-term positive consequences.

THE 2006 CONSTITUENT ASSEMBLY IN HISTORICAL AND INSTITUTIONAL CONTEXT

Unlike many countries in Latin America and elsewhere, Bolivia's transition to democracy did not include constitutional reforms. Bolivia entered its democratic history with the 1967 Constitution—a document drafted (though never implemented) during the military dictatorship of René Barrientos (1964–1969). Traditional parties incorporated grassroots demands for constitutional reform by the late 1980s, leading to two substantial reforms to the 1967 Constitution, in 1994–1995 and 2004 (referred to as the 1995 Constitution and the 2004 Constitution, respectively).[2] Both reforms were approved by the legislature, since the 1967 Constitution did not allow for a Constituent Assembly. The 1995 Constitution included significant changes—particularly in the area of multicultural reform—that were part of a broader package of institutional reforms (including electoral system reform and municipal decentralization) pursued during Sánchez de Lozada's first presidency. The issue of a Constituent Assembly was raised in and became a defining issue of the 2002 election: it was embraced by some parties (notably MAS) but rejected by others (notably the Movimiento Nacionalista Revolucionario, MNR). Still, demands for further constitutional reform were strong enough to push the issue onto the legislative agenda. Many of the 2004 reforms (including the introduction of a Constituent Assembly into the constitution) were already contemplated before the 2003 political crisis. Still, they were not enough to satisfy pent-up popular frustrations and demands for a Constituent Assembly.

Only six months into his presidency, Evo Morales fulfilled one of his principal campaign promises: to hold a national election for a Constituent Assembly. On July 2, 2006, more than 3 million Bolivian voters (more than 83 percent of eligible voters) went to the polls to elect delegates to a Constituent Assembly that would be empowered to and charged with drafting a new national constitution. Although this was not the first time Bolivia had reformed its constitution (Bolivia has seen seventeen constitutional texts), this was the first time such a body was elected under the rules of universal adult suffrage and in the framework of a competitive electoral democracy.[3] Popular expectations and fears were high—particularly as Morales's government made clear that this was not going to be merely a constitutional reform process, but rather an ambitious attempt to "refound" the country, correcting the "original sins" of the first, postcolonial republican constitution. As such, and in the euphoria of Morales's recent election as Bolivia's first indigenous president, indigenous rights—including collective political and cultural rights—were on the agenda. In particular, Morales and his supporters sought to go further than the 1952 revolution—the reference point for transformative politics in Bolivia—by infusing a twenty-first-century multicultural sensibility. Popular expectations were tempered, however, by the experiences of three previous assemblies. Those experiences in turn influenced the strategies pursued by various actors during the 2006–2008 constitutional reform process.

The Historical Context

Morales and his followers see themselves as heirs to Bolivia's revolutionary tradition. This tradition has two distinct elements: an indigenous resistance tradition that harkens back to the colonial era, but includes indigenous uprisings from the nineteenth and twentieth centuries; and a national revolutionary tradition anchored in the 1952 National Revolution. The vision promoted by the National Revolutionary Movement (MNR) during the 1940s and 1950s was an ideologically vague populist program of national unity and modernization. While it did much to improve the lives of indigenous Bolivians, it did so without a multicultural agenda. Rather, the MNR pursued an assimilationist agenda to transform "Indians" into "peasants" and "integrate" them into a common (mestizo) Bolivian national identity. For much of its history, the Bolivian Left (with its Marxist emphasis on class struggle) followed this trajectory. While the 1970s saw the emergence of explicitly "ethnic" *katarista* parties in the Andean highlands, these remained marginal political actors. Only in the 1990s, after a lengthy decline and near political extinction, did the Bolivian Left begin establishing significant ties with the indigenous movement. By the end of the 1990s, the Bolivian Left was increasingly presenting itself in "ethno-populist" terms (Madrid 2008). Morales and MAS are a product of this fusion, and claim both revolutionary traditions.

Bolivia's first truly radical constitutional break came in 1938 (Barragán 2006, 89–90). The country's unexpected defeat in the 1932–1935 Chaco War with Paraguay produced a generational crisis that reverberated for decades, leading to the 1952 National Revolution. Immediately after the war, a military coup led by Germán Busch launched an aggressive reformist effort. As a military dictator, Busch shuttered the legislature long before he called for elections for a Constituent Assembly. That assembly was, not surprisingly, dominated by Busch allies (holding 114 of 121 seats) and moved swiftly to approve a new constitution that included significant labor rights and other features consistent with the "social constitutionalism" model introduced in the 1917 Mexican Constitution. Although the principles of the 1938 Constitution survived the end of the Busch regime, the years following the mercurial dictator's suicide were immediately followed by a conservative restoration that rolled back most reforms.

Another key moment includes both the 1945 Indian Congress and the parallel Constitutional Convention, both held during the government of Gualberto Villarroel (1943–1946), another reformist military dictator. Villarroel belonged to the generational political movement (spearheaded by the newly formed MNR) and came to power in a joint civilian-military putsch. The importance of this moment is paradoxical: the 1945 Indian Congress marked the first time Bolivia's indigenous majority was formally recognized and given a voice in the political process. Many of the body's resolutions—abolishing the system of *pongueaje* (peonage) and other forms of obligatory labor, and granting indigenous people the right to move freely in cities—were incorporated into constitutional law. But it is noteworthy that the Indian Congress was separate and distinct from that year's Constitutional Convention. Thus, the Villarroel regime maintained the exclusion of the indigenous majority from full and equal political participation.

Finally, the 1971 Popular Assembly left a deep mark on the psyche of the Bolivian Left and was a significant point of reference for the 2006 Constituent Assembly. The 1971 Popular Assembly was called by another reformist military dictator, Juan José Torres (1970–1971), who came out on top in a brief but violent conflict between left- and right-wing forces within the military. But this assembly had been "produced from below" (Barragán 2006, 110). Only months in power, Torres was almost toppled by a right-wing military coup, and was only saved by spontaneous popular mobilization in defense of his government. Once the coup was put down, labor movement leaders demanded a popular assembly with sweeping powers—including drafting a new constitution. The 1971 Popular Assembly was not elected but formed by representatives of various labor and professional sectors aligned with the Trotskyite Bolivian Workers Federation (Central Obrera Boliviana, COB). Indigenous groups played a limited and subordinate role in the Popular Assembly, mostly subsumed into their role as peasants. Even though Torres granted the assembly legislative powers, it refused to support his government, calling instead for the immediate establishment of a "workers' state." One of the body's first acts was to announce a general strike, which crippled the regime and opened the door for another conservative reaction.

Despite the key similarity that all three assemblies were installed under military dictators (rather than a democratically elected president), the lessons they imparted to Bolivian reformers—particularly to those aligned with Evo Morales and his MAS party—were significant. The 1938 experience taught that even if "revolutionary forces" control a Constituent Assembly, a determined reactionary opposition can reverse its work if the revolution's leader does not maintain close ties to and actively mobilize popular support. The 1945 experience taught that it was not enough to grant indigenous people "civil rights" and incorporate them into the national dialogue without including them directly in the political process as equals. Villarroel's ignominious fall in 1946 (he was dragged from the presidential palace and hanged) offered another lesson: Despite his fascist sympathies, Villarroel's legacy was later refurbished. While he was long a pillar in the MNR's revolutionary pantheon, Bolivia's national Left also admired his national-corporatist policies, pro-labor reforms, and anti-imperialist rhetoric. The fact that the key leftist party of the time, the Left Revolutionary Party (Partido de Izquierda Revolucionario, PIR), played an active role in Villarroel's fall was a prime factor in its rapid decline—becoming a warning about "false leftists" (or *piristas*) who are manipulated into supporting conservative interests.

A similar lesson was learned from the 1971 experience: the unwillingness of leftist groups to support an existing regime—even one less radical than desired—led to failure. By the time the 2006 Constituent Assembly was inaugurated, MAS had internalized critical lessons: division within the "popular" forces or failure to actively support Morales and his regime only strengthened entrenched conservative opposition. It is because of this experience that Morales and his close supporters regularly stifle opposition within their own coalition—including indigenous communities—as undermining the regime and facilitating the interests of the conservative opposition. From the regime's perspective, the interests of indigenous communities need to be balanced against the broader national interests.

All this matters because the constitutional reform efforts were not limited to the issues of indigenous rights or multicultural recognition. Morales's supporters were also motivated—perhaps chiefly so—by broad opposition to the neoliberal status quo in place since 1985. Beginning in earnest with the 2000 "water war" in Cochabamba, where a popular protest against the privatization of the city's water utility first cracked the veneer of political stability that marked the posttransition period, and carried forward through the 2003 "gas war" that toppled Sánchez de Lozada only a year into his second presidential term, Bolivia was in a political crisis that had not yet dissipated by 2006.

The 2003 gas war is instructive: Widely understood as a popular mobilization against Sánchez de Lozada's neoliberal politics (specifically the issue of natural gas exports to the U.S. through Chile), the conflict was a much more complex convergence of different, unrelated political forces. The first stage began in July 2003, when Aymara communities led by Felipe Quispe, leader of the Indigenous Pachakuti Movement (Movimiento Indígena Pachakuti, MIP), the country's most successful indigenous party,[4] launched a protest against the government in defense of political autonomy for indigenous communities. This mobilization coincided with a protest led by the COB. It was this latter protest that raised the gas issue, as part of a broader repudiation of neoliberal policies. The government's heavy-handed repression of the indigenous protest galvanized public sentiment against the regime, leading to a cascade of mobilizations that drove Sánchez de Lozada to resign his presidency and go into self-imposed exile in the United States. By October 2003, the conflict was baptized the gas war (Guerra del Gas) and framed as a national-popular uprising in defense of the country's national resources and in opposition to a corrupt neoliberal regime (for an example of such an analysis, see Dangl 2007). Within this framework, the role of indigenous actors was marginalized and subsumed within a larger anti-imperialist, *desarrollista* perspective. By 2005, Quispe had become a marginal figure; MIP captured only 2.2 percent of the vote and did not win a single legislative seat in that year's general election.

Finally, any discussion of the historical context for the Constituent Assembly must mention the 1994 Popular Participation reforms enacted during Sánchez de Lozada's first presidency. The 1994 Ley de Participación Popular (LPP) introduced decentralized municipal governments, which were then incorporated into the 1995 Constitution (Articles 200–206). In addition to significant autonomy, they were guaranteed 20 percent of the state budget, distributed across all municipalities on a per capita basis (though this was not stipulated in the constitution, only in the LPP). The LPP was significant for two reasons. First, it was the first effort by the state to decentralize, creating constitutionally sanctioned, elected local authorities for the first time. Second, many of the rural municipalities were indigenous communities. This meant that local indigenous communities won constitutionally sanctioned autonomy in 1995 (the year the LPP went into effect and nationwide municipal elections were first held). Further, the LPP explicitly allowed for the legal recognition of *comités de vigilancia* (vigilance committees), which could be organized at the neighborhood level, as partners in municipal government administration. The later 1996 Agrarian Reform Law (Ley INRA) went further, establishing TCOs and granting them special rights over their land and its resources. Municipal decentralization was a boon for the indigenous movement, as indigenous parties and candidates—who easily won control over indigenous-majority municipalities—established their credibility as legitimate, responsible political actors. Both MAS and MIP were forged in municipal-level contests, which became springboards to national politics (see Van Cott 2007, 2008). It is noteworthy that in crafting the LPP, Sánchez de Lozada explicitly rejected department-level decentralization in favor of the more local, municipal level. Despite its limitations (e.g., municipal governments were still bound tightly within the framework of a unitary state), the intermediate steps introduced during the first Sánchez de Lozada presidency were a model—both for multiculturalism and for indigenous autonomy—for the 2006 Constituent Assembly.

A Snapshot of the Constituent Assembly

By the time Morales announced elections for a constituent assembly, MAS had successfully restructured itself into a broad, "big-tent" alliance of Left-populist forces, in which the indigenous movement was only one component—although an important one. The election for assembly delegates would also come on the heels of the December 2005 general election in which Morales and MAS won an unprecedented absolute majority (53.7 percent) of the presidential vote and secured a majority in the lower-chamber House of Deputies (though not in the Senate).[5] From the start, MAS made clear its goal of winning a supermajority in the Constituent Assembly, allowing it to freely draft a new constitutional charter without interference. The opposition, anchored by its control of the Senate and six of the country's nine prefectures, managed to wrest a number of significant concessions. These set the tone for future concessions throughout the process—many of which diluted indigenous demands.

The Ley de Convocatoria (Ley No. 3364) of March 2006 set the guidelines, both for the election of assembly delegates and for the body's procedural rules. Delegates would be elected in two tiers: 210 delegates were elected from the seventy "uninominal" districts (three from each) and forty-five delegates were elected from department-wide districts.[6] No delegates were elected to explicitly represent indigenous communities or by *usos y costumbres*, as had been proposed by indigenous leaders.[7] Additionally, seat allocation rules made it impossible for any party to win the two-thirds supermajority required to approve a constitutional text.[8] Finally, the opposition won an important concession regarding regional (i.e., departmental) autonomy: A referendum on regional autonomy would simultaneously be put before voters, and the Constituent Assembly would recognize regional autonomy for departments in which a majority voted in favor. This opened the possibility of an asymmetrical devolution process—perhaps similar to the Spanish or British examples. Beginning in 2004, a powerful pro-autonomy movement had emerged in the so-called Media Luna departments of Santa Cruz, Tarija, Beni, and Pando. Morales and MAS opposed regional autonomy, understood as a challenge to their broader national socioeconomic policy agenda and led by conservative elites. Based on results of the December 2005 election, it was clear that the opposition would do well in the Media Luna (where it won a plurality in each department) and that voters there would back regional autonomy. Thus, the Constituent Assembly would be a priori constrained by three realities: delegates would be elected in a traditional manner, favoring party representation (though parties were not required to present candidates in all districts, unlike in presidential and legislative elections); MAS would be unable to unilaterally determine the assembly's outcome; and the final document would recognize regional autonomy in at least some departments.

To overcome these obstacles, MAS pursued a complex strategy of recruiting a broad range of candidates while also building alliances with smaller, independent parties that were likely to support MAS in the assembly. This strategy was made possible by a highly fractured political landscape. A total of twenty-five parties competed in the 2006 Constituent Assembly election. Of the sixteen that went on to win at least one seat, only two could be qualified as indigenous parties: Aboriginal Popular Movement (Movimiento Originario Popular; three seats) and Movimiento AYRA (two seats). MIP, which lost its legal recognition after the December 2005 election, did not present a list of candidates. The remaining thirteen parties represented a relatively broad ideological spectrum, including some with affinities toward MAS. While MAS gathered together many social movement organizations under its umbrella, the opposition remained fragmented. PODEMOS, the principal opposition party, won the second-largest bloc of delegates—after MAS—with sixty. The MNR did well, winning a total of twenty delegates across its three electoral fronts.[9] Three other "traditional" parties associated with the pre-Morales regime won seventeen delegates.[10] A motley assortment of new parties and "civic associations" (allowed to participate in elections under the 2004 Constitution) won the remaining eighteen delegates. MAS, not surprisingly, won the lion's share of the delegates, with 137 (just under 54 percent).

One of the surprising features of the 2006 Constituent Assembly election was that "indigenous peoples" (another new category introduced in the 2004 reforms that broke political parties' monopoly over electoral politics) did not participate directly. Civic associations and indigenous peoples first participated in the December 2004 municipal elections, and both had significant successes. Nevertheless, the electoral system devised for the Constituent Assembly put grassroots indigenous organizations at a tremendous disadvantage. Whereas civic associations could be quite large, and often were formed either in large urban cities or at the departmental or provincial level, indigenous organizations (of the kind that participated in the 2004 municipal elections) were mostly micro-local. Because the uninominal districts used to elect delegates were based on population distribution, nearly half were in urban districts. The remaining rural uninominal districts often included several municipalities. Thus, indigenous representation in the Constituent Assembly was primarily channeled through other political fronts—primarily (though not exclusively) MAS.

Despite the obstacles to the "direct" participation of indigenous movements, the Constituent Assembly was remarkably diverse, according to a demographic survey of delegates by Xavier Albó (2008). When asked if they identified with any indigenous community, more than half (142 of 255 delegates) did so. This made the assembly's ethnic breakdown roughly similar to that found in the 2001 Bolivian census (see table 4.1)—though Aymara communities were noticeably underrepresented. Although all delegates spoke Spanish, nearly two-thirds of delegates also spoke at least one indigenous language—though many of the rest spoke only Spanish (58 delegates) or Spanish and another foreign language (46 delegates).[11] Interestingly, more than two-thirds self-identified as mestizo (178 delegates) and very few (9 delegates) were classified as white (Albó included in this figure 3 delegates who identified themselves as "Bolivians"). The category of mestizo (which was not included in the 2001 census) produces some interesting interactions (see Albó 2008, 56–60): most delegates who self-identified as Quechua preferred to also identify themselves as mestizo rather than indigenous, while the converse was true for those who self-identified as Aymara.

Looking across party blocs, however, Albó (2008) found significant divergence (see table 4.2). Most delegates who self-identified with one of the two Andean indigenous communities (Quechua and Aymara) were found within the pro-MAS bloc of delegates. Interestingly, more than half of those who identified with one of the other (non-Andean, lowland) indigenous communities were found within the pro-PODEMOS bloc. Not surprisingly, indigenous representation within the center (*bisagra*) bloc was about midway between the pro-MAS and pro-PODEMOS blocs. Clearly, the pro-MAS bloc could credibly claim to represent indigenous people's interests, with nearly three-quarters self-identifying with an indigenous community. Likewise, just over half of pro-MAS delegates identified themselves as mestizo, in

Table 4.1 Ethnic Distribution of Constituent Assembly Delegates Compared to Overall Population

Indigenous Community	Self-Identification			Speaks Language[a]		
	Number of Delegates	Percentage of Delegates	Percentage in 2001 Census	Number of Delegates	Percentage of Delegates	Percentage in 2001 Census[b]
Quechua	81	31.8	30.7	104	40.8	19.9
Aymara	43	16.9	25.2	45	17.6	13.3
Other	18	7.1	6.1	16	6.3	1.0
None	113	44.2	38.0			

[a] Includes those who speak two or more indigenous languages.
[b] The 2001 census only asked respondents about their "maternal" language; less than half of the delegates who spoke an indigenous language learned it as a child (see Albó 2008, 55).
Data from Albó (2008) and 2001 Bolivian census.

Table 4.2 Ethnic Distribution (Based on Self-Identification) of Constituent Assembly Delegates across Party Blocs

	Pro-MAS (%)[a]	Pro-PODEMOS (%)[b]	Center (%)[c]
Self-Identification with Indigenous Community			
Quechua	46.2	6.8	12.5
Aymara	23.4	5.6	8.3
Other	3.2	13.7	12.5
None	25.9	74.0	66.7
By Generic Categories			
Indigenous	40.5	4.1	4.2
Mestizo	57.0	90.4	91.7
White	2.5	5.5	4.2

[a] Includes MAS, ASP, AYRA, CN, MBL, and MOP.
[b] Includes PODEMOS, AAI, APB, MIR, and MNR-FRI.
[c] Includes AS, UN, MNR, and A3-MNR.
Data derived from Albó (2008).

contrast to more than 90 percent in both the pro-PODEMOS and center bloc. Albó (2008) also found that pro-MAS delegates were more likely to be rural, female, or socioeconomically disadvantaged.

A Frustrated Assembly

At the start, the Constituent Assembly had tremendous promise. Long before it was elected, the National Electoral Court (Corte Nacional Electoral, CNE) began massive civic education campaigns to prepare Bolivians for a future constituent assembly (see Ayo et al. 2007). Throughout November 2005 (a month before Morales was elected president), the CNE organized more than fifty *mesas de diálogo*, educational presentations about past constitutional reforms and forums for participants to deliberate about future reforms. In addition, the CNE also published several educational pamphlets, distributed as supplements in Bolivian newspapers, about various aspects of the Constituent Assembly process and the issues and proposals before voters. Before it formally began deliberating, groups of delegates traveled across the country on public "listening tours." Meanwhile, delegates began to organize themselves into regional or departmental caucuses, similar to those found in the legislature. Later, throughout March–April 2007, the assembly installed thirteen official "territorial forums" (*foros territoriales*), where delegates met citizens and received proposals. All this suggested that the Constituent Assembly would be a forum for open deliberations, producing an example of genuine reform from below.

Such aspirations were dashed, however, as internal divisions within the assembly were augmented by a series of mass mobilizations meant to force the body to act quickly and decisively. As early as August 2006, the country's *cocaleros* (coca farmers) announced they would march to Sucre to "supervise" (*fiscalizar*) the assembly. The move was approved by Morales (who still headed the *cocalero* movement), who went on to announce in a national press conference that he had approved the initiative of social movements to gather in Sucre to "control our [delegates]" ("Cocaleros deciden ir," 2006). In coming weeks and months, deliberations stalled repeatedly, mostly over procedural issues, increasing public anxiety and frustration.

Part of the problem, of course, was that expectations were unrealistically high. Many Bolivians believed a constituent assembly would somehow miraculously solve their social, economic, and political problems—and therefore assumed the assembly should deliberate on a wide variety of quotidian concerns. The Constituent Assembly had also been widely imagined as the antithesis of traditional "party politics" (*partidocracia*), whose cross-partisan deal making was viewed as symptomatic of corrupt politics. But grassroots reform projects undertaken in the context of weak representative institutions are complicated. After two years of near-constant political mobilization, and in the midst of one of the country's most profound political crises, many Bolivians had little patience as assembly delegates spent their first weeks organizing office space, requesting travel appropriations (ostensibly to visit their constituents), or demanding higher per diems and salaries. Such impatience extended to procedural issues facing the assembly, such as establishing a leadership structure, organizing committees, or establishing debate rules. It took the delegates nearly four months to agree on basic deliberation rules—before deadlocking on the critical question of whether a two-thirds supermajority or merely an absolute majority of delegates would be necessary to approve constitutional reforms.

In early deliberations, the Constituent Assembly confronted four distinct issues that polarized debate and set the entire process on the road to failure.[12] Without describing them in detail, it is important to enumerate them: First was the question of whether the assembly should merely modify the existing constitutional text, or whether it should have broader, plenipotentiary powers on a level footing with the legislature. The opposition resisted this, in large part because its control of the Senate was a significant check on Morales's government—which would be lost in the unicameral Constitutional Assembly (where MAS held a solid majority). On September 29, delegates approved a declaration (by simple majority) that the Constituent Assembly was "original" (and not "derived") and could order itself without any restrictions (including those stipulated by the Ley de Convocatoria). Opposition delegates opposed the move, and began legal challenges before the Constitutional Tribunal and mobilizing popular support (particularly in the Media Luna).

A second issue was the "two-thirds" question. From its conception, stipulated in the Ley de Convocatoria, the assembly was to approve changes to the constitution by a two-thirds supermajority. By November 17, 2006, the Constituent Assembly approved (by simple majority) Article 71 of its deliberation rules, stipulating that decisions would be made by simple majorities, with two exceptions: (1) the complete final text would require a two-thirds supermajority, and (2) any "observed" articles for which one-third of delegates backed an alternative proposal would require a special debate after all the other, nonobserved articles were approved. This launched a prolonged protest from opposition delegates and their supporters, who vehemently argued that "two-thirds is democracy."

A third issue involved regional autonomy. Although the assembly was charged with approving regional autonomy for those departments that voted for it in the June 2006 autonomy referendum, the issue was contested throughout the two years the body deliberated—despite the fact that the assembly had from the start established a working group (one of the twenty-one established October 30, 2006) specifically to deal with issues of autonomy (broadly defined). Morales and MAS declared that because a (narrow) majority of Bolivians had voted against regional autonomy, the issue had been decided. Opposition-backed regional movements mobilized on behalf of regional autonomy, demanding that their departments' votes in favor of autonomy (by wide majorities) be respected—as stated in the Ley de Convocatoria. These mobilizations would eventually lead to four "wildcat" referendums (unsanctioned by the CNE or Morales's government) between May and August 2008 in which voters in the Media Luna departments again approved departmental *estatutos autonómicos* (regional charters).

The fourth and final issue was the one that broke the assembly's back. Beginning in March 2007, civic leaders in the city of Sucre began mobilizing to demand that the Constituent Assembly include in its deliberations the question of moving Bolivia's capital back to Sucre.[13] Over several months, the *capitalía* movement gained traction, repeatedly disrupting the assembly's deliberations, and even forcing the resignation of the MAS prefect in favor of new elections, won by Savina Cuéllar, a MAS Constituent Assembly delegate who switched to the opposition over the issue (see Centellas 2010). The *capitalía* question became a wedge issue, as a number of MAS delegates defected to the opposition, while PODEMOS delegates from La Paz joined the pro-MAS majority in repeatedly tabling discussion. Though in many ways a relatively marginal issue (when compared to the wide range of issues before the Constituent Assembly), the *capitalía* movement prompted the rapid breakdown of the assembly's deliberations.

Ongoing protests by *capitalía* supporters throughout August–November 2007 shut down the Constituent Assembly, preventing further deliberations. By August 2007, most opposition delegates had walked out of the assembly. The decision to move the assembly's deliberations to a nearby military academy (La Glorieta) just outside the city on November 23, 2007, met with immediate opposition. This was aggravated when the 138 delegates (almost all from MAS and only slightly more than half the total) assembled at La Glorieta approved a preliminary draft of the constitution. This led pro-*capitalía* protesters to attack the police and pro-MAS groups (who had come to protect the assembly), leaving three dead and at least one hundred injured (AIN 2007).

In the aftermath of the violence, the Constituent Assembly reconvened in the city of Oruro on December 8–9, 2007. The event was televised nationally, and counted the participation of 164 delegates (less than two-thirds of the total). In a marathon session lasting fourteen hours, 411 constitutional articles were rapidly read aloud, briefly debated, and (all but one, about the maximum size of agricultural property) approved by two-thirds of the delegates assembled. Only days later, on the evening of December 14, Silvia Lazarte, the Constituent Assembly president, presented the final document (including minor revisions) to Vice President Alvaro García Linera.

While pro-MAS groups celebrated, opposition groups vowed to resist the "illegitimate," "blood-stained" document.

The document that went before voters more than a year later, on January 25, 2009, was not the document approved by the Constituent Assembly in Oruro. A heavily modified document was hammered out in an intense compromise negotiation October 8–20, 2008, between MAS and opposition party leaders, under the direction of Vice President García Linera, and with mediation from the Catholic Church. This "pacted" agreement modified more than one hundred articles of the text approved in Oruro. Many of the compromises are not directly relevant for this chapter's discussion of multicultural rights in Bolivia (e.g., the 2007 document established a unicameral legislature; the 2008 document retained a bicameral one). Yet they reflect an important pattern: Morales's government bargained away important preferences in favor of securing a necessary level of political stability. In the end, after nearly two years of uncertainty and a tumultuous Constituent Assembly process, Bolivia emerged with a new constitution that was, in many ways, only a modification of the previous charter. It was also a document drafted not, in the end, by a plenipotentiary or original Constituent Assembly, but by roughly three dozen or so ranking government and opposition leaders sitting behind closed doors.

MULTICULTURALISM'S ADVANCES AND LIMITATIONS IN THE 2009 CONSTITUTION

There can be no denying that the 2009 Constitution is a significant advancement for multiculturalism in Bolivia—and for the rights of indigenous peoples in particular. Even critics of the final document's "liberal" elements recognize it as an important "intermediate" step (Mamani Ramírez 2010). An analysis of the multicultural elements of the 2009 Constitution can be made along two dimensions: a symbolic dimension, which may have limited immediate practical impact but nevertheless signals a shift in the state's value orientation; and an institutional dimension, which subsequently requires additional reforms to ensure that state policies and institutions are in line with constitutional directives. An example of a symbolic reform is the incorporation of the Andean *wiphala* (the multicolored flag of the indigenous movement) as one of the two national flags. An example of an institutional reform is the recognition of indigenous autonomy and the use of *usos y costumbres* in such territories. While the latter (institutional) reforms commit the state to further actions (such as the modifications of statutes in the Judicial Code or to organize autonomy referendums), the former (symbolic) reforms signal a commitment on the part of the state to recognize and valorize the country's cultural pluralism.

In terms of symbolic reforms, the 2009 Constitution goes significantly further than earlier texts. It begins with a 471-word preamble (earlier documents simply started at Article 1) that presents a sweeping cultural history of the country from the creation of the world, a summary of values and principles, and a declaration in the voice of the Constituent Assembly of having upheld its duty, "strengthened by the Pachamama and thanks to God," to "refound" the country. The preamble even includes a single-sentence paragraph declaring, "We leave in the past the colonial, republican, neoliberal State." Beyond the terse repudiation of the earlier ("colonial, republican, neoliberal") state, the preamble sets a clear tone of pluralistic inclusion—particularly with regard to the country's pre-Columbian traditions—now seen as integral to the country's historical fabric and projecting the existence of "Bolivia" to a timeless past, predating the Spanish conquest and colonialism.

From there, the document launches into a substantially restructured opening Articles 1–6. The 1995 Constitution had previously made symbolic changes to Article 1, declaring Bolivia "multiethnic and pluricultural" and "founded on the union and solidarity of all Bolivians." The 2009 text significantly expands this, declaring Bolivia a "plurinational communitarian" state, founded on "political, economic, juridical, cultural, and linguistic pluralism." Previous versions of Article 2 (on sovereignty) and Article 4 (on representation) were removed; the issue of sovereignty was moved into the subsequent section of the constitution (and revised to make clear that sovereignty rested in the people, not their representatives); the issue of representation was not reintroduced in its previous formulation. The following articles introduced sweeping symbolic changes: recognition of indigenous communities with right to autonomy, ancestral territory, and cultural institutions (Article 2); recognition of Bolivia as composed of its various indigenous "nations and peoples," intercultural communities, and Afro-Bolivians (Article 3);[14] establishment of a secular state with freedom of religion, including "spiritual beliefs according to one's worldview [*cosmovisiones*]" (Article 4); recognition (and enumeration) of thirty-six indigenous languages that are (in addition to Spanish) official languages, and the stipulation that every level of government must use at least two official languages (Article 5); and an enumeration (absent in previous constitutions) of the national symbols, including the *wiphala* and the *kantuta* and *patujú* flowers (Article 6). This was shortly followed by Article 8, which enumerates the state's social values—including values and principles derived from the Aymara, Quechua, and Guaraní traditions.[15]

Such symbolic changes were a substantial leap from the pre-1995 constitutional tradition—which did not acknowledge the existence of indigenous or other cultural communities—limited to enumerating liberal or republican principles of representation, organizing formal political institutions, and framing the country's economic and social structure. The 1995 Constitution recognized the country's cultural pluralism but did little to promote indigenous cultural or political rights. In fact, the 1995 Constitution explicitly mentioned indigenous peoples only three times, in Article 171, which dealt exclusively with "agrarian and peasant" issues. That article recognized the right of indigenous peoples to cultural lands, as well as to the continued use of their culture, language, and traditions on those lands; it also recognized the "jurisdictional personhood" of indigenous communities and the use of a community's traditional *costumbres* to dictate communal norms or to appoint their leaders (so long as they conformed with the constitution). In contrast, the 2009 Constitution explicitly mentions indigenous peoples 128 times (not including the preamble) and in a wide range of contexts.

Institutionally, the 2009 Constitution includes three significant changes that substantially expand the almost exclusively symbolic multiculturalism of the 1995 and 2004 Constitutions.[16] The first is the recognition of indigenous autonomy as a distinct—yet equal—category, separate from municipal, regional, or departmental autonomy. The second is the establishment of special indigenous electoral districts. The third is the recognition of indigenous jurisdictional competence as distinct from, and equal to, the "ordinary" justice system. Despite the fanfare surrounding these three important changes, it is here that the view of the 2009 Constitution as a sweeping alteration of political power in favor of Bolivia's indigenous majority begins to break down. Even before the "pacted" modifications to the text, many proposals put forward by the indigenous movement had been scaled down, leaving Pablo Mamani Ramírez to conclude that "liberal principles are placed above communitarian indigenous principles" (2010, 707, my translation).

Although indigenous autonomy is recognized in the 2009 Constitution—ostensibly on equal terms with other forms of territorial autonomy—implementation is problematic. First, because the framework for autonomies begins with the principle of respecting departmental boundaries. This is made explicit regarding the new intermediate category of regional autonomy (see Article 280), which can only be formed by a joining of municipalities within a department; likewise, municipalities must be contained within departmental boundaries. The articles dealing explicitly with indigenous autonomy (Articles 289 and 296) are silent on the issue,[17] but the language in this section repeatedly mentions municipalities—which, in practice, became the basic units for indigenous communities. There is a possibility that indigenous communities that cross departmental lines (as many do) could come together and win legal recognition (since Articles 289 and 290 make clear that indigenous autonomy is based on "ancestral territories"), but the overall constitutional language makes department boundaries inviolable.

The impact of special indigenous electoral districts is paradoxical. The 2009 Constitution creates such districts and describes their purpose (Articles 146 and 147), but does not enumerate them—leaving that to the new Plurinational Electoral Organ (formerly the CNE). Indigenous leaders demanded fifteen special reserved seats for indigenous communities, but the 2009 legislative elections included only seven such districts (one in each of the country's departments, minus Potosí and Chuquisaca). Additionally, special indigenous districts were reserved for indigenous communities that are minorities within departments, using data from the 2001 census and the registry of TCOs. This meant that no special indigenous districts were reserved for Quechua or Aymara communities (under the assumption that ethnic Quechua and Aymara voters can easily elect representatives in rural uninominal districts in which they comprised substantial majorities). Special indigenous districts also explicitly could not cross department lines, were limited to rural areas, and included more than one indigenous community (since all recognized indigenous communities within a department were lumped together). Further, elections in special indigenous representatives were uniform, using simple majority (or "first past the post"—FPTP). Many indigenous leaders objected, arguing that the reforms only included indigenous representatives as token minorities. That objection, however, should be placed in the context of a broader electoral system in which indigenous candidates already had a record of winning elections outright in uninominal contests—as well as through the "plurinominal" (PR) lists for deputies and senators. The criticism is valid, however, since the FPTP electoral system used—rather than any recourse to *usos y costumbres*—made the districts merely additional uninominal districts (a form of political affirmative action quota system). The reality on the ground also seemed to preference large parties. Although the electoral law allows for politically organized "indigenous communities" to campaign for office, all seven special indigenous representatives were elected as representatives of MAS and the opposition PPB-CN (the current principal opposition electoral vehicle).

Another key problem with indigenous autonomy is its territorial restriction. Repeatedly—both in the 2009 Constitution and in the supplemental legal framework (such as the 2009 electoral law)—preexisting departmental boundaries are sacrosanct. This means that indigenous communities are constrained by political boundaries that had not historically taken them into account. Further, the key element of indigenous autonomy—the use of *usos y costumbres*—was restricted to "rural" areas. Critics rightly pointed out that this essentially restricts "indigeneity" to a rural context, ignoring the reality that a sizeable share of Bolivia's indigenous population today is urban—or that many of the country's major cities (including El Alto, La Paz, and Cochabamba) now have indigenous majorities. Thus, taken together, the 2009 Constitution and subsequent regulatory laws recognize the cultural rights of Bolivia's indigenous majorities, but grants them political rights only within a rural context.

Finally, a key constraint facing indigenous autonomy in Bolivia is the recognition of strong departmental governments—a clear victory for the regionalist movements of the Media Luna. The 2008 congressional comprise introduced a number of significant amendments to the draft constitution that strengthened regional governments, expanding their jurisdictional competencies. While Article 276 clearly states that the various autonomous units (departments, regions, municipalities, and indigenous communities) are of "equal constitutional rank" and not hierarchically subordinated, the reality is that they are. The 2009 Constitution grants departments a total of thirty-six exclusive (not shared) jurisdictional competencies, including the following policy areas: human development, labor, energy and transportation, regulations over social organizations or NGOs that operate in their territory, sanitation, cultural patrimony, participation in state enterprises active in their territory, and foreign investment. Since all regions, municipalities, and indigenous communities are explicitly constrained within departmental boundaries, this implies their subordination to departmental jurisdiction in a wide range of areas.

In the end, the 2009 Constitution was not the promised radical refounding of a postcolonial republic. The explicit recognition of existing departmental boundaries precluded a number of alternatives. The reformulation of departmental boundaries was never seriously discussed—and the 2009 Constitution shut the door on any such future discussion, leaving only the possibility of (de facto subordinate) autonomy for regions within the departments. Likewise, the basic structure of government remained unchanged. Bolivia retained a presidential system with a runoff system (introduced in the 2004 Constitution), a bicameral legislature (though the Senate was expanded), and a mixed-member proportional electoral system. Beyond a number of symbolic reforms that recognized Bolivia's indigenous peoples, their history, and their culture, most multicultural reforms in the constitution limited the sphere of indigenous politics to rural, small-scale communities. What the 2009 Constitution did produce—which is a significant break from Bolivia's political tradition—is a "federalized" (or devolved) state, but one giving significant weight to departmental autonomy. The autonomy of smaller subnational units—municipalities and indigenous TCOs—is more fragile and, as the TIPNIS example suggests, in practice tends to privilege the interests of the central state's national development agenda.

CONCLUSION: IS BOLIVIA'S NEW CONSTITUTIONAL FRAMEWORK CONSOCIATIONAL?

It is difficult to place Bolivia's current political system within the power sharing or consociational model—particularly in relation to ethnic or indigenous communities and the state. Certainly, the devolved jurisdictional authorities specified for the various levels of autonomy (department, region, municipality, and indigenous community) suggest that Bolivia's previously unitary state is now sharing power by dispersing significant policy- and decision-making authority. In reality, ultimate authority still resides very clearly in the central government, not autonomous subunits. One clear example is the 2010 anticorruption law, which strips any elected official of his or her position if state prosecutors raise formal charges. In principle, the law is meant to give elected officials a chance to defend themselves at trial without interfering with their duties; in reality, the law has been used to reverse opposition gains at the ballot.

Arend Lijphart's model of consociational democracy includes four key principles: grand coalition, autonomy, proportionality, and minority veto (Lijphart 2007, 7). Of these, only autonomy is clearly represented in the 2009 Constitution—though in a slightly more limited form than the kind envisioned by Lijphart, who clearly had in mind a more federal system—in which states shared sovereignty (not just competencies) with the central state. If anything, Bolivia has consistently moved away from the other three principles in the last several years. The 1995 electoral reform that introduced the mixed-member proportional electoral system was a shift away from PR and toward FPTP (a typically majoritarian electoral system). In the intervening years, the reduction of PR seats in the lower house has meant a continued shift further toward a majoritarian electoral system. Similarly, the 2009 Constitution introduced a runoff system for president (as well as for governors and mayors—who are now elected directly).[18] This was a decisive shift away from the previous system, in which presidents were elected by a legislative vote (in the case no candidate won an absolute majority—which did not happen in any election between 1979 and 2002). This "parliamentarized presidential" system (Mayorga 1997) relied on broad, multiparty coalition cabinets (a consociational feature). Since 2005, Bolivia has been governed by a single-party government for the first time since its transition to democracy (signaling a move toward majoritarianism). Last, minority veto has never been part of Bolivia's institutional framework.

Looking at the ten variables included in Lijphart's (1999) description of consensus democracy, we again see evidence of Bolivia moving away from—rather than closer to—this model. The strengthening of the presidency, which is now clearly independent from the legislature (see Centellas 2008), shows a concentration of executive power. Morales is a much more powerful president than any of his predecessors. He may be no more of a caudillo within his own party than previous leaders (Banzer over ADN, Sánchez de Lozada over MNR, or Jaime Paz Zamora over MIR)—but these others all secured the presidency only after forging alliances ("pacts") with their rivals, establishing multiparty coalition cabinets. Bolivia has not yet moved clearly to a two-party system, but it is no longer a truly multiparty system, either. Increasing polarization has created the building blocks for a future two-party system, though Bolivia is today best described as a "dominant-party" system. The system for interest group representation is more difficult to classify, since MAS is a corporatist alliance of various social movements, unions, and civic organizations (including indigenous communities) tied together by the personality of Evo Morales (see Stefanoni 2010). But Morales's government has seen independent interest groups—even those that are component parts of the MAS "big-tent" alliance—challenge the state directly with a wide variety of demands. This suggests that interest group pluralism is alive and well in Bolivia.

Along the five variables associated with the "federal-unitary" dimension of Lijphart's (1999) consensus democracy model, there are some positive signs. Bolivia's 2009 Constitution is a radical departure from the unitary model and may lead to a more strongly devolved—even federal—future Bolivian state. The retention of a bicameral legislature is one variable in which Bolivia did not move toward majoritarianism. The rest of this dimension is mixed, however. Ostensibly the central banks and judiciary remain independent, from both the executive and legislative branches of government, but the reality is that both are strongly controlled by the executive. Likewise, the constitution continues to dictate the need for supermajorities on key policy areas or for major issues (such as revisions to the constitution), yet experience has shown that MAS attempts to govern with few constraints.

The way the 2009 Constitution emerged, however, offers an interesting example of the possibilities of informal consociationalism in Bolivia. On the one hand, the formal process showed significant majoritarian tendencies—as the MAS majority tried to sideline the opposition. Much of the blame can be handed to the opposition, of course, which used a variety of tactics to stall the process and showed itself willing to engage in brinksmanship. But some of this may have been unnecessary if MAS delegates accepted that a consensus would require the very kind of despised "pacts" that were common during the 1985–2002 period. In the end, ironically, the process was rescued by an extrainstitutional negotiation carried out largely behind closed doors in meetings in which the opposition was overrepresented. Most political actors broadly saw the final text of the 2009 Constitution as legitimate precisely because it was hammered out through the kind of "grand bargaining" envisioned by Lijphart. But there are no institutional guarantees that future divisive issues will receive similar treatment.

Looking explicitly at the relationship between Bolivia's indigenous peoples and the state, there is little evidence of a multicultural consociational model. Indigenous peoples are now constitutionally granted autonomy, but in a rather limited way: it is restricted by preexisting territorial boundaries; it is limited to small rural communities; it places significant restrictions on the use of *usos y costumbres*; and it does not grant communities veto rights on decisions involving their resources. The restrictions on *usos y costumbres* are both complex and problematic. Like people in many other countries, Bolivians have been forced to wrestle with potential conflicts between practices that fall under *usos y costumbres* and their commitments to human rights. Thus, for example, one can understand restrictions on the use of capital or corporal punishments—a practice sometimes defended as falling under the category of *usos y costumbres*. However, it is less understandable why far less controversial elements of *usos y costumbres*—such as traditional ways of selecting community leaders—should be brushed aside. This is particularly puzzling when it comes to electoral representation.

National-level elections do little to promote a consociational mode of politics for two reasons. First, representatives from all seven special indigenous districts are elected using simple plurality, in competitive multiparty elections. Since these districts comprise two or more distinct indigenous communities, rival communities will inevitably challenge each other. Without any consociational electoral mechanism—such as the use of preferential voting methods recommended for ethnically plural societies (Reilly 2002)—this is a recipe for the largest group to dominate. Further, the experience of the 2009 legislative election suggests that these special districts are little more than additional uninominal districts. All seven districts were won by one of the two major parties (six by MAS, one by the opposition PPB-CN). The experience of the uninominal districts in Bolivia also does not support a consociational mode of politics. The use of single-member districts in which representatives are elected by plurality is the most traditional of majoritarian electoral systems. The changes to the senatorial electoral rules do not seem to alter the balance significantly: senators are still elected from multimember districts (increased in number from three to four) with a system that privileges any district's dominant party.

Even within autonomous indigenous communities, the new institutional rules do not seem to actively encourage consociationalism. Eleven municipalities voted in 2009 (in a referendum attached to the December 2009 general election) to declare themselves autonomous indigenous communities. Soon after, many went forward with steps to select their own authorities using *usos y costumbres*. Surprisingly, the Morales government intervened, requiring all eleven newly recognized autonomous indigenous communities to participate in the April 2010 municipal elections—and to use the same electoral system as all other municipalities. This is particularly ironic because many of the methods of electing leaders within these communities were much closer to the consociational model: Using *usos y costumbres*, communities had named governing councils that would explicitly include a representative from each of the various subgroups within their community. Instead, these autonomous indigenous communities were forced to use an electoral system that defined politics as interparty competition. Following the law, these communities created and registered "indigenous communities" with the electoral court with slates comprised of the leaders they had chosen by *usos y costumbres*. These slates then faced off against other legally recognized electoral vehicles—including MAS. The resulting electoral campaigns tore many communities apart, particularly after results left some groups excluded from representation.

The 2009 Bolivian Constitution is a significant advance in the recognition of Bolivia's multiculturalism. It also marks a significant—albeit incomplete—departure from the country's centralist tradition as a unitary state. But it is difficult to qualify the emerging model as one of consociational politics. In various forms, the electoral system continues to encourage interest group fragmentation. And while MAS has evolved into a party that may be described internally as consociational (in terms of its internal party organization—although the dominant role played by Evo Morales casts a significant shadow), the party does not include all relevant political sectors—which are left out and increasingly marginalized. If anything, the last few years have seen Bolivia move further toward a majoritarian model of democracy, rather than toward one based on power sharing or consociationalism. This is particularly true when it comes to Bolivia's indigenous peoples, who are now better recognized and included in the political process, but still enjoy only limited (albeit expanded) political autonomy.

NOTES

1. These and all subsequent election results come from CNE (2010).
2. A third, but relatively minor set of reforms was enacted in 2002.
3. Delegates to previous constitutional conventions had been elected indirectly and/or with the franchise limited to literate men. The 1967 convention was the first after universal adult suffrage was installed, but it took place under a military dictatorship.
4. MIP was the first explicitly ethnic indigenous party to win more than 2 percent of the vote in a national election, winning 6.1 percent and placing fifth in the 2002 contest.
5. The electoral formula used to elect senators (three per department, with the first-place party winning two seats and the second-place party automatically winning the third seat, on the basis of that department's presidential vote) favored the opposition. Despite winning only 28.6 percent of the vote, the principal opposition party, Democratic and Social Power (Poder Democrático y Social, PODEMOS), won thirteen seats in the twenty-seven-member Senate. In contrast, MAS, with 53.7 percent of the vote, won only twelve seats; two other opposition parties won the two remaining seats.
6. The uninominal single-member districts were introduced in the 1995 electoral system reforms that shifted Bolivia from a list-PR to a mixed-member proportional electoral system. The use of the term "uninominal" to refer to districts that elected multiple representatives is, strictly speaking, incorrect. But the term is widely used in Bolivia to refer to those districts.
7. For example, the Confederation of Indigenous Peoples of Bolivia (Confederación de Pueblos Indígenas de Bolivia) proposed two seats per uninominal district, plus an additional sixty-eight seats elected in specifically ethnic districts using *usos y costumbres*. A number of other indigenous organizations backed the proposal, or presented alternative proposals that similarly included specifically reserved seats for indigenous peoples to be filled according to their community's *usos y costumbres* (see Cordero 2005, 71–81).

8. Seats were allocated as follows: in uninominal districts, two seats would go to the first-place party, with the second-place party winning the remaining seat. In department-wide districts, the first-place party would win three seats, with the second- and third-place parties winning the remaining seats. Even if one party placed first in each district, it could only win 167 of 255 seats (65.4 percent), falling short of the 169 required for a supermajority.
9. The MNR competed in all nine departments, but ran under different banners (representing different regional alliances) in Santa Cruz (where it ran as A3-MNR) and Tarija (where it ran as MNR-FRI). MNR won eight delegates (seven in Beni, one in Pando); MNR-FRI won eight delegates in Tarija; A3-MNR won two delegates in Santa Cruz.
10. These were MBL, a center-left party that had been part of the MNR-led coalition that had nominated Sánchez de Lozada in the 2002 presidential election (it won eight delegates); UN, a relatively new party founded in 2004 by a Bolivian business magnate with long-standing ties to the center-left party MIR (eight delegates); and the party of former president Jaime Paz Zamora, MIR (one delegate).
11. Perhaps as a sign of the body's cosmopolitanism, thirty-two delegates (12.5 percent) reported speaking Spanish, an indigenous language, and a foreign language. This meant that a total of seventy-eight delegates (nearly a third of the assembly) spoke a foreign language.
12. For a chronology, see Carrasco and Albó (2008), included in a special double issue of *T'inkazos* devoted entirely to the Constituent Assembly.
13. Sucre had been the original capital of Bolivia until 1899, when the seat of government was moved to La Paz at the end of the 1898–1899 Federalist War. Sucre has remained the judicial capital, housing the Supreme Court.
14. This is the first time the Afro-Bolivian community was ever included in a constitutional text. The 2009 Constitution mentions them explicitly in three other places: Article 32 (in the section on indigenous and campesino communities), Article 100 (in the section on cultures), and Article 395 (in the section on land and territory).
15. These are *Ama qhilla, ama llulla, ama suwa* (Quechua for "don't be lazy, don't lie, don't steal"); *Suma qamaña* (Aymara for "live well"); *Ñadereko, teko kavi, ivi maraei* (Guaraní for "harmony, good life, good earth"); and *Qhapaj ñan* (Quechua for "noble path").
16. The 2004 Constitution expanded indigenous rights only by granting "indigenous communities" the right to participate in elections. They were still required, however, to register with the CNE.
17. Curiously, this section does not immediately follow the sections on departmental, regional, and municipal autonomy, but rather falls between the sections on executive (Articles 285 and 286) and legislative (Articles 287 and 288) organs for autonomous governments, and the section on the distribution of competencies between the four kinds of autonomous units and the central government (Articles 297–305).
18. When municipal elections were introduced in 1995, voters cast ballots only for a party list of municipal council candidates. The newly elected municipal council then chose a mayor from among its members (essentially, a parliamentary system on a small scale). As in presidential elections, if no party list won an absolute majority of the votes, mayors were chosen from multiparty coalitions. The introduction of separate, direct elections for mayors moved municipal governments from a parliamentary model to a presidential one.

REFERENCES

AIN (Andean Information Network). 2007. "Bolivia: Three Dead in Capital Conflict." November 26. http://ain-bolivia.org.

Albó, Xavier. 2008. "Datos de una encuesta: El perfil de los constituyentes." *T'inkazos* 11 (23/24): 49–64.

Ayo, Diego, Yuri Tórrez, and Juan Carlos Velásquez. 2007. *La agenda de la Asamblea Constituyente*. La Paz: CNE.

Barragán, Rossana. 2006. *Asambleas constituyentes: Ciudadanía y elecciones, convenciones y debates (1825–1971)*. La Paz: Muela del Diablo.

BIF (Bolivia Information Forum). 2011. "Blocking the Road: Indigenous Groups Challenge Government Policies in the TIPNIS." *BIF Bulletin* 20. http://www.boliviainfoforum.org.uk.

Carrasco Alurralde, Inés Valeria, and Xavier Albó. 2008. "Cronología de la Asamblea Constituyente." *T'inkazos* 11 (23/24): 101–124.

Centellas, Miguel. 2008. "From 'Parliamentarized' to 'Pure' Presidentialism: Bolivia after October 2003." *Latin Americanist* 52 (3): 2–30.

Centellas, Miguel. 2010. "Savina Cuéllar and Bolivia's New Regionalism." *Latin American Perspectives* 37 (4): 161–176.

CNE (Corte Nacional Electoral). 2010. *Atlas Electoral de Bolivia*. La Paz: CNE, UNDP-Bolivia, and International IDEA.

"Cocaleros deciden ir a Sucre y fiscalizar a Constituyentes." 2006. *Los Tiempos*, August 13.

Cordero Carraffa, Carlos. 2005. *La representación en la asamblea constituyente: Estudio del sistema electoral*. La Paz: Corte Nacional Electoral.

Dangl, Ben. 2007. *The Price of Fire: Resource Wars and Social Movements in Bolivia*. Oakland, CA: AK Press.

Lijphart, Arend. 1977. *Democracy in Plural Societies: A Comparative Exploration*. New Haven, CT: Yale University Press.

Lijphart, Arend. 1999. *Patterns of Democracy: Government Forms and Performance in Thirty-Six Democracies, 1945–1990*. Oxford: Oxford University Press.

Lijphart, Arend. 2007. *Thinking about Democracy: Power Sharing and Majority Rule in Theory and Practice*. London: Routledge.

Madrid, Raúl L. 2008. "The Rise of Ethnopopulism in Latin American." *World Politics* 60 (3): 475–508.

Mamani Ramírez, Pablo. 2010. "Lo indígena en la nueva Constitución Política del Estado 'Constitución intermedia.'" In *Miradas: Nuevo Texto Constitucional (A Closer Look: Bolivia's New Constitution)*, 703–711. La Paz: International IDEA and Vice Presidency of Bolivia.

Mayorga, René Antonio. 1997. "Bolivia's Silent Revolution." *Journal of Democracy* 8 (1): 142–156.

Reilly, Benjamin. 2002. "Electoral Systems for Divided Societies." *Journal of Democracy* 13 (2): 156–170.

Stefanoni, Pablo. 2010. "Radiografía del MAS: Las ambivalencias de la democracia corporativa." *Le Monde Diplomatique* 26 (May): 4–6.

Van Cott, Donna Lee. 2007. *From Movements to Parties: The Evolution of Ethnic Parties*. Cambridge: Cambridge University Press.

Van Cott, Donna Lee. 2008. *Radical Democracy in the Andes*. Cambridge: Cambridge University Press.

5 The Backlash against Indigenous Rights in Ecuador's Citizen's Revolution

Carmen Martínez Novo

INTRODUCTION: TWENTY-FIRST-CENTURY SOCIALISM AND INDIGENOUS PEOPLES

Ecuador is one of the countries in Latin America that has apparently turned toward the Left in the last few years (French 2009; Weyland 2009; de la Torre 2010; Escobar 2010). Since 2007, Rafael Correa, a president who questions both neoliberalism and North American hegemony, has governed Ecuador. Correa claims to rule for the vulnerable and the dispossessed, and argues that he is radically changing the country through what his party, Alianza País, calls a "Citizen's Revolution." Initially, Correa sought the support of the indigenous movement for this transformation: He gave speeches in the Kichwa language, wore an outfit with native symbols, and started his first presidency with an event in an indigenous community in rural Cotopaxi, located in the central highlands of Ecuador. Two years later, however, the Confederation of Indigenous Nationalities of Ecuador (Confederación de Nacionalidades Indígenas del Ecuador, CONAIE), the largest indigenous organization, began to confront Correa's government. In 2009, CONAIE staged demonstrations against the approval of the water and mining laws designed by the government. On February 26, 2010, CONAIE decided in a general assembly to start an uprising against Rafael Correa and to seek an alliance with other sectors and social movements to fight the government's policies. CONAIE also decided not to let any government officials enter indigenous territories or communities without permission of the organizations. In June 2010, CONAIE was not invited to the meeting of ALBA in Otavalo, Ecuador.[1]

At this meeting, representatives including presidents Rafael Correa, Hugo Chávez of Venezuela, and Evo Morales of Bolivia were discussing how to implement plurinational states and interculturalism at a continental level. CONAIE staged a demonstration at the doors of the meeting asking to be received, particularly by President Morales. Indigenous leaders were not received at the meeting and their demonstration was repressed by the police. Then the provincial prosecutor accused Marlon Santi, president of CONAIE, and Delfin Tenesaca, president of Ecuarunari, of terrorism.[2] Why is a government whose agenda would be expected to coincide with that of the indigenous and other social movements involved in such a conflict? Why are social movements fighting the government instead of supporting it?

In this chapter, I first discuss the current state of the indigenous movement in Ecuador, which according to observers went through a period of relative weakness and internal division starting roughly in 2004 (Zamosc 2007; Van Cott 2009). However, the indigenous movement, or at least some branches of it, seems to have started a new stage of consolidation in its opposition to the current government. I then analyze the advances and ambiguities of the 2008 Constitution regarding indigenous rights. I argue that the tensions in the constitution reflect struggles among different currents within the governing coalition. Finally, I focus on the conflict between the government of Rafael Correa and CONAIE, which culminated in the death of a Shuar teacher in demonstrations on September 30, 2009. The government is making its agenda known through executive decrees, secondary legislation, and the practices of government. According to the indigenous movement, this agenda very much contradicts what is stated in the 2008 Constitution. This postconstitutional conflict is centered around two main issues: the discontinuation of the autonomy of indigenous organizations to manage the System of Intercultural Bilingual Education and other state institutions that focus on indigenous welfare, and the new mining and water laws that, according to CONAIE, have been written without the participation and consent of social movements, strengthen the role of the state in the management of natural resources at the expense of communities, and present the risk of privatization of these strategic resources. In these two issues (control of state institutions for indigenous development and control of natural resources), what seems to be at stake is a process of reinforcement of the central state that implies the reduction of the participation and autonomy of social movements in the policies that affect them.

I argue that in Ecuador, a very strong indigenous movement was able to gain autonomy through a bottom-up process of democratization of society. However, this movement was partially co-opted during the 1990s. Indigenous organizations were granted autonomy by the state, but not enough resources to make it effective. This shallow multiculturalism engineered from above led to the co-optation of the leadership of the indigenous movement, which benefited from tokenism and achieved a few positions in the state apparatus, development projects, and international organizations. However, indigenous individuals at the grassroots level did not see enough change, and some felt that indigenous leaders no longer represented them. As a result, these communities were easily drawn toward President Correa's project after 2007. Correa's government has carried out a process of state formation that has sought to reinforce the central state, reducing the spaces of autonomy for indigenous organizations. Meanwhile, individual rights have been privileged instead via antidiscrimination and affirmative action laws associated with the term *interculturalidad*. However, these antidiscrimination policies will hardly be implemented without a strong social movement requesting that they are made effective in a country in which whites and mestizos still hold most power, including within Correa's so-called Citizen's Revolution.

Other scholars are also showing doubts regarding the commitment of so-called twenty-first-century socialists to the rights of indigenous peoples. It has been argued that the turn toward the left in Latin America in the twenty-first century may produce a fruitful combination of ethnic and class objectives that could be positive for indigenous rights, particularly in the case of Bolivia. For Nancy Postero (2007), the new moment of postmulticultural citizenship is characterized by a combination of the ethnic recognition and participation afforded during the neoliberal period with a struggle for greater redistribution of the nation's resources. However, in her later work, Postero (2010) has recognized that tensions are mounting between indigenous organizations, particularly those of the Amazon, and the Evo Morales regime. According to Postero, the Morales government displays a radical agenda of protection of the natural environment for international consumption while focusing its local development strategy on forms of extraction of natural resources that degrade the environment and negatively affect indigenous groups living in the frontiers. This process is producing divisions between popular groups (mostly indigenous) interested in the exploitation of resources to fund social programs, and indigenous groups directly affected, polluted, and displaced by extractive activities.

Donna Lee Van Cott (2008) was not optimistic either about the relationship between the twenty-first-century Left and indigenous peoples, but considered that after the indigenous gains of the 1990s, the Left could not afford to ignore ethnicity-based demands. In a more recent article, however, Van Cott (2009) warned that the rise of populist-leftist governments in the Andes could take space from indigenous movements in leading the struggle against neoliberalism and could erode the support of mestizos for these movements.

In an interesting and thorough article that surveys changes in Venezuela, Bolivia, and Ecuador, Arturo Escobar (2010) highlights important transformations at the level of constitutions and plans of government that include a reversal of neoliberal policies, a renewal of democracy, and the inclusion of proposals of social movements like *sumak kawsay*, Kichwa for good living, which prioritizes human welfare over accumulation of wealth and proposes a new relation to nature. However, he also has some reservations in relation to these changes: For example, he sees a tendency toward the concentration of power in the state and a continuation of traditional understandings of development based on the extraction of natural resources. He also perceives a tension between states trying to use the creative energies of social movements and contrary tendencies to exclude social movements from government and to try to control them. Finally, he also acknowledges a tension between radical discourses and whether there is enough political will to translate these discourses into practices.

In the case of Venezuela, according to some authors, there is less tension between Chávez's government and ethnic or nonwhite groups (Gottberg 2011). Gottberg argues that the conservative opposition has adopted a racist discourse to delegitimize Chávez's supporters. In the context of this confrontation, Chávez has emphasized his nonwhite (Zambo, a mixture of indigenous and Afro-descendant) origins and has labeled the opposition white and therefore foreign to the Venezuelan nation. This symbolic inclusion of nonwhites as the real Venezuelans has resonated with supporters. However, other authors argue that the Venezuelan state is not allowing indigenous peoples to keep their autonomous organizations and alternative ways of life. The state is encouraging indigenous peoples to organize through communal councils like the rest of the population and to integrate into the Venezuelan economy (Angosto 2008). Esteban Mosonyi (2012), president of the Association of Anthropologists and Sociologists of Venezuela, adds that the Chávez government is not doing enough to protect forest peoples like the Yanomami from the encroachment of mining interests.

This chapter builds on these insights to discuss some of the nuances of the conflict between the new Latin American Left and indigenous organizations through the examination of the Ecuadorian case. I now turn toward the previous internal problems of the indigenous movement in order to understand why the later backlash against indigenous rights has been possible.

THE CRISIS OF THE ECUADORIAN INDIGENOUS MOVEMENT

Until recently, the indigenous movement of Ecuador has been called the strongest indigenous movement in Latin America (Yashar 2005; Zamosc 2007). Its modern manifestations started in the 1940s in collaboration with the Left, particularly with the Communist Party (Becker 2008). At the time, the movement focused on the struggles for the improvement of conditions under the hacienda system, for the eventual demise of this system, for access to land, and for education. Access to education was also linked to citizenship rights because the illiterate could not vote or be elected until 1979. In the 1970s, the indigenous movement worked more closely with the Catholic Church, which, after the Second Vatican Council (1962–1965), started to practice Liberation and later Inculturation theologies.[3] During this period, the priorities were the struggle for agrarian reform and agrarian development, to overcome exclusion from education, against discrimination, for cultural rights, and for indigenous territories (Martínez Novo 2009).

CONAIE, a strong nationwide organization, was created in 1986, and intercultural bilingual education was made official in 1988. The System of Intercultural Bilingual Education in Ecuador has been unique in Latin America because indigenous organizations nominated its authorities and administrators, hired its teachers, and designed its curriculum with relative autonomy (Abram 2004). However, the central government still supervised the system and controlled its finances. The creation of this autonomous system of education took place at the same time that different governments implemented sharp budget cuts in education (Montaluisa 1990). The poorly financed system became an example of what has been called recognition without redistribution (Fraser 1996).

The indigenous movement in Ecuador has been considered stronger than others in the region because it was able to unify organizations from the community to the national level, and because its massive uprisings were able to deeply affect state policy (Yashar 2005; Zamosc 2007). Starting in 1990, the indigenous movement staged a series of national uprisings that were able to halt the implementation of neoliberal reforms and that contributed to ousting two presidents, Abdalá Bucarám in 1996 and Jamil Mahuad in 2000 (Zamosc 2007). It is less often noted that the movement also achieved the creation of a series of state institutions for education, health, and development that were managed directly and autonomously by indigenous organizations. Political participation was another strength. In 1996, CONAIE, in alliance with other social movements and sectors, created the political party Pachakutik. That same year, Pachakutik was able to win 10 percent of congressional seats. Pachakutik also had considerable impact in the 1998 Constituent Assembly, where it also controlled 10 percent of the seats. The 1998 assembly declared Ecuador a pluricultural and multiethnic state and asserted the right of communities to preserve their culture, forms of political organization, and administration. The 1998 Constitution also had provisions regarding the adjudication of indigenous territories. However, many of these rights depended on the implementation of further legislation, and this task became difficult because Pachakutik was a minority in Congress (Zamosc 2007). The national representation of Pachakutik in Congress has been from 10 percent to 7.5 percent of congressional seats (Zamosc 2007). The party was also able to achieve important representation at the regional and local level. For example, in the 2000 elections Pachakutik won four governorships and seventeen mayoralties. In 2004, it won three governorships and twenty mayoralties, plus wide representation in provincial, municipal, and parish councils (Zamosc 2007).

The relative crisis of CONAIE from roughly 2004 is multidimensional, and different authors emphasize different reasons for it (Ospina 2009). Many point to the ill-conceived alliance of the indigenous movement with Colonel Gutiérrez, who instigated a coup d'état in 2000 with CONAIE's support. The lack of solid democratic values demonstrated by the indigenous movement through participating in this coup has been criticized (Zamosc 2007). In 2002, Gutiérrez won the presidential elections in alliance with Pachakutik. This allowed CONAIE to participate in government and some of its leaders to become ministers of state. For example, Nina Pacari became minister of foreign relations, and Luis Macas became minister of agriculture. However, a year after the election the alliance broke up as Gutiérrez reinforced neoliberal policies and started to negotiate a free-trade agreement with the United States, and the indigenous movement tried unsuccessfully to become an opposition from within. In 2003, Pachakutik was forced to leave the government and Gutiérrez started a policy of dividing the indigenous movement. This consisted of clientelism at the community level to try to bypass CONAIE's organizational structures. Another strategy was to make alliances and give positions in state institutions to other smaller indigenous organizations such as FEI (Federación Ecuatoriana de Indios, Ecuadorian Federation of Indians, linked to the Communist Party), FEINE (Federación Ecuatoriana de Indígenas Evangélicos, Ecuadorian Federation of Evangelical Indigenous People, a Protestant indigenous organization), and FENOCIN (Federación Nacional de Organizaciones Campesinas Indígenas y Negras, National Federation of Peasant, Indigenous, and Black Organizations, linked to the Socialist Party). The exacerbation of internal divisions among indigenous populations by different governments and the co-optation of the grassroots and some part of the leadership are among the reasons for the crisis of CONAIE.

Some authors point out that the crisis of the indigenous movement may be related to its institutionalization and participation in politics (Zamosc 2007; Van Cott 2009; Ospina 2009). Zamosc argues that the struggle to control the state led the indigenous movement to carry out some opportunistic moves such as the 2000 coup d'état, which cost it legitimacy. Van Cott argues that indigenous elected authorities might have been subjected to unrealistic expectations on the part of voters that may not have been fulfilled. Moreover, according to Van Cott, indigenous parties may no longer be perceived as fresh and corruption-free options. Finally, competition over government positions has produced fragmentation in the organization. Ospina suggests that the indigenous movement was perhaps unprepared for its political success. The best cadres of CONAIE moved to government positions, leaving the social movement unattended. Those in government positions might not have been prepared for the tasks they needed to complete (Ospina 2009). This last argument is problematic because mestizo candidates may also be unprepared, and experience in government has to be acquired by doing it.

Another reason for the crisis is that the indigenous movement seems to have lost its relevance as an avant-garde of anti-neoliberal and radical struggles with the rise of Correa's post-neoliberal project. For instance, Correa's project attracted a good number of intellectual collaborators of Pachakutik and CONAIE, further weakening the indigenous movement. Nevertheless, now that social movements and environmentalists and their agendas have been marginalized from the governing coalition, CONAIE has the potential to again lead Ecuadorian oppositional movements.

According to Donna Lee Van Cott (2009), the indigenous movement needs to reassess the political scenario since the Left has come to power. It was easier to be in opposition to conservative governments than to relate to the populist Left that is depriving the indigenous movement of wider political support. In addition, the inward turn of Ecuador's indigenous movement toward a more restricted indigenous agenda and the expulsion of mestizos from Pachakutik did not help either. This happened after the failed alliance with Lucio Gutiérrez made activists think that they had overstretched their movement. However, this strategy further deprived Pachakutik of mestizo and urban support.

Víctor Bretón (2005) adds further reasons for the crisis of the indigenous movement. He has emphasized the role of a World Bank program called PRODEPINE (Programa de Desarrollo de los Pueblos Indígenas y Negros del Ecuador, Program for the Development of Indigenous and Black Peoples of Ecuador) in weakening the indigenous movement. PRODEPINE has granted money to indigenous organizations for local development projects. According to Bretón, the World Bank has encouraged indigenous organizations to privilege a technocratic instead of a political leadership and to focus on short-term goals instead of long-term political projects. This has resulted in the depolitization and demobilization of CONAIE.

Another explanation is the growing gap between the leaders and the grassroots. Some leaders have become technocrats focused toward national and international contexts and have lost contact with the communities. In addition, the communities have not seen enough change at the grassroots level after more than a decade of uprisings and political participation. This has led indigenous people to complain about the corruption of the leadership and to become tired of organizing and demonstrating without seeing clear results (Tuaza 2009).

Rudi Colloredo-Mansfeld (2009) has argued that class differentiation in indigenous communities has strengthened the indigenous movement. Through long-term fieldwork in the northern highlands of Ecuador, Colloredo discovered that urban and professionally oriented indigenous people contributed a great deal with their vision and resources to make the political movement more effective. While agreeing with Colloredo that mobile and richer indigenous individuals may be powerful political resources, class differentiation and differential access to the benefits of identity politics may also produce resentment in communities that have perceived this differentiation as corruption on the part of the leadership. In addition, indigenous community members may grow tired of local statecraft strategies that have often mobilized their collective labor to work or protest without providing enough advantages for everybody involved.

Finally, the grassroots seem to be more interested in economic mobility and inclusion, and therefore in individual rights, than in reinforcing indigenous culture and collective autonomy. Ethnicity is a strategy that seems to have benefited indigenous leaders, but communities and the grassroots much less. This is because the politics of recognition and the tokenism associated with them may have created a few jobs for leaders while precluding greater structural transformations that might have reached indigenous communities more deeply. This is yet another reason for the grassroots to be attracted to Correa's political project. Unlike the case of Bolivia, in this case the deficiencies of neoliberal multiculturalism were blamed on indigenous leaders.

The crisis of the indigenous movement in the second half of the decade of 2000 is reflected in electoral results. In the 2006 elections, Pachakutik ran its own indigenous candidate, Luis Macas, trying to replicate Evo Morales's 2005 victory in Bolivia. However, Macas obtained less than 2 percent of the national vote (Báez and Bretón 2006) and only 25 percent of the indigenous vote (Van Cott 2009). Pachakutik's delegation to Congress diminished from eleven to six deputies. This relative electoral failure has led some regional and local indigenous leaders to ally with Alianza País, Correa's political party, while many of them also remain members of Pachakutik and CONAIE.

Pachakutik's lack of support for Correa's candidacy in 2006 is at the root of the separation between Correa's project and the indigenous movement. It is also at the root of the division of CONAIE, since some branches like the Indigenous and Peasant Movement of Cotopaxi (Movimiento Indígena y Campesino de Cotopaxi, MICC) wanted to ally with Correa, whereas other regional leaders like Auqui Tituaña, former mayor of Cotacachi, opposed this alliance. These divisions have reached the indigenous movement in intimate ways, dividing kin against kin: for example, Marlon Santi, former president of CONAIE, has become a radical opponent of Correa's government, whereas his first cousin, Carlos Viteri, distributes subsidies in the Amazon to increase support for the government among Amazonian peoples.

Despite this situation, some branches of the indigenous movement have become stronger and more unified in the confrontation with Rafael Correa's government. In particular, Amazonian indigenous peoples are becoming unified against what they perceive as a renewed offensive of oil and mining companies that want to penetrate their territories with the support of the government. In the highlands the main issues radicalizing indigenous populations are the unequal distribution of water, which they do not see remedied by the new water law; the control of state institutions for indigenous education, health, and development; and the expansion of mining. Also, Correa's lack of respect for indigenous leaders, whom he calls *pelucones* and *ponchos dorados* (preppies and golden ponchos) who are unprepared to lead a social movement, has had an effect in radicalizing CONAIE's position.

THE 2008 CONSTITUTION: ADVANCES AND AMBIGUITIES IN INDIGENOUS RIGHTS

The 2008 Constitution has meant some apparent advances for indigenous rights over the 1998 Constitution. However, due to tensions in the ruling coalition, some points have been kept intentionally ambiguous, some advances have not been possible, and even some setbacks are taking place, mainly through the presidential decrees and statutory legislation that have been issued since the constitutional text was approved.

The 1998 Constitution declared Ecuador a pluricultural and multiethnic state. Although the idea that Ecuador should be plurinational was an indigenous demand since the early 1990s, it was not accepted in the 1998 Constitution because some sectors feared that this could become grounds for the division of the fatherland. In the Constituent Assembly of 2008, there was a debate on whether Ecuador should be plurinational or intercultural.[4] The plurinational side got support from the ideas of Portuguese intellectual Boaventura de Sousa, who is an icon of the Latin American Left, and an organizer of World Social Forums, which, according to John French (2009), have been able to successfully articulate the New Left in Latin America. On the indigenous activist side, the position of plurinationality was championed by Mónica Chuji, an Amazonian indigenous woman who became secretary of communication in Correa's government and later a representative of Alianza País to the 2008 Constituent Assembly while remaining a member of CONAIE. For de Sousa (2007), plurinationalism did not mean the division of the state, but it did mean self-determination, celebration of diversity, antidiscrimination, and a transitional period of affirmative action, as well as redistribution of resources. Plurinationality should also imply, according to de Sousa, sharing decisions about natural resources. According to Monica Chuji (interview by author, April 11, 2008), plurinationality is a political process that seeks to restructure the state through a new geographical organization in which indigenous territories have equal privileges with traditional geographical divisions such as provinces or municipalities. She also proposed special representation of the indigenous nationalities in all structures of the state such as Congress, the Supreme Court, the Electoral Court, and so on. Finally, she emphasized that indigenous peoples should be consulted regarding natural resources and that their decisions should be binding for the state.

The intercultural side was led by Ecuadorian intellectual Galo Ramón and by indigenous peasant activist Pedro de la Cruz, president of FENOCIN, an indigenous organization linked to the Socialist Party. According to Ramón (2008), *interculturalidad* recognizes the right to difference and diversity, but emphasizes a process of living together and the construction of unity. *Interculturalidad* is based not on autonomy of indigenous peoples in their own territories, but on inclusion and equality in diversity that pervades all institutions of society. Therefore, *interculturalidad* focuses more on the individual rights of diverse or disadvantaged populations than on their collective autonomy. This project is particularly relevant for territories that are shared by mestizos and diverse indigenous groups. Also, according to Ramón, *interculturalidad* is more relevant for Afro-Ecuadorians than plurinationality since few of them live in their own territories. Pedro de la Cruz (interview by author, April 11, 2008) adds that autonomy can be used by the conservatives to strengthen their power and to resist change, and emphasizes the need for unity as well as equality. Although de la Cruz, given the socialist tradition he comes from, emphasizes class unity among the poor regardless of their ethnic or racial background, he is also for antidiscrimination and affirmative action laws.

Catherine Walsh (2009) claims that both *interculturalidad* and plurinationality should be implemented because both are complementary processes. According to the author, plurinationality should be understood not as division, but as a more adequate way to unite and integrate. *Interculturalidad* is understood by Walsh not only as a public policy but as work that needs to be done both at the level of the state and within society. This can be achieved through policies and attitudes that encourage inclusion.

After this debate, a consensus was reached in the governing party and both terms, plurinationality and *interculturalidad*, were included in the constitution, but some of the demands of the first as well as of the second seem to have been somewhat diluted (Asamblea Constituyente 2008). Plurinationality was accepted as a term, but emphasizing the unity and predominance of the central state. The sovereignty of the state superseded territorial autonomy, and special representation of indigenous nationalities beyond regular democratic representation was not accepted. Furthermore, nonrenewable natural resources belong to the central state. Indigenous peoples should be consulted, but it is in dispute whether the state needs to follow these recommendations. This led some critics to argue that the term plurinationality was accepted but not the meaning (DINEIB 2008a). Furthermore, in the 2008 Constitution's section on indigenous rights, collective autonomy was limited by the constitution, human rights, and women's rights. Therefore, Correa's government adopted what Todd Eisenstadt calls "conditional multiculturalism" in the introduction to this volume. As the term "plurinationality" was emptied of meaning through conditions, the reinforcement of the state, and secondary legislation, the government turned toward an individual rights approach represented by the term *interculturalidad*.

Another issue that created tensions in the governing coalition was whether to declare Kichwa an official language together with Spanish. Many deputies to the Constituent Assembly wished to do so, but the final consensus reached by Correa's party was to leave Spanish as the only official language and to declare native languages "languages of intercultural communication." The reasons given by Alianza País and President Correa to keep Kichwa in an inferior status in relation to Spanish were that Kichwa is an oral language, that it is not a national language, that it would be very costly to make Kichwa an official language, that the imposition of Kichwa on the coast would generate resentment, and that the population should rather learn English (DINEIB 2008b).

Antidiscrimination and affirmative action legislations are important advances in the 2008 Constitution. Antidiscrimination principles appear throughout the constitutional text and have been further developed through Presidential Decree 60, issued on September 28, 2009, which is based on a previous academic plan for public policy requested by the government (Antón and García 2009). Presidential Decree 60 is very radical concerning race relations. For example, it reads, "the state will try to achieve [*procurará*] the hiring of Afro-Ecuadorians, Indigenous, and *montubios* [mestizo peasants from the coast] in all its institutions in a proportion that will not be less than their participation in the total population" (Correa 2009b, my translation). This decree, however, has not been sufficiently implemented.

The question of indigenous territories and control of nonrenewable natural resources remains a problematic and ambiguous arena in the constitutional text. As in the 1998 Constitution, indigenous territories (*circunscripciones territoriales indígenas*) are included in the text. However, these territories do not pertain to the regular territorial organization of the state and in principle do not have equal rights (including budgets) as provinces, counties (*cantones*), and municipalities. Their legal status was later defined by statutory legislation. To generate an indigenous territory, interested groups should base their petition in the divisions of the state that already exist, such as parishes, counties (*cantones*), and provinces. In those territorial divisions they should carry out a referendum that they should win by two-thirds of the vote (Asamblea Nacional del Ecuador 2008, 158). The problem with this method is that the current divisions of the state are based on the distribution of mestizo population and not on the distribution of its indigenous inhabitants. Typically, indigenous populations are distributed in the margins of such a division, the center of which is the mestizo town or small city (Julian Larrea, personal communication). This would make the official approval of indigenous territories very difficult unless the divisions of the state are legally changed, which is a tortuous legal and political process that may take decades to complete.

Furthermore, it is clear in the constitutional text that nonrenewable resources belong to the central state.[5] The chart of indigenous rights in the constitution establishes that communities should be consulted when their territories or rights are affected, but it is not clear whether this consultation is binding for the state. Alianza País did not accept unambiguous binding consultation for indigenous peoples in the constitution. This point created tensions between a section of the ruling coalition led by Alberto Acosta and close to environmentalist and proindigenous concerns that promoted autonomy and the importance of binding consultation with communities, and another sector of the ruling coalition led by President Correa that prioritized national development and the extraction of natural resources. Alberto Acosta and his follower environmentalists and supporters of indigenous rights lost this battle, but introduced an ambiguity into the constitutional text that they are trying to use in favor of communities. They included in the constitutional chart of indigenous rights that Ecuador would respect all international treaties regarding indigenous and human rights. That would include the 2007 United Nations Declaration of Indigenous Rights, which stipulates that the consent of indigenous communities is needed in order to extract natural resources from their territories.

POSTCONSTITUTIONAL CONFLICTS OVER THE CONTROL OF STATE INSTITUTIONS FOR INDIGENOUS DEVELOPMENT AND NATURAL RESOURCES

The 2008 Constitution contained advances and also ambiguities that created expectations on the part of indigenous peoples, but that also heralded conflicts. The first strong conflict pertains to the system of intercultural bilingual education. In February 2009, through Executive Decree 1585, the Correa government abolished the autonomy of indigenous organizations to elect the authorities of DINEIB (Dirección Nacional de Educación Intercultural Bilingüe) or to decide on educational policies (Correa 2009d). This decree established that the intercultural bilingual system would be managed by the minister of education, a mestizo, according to national public policies. All authorities including the national director of intercultural bilingual education and the provincial directors would be freely nominated and removed by the minister. This meant a big change and a setback for indigenous organizations because since 1988, according to how representative they were among indigenous peoples, these organizations had been able to elect the authorities of the system, to design the curriculum and educational policies, and to hire its teachers. This decision, which contradicts the concept of plurinationality declared in the 2008 Constitution, caused great discontent in the indigenous movement. It is important to note that many of the movement's cadres are bilingual teachers. The intercultural bilingual system is also one of the main sources of employment for indigenous professionals in a very discriminatory labor market. Furthermore, the autonomy of the intercultural bilingual system of Ecuador is unique in Latin America (Abram 2004). Indigenous organizations in many countries are struggling to achieve what Ecuadorian indigenous nationalities already had.

Several reasons were given for this change, which goes against the idea of autonomy that the declaration of the plurinational state implies. According to the Ministry of Education, intercultural bilingual education had been delegated to indigenous organizations in the context of the neoliberal retrenchment of the state. For this reason, bilingual education had become the booty of a handful of corrupt leaders who had used the system for their own profit, who had politicized it, and who were the cause of the deep problems of quality in the system. The ministry also accused CONAIE of being racist, because they had monopolized intercultural education for the sake of indigenous organizations, had taught children about indigenous struggles, and had not included mestizos. "Corporatist organizations" such as the indigenous movement were accused of causing all the system's problems, and the context of neoliberal budget cuts and constraints in which indigenous organizations had to operate was not mentioned (Ministerio de Educación del Ecuador 2009). Thus, the individual rights of those using the educational system (indigenous children) were allegedly favored over the collective rights of indigenous organizations to have an autonomous education.

This presidential decree was renegotiated after demonstrations that culminated in the death of a Shuar teacher in September 2009. As a result of the negotiations between the government and CONAIE, the executive issued Decree 196 in December 2009 to substitute for the earlier legislation (Correa 2009c). This decree keeps the authority of the minister of education over the intercultural bilingual system and the election of its authorities. The government, however, accepted CONAIE's proposal that indigenous authorities be chosen by the minister through a competition based on merit. A National Commission of Intercultural Bilingual Education composed of representatives of the fourteen indigenous nationalities that exist in Ecuador was also added. However, this institution will only have an advisory character, and will not be elected by indigenous organizations but by the Council of Citizen's Participation and Social Control.[6] Decree 196 also stipulates that persons who have twice been provincial directors of intercultural bilingual education cannot be elected to be national or provincial directors, and that those who have challenged authority or participated in an unconstitutional strike cannot be chosen. It is clear that what these stipulations are seeking is to exclude the established leadership of the indigenous movement who have already held high positions and who have challenged the government in demonstrations and strikes. In 2011, the executive and legislative branches issued the Organic Law of Intercultural Education. This law kept the control of indigenous education in the hands of the executive but expanded an intercultural curriculum to the whole school population of Ecuador.

Even though the government claims to have an interest in the reinforcement of central state control and in eliminating the historically delegative nature of the Ecuadorian state that intensified under neoliberalism (Martínez Novo 2007), the president issued another decree (Correa 2009e) delegating the administration of education, health, development, and infrastructure in the Amazon to the Catholic missions with the economic and political support of the state. This happened despite the fact that, after many heated debates, the 2008 Constitution declared Ecuador a secular state, allowed religious pluralism, and required equality and nondiscrimination of different faiths in the country. Interestingly, the Catholic missions are perceived as depositories of the "general interest," whereas indigenous organizations and other social movements are perceived as private interests and corporatist.

The suppression of autonomy in the control of state institutions for indigenous welfare has been accompanied by a strong campaign delegitimizing indigenous leadership in presidential speeches, government-owned media, and by intellectuals who are close to the government. For example, President Correa has asserted:

What legitimacy does CONAIE have?...We, the majority must decide how we want to organize and how we want to live. And a few stone throwers should not impose their will. Thirteen million Ecuadorians should rise against these troglodyte attitudes that want to keep our country in the past.... What CONAIE does is not resistance; it is aggression. (quoted in Amnesty International 2012, 21; my translation)

A document by Minister of Culture Erika Sylva and Undersecretary of the Ministry of Foreign Affairs Rafael Quintero, both recognized social scientists and professors of the Central University in Quito, claims that since 2009 CONAIE has been attempting to conspire against President Correa and the constituent process in alliance with the extreme Right and with financial help from U.S. institutions that seek to destabilize the Latin American Left. According to the authors, the indigenous movement and the teachers' union form part of a corporatist Left that defends private interests, has abandoned the struggle for social reform, and is functional to neoliberalism (Quintero and Sylva 2010). In the state-owned newspaper *El Telegrafo*, opinion writer Guido Calderón has argued that the ancestral cultures of Ecuador lack a historical contribution:

They are only characterized by a rosary of complaints and resentments....I do not see either their historical nor their contemporary contribution. Their actions are limited to threats, social disruption, and the exhibition of a permanent violence....They want us to accept by force their barbarism as part of our lives. Even more, they expect our laws to lie below their brutal indigenous law. A bunch of leaders addicted to substances does not create cultures and even less ancestral cultures. (2010, my translation)

Are we witnessing a backlash against the indigenous movement by resentful mestizos who only unwillingly had remained silent and accepted the respect required by the recognition policies of neoliberal multiculturalism? Unfortunately, after listening to presidential speeches, individuals like Calderón feel justified in revealing points of view such as those reproduced above. Paradoxically, some of the most severe critics of the indigenous movement are intellectuals like Sylva that not so long ago were its advocates and wrote influential pieces on it.

In addition, government practices at the community level are eroding the organizational structures of the indigenous movement, according to CONAIE. The government is distributing money at the community level through a myriad of social programs like the bonus for human development (a small cash transfer to low-income elderly and low-income mothers), a bonus for housing, credits for agriculture and small businesses, and the programs Socio Páramo (Member for the Highlands) and Socio Bosque (Member for the Forest), which subsidize communities that protect their natural environment. Indigenous activists claim that these programs aim to co-opt the grassroots through bypassing CONAIE's organizational structures. Correa has also allied with FEI, FEINE, and FENOCIN, the smaller indigenous organizations. To solve this problem, CONAIE has denied government officials access to indigenous territories. Leaders argue that these officials come to divide indigenous people and to destroy their organizations (CONAIE 2010).

Finally, the government, through the Ministry of Peoples and Social Movements, is attempting to create parallel social movements from above. This strategy became more urgent for the government after a police strike on September 30, 2010, that caused chaos in Ecuador because the president was allegedly held hostage at the Police Hospital (see de la Torre 2011 for an explanation of this strike). Quintero and Sylva (2010, my translation) note:

> To confront the coup attempt, the political response of the government has been to radicalize the process, to empower its Left tendency. In addition, the government has realized the urgent need to work in the political organization of the people, . . . in the efficiency of mobilization. The organizational strategy is central because, as long as change is in the agenda, conspiracy and attempted coups will continue.

Doris Solís, minister of political coordination, added in a speech reporting the achievements of her first six months in office:

> The General Coordinator of Social and Political Actors promotes the construction of long-term sustainable processes that allow for the implementation of the second stage of the Citizen's Revolution. This means to promote the self-construction and self-determination of social actors so they become social subjects of change. These alliances are meant to reverse the confrontational positions of indigenous elites who have also co-opted the leaders of some organizations. They must be substituted by renewed processes of dialog and construction of agreements so that government's public polices can be implemented.

Another source of conflict between the government and indigenous organizations is the administration of natural resources such as oil, minerals, and water. The discussion of the mining and water laws has provoked demonstrations by CONAIE, and the reform of these laws is a central point in its political agenda. One complaint is that these laws were written without the participation or consent of the indigenous communities that will be affected by them.

CONAIE started a lawsuit to declare the new mining law unconstitutional with the help of an environmentalist group. CONAIE's arguments are that according to the constitution, indigenous peoples should have been consulted before the law was written and they were not. The mining law contemplates consultation after the concessions to companies are made and not before, as mandated by the constitution. The mining law claims to prevail over all other laws. However, an ordinary law cannot prevail over organic laws. During the constituent process, representatives were careful to name economic laws ordinary and those laws that pertained to human and social rights and the rights of nature as organic. The rationale for this was that the economy should be at the service of the human being and not the reverse (Acosta 2009). However, the government, by giving preeminence to the mining law and by calling mining a national priority, is trying to reverse this principle, according to CONAIE's lawyers. Furthermore, the mining law obliges the owners of the land to allow mining companies to carry out prospecting and extractive activities on their property in exchange for monetary compensation. CONAIE argues that this regulation violates the integrity, indivisibility, and the right to customary use of indigenous territories established both in the constitution and in international treaties such as the 2007 United Nations Declaration on the Rights of Indigenous Peoples. Finally, the law allows the government and the mining companies to prosecute and repress the inhabitants of the areas where these activities take place if they oppose them (Acosta 2009). The Constitutional Court has already ruled in this case and has decided that the mining law is only conditionally constitutional in indigenous territories, and it is unambiguously constitutional in nonindigenous territories. The condition is that in indigenous territories, companies need to carry out a process of consultation with communities before beginning prospecting activities. Despite this legal complexity, according to informants working in the mining sector, companies operate in Ecuador under this law.

CONAIE and ecologist groups such as Acción Ecológica (Ecological Action) have criticized the draft of the water law. A source of dispute is that the government wants to create a single water authority that would eliminate the autonomy that indigenous communities used to enjoy in regulating the use of water. This would again threaten the plurinational character of the Ecuadorian state because the law does not respect the rights of communities, peoples, nationalities, and peasants who have their own forms of organization of water distribution and use. Although the constitution establishes that water cannot be privatized, the water law, according to indigenous activists and environmentalists, gives priority to the industrial use of water by hydroelectric and mining companies. Also, the water law establishes that the use of water can be transferred with a property and that water that is naturally retained in a property belongs to the owner of the land. This is considered a form of privatization of water that contradicts what is mandated by the constitution, which is that water cannot be privatized. An important issue is that the law ratifies previous concessions, which, according to CONAIE, again allows for the privatization of water and also hinders its redistribution to common people, which is required by the constitution. Currently, water is very unequally distributed in Ecuador. Peasants have little access to water, while it is hoarded by agribusinesses, large landowners, and hydroelectric and mining companies. Thus, the redistribution of water is an important issue for social movements. Moreover, the law does not sanction those who pollute water and does not establish mechanisms of recovery of waters and ecosystems that have been already polluted. Finally, the law establishes tariffs for the use of water to subsidize water systems. Since indigenous peasants built these systems with communal work, they do not agree with this last point either.

CONCLUSION: WHATEVER HAPPENED TO COLLECTIVE INDIGENOUS RIGHTS IN ECUADOR IN THE TWENTY-FIRST CENTURY?

The indigenous movement of Ecuador is confronting a radical new project of state formation in a moment of relative organizational weakness. This government has allowed for some apparent advances in indigenous rights like the legislation on plurinationality, antidiscrimination, affirmative action, and the rights of nature. However, these principles have been weakened through executive decrees, statutory legislation, and the practices of government. One reason for this is that the government has been constituted by different currents, some environmentalist, for indigenous rights, and participatory, some centralist and developmentalist. Unfortunately, the second current seems to be gaining strength at the expense of the first. The high expectations that the process of change raised in indigenous peoples contrast with centralization practices, ambiguities, and setbacks in some important issues. Collective rights and autonomy have been progressively dismantled and apparently substituted by "conditional multiculturalism" limited by the constitution, human rights, and women's rights or displaced by the individual rights promised by antidiscrimination laws and the project of *interculturalidad*. However, although these changes might seem to help achieve a better balance between collective and individual rights, without a strong, well-led collective organization it is likely that not even individual rights will be implemented. Furthermore, the discourses of conditional multiculturalism or *interculturalidad* do not seem to originate in a sincere attempt to solve the drawbacks of multiculturalism, but in an attempt to dismantle collective autonomy without replacing it with another set of solid principles that would be implemented in favor of disadvantaged and colonized groups.

Kurt Weyland (2009) differentiates two kinds of political styles in those governments that have turned toward the Left in Latin America since the late 1990s: a group of governments are more blunt and radical both in their political discourse and in their policies. Others are more moderate and, although they seek to implement social policies and to carry out some redistribution, still follow neoliberal economic prescriptions. According to Weyland, the governments that can allow themselves to be more radical and openly challenge neoliberalism and U.S. hegemony are those who possess large deposits of nonrenewable natural resources, particularly Venezuela, Bolivia, and Ecuador. Therefore, the extraction of natural resources is a key issue for these governments. The majority of these resources are located in indigenous territories. As governments struggle to extract more nonrenewable resources to be able to sustain social policies and to stay relatively independent of U.S. sources of funding, they are likely to provoke conflict with indigenous movements. Paradoxically, damage to indigenous territories and communities is carried out or allowed to happen precisely to fuel the innumerable small programs that are keeping the government quite popular within and outside indigenous communities. The result is a fragmentation of the indigenous movement between those who resist forcefully and those happy with small policies of redistribution. However, in the case of Venezuela, it seems that the polarization between the racist claims of the political opposition and the ethnopopulist discourse of Chávez (Gottberg 2011), the existence of more and more efficient mechanisms for popular participation (López Maya and Lander 2011), and the fact that indigenous groups are smaller and weaker, has not led yet to the kinds of confrontations between post-neoliberal governments and indigenous organizations that we find in Ecuador and Bolivia.

Bebbington and Humphreys Bebbington (2011) argue that extractive activities are expanding aggressively in Andean-Amazonian countries in recent years. Extractive industries are opening new frontiers and deepening their work in already exploited areas. This process is exacerbating social conflict as extractive activities clash with social movements in frontier areas. Interestingly, the authors argue that neoliberal and post-neoliberal governments have responded in similar ways to this wave of global expansion of extractive activities: governments desperately need and take advantage of the profits generated by these activities and claim that they use the revenues to improve the standard of living of the general national population, even when affecting the rights of the groups who live in the frontier. Governments also confront social movements in frontier areas with increasing intolerance and in some cases with violence, and tend to criminalize and stigmatize those who oppose extraction. In this context, indigenous rights and autonomy, even of the more restricted kind, seem to directly threaten this intensified focus on extraction. Will the renewed focus on extraction set a limit to both neoliberal and post-neoliberal kinds of multiculturalism?

However, this logic does not explain the need to rescind the autonomy of indigenous organizations to manage state institutions for indigenous issues. This is explained by the government in terms of the need to strengthen the state to rescue it from its neoliberal retrenchment. This resonates with John French's (2009) argument that what characterizes the New Left in Latin America is its rejection of neoliberalism as well as its desire to return to an earlier period of stronger states such as those that characterized the import substitution period in Latin America. The New Left, according to French, is not anticapitalist, only anti-neoliberal. This process of reinforcement of the central state seems to imply, in the case of Ecuador, reducing the autonomy of social movements and even suppressing them as autonomous organizations and replacing them with groups faithful to the government.

Then what could be the ethnic project of the post-neoliberal Left in Ecuador? On the one hand, as Van Cott (2008) predicted, this Left still needs to claim indigenous rights to legitimate itself, and those appear throughout the Ecuadorian constitution as well as in development plans that emphasize the Andean concept of *sumak kawsay* or the good life. On the other hand, the nonindigenous Left is taking space and support away from the indigenous movement. With a weaker indigenous movement, it is less likely that indigenous constitutional rights will be implemented.

I would like to end with a quote from Rafael Correa's book *Ecuador: From Banana Republic to No Republic*:

Because of the absence of motivated and cohesive societies, solid formal institutions, and values and attitudes that would accelerate progress, the role of adequate leadership is fundamental. Leadership is simply the ability to influence other people, and can be used to serve them.... Good leaders may be fundamental to compensate for the absence of social, institutional, and cultural capital, and their importance will diminish precisely when they help to consolidate this capital. (2009a, 195, my translation)

It is important to note that Correa is writing in a country that produced what has been called the strongest indigenous movement in Latin America. But he does not acknowledge the existence of this social capital while new social capital, the "permitted Indian" of post-neoliberalism,[7] is to be molded by an enlightened and strong leadership.

ACKNOWLEDGMENTS

This research was carried out with the help of a 2008 post-PhD grant from the Wenner-Gren Foundation for Anthropological Research for fieldwork on "the indigenous movement of Ecuador and its nonindigenous allies" and funds from a project of the Ministerio de Economía y Competitividad of Spain titled Hegemonía, Dominación, y Administración de Poblaciones en América Latina (CSO2011–23521), led by Víctor Bretón. Grinnell College provided a perfect environment for writing. I thank David Harrison and David Cook-Martín for this opportunity.

NOTES

1. ALBA is the Bolivarian Alliance for the Peoples of Our America, an organization that imitates and opposes free-trade agreements with the United States.
2. Ecuarunari is the indigenous organization for the Ecuadorian highlands.
3. Inculturation theology consists of the respect of the Catholic Church for non-Western cultures. These cultures are supposed to contain the "seeds of the verb," or manifestations of God's will and Catholic values. The Catholic Church is expected to use the languages and other cultural manifestations of native peoples in its liturgy.
4. The term *interculturalidad* appeared in Latin America and Ecuador in the 1980s and 1990s to describe experiences of coexistence of social groups and cultures within alternative educational systems for indigenous peoples and in municipal governments where indigenous politicians gained prominent positions. This idea emphasizes a process of coexistence and interrelation among diverse groups in conditions of equality. Some scholars, like Rappaport (2005), have spoken of *interculturalidad* as a genuine Latin American concept that they oppose to multiculturalism, which in Latin America is more often associated with a U.S. origin.
5. This legal concept is not new in the constitutions of Ecuador or most other Latin American countries. The idea that states retain the rights to all subsoil (mineral, fossil fuel) resources has very deep legal foundations in Latin America.
6. The Council of Citizen's Participation and Social Control is selected through a system of merits as reflected on résumés and multiple-choice exams given to the candidates. The press asserts that the process of selection is closely supervised by the executive.
7. For a discussion of the "permitted Indian" of neoliberalism, see Charles Hale (2002).

REFERENCES

Abram, Matthias. 2004. "Estado del arte de la educación bilingüe intercultural en América Latina." Washington, DC: Interamerican Development Bank.

Acosta, Alberto. 2009. "Comunicación a los miembros de la Corte Constitucional sobre los efectos económicos, medioambientales, sociales y culturales de la Ley Minera." Corte Constitucional del Ecuador, June 9.

Amnesty International. 2012. *Para que nadie reclame nada: ¿Criminalización del derecho a la protesta en Ecuador?* London: International Secretariat of Amnesty International.

Angosto, Luis Fernando. 2008. "Pueblos indígenas, guaicaipurismo y socialismo del siglo XXI en Venezuela." *Antropológica de la Fundación Lasalle de Ciencias Naturales* 110: 9–33.

Antón, Jhon, and Fernando García. 2009. *Plan plurinacional para eliminar la discriminación racial y la exclusión étnica y cultural.* Quito: Secretaría de Pueblos.

Asamblea Constituyente. 2008. "Ecuador: Estado unitario intercultural y plurinacional." Press communication, Montecristi, Ecuador, April 13.

Asamblea Nacional del Ecuador. 2008. Constitución de la Republica del Ecuador. Comisión Legislativa y de Fiscalización.

Báez, Sara, and Víctor Bretón. 2006. "El enigma del voto étnico o las tribulaciones del movimiento indígena." *Ecuador Debate* 69: 19–36.

Bebbington, Anthony, and Denise Humphreys Bebbington. 2011. "An Andean Avatar: Post-neoliberal and Neo-liberal Strategies for Securing the Unobtainable." *New Political Economy* 16 (1): 131–145.

Becker, Marc. 2008. *Indians and Leftists in the Making of Ecuador's Modern Indigenous Movements.* Durham, NC: Duke University Press.

Bretón, Víctor. 2005. *Capital social y etnodesarrollo en los Andes.* Quito: CAAP.

Calderón, Guido. 2010. "Mestizos trasnochados." *El Telegrafo*, June 13.

Colloredo-Mansfeld, Rudi. 2009. *Fighting Like a Community: Andean Civil Society in an Era of Indian Uprisings.* Chicago: University of Chicago Press.

CONAIE. 2010. "Resolución de la Asamblea Extraordinaria de CONAIE." CONAIE, www.conaie.nativeweb.org, February 26.

Correa, Rafael. 2009a. *Ecuador: De banana republic a la no republica.* Bogota: Random House Mondadori.

Correa, Rafael. 2009b. "Executive Decree 60 (On the Elimination of All Forms of Racism and Discrimination)." September 28. Presidencia de la República del Ecuador, www.presidencia.gob.ec.

Correa, Rafael. 2009c. "Executive Decree 196 (Regulation of the Intercultural Bilingual System of Education and Designation of Its Authorities)." December 29. Presidencia de la República del Ecuador, www.presidencia.gob.ec.

Correa, Rafael. 2009d. "Executive Decree 1585 (On the Transfer of the Intercultural Bilingual Education System to the Ministry of Education)." February 18. Presidencia de la República del Ecuador, www.presidencia.gob.ec.

Correa, Rafael. 2009e. "Executive Decree 1780 (On Catholic Missions)." June 12. Presidencia de la República del Ecuador, www.presidencia.gob.ec.

de la Torre, Carlos. 2010. *Populist Seduction in Latin America*, 2nd ed. Athens: Ohio University Press.

de la Torre, Carlos. 2011. "Corporatism, Charisma, and Chaos: Ecuador's Police Rebellion in Context." *NACLA* 44 (1): 25–29.

de Sousa, Boaventura. 2007. *La reinvención del estado y el estado plurinacional.* Santa Cruz de Bolivia: CENDA.

DINEIB (Dirección Nacional de Educación Intercultural Bilingüe). 2008a. Communication: "¿Plurinacionalidad sin instituciones indígenas tiene sentido?" July 7, www.dineib.gob.ec.

DINEIB. 2008b. "El Quichua es una novelería según Correa." July 23. www.dineib.gob.ec

Escobar, Arturo. 2010. "Latin America at a Crossroads: Alternative Modernizations, Post-liberalism, or Post-development." *Cultural Studies* 24 (1): 1–65.

Fraser, Nancy. 1996. *Justice Interruptus: Critical Reflections on the Postsocialist Condition.* New York: Routledge.

French, John. 2009. "Understanding the Politics of Latin America's Plural Lefts (Chavez/Lula): Social Democracy, Populism, and Convergence on the Path to a Post-neoliberal World." *Third World Quarterly* 30 (2): 349–370.

Gottberg, Luis Duno. 2011. "The Color of Mobs: Racial Politics, Ethnopopulism, and Representation in the Chavez Era." In *Venezuela's Bolivarian Democracy*, edited by David Smilde and Daniel Hellinger. Durham, NC: Duke University Press.

Hale, Charles. 2002. "Does Multiculturalism Menace? Governance, Cultural Rights and the Politics of Identity in Guatemala." *Journal of Latin American Studies* 34: 485–524.

López Maya, Margarita, and Luis Lander. 2011. "Participatory Democracy in Venezuela: Origins, Ideas, and Implementation." In *Venezuela's Bolivarian Democracy*, edited by David Smilde and Daniel Hellinger. Durham, NC: Duke University Press.

Martínez Novo, Carmen. 2007. "¿Es el multiculturalismo estatal un factor de profundización de la democracia en América Latina?" In *Ciudadanía y exclusión: Ecuador y España frente al espejo*, edited by Víctor Bretón, Francisco García, Antoni Jové, and Maria José Vilalta, 182–202. Madrid: Catarata.

Martínez Novo, Carmen. 2009. "The Salesian Missions of Ecuador: Building an Anti-neoliberal Nation through the Cultural and Political Construction of the Indigenous Movement." In *Bridging the Gaps: Faith-Based Organizations, Neoliberalism, and Development in Latin America and the Caribbean*, edited by Tara Hefferan, Julie Adkins, and Laurie Occhipinti. New York: Lexington Books.

Ministerio de Educación del Ecuador. 2009. "El gobierno de la Revolución Ciudadana fortalece la educación intercultural bilingüe." Ministry of Education, www.educacion.gob.ec.

Montaluisa, Luis. 1990. "La educación intercultural bilingüe en el Ecuador." In *La educación indígena en el Ecuador*, edited by Consuelo Yánez, 163–179. Quito: Abya Yala.

Mosonyi, Esteban. 2012. "La situación Yanomami en la cultura actual." E-mail communication to the Section of Ethnicity, Race, and Indigenous Peoples of the Latin American Studies Association, September 14.

Ospina, Pablo. 2009. "Nos vino un huracán político: La crisis de la CONAIE." In *Los Andes en Movimiento*, edited by Pablo Ospina, 123–146. Quito: Corporación Editora Nacional.

Postero, Nancy. 2007. *Now We Are Citizens: Indigenous Politics in Postmulticultural Bolivia.* Stanford, CA: Stanford University Press.

Postero, Nancy. 2010. "After the Revolution: Shifting Notions of Indigeneity in Evo Morales's Bolivia." Paper presented at the conference Repositioning Indigeneity in Latin America," Johns Hopkins University, Baltimore.

Quintero Lopez, Rafael, and Erika Sylva Charvet. 2010. "Ecuador: La alianza de la derecha y el corporativismo en el putch del 30 de septiembre de 2010." Partido Socialista Frente Amplio del Ecuador, www.psfaecuador.org.

Ramón Valarezo, Galo. 2008. "¿Plurinacionalidad o interculturalidad en la Constitución?" Unpublished manuscript, Constituent Assembly of Montecristi, Ecuador.

Rappaport, Joanne. 2005. *Intercultural Utopias: Public Intellectuals, Cultural Experimentation and Ethnic Pluralism in Colombia.* Durham, NC: Duke University Press.

Tuaza, Luis Alberto. 2009. "Cansancio organizativo." In *Repensando los movimientos indígenas*, edited by Carmen Martínez. Quito: FLACSO.

Van Cott, Donna Lee. 2008. "Indigenous Peoples and the Left: Tentative Allies." *Global Dialogue* 10.

Van Cott, Donna Lee. 2009. "Indigenous Movements Lose Momentum." *Current History* 108 (715): 83–89.

Walsh, Catherine. 2009. "Plurinacionalidad e interculturalidad." In *Interculturalidad, Estado, Sociedad: Luchas (de)coloniales de nuestra época.* Quito: Abya Yala.

Weyland, Kurt. 2009. "The Rise of Latin America's Two Lefts: Insights from Rentier State Theory." *Comparative Politics* 41 (2): 145–164.

Yashar, Deborah. 2005. *Contesting Citizenship in Latin America*. Cambridge: Cambridge University Press.

Zamosc, León. 2007. "The Indian Movement and Political Democracy in Ecuador." *Latin American Politics and Society* 49 (3): 1–34.

PART THREE
MULTICULTURAL AND AUTONOMY MOVEMENTS IN OAXACA, MEXICO

6 What We Need Are New Customs

Multiculturality, Autonomy, and Citizenship in Mexico and the Lessons of Oaxaca

Víctor Leonel Juan Martínez (translated by Michael S. Danielson)

Latin America's first wave of constitutional reforms to recognize the rights of indigenous peoples and communities in the final decades of the twentieth century was followed by significant normative progress in the first decade of the twenty-first century with the approval of the United Nations Declaration of the Rights of Indigenous Peoples. Following these changes in the rights of indigenous peoples, the discussion has been increasingly focused on making these legislative advances concrete in practical terms.

The indigenous rights debate is all the more dynamic because of the advances made by the indigenous movement, its political triumphs, and its internal contradictions. The triumphs include the winning of the Bolivian presidency by Evo Morales and his subsequent disputes over the autonomy of the opposition strongholds of the eastern Media Luna region (see chapter 3, this volume). Other important examples include the emergence—and subsequent retreat from the national stage—of the Zapatista National Liberation Army (EZLN, by its Spanish acronym) in Mexico, as well as the variants of the Pachakuti movement in Ecuador. Finally, this debate becomes even more dynamic when we consider the complexities of guerrilla conflict, drug trafficking, indigenous and Afro-Colombian self-determination struggles, and the dynamics expressed by the "Mingas" in Colombia and the contradictions presented by the autonomous regions of Nicaragua.

Discussions about the daily exercise of the right to difference, and the specific practices that make it possible, are guided by several axes, including the exercise of the right to self-determination, the ever-present conflict between collective and individual rights, and sociopolitical conflict that sometimes results in violence.

The southeastern state of Oaxaca, Mexico, brings together these different axes, and is a paradigmatic case of how the politics of recognition in Mexico has worked in practice. There have been a number of changes to the state's constitution since 1990, but the most important of these was the recognition of the so-called *usos y costumbres* (indigenous customary law, literally: usages and customs, or UC) for the election of local authorities. This reform, approved in 1995, allowed 418 of the state's 570 municipalities to elect their local governments using different rules than the liberal ones that prevail nationally.

In addition, it is important to view this recognition as opening a necessary space for the construction of intercultural dialogue. This is particularly evident if we consider that the daily practice of citizenship in these municipalities and communities ranges from the liberal (as established in the national legal framework) to the differentiated. On the one hand, communities resort to state and federal electoral institutions to attend to and resolve conflicts. At the same time, however, communities address internal problems themselves. This coexistence of these different spaces, which cause conflicts in many cases but also offer practical solutions, constitutes an intercultural exercise.[1]

The reform that was approved in 1995 under the name of *usos y costumbres* and in 1997 as "norms of customary law" recognizes the existence of differentiated systems of sociopolitical organization and different rules of citizenship construction.[2] For this reason, more than as an appeal to the conservation of "the indigenous tradition," it is necessary to know what happens in the present and how citizenship is constructed as a result of quotidian practices of the forms of social organization in force in the community.

Oaxaca's municipalities are experiencing intense sociopolitical change. This dynamic translates into contradictions, conflicts, and consensus. These changes pose challenges to the preservation of the traditions of indigenous communities, which is reflected in the constant and passionate debates on the subject. In municipalities, this debate and these challenges often devolve into conflict, which is most typically manifested in the competition for municipal power. A focus on political competition and conflict makes possible a concrete appreciation of how communal rights to difference and self-determination are exercised, or not.

In this chapter, though it is assumed that this collection of practices, structures, and norms constitutes differentiated modes of sociopolitical organization, I employ the popularized term *usos y costumbres* (UC), because the communities themselves have adopted the term, giving it a new meaning, as well as to avoid confusion when explaining the processes to which we refer.

MULTICULTURALITY, AUTONOMY, AND SUBNATIONAL INSTITUTIONS

Local spaces are of great importance to the struggle for self-determination of indigenous peoples because they have constituted contested spaces. First, there are concrete experiences of autonomy in subnational spaces. On the other hand, nation-states have focused on these local spaces both to advance the politics of recognition and for the instrumental utility of isolating the demands of the indigenous movement (see chapter 2, this volume).

Examples of the former include alternative local governance, such as that created in Ecuador by the Council of Indigenous Nationalities of Ecuador (Consejo de Nacionalidades Indigenas de Ecuador, or CONAIE), which mandated that local governments generate a new development model based on three fundamental pillars: the democratization of local power; transparency in public administration and politics; and the management of economic, social, political, and cultural development (Tibán and García 2008, 151–187). Examples of the latter include Bolivia, where there have been strong criticisms of the model employed by the State, which in the 1990s made use of multicultural practices to neutralize the growing autonomy movement of the Andean communities. In this case, government policy was not motivated by the fundamental objective of recognizing cultural difference, but rather to incorporate an ethnic dimension within state institutions (Regalsky and Quisbert 2008).

In Chile, the dictatorship of Augusto Pinochet instituted a reform in 1980, creating various municipalities with indigenous populations in the Andean region. At the start of the 1990s, the democratization of local governments coincided with a rapid increase in indigenous consciousness and level of organization. In these cases, ethnic identity was actively present among local actors. It was used as an instrument with which to promote and confront different interests, including those that had been established in Andean municipalities and those emerging from relationships to the State and with capital (Gundermann 2003, 55–57).

There are many examples of this in Latin America. In Mexico, the Zapatista project has grown in autonomous territories and through the practices of local governments (autonomous municipalities, the *caracoles,* and the Juntas de Buen Gobierno).³ As with the Zapatista communities, other places in the country have had locally constructed experiences of difference-based autonomy without being recognized under a legal framework. The absence of legal recognition of autonomy in much of the country makes the study of the Oaxaca experience of particular importance.

Autonomy in Oaxaca: Resistance or Concession?

Two decades since the beginning of the process of recognition of indigenous rights in Oaxaca, the causes of this process continue to be debated. On one side, this process has been marked by political and electoral conflict at the municipal level. The isolation of demands to the community space has subordinated local agendas of microregional or state-level impact (such as projects to extract natural resources). These facts support arguments that multiculturalism is used as a tool of state policy to limit rather than expand the rights of indigenous communities. In this way, essential rights like that to territory are excluded, and only the cultural rights of the "acceptable Indian" (Hale 2007) are recognized. As such, it would seem that recognition was a concession by the State from "above" to guarantee the control and subordination of indigenous peoples and communities. However, the legislation in Oaxaca was a pioneer among policies of concrete recognition of the political rights of indigenous peoples.

Nonetheless, in the Oaxacan case the practice of autonomy goes beyond the recognition politics of the end of the last century. Oaxaca has a long history of recognition policies. Since Mexico's independence the coexistence of at least sixteen different ethnic groups has been recognized. This situation is also reflected in the territorial composition of the state, as almost 80 percent of property is collectively titled (*ejido* or *communal,* as opposed to private; Atlas Agrario del Estado de Oaxaca 2002).

In Oaxaca, de facto, and in many cases de jure, recognition arose out of a historical relationship. From the perspective of the state, this relationship was one of respect and control over indigenous communities. From the perspective of the indigenous communities, this relationship combined compliance with autonomy. It was not the unconditional acceptance of liberalism, a capitulation to the new elites, that explained the acceptance of this peculiar relationship with the state. Rather, indigenous peoples and communities accepted this relationship as an opportunity to exercise a camouflaged resistance within the institutions and the norms created by them. This is demonstrated by the strength of communities, for example, in their successful defense of territory and natural resources (see Bailón Corres, 1999).

The constant resistance of the indigenous peoples has been translated into a dynamic of mobilization through the actions of indigenous and social organizations, or through the communities and municipalities themselves. Because of this, legal changes to recognize their rights have also come from this constant pressure (which fluctuates in strength) in Oaxaca. So the recognition of autonomy is a "bottom-up" process, constructed through the resistance and struggle of the indigenous movement.

With the 1995 legislative reform recognizing UC, different sets of actors saw a way to serve their own interests. The state and federal governments saw the reforms as a means to preserve stability and political control when faced with the fear that the Zapatista rebellion in Chiapas would motivate similar actions in Oaxaca. The Party of the Institutional Revolution (PRI) saw recognition as an instrument with which to maintain its hegemony and to contest the advance of opposition parties. The opposition parties saw UC recognition as the crack through which they could increase their influence. The indigenous movement saw it as a response to its demands for autonomy and its recognition as a social subject. The communities saw in the reforms a reaffirmation of their autonomy and a recognition of their daily practices. Social organizations saw the UC municipalities as new spaces of influence and the recognition of their autonomy as an opportunity to displace the parties. Finally, indigenous leaders and intellectuals viewed the recognition of autonomy as the materialization of their utopias.[4]

The politics of recognition in Oaxaca responds, in certain circumstances and spaces, to these many visions and interests. These interests converged in the constitutional recognition of 1995, which political elites used to maintain governability in the state and thus protect their own interests, but that at the same time met the objectives and responded to the demands for which indigenous communities had struggled. As such, the 1995 recognition was an interactive situation that derived from a historical goal of the state as well as through the resistance of indigenous local communities.

Federalism: The Door to Recognition

The politics of the recognition of difference and of the right to self-determination of the indigenous peoples in Mexico and Latin America has been constrained to subnational spaces—community, municipality, region. Indeed, the recognition of autonomy was created by many actors, all with their own agendas. From the perspective of the State, multicultural policies have been used as strategies to "domesticate difference," as a mechanism to depoliticize indigenous struggles for autonomy (Leyva et al. 2008). Also, as in the Oaxaca case, multicultural policy constituted the recognition of the existence of differentiated rules and practice.

The Mexican case exemplifies how both processes have occurred and how constitutional and institutional design is used both to recognize the exercise of autonomy and to inhibit its true realization. In Oaxaca, the recognition in 1995 of UC elections and the 1997 passage of the Law on the Rights of Indigenous Peoples and Communities were made possible because the federal door was opened, as the constitution establishes the autonomy of states to pass legislation with respect to their internal regimes (*Dictamen de la Ley de Derechos* 1998).

Later, in 2001, the federal government closed the door with a constitutional reform which established in Article 2 that "the recognition of indigenous peoples and communities will be done in the constitutions and laws of the states, which should take into account ethnolinguistic characteristics and the physical settlement of communities, in addition to general principles established in previous paragraphs of this article."[5] This power is limited by the federal constitution itself. As Article 124 of the constitution establishes, the powers that are not expressly conceded to the federation are understood to be reserved to the states, which cannot contradict or go beyond that which is established in the federal order. In practice, internal electoral norms or indigenous jurisdictions can be interpreted (and judges have done so) to be in conflict with that which is established in the federal constitution. For this reason, Article 2 of the constitution is, on the one hand, an opening through which our country might advance. On the other hand, however, it is a straitjacket that constrains further advances.

Municipalities: The Floor and the Ceiling of Autonomy

Considering subnational spaces, multiculturalist institutions also represent cracks subject to ethnicization by communities and municipalities and are used to generate new relationships with the State. Additionally, acting in accordance with institutional boundaries, communities struggle for and generate new mechanisms of political representation (e.g., municipal associations or political parties, through the election of state and federal deputy candidates). This double game in which communities reconstitute themselves at the same time as they impact the reconfiguration of the state is what Sousa calls interlegality (Leyva et al. 2008), and is created starting with subnational institutions.

The category of citizenship permits us to continue this process, given that it not only refers to the formal structure of a society but also indicates the struggle for recognition of others as subjects with valid interests, relevant values, and legitimate demands (Sojo 2002). Further, a common criticism of the conventional vision of citizenship is that belonging to a nation-state often means very little to its members in comparison to belonging to subnational communities with which some identify and through which they are able to exercise their rights and obligations (Kabeer 2007). And if it is indeed the case that the idea of citizenship is practically universal, its meanings and the ways in which it is lived are not. One limit to the theoretical debate is that much of it is not empirically grounded as scholars do not know what citizenship means to people, what the perspectives of "common" citizens are, or what those meanings might tell us about the construction of inclusive societies (Kabeer 2007). Hence, it is necessary to situate the discussion in specific contexts, because even if there are convergences in the analytical concerns, there are notable regional differences in theoretical orientation and empirics that reflect different histories and particularities in the contexts in which the processes are framed (Maitrayee and Singh 2008).

From here, we may proceed to the relevance of the Oaxacan experience. The most important fact is that the legislation recognizes the right to self-determination for Indian peoples but limits the exercise of this right to a specific territorial delimitation: the municipality. This double process has had different impacts. First, the PRI, which used to rely on these communities as a reservoir of votes, saw a significant decline in its electoral share in those places, permitting the expression of greater political pluralism.[6] This has generated and consolidated new mechanisms of political representation, including intermunicipal associations, social organizations, and participation in political parties. It has demonstrated that the defense of the community, as a base from which to exercise the right to self-determination, does not impede, but rather strengthens the construction of broader spaces for political representation and government, such as microregions and intermunicipalities.

Second, recognition has created new ways to recuperate political control and to restrain indigenous populations. These new practices include the offering of public resources on a conditional basis and an increased corporatization of new political subjects—women, youth, elderly, small producers—through clientelistic practices employed by governments and political parties. Recognition has also stimulated corrupt practices that benefit individuals or groups, divert funds from the municipal treasury for political campaigns, or a combination of both. Finally, there have even been changes following recognition that diminish or violate municipal autonomy.

These facts lead us to the conclusion that the defense of self-determination ends up converting the municipality into an island, strengthening its internal life but generating few strong relationships with external processes. These factors help to explain the retreat of the indigenous movement and the persistence of authoritarian practices seen in Oaxaca over the past decade, and which in 2006 led to the outbreak of social conflict.[7] These processes, which are not homogeneous and should be appreciated in their full diversity, show that the municipality has become the "floor" and the "ceiling" for the exercise of autonomy.

FROM DIFFERENTIATED CITIZENSHIP TO MULTIPLE CITIZENSHIPS

In Oaxaca's UC municipalities, citizens join together in the public space, not as individuals subject to rights and obligations in full equality, but rather as members of a political community (the municipality, the community), governed by criteria of ethnic or cultural identity. Accordingly, they find themselves governed by legitimation mechanisms based on the collective in which fulfilling obligations antecedes the exercise of rights. It is these guiding axes that are being transformed by a series of external and internal factors and, simultaneously, by their relationship with the State. At the same time, members of UC municipalities continue to participate as citizens of the nation-state, which generates the exercise of multiple citizenships. For this reason, it is necessary to understand if these transformations come from a change in indigenous communities' conception of citizenship, through a process of modernization of their own cultural codes, and if they enhance autonomy or favor state control.

Until a few years ago it was not a problem to comply with these principles: subjects living in a rural community dedicated themselves to productive activities (agriculture, fishing, forestry). Insofar as they had subaltern identities (peasant, woman, *comunero*, youth, elderly),[8] these identities did not create serious contradictions and one's characteristics as a member of the community were prioritized. However, reality has now become complicated and one can simultaneously hold various identities, which vary depending on sociopolitical context and can have equivalent hierarchies or work to the detriment of one's identity as a member of a community. Such situations can create a range of tensions.

Recognition impacts the internal lives of municipalities. First, legal recognition equips municipalities with mechanisms with which to exercise their autonomy. At the same time, recognition of autonomy creates new conditions in the competition for local power, as disagreements that were previously repressed are now openly discussed. Although these contradictions come to a head in electoral processes, UC systems of community organization are about much more than elections, and practically encompass the entire community life.

Together with this, structural problems, such as the exclusion from power of certain sectors of the population, become visible with the recognition of autonomy. This situation coincides with other processes, both internal (e.g., generational renewal, changes of productive activities, professionalization of community members, and rural-urban transit, among others) and external (e.g., migration, decentralization policies, globalization, struggles for women's and human rights, the appearance of new religions, etc.).

Although indigenous municipalities and communities have always had to adapt to new contexts, they have never been simultaneously permeated by as many forces to the extent that they are now. These forces necessitate concrete responses that conserve the essential principles of their differentiated systems. In addition, we must consider that UC municipalities are embedded within broader communities (i.e., the state and the national) and, because of the phenomenon of migration, some community members are simultaneously citizens of another nation (such as the migrants that have acquired U.S. citizenship). So these communities must develop within distinct spaces and times, and they respond to different conceptions of citizenship (differentiated citizenship in the communal space, and liberal citizenship in the other spaces). This generates tensions in community life, including serious conflicts, with new pragmatic responses to situations of conflict.

Using different conceptions of citizenship is the best way to give form to the dissent over the interpretation of the principles that mobilize subjects and provide clearer points of identification (Mouffe 1999). An example of this can be found in those municipalities' citizens who have switched from fulfilling community obligations, the basis of differentiated citizenship, to exercising the attributes of liberal citizenship. Another clear case can be seen when municipal elections by *usos y costumbres* and state or federal elections are held on a single day. These elections differ not only in procedure but also in their political and cultural conception. So the community citizen can leave an assembly to go to the ballot box and deposit her vote as a Mexican citizen. Alternatively, she can participate in the election of municipal authorities under the system of political parties, and then participate in an assembly of *comuneros* or *ejidatarios*, where the defense of the territory makes it possible to put differences aside and build consensus.

Other situations have emerged that also demonstrate these mechanisms of joining together or collaboration between two distinct normative orders. For example, participation as a precinct official for state or federal elections counts in some UC communities as *tequio*.[9] In 2006 the Assembly of the Municipal Authorities of the Zoogocho Sector (Asamblea de Autoridades Municipales del Sector Zoogocho), which groups nineteen communities, and the Liberal Union of Municipal Governments (Unión Liberal de Ayuntamientos, or ULA), which encompasses twenty-six municipalities, together with indigenous intellectuals and leaders from the Northern Sierra (Sierra Norte),[10] called upon the political parties to select their candidates for federal deputy in consultation with the indigenous population and in accordance with their internal mechanisms and rules. Only the Party of the Democratic Revolution (Partido de la Revolución Democrática, or PRD) complied with this call, and the candidate was then the mayor of Guelatao de Juarez. In the election the support of the communities and their authorities was visible, and he won the election.

In addition, both of the above-mentioned associations have become fundamental spaces of representation and political intermediation between the indigenous peoples of the region and state and federal authorities. Their capacity and legitimacy provide them with great strength in negotiations (see Hernández-Díaz and Juán Martínez 2007).

Before the 1995 reform, serving on the Municipal Committee of the PRI was recognized as a *cargo* in the structure of communities.[11] This is a demonstration of the paradoxical "double game" of indigenous communities to maintain their political autonomy. Ties to this party permitted the subsequent legal recognition of authorities elected in accordance with internal rules, which contradicted the existing legal framework. With the recognition of UC and the increase in political competition in the state, this particular practice has disappeared. But UC municipalities continue to show their adaptability, and in the new context are increasingly substituting the practice of public voting by show of hands in community assemblies with the electoral mechanisms typical of representative democracies, such as ballots, precincts, the secret vote, party tickets, and election officials.

There are many examples of the creation of new rules and agreements that allow for the maintenance of the principles of the collectivity:[12] the substitution of *tequios* with other obligations, the option for migrants to designate family members or to pay a replacement when one is named to serve in a *cargo*, the separation of the formerly interwoven religious and civil structures of communities to allow those who practice non-Catholic religions to fulfill their duties and exercise their community rights while guaranteeing the freedom of religion, and the incorporation of actors previously excluded from the exercise of citizenship.

It is not only in the area of elections that these transformations have occurred. With respect to the implementation of justice, judicial aldermen (*síndicos*)[13] and local judges (*alcaldes*) have demonstrated their autonomy to make rulings, at least those related to certain legal formalities (e.g., citations, acts), and to ensure they are complied with, though they must be careful that the sanctions they enforce do not violate human rights norms (DPLF 2007). Even in such a liberal sphere as the market, there are examples of communal business based on collective property and managed in ways very different from standard business practices. That said, such businesses have made solid and successful inroads in such places as the forest communities of Ixtlán de Juárez, San Pedro El Alto, and Textitlán in Oaxaca, and San Juan Pueblo Nuevo in the state of Michoacán (Garibay Orozco 2008).

Of course, this is a double process. From the state perspective there have also been adjustments; whereas the state previously tolerated differentiated practices, they have since implemented legal reforms to recognize them. There are de facto situations that must be made to fit legal formalities by government agents, and new political actors whose points of view are recognized and respected. In many cases, such as public transportation concessions, authorization is given only with the approval of affected communities, and communities are even permitted to own their own transportation services. In quotidian political practice, it is necessary to make adjustments to guarantee harmonious relations, or at least governability.

Between Agreement and Breakdown: The Conflicts

It is common that upon arriving in Oaxacan municipalities and communities, and upon learning about their characteristics, when the moment to touch upon their political organization arrives, their inhabitants or authorities indicate that they have a certain number of citizens. The "children of the *pueblo*," of which we are told in many ethnographic descriptions, are now referred to as "citizens," a conceptual category used, with the opposite meaning of the liberal usage, to name those who sustain the collectivity and fulfill their obligations to it. Accordingly, they are considered to be the foundation of the organizational structure of the community, and some use the synonym "contributors" to describe those who are up to date on their financial contributions (*cooperaciones*), *tequios*, and community responsibilities. Community citizens, then, are defined as those people (normally men) that fulfill their obligations, *tequios*, and *cooperaciones*, participate in community assemblies, and are eligible to be named to posts in the system of *cargos*. This is the case, independently of where a community member may be living at the time, as residency has ceased to be a necessary requirement to acquire the character of community citizen everywhere.

In the same way, the term *usos y costumbres* has been ethnicized. To differentiate this political regime from the regime based on party competition, as well as to describe the norms of community coexistence and the ways in which differences are resolved, justice is applied, or contributions to collective well-being are made, residents of those communities often use the phrase: "Here we follow *usos y costumbres*."

But citizenship also means exclusion. Accordingly, there are population groups that are not recognized as citizens, despite having the ability to comply, or actually complying, with the norms of community coexistence.

Municipalities and communities with this system of social organization are affected by different internal and external processes, which generate a series of dynamics that require changes to the rules of their organizational systems and the ways in which citizenship is exercised. These transformations have caused a multiplicity of conflicts to arise in the recent past, leading communities to come to new internal agreements to make it possible for these differentiated systems to remain in place.

We can better understand the multiplicity of conflicts if we consider that there is a de facto coexistence of two normative orders with diametrically opposed and theoretically irreconcilable origins: collective rights against individual rights. This situation intensifies conflicts, but it also makes it necessary to search for alternatives or pragmatic solutions that make it possible to find mechanisms that permit day-to-day coexistence.

With the daily process of citizenship construction in these municipalities, we assume that if this category is considered to have legal-moral status (normatively as a collection of rights and ethically as a collection of responsibilities) and provides an identity through which a person recognizes and feels a sense of belonging to a society (Cortina 1998), we must then see how these bases are established. This is especially important considering that in the present case, the ethical-normative aspect begins with the rights of the collectivity, whether a priori or as an indispensable condition to be able to exercise individual rights. Upon understanding that community citizenship is in permanent construction, we can assess the causes of conflict in these municipalities and the particular forms of conflict resolution.

The number of conflicts in the past fifteen years demonstrates this dynamic of the reaccommodation and restructuring of these normative systems, since, even when differences do not emerge during electoral processes, it is precisely through the competition for local power that the renegotiation of rules becomes visible. The high number of conflicts in recent years demonstrates this dynamic.

According to data from the State Electoral Institute (Instituto Estatal Electoral, IEE), ten municipalities experienced conflicts and fifty-nine had "problematic situations" in 1995.[14] In 1998, eighty municipalities experienced conflicts. In 2001, the number of conflicts reached 107, and elections were annulled in eighteen municipalities. In addition, between 2002 and 2004 municipal power was dissolved in twenty-nine municipalities and nine mayors left office early to seek another office (*solicitaron licencia*). In 2004 there were around twenty "problematic situations"; elections were annulled in ten municipalities; and in five more they did not occur. Of those fifteen municipalities, only three held special elections. In 2005, some thirty municipalities were considered to be "hot spots" (*focos rojos*, i.e., in danger of devolving into conflict). In 2007, elections were nullified in ten municipalities and in fifteen the Electoral Tribunal of the Federal Judiciary (Tribunal Electoral del Poder Judicial de la Federación, or TEPJF) filed a constitutional challenge to the decision of the Electoral College (of the state of Oaxaca) to validate or annul different elections.

In 2010, fifty elections were annulled in UC municipalities, the highest number in history. To explain this atypical case, it will be necessary to review the actions of the state electoral bodies. The IEE and the State Electoral Tribunal (Tribunal Estatal Electoral, or TEE) annulled forty elections and the TEPJF annulled ten, which is analyzed below.

Though these data give us some sense of the issue, it is important to recognize that the IEE uses discretionary criteria to determine if a municipality is in conflict. In some cases the slightest formal violation of the rules is counted by the IEE as a conflict, even when it requires only a minor correction. On the other hand, for reasons of procedural timing, some conflicts that result in violent confrontations (like Amoltepec and Quetzaltepec between 2001 and 2004) are not classified as such by the IEE.

Finally, the frequency of conflict in UC municipalities is related to internal and external structural problems of the system that are manifested in the following:

1. The exclusion of certain population sectors or emergent actors: women, youths, migrants, and practitioners of the nonmajority religion, among others
2. The absence of mechanisms to ensure the political representation of minorities
3. Election requirements and procedures
4. Community autonomy, which, in opposition to municipal unity, causes problems between the municipal seat (*cabecera*) and *agencias*[15]
5. A lack of legal and institutional mechanisms to improve access to electoral justice (*jurisdicción electoral*)
6. The changes in the regional system of dominance

To demonstrate these municipal dynamics, I refer to the most fundamental and evident causes of this conflict.

Community versus Individual: The Principle of Construction and the Root of the Problem

The act agreed to by the general community assembly of the Zapotec municipality of Santa María Quiegolani on May 11, 2008, stated the following: "The community in general and especially the women of Quiegolani categorically disown Eufrosina Cruz Mendoza as a citizen and resident, given that she has never lived in this municipality and its members do not feel supported by what she has said and done with the news media and before any government agency" (CNDH, 2008).[16] This occurred as a community response to the activism of Eufrosina Cruz, who one year previously attempted to run for the office of mayor. On November 4, 2007, when municipal elections were held in Quiegolani, Eufrosina sought the nomination, for which she had campaigned previously in the community. In the electoral procedures of the municipality, each citizen writes on a ballot the name of the person for whom he or she is voting for the post and deposits it in an urn. When the ballots were counted, all votes in favor of Eufrosina Cruz were annulled, as she was considered to be ineligible because she had not fulfilled the requirements to serve in the post. Faced with these facts, she publicly announced that she was denied the right to participation because she is female (Juan Martínez 2008).

Even so, the news media published the story that she had won the election and that her triumph was not recognized. Although she did not win the election and had not fulfilled the prerequisites to be eligible to run—as she had left the community fifteen years earlier and had not lived there since, and had not been involved in the constant construction of the collectivity—she argued that the recognized winner of the elections did not live in the community either and had not met various community obligations (Cruz Mendoza 2007).

The case of Eufrosina is evidence of the most complicated aspect of UC systems, the fact that some individuals are excluded. Her subsequent activism demonstrates the antagonism between individual and collective rights, and accounts for the formal and real context within which differentiated systems of organization develop along with the intervention of internal and external agents (news media, deputies, parties, and a diversity of other political actors). It is particularly necessary to call attention to a false argument that presents the requirements of community eligibility as synonymous to exclusion. Because of this, beyond questions of the legitimacy of Eufrosina's struggle, it is important to be careful of government actions that overgeneralize and disqualify the system without considering the context and its internal characteristics (Sierra 2009, 73–96).

This explains the community response. They felt that their rights to self-determination as a collectivity—to govern themselves according to their own rules—were being threatened. Faced by this siege, the municipal authorities convened an assembly to step down from their posts and "turn in the *bastón de mando*" to whomever the citizens chose.[17] So although Eufrosina may be recognized elsewhere, in Quiegolani they do not see things that way. For her community, the mayor was legitimately elected and Eufrosina, through her political activism, could have caused him to be stripped of his rightful post. The community responded by revoking

Eufrosina's citizenship. Although, as was subsequently documented, no concrete actions were taken to impede Eufrosina's transit, local services (e.g., water, electricity) were not cut off to her family members, nor has she suffered other aggressive actions, the truth is that her banishment was a symbolic act for the community.

Without diminishing the extent of this problem, it is necessary to calmly review this type of situation. Tlalixtac de Cabrera, another Zapotec municipality, was from 2008 to 2010 governed by a woman. The mayor had a long history of service to her community, even though formally, as in Quiegolani, women were not considered to be holders of citizenship rights. Nevertheless, Rafaela Hernández Chávez's career of *cargo* service in her community crossed many different spaces: the church, the school, and health services, until it reached the community and *ejido* assemblies (Hernández Chávez et al. 2010).

In contrast to Eufrosina, her residency in the community, despite the fact that she worked outside of it, allowed her to weave this complex web of relationships and to comply with the obligations of citizenship before she was proposed as a mayoral candidate for the first time in 2004. Because of her choice not to seek the position at that time, as well as the strength of the other candidates, she did not win that election. In 2007, however, she was nominated again and won the mayoral election easily. Not only was female leadership accepted despite iron rules and community structures, but these structures and rules have now taken on a new dynamic.

In San Juan Guelavía, faced with high rates of migration, women began to cover their husbands' community obligations and, after becoming visible in the public space, gradually began to have a greater presence. Since 2004, the symbolic message of the assemblies has been revelatory. Women occupy the center of the main plaza when community assemblies are held. Until a few years before, women were rarely even present in the places where assemblies were held. Their first steps were simply making it to the assembly, but remaining on the margins, outside of the center. The situation changed. Now men are the ones that stand on the margins, some even completely at the outer edge of those meetings (Zafra and Juan Martínez 2010).

The fact that advances have been made in some communities does not mean that women no longer face marginalization, inequality, and exclusion. Although women now participate in many municipalities and have even been elected as mayors, in a large number of places they are relegated to lower positions or the *cargos* in which their service counts toward the service requirements of related men (e.g., fathers, husbands, brothers). In others, due to the conditions under which their service unfolds, the context, and the demanding nature of the system, some women do not wish to participate, as this often adds additional burdens to those they already have (Hernández Cárdenas 2009). In many places, women are still openly marginalized and discriminated against.

Exclusion and Inclusion: A Question of Faith?

In some communities, conflicts occur because some members practice a religion different from that of the majority (as a general rule, Catholicism). These conflicts are not necessarily because some profess a different faith; rather, they emerge when a community's system and internal rules are such that the structure of *cargos* and community service combines that of the administrative and public order and, due to colonial inheritance, that of the religious sphere. When both types of service overlap, citizens are required to serve both structures without distinction (civil and religious).

In San Juan Bosco Chuxnabán, a municipal *agencia* in San Miguel Quetzaltepec (CEDHO 2011), as well as in Capulapam de Méndez, Santa María Yohueche, San Juan Juquila Mixe (CEDHO 1997) and other communities, those who practice other religions have alleged harassment and have even been expelled for refusing to serve in *cargos* or to serve the Catholic Church. Contrary to what it seems, what is sanctioned is the failure to fulfill community obligations more than religious beliefs (even when separation is weak). Nevertheless, this variable again shows the confrontation between the rights of the collectivity and those of individuals.

It is necessary to look at how this situation has been resolved in other places. In the 1980s, some of the inhabitants of Villa Díaz Ordaz converted to new religions, mainly Jehovah's Witnesses and evangelicals. Before a split could occur in the internal system of organization, the community decided to separate the religious *cargos* from the civil *cargos*. Under the new norms, even when accounted for in the notebook of community services, those that fall within the religious structure are only obligatory for Catholics. Those of other religions only give service to different committees, the Commission of Communal Resources, and the municipal government—so much so that many of those of other religions have served as aldermen (one as judicial alderman or *síndico*, the most powerful member of the municipal government after the mayor) or *alcaldes* (local judges) and participate without problems in various public spaces of community decision making.

These cases illustrate the complexity entailed by these differentiated systems, their contradictions, and structural problems, but also of the capacity of communities to adapt to these new challenges, contexts, and conditions. Those that idealize the governability achieved by this system, as much as those who only emphasize its problems, are at risk of overgeneralizing.

These cases also illustrate the agreements that allow for rule changes and to make compatible that which appears to be irreconcilable: collective and individual rights. Even so, this alerts us to the risks that occur when consensus is not reached and there is no capacity for the two rights regimes to adapt to each other.

The Local and the Global: Tension Factors

In the assembly to elect municipal authorities, the inhabitants of San Pablo Macuiltianguis have used an interesting process since 2004. Despite the fact that people vote by a show of hands, counted immediately, the final result is not determined until the vote tally is sent, via fax, from community members who simultaneously hold an assembly in Los Angeles, California. Candidates are proposed by people in Los Angeles as well as in an assembly held in the community, and the candidate list is put to a vote on both sides. Those in the community speak to their counterparts in Los Angeles over the phone to report the results of their respective assemblies. At the end, the votes cast in both assemblies are counted and the winner is determined.

More than half of the population of the municipality lives outside of the community, the majority in the United States. Rather than becoming disengaged from their community of origin, in many senses migrants have become what sustains the community: they remain current on their duties; they search for new ways to preserve their organization; and they have re-created the community in their destination. This confers upon them the right to participate in decisions, such as the election of the local government.

Migration has caused many transformations in these differentiated systems of organization and in the construction of communitarian citizenship. In some cases, like Macuiltianguis, there was a gradual adaptation to the new reality. In other places, contrary processes are generated.

In Santa Ana del Valle, migrants resisted complying with the obligations imposed upon them, particularly the obligation to return home from abroad when they were named to serve in a *cargo* (Aquino Morales 2002). This situation generated an interesting process of internal reflection between 2002 and 2004, which utilized a mechanism that had been specifically designed to revise the organizational structure and system in which different sectors of the population were represented. The result of a two-year process, which even included a public consultation, was the restructuring of the community's system of *cargos*, obligations, and the acceptable forms of compliance (Morales and Camarena 2002).

This exercise motivated broad participation among those living in the community and the migrants; they discussed a diverse range of topics concerning the community, its organization, and its rules. Beyond the changes made, there was a reaffirmation of the community's ethnic identity, a resumption of its *usos y costumbres* as a way of preserving it, but also to maintain governability. In this case, migration generated a process of internal reflection and a dynamic of participation to resolve the new issues.

In both San Andrés Solaga and San Pedro Cajonos, and in many other communities, the tension between migrants and those who remain in the communities is a constant, which has devolved into the suspension of the rights of migrants, the rejection of the migrants, and even in the suspension of rights and/or the expulsion of some who attempt to return to their community, in a topic that is still without resolution (e.g., see Molina 2006; Mateos 2005).

These are not the only intervening variables. In Villa Díaz Ordaz, it was necessary to reform the Parents' Committee (Comité de Padres de Familia), which moved from the general assembly in which it was conducted to the realm of parents of children who studied in one of the community's schools. This was due to the increasing presence of children from a nearby housing development in the neighboring municipality of Tlacolula, but who made use of the educational services of Villa Díaz Ordaz.

Precisely because of problems related to urbanization, the creation of new human settlements and the growth of populations have meant that in San Sebastián Tutla, with a population of greater than fifteen thousand in the whole municipality, the majority lack citizenship rights and are not permitted to participate in decision making or assemblies, much less in the election of municipal authorities. Only community citizens possess these rights, some hundreds of people native to the municipal seat, who even there are becoming a minority compared to the number of settlers that have arrived in the past decade. Most of the population is concentrated in a housing development, El Rosario, created in the 1980s to meet the growing housing demand of the metropolitan zone of the state capital (see Recondo 2007b).

In 1998 this situation led to a mobilization of the residents of the housing development, which was followed by an IEE resolution to change the local electoral regime from UC to political parties. This situation motivated the PRI to mount a legal challenge before the TEE, which revoked the decision of the IEE and resolved that Tutla would continue to be governed by *usos y costumbres*. Beyond what may have been the PRI's true motivations for this decision, its behavior reveals the gaps in electoral law, as citizens of UC municipalities possessed no means of legal challenge. The lack of institutional channels to adjudicate differences explains, in large part, why these differences have to be resolved by means of pressure and political mobilization.[18]

The Rebellion of the Villages: Disputes over the Autonomy of Communities

In many other municipalities, the competition for local power has increased, as public funds now automatically arrive and allow those in power to work toward the benefit of the collectivity, while also generating processes of corruption that have taken various municipalities to the point of political and social decomposition. In addition, the arrival of these resources has led to a decline of *tequio* and an increase in the likelihood that *cargo* service is remunerated.

Among the most visible tensions in UC municipalities are those between the municipal seat and the autonomous communities within municipal borders. The most common disputes at the root of these tensions have to do with the federal funds directly transferred to municipalities (from federal funding branches 28 and 33), as submunicipal communities mobilize to demand an equitable distribution of these resources. It is important to point out that, in the case of Oaxaca, multiple preexisting communities—historically recognized as the centers of local governance, autonomy, and sustenance within the state structure—were often brought together into the administrative body of the municipality. As such, in some cases, municipalities consist of various distinct population centers, while in others, the majority of the community lives in a single population center.[19]

Until a couple of decades ago, the relationship between different communities in a municipality was one of complete respect for autonomy and was without problems. In addition, the municipal seat, which was one of several communities that made up the municipality, was not distinguished from the others except by its size or its better geographic position with respect to transportation. However, neither the municipal seat nor the submunicipal villages (*agencias*) received any external public resources.[20] In an important number of municipalities (around one hundred), the municipal government is only the authority for the community located in the municipal seat, as citizens of the submunicipal villages do not vote and cannot be elected in municipal elections. This has been a historic arrangement based on respect of community autonomy.[21]

In other cases, such as those of Santa Catarina Ixtepeji (with a seat and four villages), San Juan Lalana (fifty-seven localities), and Mazatlán Villa de Flores (with eighteen agencies and thirty-four congregations and small ranches), the inhabitants of all of these population centers form a part of the community and participate in local elections accordingly.

This conflict began with the decentralization of the Mexican state, a positive fact that, by not considering state and local particularities, became a cause of disputes. These disputes center on the intramunicipal distribution of federal funds (Branches 28 and 33), which the municipal government has the power to spend on public works and municipal services within the municipal boundaries. However, the government often privileges the municipal seat in the distribution of resources. Because of this, many of the political mobilizations of the past decade have been led by citizens of submunicipal villages asking for a just and equal distribution of the resources who, upon seeing that this does not occur, demand to participate in municipal elections as a pathway to accessing these resources.

The case of the municipality of Santiago Matatlán and the submunicipal village of San Pablo Güilá illustrates this situation. Güilá lost its status as a municipality at the beginning of the twentieth century and has since been subordinated to Matatlán. Nevertheless, the two communities are similar in population and sociopolitical importance. They maintained a mutual respect of each other's autonomy until federal resources arrived. Since then, Güilá has demanded an equitable distribution of these funds; upon not receiving them, they sought the opportunity to vote in municipal elections (Bautista et al. 2007).

Faced with this situation, in 2004 a pragmatic agreement was reached. The federal resources received by the municipality are split in two: 50 percent for the municipal seat and 50 percent for the village. Because the cause of the conflict was thus removed, Güilá no longer demanded to participate in municipal elections and each community reclaimed its autonomy. Agreements like those between Güilá and Matatlán have not been reached by all: the 2001 elections in Santiago Yaveo were annulled and in 2004 and 2007 elections could not be held due to the failure of the municipal seat and the *agencias* to come to an agreement. This municipality has been governed by a municipal administrator, named by the state government, for almost the entire decade. Many other municipalities have shown similar dynamics. There are partial accords, but they must be negotiated in each election, even sometimes beforehand if one of the parties breaks the agreement.

Given the fact that this is the cause of conflict in a large number of municipalities, some have proposed establishing the community as a fourth level of government or even enacting legislative reforms to establish clear mechanisms for the distribution of federal resources that, as a result of decentralization, are transferred to states and municipalities.

There are many examples like this one of rupture and change in Oaxacan communities and municipalities that struggle to preserve their systems of sociopolitical organization. The forms in which citizenship is acquired and exercised are also transformed. They respond to new realities that demand unprecedented responses, rule changes, and changes in the principles that are their foundation and their sustenance.

CONFLICT, INSTITUTIONALIZATION, AND NEW AGREEMENTS

The idealized vision of UC communities is characterized by citizens climbing a ladder of service to their community, and there is no struggle for local power. Accordingly, there are no political campaigns; candidates do not seek power of their own initiative; and there are no factions that seek municipal control. This vision does not necessarily correspond to reality. In many cases, even, the culture of participation through political parties has been mimicked in the internal rules and procedures of communities. This is the case, for example, in San Miguel Chimalapas. In 2010, two candidates competed in the electoral process in this municipality. One candidate was identified with the incumbent group in control of the municipal government, signaling his ties with the PRI. The other, who belonged to the local power group that controlled the Commission of Communal Resources, sought out the support of the PRD and the Convergence Party (Partido Convergencia, or PC). These two factions disagreed about the voting mechanism that would be used. In the municipality, voting by show of hands had previously changed to voting with ballots and urns. However, this did not eliminate the public nature of voting in Chimalapas, as a different urn was installed for each candidate. To vote for a candidate, then, citizens placed their ballot in the box bearing his name, in plain sight of everyone present. One of the competing groups struggled to change this procedure to guarantee that the vote would be secret.

In the past two decades, two variables have influenced the forms of participation and citizenship construction in communities: requirements and procedures for the election of their authorities and the intervention of political parties and external social organizations in the community. Beginning with UC recognition, political parties have had a hidden presence in some municipalities. San Juan Mixtepec, for example, is the site of a struggle every election between a ticket identified with the National Peasant Confederation (Confederación Nacional Campesina, or CNC), which is affiliated with the PRI, and the International Network of Indigenous Oaxacans (Red Internacional de Indígenas Oaxaqueños, or RIIO), previously identified with the PRD. In 2007, following a failed community assembly, as public voting was not viable because of high levels of participation and polarization, it was decided that the election process would use candidate tickets, urns, and the secret ballot (Blas López 2005).

This change in the electoral process also influenced a deeper change. First, due to the influences of the Mexican political system, factions begin to seek external support, as campaigns require resources. Second, because this changes the relationship between candidates and citizens, it is not always the case that prestige, a spirit of service, and leadership capacity are what determines who the candidates will be. Rather, new practices are incorporated, including clientelism, vote buying, and coercion.

In municipalities where communitarian institutions and identity are solid, the presence of factions does not cause great difficulty. At the end of the electoral process the members of the losing faction are incorporated into the community structure and bind themselves to the rules of the system. This does not happen, however, when the factions resist or question these structures. Outside of the electoral period, rivalries continue. The militants of the losing group do not participate in community work, nor do they participate in *tequio* or serve in *cargos*.

It is necessary to consider the fact that internal divisions in communities are often caused by the arrival of external agents. Faced with the exclusion that community members suffer from or because they will have to negotiate outside of the realm of their communities, they seek the support of social organizations and political parties that offer to serve as political intermediaries before other authorities. These include the state electoral body, the Chamber of Deputies (which until 2007 was in charge of approving municipal elections), and state and federal governments, from whom local leaders seek resources during elections, and even outside of them (as receiving these funds allows them to sustain and grow their bases of support). Nevertheless, more than representing the ideology of political parties, the constitution of these factions reflects the presence of different interests in the struggle for local power, or the existence of internal differences and fractures that have led to the organization of displaced or excluded actors.

The False Dilemma: Parties or *Usos y Costumbres*

This situation has reopened the debate about the existence of an antagonism between the principles of these differentiated systems of organization, autonomy, and the intervention of political parties. Such a basic opposition does not necessarily exist. It is important to remember that what is being recognized is the right to self-determination of these municipalities; that is, the authority to govern themselves in accordance with their own norms and to elect their authorities using internal rules. Hence, a decision by the community to hold elections with the participation of political parties or employing rules and tools characteristic of representative democracy does not infringe upon this right.

In fact, in 1995, upon defining which municipalities would fall under the UC system and which would be under the regime of political parties, some municipalities with systems of differentiated organization opted for the party-based system, including Magdalena Ocotlán, Pinotepa de Don Luis, Ihualtepec, and San Baltazar Chichicapan. In these municipalities the majority of the population is indigenous. Their internal rules are sustained by principles of differentiated systems, including unremunerated *cargos*, a system of *cargos* or services, and collective rights. Nevertheless, when competing for local power, because of internal conflicts, the vulnerability caused by the existence of conflicts with other communities, and the nonviability of traditional procedures, they decided to maintain the principles and rules for community life, with the exception of the competition for local power, which follows the regime of political parties.

Some of these reasons and conditions have led other municipalities to renegotiate their internal rules. This negotiation is reflected in electoral contests, but, as I have shown, it is founded upon the community's system of sociopolitical organization. In the past fifteen years, various municipalities have adopted mechanisms of representative democracy, such as urns, ballots, candidate tickets, and campaigns, to elect their local governments. Prominent cases include Mazatlán Villa de Flores, Santa María Chilchotla, Tlacochahuaya, and San Juan Mixtepec, among others.[22]

Therefore, the decision to elect local governments by political parties or by assembly, systems of cargos, and so forth, does not define the right to political autonomy in and of itself. The defining element, rather, is that the form and procedure should be a product of agreements based on communitarian consensus. The challenging of the authenticity of UC municipalities "that are, in reality, electing based on parties" rests upon this confusion.[23]

In many UC municipalities, factions organize to compete for local power which is not necessarily a problem. Problems present themselves when they seek support from (including economic resources and political intermediation), or support is offered to them by, political parties, social and civic organizations, state politicians, and regional caciques (political bosses or strongmen). This situation was perverted by the institutional structure of the Electoral College, which was subsumed to the Chamber of Deputies. Those who made the final decisions about the validity of municipal elections were the political parties themselves. For this reason, municipal factions established ties with the political parties, principally with the PRI and the PRD.

The typical solution offered to remedy this type of conflict—that municipalities should move from the UC system to the party system—is based on the confusions discussed above, and wrongly assumes that these problems, which are rooted in the structure of the system, could be solved by changing systems. The change of regime by decree would only hide the problems, as before 1995, without resolving them.

To show the relevance of such a measure, it is argued that conflicts have diminished in party system municipalities. Although this is true, it neglects the high level of conflict that these municipalities had in previous decades, when violent confrontations and the occupation of town halls was part of the daily landscape until 1995. The party-system municipalities of Miahuatlán, Tlacolula, Ocotlán, and Juchitán, among others, had recurring violent postelectoral conflicts, and it was not their status as party-system municipalities that resolved this problem, as they always elected their authorities under this regime (see Bailón Corres 1999; Díaz Montes and Martínez Vásquez 2001). What happened was that electoral reforms (federal in 1994 and local in 1995) established norms and institutional mechanisms to attend to conflicts, including means of challenging the results, an autonomous electoral body, state and federal electoral tribunals, and legislation that dealt with the variables that were the cause of conflicts.

This is far from being the case under the UC regime. There are no institutional channels through which to process conflicts. While those from party-system municipalities have representatives to defend their rights before the IEE, UC municipalities are subject to the discretion of the electoral councilors. Before the electoral reform of 2008, no legal remedies were available to challenge the results of an election.

The variables considered over the course of this chapter have combined to produce an intense dynamic in Oaxaca's municipalities. In various cases, systems are unable to respond to new problems; internal institutions are surpassed and the external institutions are unable to help. This has led to cases of violent confrontation, with high costs to the municipalities in question, as these conflicts not only make the right to self-determination vulnerable but also lead to social fracture and even the loss of human lives. The cases of Santiago Amoltepec (HRN 2002), San Miguel Quetzaltepec (Morales Canales 2002), and Tanetze de Zaragoza (Ramos Morales 2002), among others, alert us of the extremes that can occur if accords between the parties to the conflict are not reached. In other cases, exclusion prevails and leaves minorities without defenders of their rights.

However, it is from the municipalities that we might seek institutionalization before conflict. All signs indicate that after fifteen years of recognition, some lessons have been learned. The failure to resolve conflicts fractures the social fabric of communities and nullifies the right to self-determination, since this means that the municipality is governed by a municipal administrator, an external agent designated by the state government.

Because of this, while only six cases reached the TEPJF between 1995 and 2004, in 2007 the citizens of fifteen UC municipalities filed cases before the TEPJF. In 2011, twenty cases were filed, which demonstrates the lack of institutional channels to resolve conflicts and the limits of those that exist.

On the other hand, the legislative changes of recent years in Oaxaca and Mexico are moving in the wrong direction to solve this problem. First, the regulation of legal remedies was omitted for elections held under the UC regime. In 2008, when the electoral code was finally established, it was done in a limited and mechanistic fashion. When this is combined with the limits to the effective autonomy of the electoral body, the outlook becomes more complicated, which can be seen by considering that the number of conflicts increased following the last reform.

THE POLITICAL SYSTEM: FROM AUTHORITARIANISM TO PLURALISM

On January 1, 2011, Oaxaca awoke with countless municipal halls occupied by groups that intended to impede new local authorities from being sworn into office. By that point, the electoral bodies (IEE, TEE, and TRIFE) had annulled a total of forty-seven elections, forty-six in UC municipalities and one in a political parties municipality—a figure never seen before. The list would grow to fifty, as elections in three additional municipalities were annulled.

Although the conflicts were caused by a diversity of factors, processes, and conjunctures, in the specific case of 2010–2011, a large number of the conflicts had to do with a new balance of power and the reshuffling of power groups within the state's political landscape. The regional system of domination, that is, the networks of relationships and reproduction of the dominance and legitimacy of the political system (Bailón Corres 1999), experienced important changes that impacted municipal life. Transformations occurring at the local level, such as increased pluralism and the exercise of self-determination, have been essential to the reconfiguration of state politics.

The Authoritarian Decade

The strong indigenous movement of the 1980s and 1990s seemed to have become lethargic during the first decade of the twenty-first century. In the previous years, in addition to becoming a social subject and a fundamental political actor in Oaxaca, the indigenous movement had important triumphs, including the recognition of political autonomy, the indigenous law, and several ordinances that incorporated the rights of indigenous communities.

With the people's demands having been formally recognized, the arrival of the new century coincided with a move backward to authoritarianism, which was incarnated in governors José Murat and Ulises Ruiz Ortiz. The governments of both demonstrated the disparities within Mexico's democratic transition. As this process accelerated on the national level, political life remained under the control of authoritarian elements at the state and local levels. Oaxaca is an example of these authoritarian enclaves, or of what is considered to be subnational authoritarianism.[24]

With the administration of Governor Murat, the indigenous agenda was dismissed and there was a Manichean view of the indigenous rights discourse, establishing the state government's Secretariat of Indigenous Affairs (Secretaría de Asuntos Indígenas), which became a bureaucratic entity without powers or resources with which to operate.

During Murat's six-year term in office, municipal governments were dissolved and the powers of mayors were revoked in more municipalities than before or since. The state Congress possesses the power to use these legal measures to resolve local conflicts, but they were used in an instrumental fashion in violation of municipal autonomy. In numerous cases, these measures were used by the state government to reward or punish municipal authorities and political actors. In the municipalities of Juchitán and Ciudad Ixtepec between 2002 and 2003, the mayors' powers were revoked so that Governor Murat's allies could be installed as mayors of the new Municipal Administration Councils (Consejo de Administración). On the other side, ungovernable situations in San Miguel Quetzaltepec and Santiago Amoltepec led to ten deaths in violent political clashes before municipal governments were dissolved by the state government (see Hernández-Díaz and Juan Martínez 2007).

In addition, in a dozen more municipalities, mayors requested leave in order to resolve conflicts without the need for the state legislature to intervene. During this period, a spurious municipal law was announced in the official record of the state government, without having been approved by the Congress. The law violated autonomy and established mechanisms though which the governor could control municipalities politically.

The regime of Governor Ulises Ruiz violated municipal autonomy, strengthened *cacicazgos* (regional and local personalistic "chiefdoms"), converted institutions into electoral appendages of the PRI, and repressed social movements. While Murat's term in office was marked by the disruption of social and indigenous organizations through co-optation and repression, the following regime of Ulises Ruiz simply opted for repression. Dozens of leaders were imprisoned and the police impeded all demonstrations. The excesses of power violated the rules of the system, swept away political codes and symbols,[25] and broke the agreements that had prevailed between the state government and the principal social sectors. Following the repression of the annual mobilization of Section 22 of the Oaxacan teachers' movement, this situation led to the largest outbreak of social conflict in the state's history.

The social organizations that had previously suffered state repression aligned themselves with the teachers' movement, a social actor with a great capacity for organization and mobilization, constituting the Popular Assembly of the Oaxacan People (Asamblea Popular de los Pueblos de Oaxaca, or APPO). At its peak, the APPO had control of the capital city and the surrounding urban area, and occupied dozens of municipal halls around the state. Governor Ulises Ruiz became the focus of all grievances, including those caused by the bad actions of municipal authorities.

The conflict of 2006 demonstrated the degree to which the axis of state governability was the municipal structure. While the capital city and the surrounding metropolitan area lived through a critical situation, in the municipalities and communities—although the dynamics of popular mobilization manifested in local spheres, as they were integrated in municipal assemblies—with few exceptions, these did not overwhelm municipal authorities. Likewise, the APPO was supported by the Assembly of Municipal Authorities of the Zoogocho Sector (Asamblea de Autoridades Municipales del Sector Zoogocho), leading to a series of internal disagreements that, though they were intelligently processed, injured intercommunity relations. Although leaders and organizations from the indigenous movement did join the APPO, the agenda of the indigenous movement remained marginal in the face of the dynamics deployed by the other members.

Within the APPO, organizations with antidemocratic roots, such as the teachers' movement itself, coexisted with committed indigenous, social, and civic organizations, urban settlers (*colonos*), and regional and local leaders, who worked in different social sectors. The APPO was a symbol of popular power, even when it lacked a clear political plan beyond the demand that Governor Ruiz be removed. In the end, this deficiency together with repression ended the popular mobilization.[26] In the midterm election the following year, Ulises Ruiz's regime and the PRI won every single-member district seat in the local legislature and won a surprisingly large number of mayorships. This triumph of the PRI was repeated in the 2009 federal elections. Nevertheless, the regime's excesses ultimately led to the loss of power, as the PRI lost control of the governorship, its majority in the state legislature, and the largest municipalities in the state in the 2010 elections.

Municipalities and the Regional System of Domination

One of the most common hypotheses put forth to explain UC recognition in 1995 was that it had to do with a PRI strategy to inoculate municipalities against the growing presence of opposition parties. Although the authoritarian control exercised in subsequent years and the electoral triumphs of the PRI in state and federal elections would seem to shore up this argument, a thorough reading of what occurred in Oaxaca demonstrates that if indeed this was the goal of the law, it was far from being reached.

In the municipal realm, political pluralism had begun to express itself starting in the 1970s and 1980s. The first victories of opposition parties were in municipalities, largely thanks to the ties they established with regional or local social movements. These included the Student-Worker Coalition of the Isthmus (Coalición Obrera Estudiantil del Istmo), which registered with the United Socialist Party of Mexico (Partido Socialista Unificado de México) and won the mayorship in the municipality of Juchitán. This is the clearest example, but not the only one (Bailón Corres 1999; Díaz Montes and Martínez Vásquez 2001). With UC recognition in 1995, one can observe a sustained fall in the vote share of the PRI, whose vote share declined election after election.

Nevertheless, as mentioned above, authoritarian mechanisms for municipal control were strengthened at the same time. With respect to UC municipalities, the politics of recognition had a double effect. The first effect was exemplified when former presidential candidate Andrés Manuel López Obrador visited all 570 Oaxaca municipalities. His trip was obstructed, at times publicly, by local authorities, who argued that this standard bearer of the PRD "violated the *usos y costumbres* of the communities."[27] This was a campaign of harassment orchestrated by the state government, which reveals the submission of local authorities.

On the other hand, and precisely because of actions like those described above, some years ago, the rural indigenous vote formed a part of the PRI's nucleus of solid votes (*voto duro*). However, a review of the electoral statistics shows that over this past couple of gubernatorial terms, the voting behavior of the 418 UC municipalities has been similar to that of the 152 municipalities governed under the system of political parties. The old loyalties of these communities to the regime and to the PRI changed with the 1995 recognition, to the benefit of greater autonomy. In these municipalities, voting became continuously more plural, and the PRI, despite its clientelistic practices and its efforts to corporatize the municipal authorities, lost points election after election (see Juan Martínez 1998, 2004b; Recondo 2007a). The fact that the PRI won sweeping victories in 2007 and 2009 can be explained by the high level of abstention and the retreat of social mobilization in the wake of the 2006 repression.

This situation was tested with the 2010 gubernatorial elections. In the two electoral districts in which all municipalities are under the UC system, Ixtlán and Ayutla, the alliance in opposition to the PRI won by ten and fifteen points, respectively. This happened despite low turnout (45.1 percent in Ixtlán and 38.8 percent in Ayutla), typically ideal levels for the imposition of the "hard vote" for the PRI. The triumph of the alliance candidate, Gabino Cué, resulted from high citizen participation and the concurrence of political parties and social and civic organizations. But the fall of the hegemonic party (the PRI) happened because of the breakdown of their old ties and alliances to municipalities and indigenous communities (see Juan Martínez 2010b).

The New Political Map in Oaxaca

The loss of the power of the PRI and the governing political elites led to different processes, which have impacted the regional system of domination and influenced the municipal space. The PRI seeks to reconstitute itself with a base in the municipalities, by obtaining control of local governments, increasing their numbers on municipal councils and in positions of municipal management, or, in more adverse contexts, by provoking problems of governability, which, if they occur within the municipal space, can have consequences at the state level. At this juncture, with the weakness of the PRI, the other parties see the possibility of increasing their influence in the municipalities. This situation was evident at the end of 2010 when, faced with high levels of conflict, the state government convened a meeting of political parties. The problem is that they did not intervene only to negotiate settlement of the conflicts in the party system municipalities, but also those under the UC system.

It is also important to note the serious problem of an antidemocratic political culture that deprives the political system and for which political parties and social organizations are equally at fault. In some cases, such as Santiago Laollaga, the results of elections were challenged, despite the decisiveness of the defeat. In others, such as Tlacolula, Santa Lucía del Camino, Pochutla, Mitla, and many more, demands are made (and received) to allow more members on the municipal council than is established in the law, or rather a joint composition of the municipal council is asked for (the same number of aldermen for each competing party), putting the legal framework of representation to the side.

However, an opposite process occurred as well. As the PRI lost state political power, local caciques lost an important source of protection in many communities. As a result, in 2010 and 2011, many communities resisted the imposition of mayors by caciques in a way that they would not have dared just a couple of years earlier, when the state-level protection enjoyed by the caciques meant they would have been condemned to failure and placed at a great risk of repression. In Santos Reyes Nopala, San Andrés Cabecera Nueva, and Santa María Petapa, among others, the old cacique-based regimes have now been confronted by serious resistance from the populations.

Absent Institutions

An important characteristic of the previous regime was the authoritarian control of institutions, which were placed at the service of the governing group and its party. As I demonstrate below, this was the case with the electoral institutions.

In January 2011, the president and secretary of the Municipal Electoral Council of Tlacolula, accused by the Special Prosecutor for Electoral Crimes (Fiscalía Especial de Atención a Delitos Electorales) for the falsification of documents, as they had recorded two people as winners of seats on the municipal council who had not been registered on any of the competing party lists (Proceedings 29/FEPADE-OAX 2010; see also Juan Martínez 2010a).

The TEE annulled the election in San Pedro Ixtlahuaca, with the following ruling: "It is ordered that the aforementioned General Council (of the IEE) which over a period not to exceed forty-five days should exercise the necessary, sufficient, and reasonable means to avoid violence or any type of social disorder in the municipality of San Pedro Ixtlahuaca and carry out a special election of authorities there" (Yescas 2011).[28] Opposing this resolution, the IEE resolved to "ratify in all senses" its November 22 agreement, in which it had qualified the election as valid.

These examples reveal the old framework of operation of institutions and elections in Oaxaca. With this, as with other issues, one could count on the complacency of electoral and government authorities and of political parties, as the unwritten rule of the political system was to preserve social peace and negotiate political agreements.

These cases demonstrate the behavior of the electoral bodies, which in practice nullified the means to challenge elections.[29] Taking cases to the federal tribunal places limits on the right to self-determination and difference, as this body bases its analysis of cases on the criteria and procedures established for party-system elections. Accordingly, this interjects a constitutional challenge that, given its inadmisability, is supplemented by the Judgment for the Protection of the Political Rights of Citizens (Juicio de Protección a los Derechos Políticos de los Ciudadanos), which is designed to defend the rights of citizens as individuals, with the limitations identified above. As can be appreciated, then, the state political system and the gaps in the legislation also play a role in municipal electoral conflicts.

CONCLUSION

During the 2000s in Latin America, the dynamic of indigenous peoples and the indigenous movement shifted from the fight for recognition to the practical realization of their demands from the spaces they won, the laws that recognize the right to difference and to exercise the different practices that make this possible.

Among the many experiences generated, two processes can be observed: (1) the attempts by nation-states to isolate the indigenous movement and/or to control it at the level of subnational institutions (e.g., municipality, community, reservations, autonomous regions) in which the exercise of their differentiated rights is constrained; and (2) the capacity of ethnic reconstitution within and from these same spaces by populations and communities to fully exercise the right to self-determination.

In the Mexican case, the clearest example of these processes is found in the southern state of Oaxaca, where a 1995 law recognized the existence of systems of sociopolitical organization with ethical and normative principles different from those prevalent in national laws: the so-called *usos y costumbres*.

In UC municipalities, the politics of recognition coincides with other internal and external processes that generate a series of dynamics and lead to the transformation of rules and organizational systems, as well as of the construction and exercise of citizenship. This explains the multiplicity of conflicts that have arisen in the state's recent history, the visibility of the system's structural problems, and the new internal accords that are allowing these differentiated systems to remain.

In reality, the coexistence of two normative orders with diametrically opposed and theoretically insoluble origins (collective versus individual rights) requires pragmatic solutions that show that it is possible to find mechanisms that permit coexistence of the two regimes. One possibility is the exercise of multiple citizenships, which correspond to distinct times and places, but manage to adjust to reconcile community belonging with acting like a member of the national community.

The different experiences reviewed here show the day-to-day exercise of multiple citizenships. First, there is the constant historical struggle and search for the recognition of multiculturality in nation-states and, accordingly, of the rights of indigenous communities and populations. This implies the exercise of an ethnic or multicultural citizenship that is based on the collectivity and amounts to the recognition of difference and the distinct practices that make difference possible. Second, although ethnic identity is defended, there is also a clear sense of belonging to the nation-state. The nationalization of oil by the Mexican government in 1938 provides a clear example of this construction of national unity and participation in a common identity. Many communities remember the solidarity with and disposition to defend Mexico's resources. A Zapotec remembers it as follows:

I was an adolescent, but I remember that my father and many people raised coins, and some silver and gold pieces. They walked to Oaxaca city to deliver them. In those days the walk took about a day and a half. And what they said was that "if we are Mexican citizens then it is our responsibility to contribute. We had also already decided to ask them to tell us if we need to defend our country and we will. It's not for nothing that we call ourselves Mexicans." (Martínez Santos 2008)

In this way, they demonstrated their membership and accepted the responsibility to defend the nation that did not recognize their difference.

Even so, the politics of indigenous rights recognition makes possible the discussion, confrontation, and internal agreements between different conceptions and practices of citizenship. With respect to women, the politics of recognition is used as an instrument to overcome exclusion, struggle for rights, and seek out gender-based political representation. In some cases, communities have reformed their systems of community organization internally. In other cases, such as that of Eufrosina Cruz summarized above, appeals are made to individual rights and liberal citizenship as provided by the state.

With respect to conflicts between municipal seats and submunicipal villages, the parties do not make appeals to citizenship as exercised by individuals. These quarrels, rather, are understood as a confrontation between the different communities that make up the municipality and are asserting their rights, often the right to receive a just portion of federal funds distributed to each municipality.

Migration provides a clear example of the simultaneous exercise of multiple citizenships. First, those migrants who have been naturalized as citizens in the receiving country (typically the United States) exercise these rights and fulfill the corresponding obligations. At the same time, they continue to be members of the Mexican nation and have the right to vote in presidential elections from abroad and to participate in various transnational social networks. In the case of Oaxacan municipalities, migrants must continue to fulfill their obligations in order to protect both their community rights and their ethnic-cultural identity, which belonging to the community makes possible.

The fact that many people simultaneously exercise their different citizenships is constantly evident. Although principles of individual or community rights may be violated by this coexistence of multiple citizenships, this situation also makes possible an intercultural dialogue that permits the discovery of unprecedented solutions to irreconcilable theoretical problems. Indeed, this is what explains the intensity of the dynamic prevalent in Oaxacan communities.

Some of the variables causing these changes, even when a sharp division between the local and the global does not exist, are more related to internal dynamics, such as the change of productive activities (migration), improvements in rural-urban transit, intergenerational struggles, or the struggle for women's rights. These internal dynamics adjust to new contexts that have to do with the direct mobilization of local actors.

Other processes correspond more to the global realm, given that they come from state decisions or are inscribed in processes in which the community is unable to intervene, except when these processes have direct community impacts: migration, federal policy (such as decentralization), urbanization, rural-urban transit, and changes to the Mexican political system and its correlate regional system of domination, among others.

In addition, there are structural problems, such as exclusion, the hybrid civil-religious structure, and collective authoritarianism. Of course, this does not occur in all cases and there is variation in the degree to which some of these problems present themselves. But it is necessary to attend to internal problems inherent to the organizational system of the community and the municipality.

If communities are to preserve their right to difference and self-determination when faced with the processes that are occurring, the problems of the system, and the new context within which they are unfolding, it is necessary to make adjustments to their systems of sociopolitical organization and to the principles that sustain the citizenship of their inhabitants. Also, the Mexican state should respect and guarantee the exercise of these rights, making the legislative and institutional changes to make these rights viable. The success of both processes depends on the decline in the level of sociopolitical conflict in these municipalities.

A failure to take on this mutual responsibility places the permanency of the community as such at risk. Not its physical disappearance, but the loss of its collective ethnic identity, which is based on the defense of its culture and its capacity for self-government (a necessary base for the acquisition of political autonomy), as well as the ethnic diversity of nation-states.

In addition, this risks municipal and state governability and generates the conditions for violent conflicts, with the high social and political costs they bring with them. A quotation from one of the participants at a negotiation (*mesa de negociación*) to resolve one of the many conflicts between municipal factions illustrates the need for an internal readjustment of the rules and the establishment of external institutional channels. Faced with the absence of advances in the negotiations, given that both groups claimed to be defending "authentic customs," one of the participants exclaimed: "What we have doesn't work anymore; what we need are new customs."[30]

NOTES

1. We characterize interculturality as the desirable dialogue between different cultural groups under symmetrical conditions, which offers, beyond peaceful coexistence, a constructive "living together" (*convivencia*) for all, leading us to a more just and equitable society (Díaz-Polanco 2006).
2. Translator's note: the Spanish phrase for "norms of customary law" was "normas de derecho consuetudinario."
3. The *caracoles* (literally, snails) are the regional capitals of the Juntas de Buen Gobierno or Councils of Good Government (see Inclán 2008, 1316–1350).
4. On this topic, see different works that analyze the factors that made the 1995 electoral reform possible: Recondo (2002), Anaya Muñoz (2002), Morales Canales (2007), and Hernández-Díaz and Juan Martínez (2007).
5. In Spanish, the quotation is as follows: "El reconocimiento de los pueblos y comunidades indígenas se hará en las constituciones y leyes de las entidades federativas, las que deberán tomar en cuenta, además de los principios generales establecidos en los párrafos anteriores de este articulo, criterios etnolingüísticos y de asentamiento físico."
6. On this topic, see Juan Martínez (2007) and Recondo (2007a).
7. For a broader analysis of the causes of the social conflict of 2006, see Juan Martínez (2007), Martínez Vásquez (2007), and other texts of the conflict of 2006 published in *El cotidiano: Revista de la realidad mexicana actual* 148 (March–April 2008).
8. *Comuneros* are members of collectively held "communal" lands prevalent in Oaxaca.
9. *Tequio* is voluntary labor to benefit the community, which is often a requirement of community citizenship in UC communities.
10. This is a mountainous region of Oaxaca located to the north of the capital city, made up of Zapotec (of the Sierra Norte) and Mixe indigenous communities.
11. *Cargos* are unremunerated service jobs that community members are typically required to perform.
12. On this subject see Juan Martínez (2004c), Hernández-Díaz and Juan Martínez (2007), Recondo (2007b), and Hernández-Díaz (2007).
13. The *síndico* is the second most powerful member of the municipal authority, after the mayor, and is in charge of all internal security matters.
14. I consulted the *Proceedings of State and Municipal Electoral Processes* (*Memorias de los Procesos Electorales Estatales y Municipales*) from 1995, 1998, 2001, and 2003. For 2005 and 2007, these proceedings were not published, and the information here comes from published press accounts.
15. *Agencias* are outlying villages within municipalities but outside of the municipal seat.
16. In Spanish, this section of the act reads: "El pueblo en general y muy en especial por el sentir de las mujeres de Quiegolani, desconocen categóricamente a Eufrosina Cruz Mendoza como ciudadana y vecina de esta población, ya que ella nunca ha vivido en este municipio y no se sienten respaldadas por lo que ella dice y hace ante los medios de comunicación y ante cualquier Dependencia Gubernamental."

17. *Bastón de mando* is the ceremonial baton that symbolizes the power of the office of mayor.
18. This theme is developed in depth in Juan Martínez (2004c).
19. For statistical data on the makeup of municipalities, including the communities that constitute them and issues of land tenure, see Velásquez (2000).
20. I use "villages" here and throughout this chapter as the translation of *agencias*. These villages are submunicipal communities in Oaxaca, which maintain a strong community identity and contain their own differentiated systems of community organization. However, they remain subsumed by the municipal governments, and their autonomy has not been recognized in the state constitution.
21. See Hernández-Díaz and Juan Martínez (2007), particularly chapter 5, "Agencias contra cabecera, la disputa por los recursos," and Hernández-Díaz and Juan Martínez (2011).
22. Examples of this can be found in the cases analyzed in Recondo (2007b), Hernández-Díaz (2007), Hernández-Díaz and Juan Martínez (2007), and Juan Martínez and Salazar Luzula (2009), among others.
23. In Spanish: "están en realidad eligiendo por partidos."
24. The concept of "authoritarian enclave" is developed by Cornelius (1999). Edward L. Gibson (2005) coined the term "subnational authoritarianism," signaling Oaxaca under Governor José Murat as one of the best examples of this.
25. His first act as governor was to convert the government palace into a museum, thus abandoning the most important symbol of political power in Oaxaca and unconstitutionally moving it to a municipality in the Oaxaca metropolitan area outside of the capital city. To subsequently resolve this constitutional irregularity, eighteen municipalities in the metropolitan area were declared permanent headquarters of the state authorities.
26. For a broader analysis of the causes of the 2006 conflict and its aftermath, see Juan Martínez (2007), Martínez Vásquez (2007), Blas López, Juan Martínez, and López Alegría (2010), and works published in *El cotidiano: Revista de la realidad mexicana actual* 148 (March–April 2008).
27. In an open letter, municipal authorities from the Mixteca region of Oaxaca (San Juan Teita, Santa María Tataltepec, San Bartolomé Yucuañe, San Miguel Achuitla, San Juan Achuitla, Santa Catarina Tayata, Santa Cruz Tayata, Santa María del Rosario, and San Martin Huamelupam), with reference to AMLO, "Energetically manifested to not be responsible for any harm that befalls this person" (in Spanish: "Manifestamos enérgicamente no hacernos responsables de que algo suceda a esta persona"). The mayors signaled that López Obrador "only comes here to divide and confront our communities, as he has done with his party" (in Spanish: "sólo viene a dividir y confrontar a nuestras comunidades, como lo ha hecho con su partido"). They affirmed that "this microregion works alongside Ulises Ruiz…and there is no doubt that we will continue to do so" (in Spanish: "esta microregión trabaja al lado de Ulises Ruiz…y sin duda alguna seguiremos haciéndolo").
28. Translator's note: in Spanish, the ruling reads as follows: "Se ordena al citado Consejo General (del IEE) que en un plazo no mayor de cuarenta y cinco días disponga las medidas necesarias, suficientes y que resulten razonables para evitar la generación de violencia o la comisión de cualquier tipo de desórdenes sociales al seno del municipio de San Pedro Ixtlahuaca y lleve a cabo la elección extraordinaria de concejales en el municipio referido."
29. An example is San Miguel Chimalapas, where the voting mechanism was the focus of disagreements. Because of this, an electoral challenge was filed and, as required by law, the electoral body was required to mediate the conflict. Far from being the case, the

IEE imposed conditions favoring one of the parties to the disagreement, and a conflict erupted. It was demonstrated that an impartial and mediating presence of the IEE would have worked after the parties to the conflict were able to agree upon electoral rules in negotiations convened by the municipal administrator.

30. In Spanish: "es que lo que tenemos ya no funciona; lo que necesitamos son nuevas costumbres."

REFERENCES

Anaya Muñoz, Alejandro. 2002. "Governability and Legitimacy in Mexico: The Legalization of Indigenous Electoral Institutions in Oaxaca." Doctoral dissertation, University of Essex, England.

Aquino Morales, Agustín. 2002. "A los oriundos de Santa Ana del Valle radicados en los Estados Unidos." *El Oaxaqueño Newspaper*, September 30.

Atlas Agrario del Estado de Oaxaca. 2002. Mexico City: SAI, INI, SRA.

Bailón Corres, Moisés Jaime. 1999. *Pueblos indios, élites y territorio*. Mexico City: El Colegio de México.

Bautista, Juan Antonio, Javier Ramírez Juárez, Beatriz Martínez Corona, Benjamín Peña Olvera, and Tomás Martínez Saldaña. 2007. "El sistema de usos y costumbres bajo el poder económico y político en el municipio de Matatlán, Oaxaca." In *Ciudadanías diferenciadas en un estado multicultural: Los usos y costumbres en Oaxaca*, edited by Jorge Hernández-Díaz, 131–150. Mexico City: Siglo XXI-IISUABJO.

Blas López, Cuauhtémoc. 2005. "Vence RIIO a CNC en elecciones extraordinarias: Elecciones y emigrantes en San Juan Mixtepec." *En Marcha* 70 (January–February): 42–43.

Blas López, Cuauhtémoc, Víctor Leonel Juan Martínez, and Juan Manuel López Alegría. 2010. *Oaxaca 2006: Autoritarismo, mitos y daños*. Oaxaca, Mexico: Editorial Siembra.

CEDHO (Comisión Estatal para la Defensa de los Derechos Humanos Oaxaca). 1997. "Recomendación CEDHO, No. 1/97." http://www.derechoshumanosoaxaca.org/newcddho/recomendaciones/1997/1-199700031.pdf.

CEDHO (Comisión Estatal para la Defensa de los Derechos Humanos Oaxaca). 2011. "Recomendación CEDHO, No. 23/2011." http://www.derechoshumanosoaxaca.org/newcddho/recomendaciones/contenedor_rec1.php?idreco=432.

CNDH (Comisión Nacional de Derechos Humanos de Mexico). 2008. *Informe especial de la Comisión Nacional de los Derechos Humanos sobre el caso de discriminación a la Profesora Eufrosina Cruz Mendoza*. http://www.cndh.org.mx/node/35.

Cornelius, Wayne A. 1999. "Subnacional Politics and Democratization: Tensions between Center and Periphery in the Mexican Political System." In *Subnational Politics and Democratization in Mexico*, edited by Wayne A. Cornelius, Todd A. Eisenstadt, and Jane Hindley, 3–16. La Jolla: Center for US-Mexican Studies, University of California, San Diego.

Cortina, Adela. 1998. *Ciudadanos del mundo: Hacia una teoría de la ciudadanía*. Madrid: Alianza.

Cruz Mendoza, Eufrosina. 2007. Interview, Oaxaca, Mexico, November.

Díaz Montes, Fausto, and Víctor Raúl Martínez Vásquez. 2001. *Las elecciones municipales en Oaxaca*. Oaxaca, Mexico: IEE.

Díaz-Polanco, Héctor. 2006. *Elogio de la diversidad: Globalización, multiculturalismo y etnofagia*. Mexico City: Siglo XXI.

Dictamen de la Ley de Derechos de los Pueblos y Comunidades Indígenas del Estado de Oaxaca. 1998. Cuadernos de la Comisión Permanente de Asuntos Indígenas No. 5. LVI Legislatura del estado de Oaxaca.

DPLF (Due Process of Law Foundation). 2007. *Memoria de la Reunión-taller de Expertos: Unificando Derecho y Sociedad en Oaxaca Indígena*. Due Process of Law Foundation.

Garibay Orozco, Claudio. 2008. *Comunalismos y liberalismos campesinos: Identidad comunitaria, empresa social forestal y poder comporado en el México contemporáneo*. Morelia, Michoacán: El Colegio de Michoacán.

Gibson, Edward L. 2005. "Boundary Control: Subnational Authoritarianism in Democratic Countries." *World Politics* 58 (October): 101–132.

Gundermann K., Hans. 2003. "Sociedades indígenas, municipio y etnicidad: La transformación de los espacios políticos locales andinos en Chile." In *Estudios Acatameños* no. 25: 55–77. San Pedro de Atacama, Chile: Revista de la Universidad Católica del Norte.

Hale, Charles R. 2007. "¿Puede el multiculturalismo ser una amenaza? Gobernanza, derechos culturales y política de la identidad en Guatemala." In *Cuaderno de Futuro No. 23. Antropología del Estado: Dominación y prácticas contestatarias en América*, edited by María L. Lagos and Pamela Calla, translated by Hernando Calla Ortega. La Paz, Bolivia: INDH/PNUD. Originally published in 2002 as "Does Multiculturalism Menace? Governance, Cultural Rights and the Politics of Identity in Guatemala." *Journal of Latin American Studies* 34 (3): 485–524.

Hernández Cárdenas, Ana María, ed. 2009. *Diagnóstico: Participación política y comunitaria de mujeres mixes*. Consorcio para el Diálogo Parlamentario y la Equidad en Oaxaca.

Hernández Chavez, Rafaela. 2010. Interview, Tlalixtac de Cabrera, Oaxaca, November 8.

Hernández-Díaz, Jorge. 2007. *Ciudadanías diferenciadas en un estado multicultural: Los usos y costumbres en Oaxaca*. Mexico City: Siglo XXI-IISUABJO.

Hernández-Díaz, Jorge, and Víctor Leonel Juan Martínez. 2007. *Dilemas de la institución municipal: Una incursión en la experiencia oaxaqueña*. Mexico City: Miguel Ángel Porrúa-IISUABJO.

Hernández-Díaz, Jorge, and Víctor Leonel Juan Martínez. 2011. "De la lucha por las autonomías a la disputa entre las autonomías: el municipio y la comunidad en Oaxaca." In *De autonomías, patrimonios y ciudadanías: Etnia y género en el campo en el siglo XXI*, edited by Verónica Vásquez García and Ivonne Vizcarra Bordi, 23–49. Mexico City: Colegio de Postgraduados-AMER.

HRN (Human Rights Network, EDUCA, and Pastoral Social). 2002. *Amoltepec: Impunidad y estado de excepción*. Oaxaca, Mexico: Human Rights Network, EDUCA, and Pastoral Social.

Inclán, María de la Luz. 2008. "From the ¡Ya Basta! to the Caracoles: Zapatista Mobilization under Transitional Conditions." *American Journal of Sociology* 113 (5): 1316–1350.

Juan Martínez, Víctor Leonel. 1998. "El Voto Indígena." *En Marcha* 8 (October–November): 5–9.

Juan Martínez, Víctor Leonel. 2004a. "Elecciones municipales por usos y costumbres; la necesidad de una reforma legislativa para el acceso de los indígenas a la jurisdicción electoral." Undergraduate thesis, Benito Juárez Autonomous University of Oaxaca.

Juan Martínez, Víctor Leonel. 2004b. "Paulatina caída del 'voto verde' para el PRI." *En Marcha* 67 (October): 33–35.

Juan Martínez, Víctor Leonel. 2004c. "Usos y costumbres: ¿Paraíso democrático o autoritarismo arcaico? Consensos y conflictos en las elecciones por normas de derecho consuetudinario." In *Género, indígenas, elecciones: Memoria del IV Congreso Internacional en Derecho Electoral*, 149–163. Mexico City: TRIFE-IFE-PNUD-IIJUNAM.

Juan Martínez, Víctor Leonel. 2007. "¡Ya cayó, ya cayó! Colapso del sistema político en Oaxaca." *Cuadernos del Sur* 22–23 (November): 81–94.

Juan Martínez, Víctor Leonel. 2008. "Eufrosina y la exclusión de mujeres." *En Marcha* 98 (January): 12–13.

Juan Martínez, Victor Leonel. 2010a. "IEE: La última y nos vamos?" *Noticias*, December 30.

Juan Martínez, Víctor Leonel. 2010b. "Y finalmente cayó." In *Oaxaca 2010: Las voces de la transición*, edited by Claudio Sánchez and Isidoro Yescas, 121–134. Oaxaca, Mexico: Carteles Editores.

Juan Martínez, Víctor Leonel, and Katya Salazar Luzula, eds. 2009. *Derecho y Sociedad en Oaxaca Indígena*. Washington, DC: Due Process of Law Foundation.

Kabeer, Naila, ed. 2007. *Ciudadanía incluyente: Significados y expresiones*. Mexico City: Universidad Nacional Autónoma de México.

Leyva, Xochitl, Araceli Burguette, and Shannon Speed, eds. 2008. *Hacia la investigación de co-labor*. Mexico City: Centro de Investigaciones y Estudios Superiores en Antropología Social, Facultad Latinoamericana de Ciencias Sociales.

Maitrayee, Mukhopadhyay, and Navsharan Singh. 2008. *Justicia de género, ciudadanía y desarrollo*. Colombia: Mayol Ediciones/IDRC.

Martínez Santos, Ismael. 2008. Interview in Villa Díaz Ordaz, in Zapotec, August 10.

Martínez Vásquez, Víctor Raúl. 2007. *Autoritarismo, movimiento popular y crisis política: Oaxaca 2006*. Oaxaca, Mexico: IISUABJO, Centro de Apoyo al Movimiento Popular Oaxaqueño, A.C., Servicio para una Educación alternativa (EDUCA), Consorcio para el Diálogo Palamentario y la Equidad, A.C.

Mateos, Askari. 2005. "Cuando el regreso es tragedia: Un migrante desterrado de su pueblo." *Masiosare* 416 (December 11).

Molina, Tania. 2006. "Migrantes, nuevos vientos que soplan del norte: El caso de Santa Ana del Valle." *Masiosare,* supplement to *La Jornada*, January 15.

Morales, Teresa, and Cuauhtémoc Camarena. 2002. *Negociando el futuro: Los cambios en el sistema de cargos de Santa Ana del Valle*. Mimeo. Oaxaca, Mexico: Centro INAH-Oaxaca.

Morales Canales, Lourdes. 2002. "En San Miguel Quetzaltepec, transgresión de la costumbre." *En Marcha* 45 (December): 10–13.

Morales Canales, Lourdes. 2007. "Le système politique de Oaxaca (Mexique) et la représentation politique des indigènes." Doctoral dissertation, Universite de La Sorbonne Nouvelle–Paris.

Mouffe, Chantal. 1999. *El retorno de lo político: Comunidad, ciudadanía, pluralismo, democracia radical*. Paidós.

Ramos Morales, Fernando. 2002. "Tanetze, el intento de un nuevo cacicazgo." *En Marcha* 37 (March): 6–7.

Recondo, David. 2002. "Etat et coutumes électorales dans l'Oaxaca (Mexique): Réflexions sur les enjeux politiques du multiculturalisme." Doctoral dissertation, Université Montesquieu-Bordeaux IV, France.

Recondo, David. 2007a. "Crónica de una muerte anunciada: El ocaso del partido de Estado en Oaxaca." *Desacatos* 24 (May–August): 123–134.

Recondo, David. 2007b. *La política del gatopardo: Multiculturalismo y democracia en Oaxaca*. Mexico City: Publicaciones de la Casa Chata.

Regalsky, Pablo, and Francisco Quisbert. 2008. "Bolivia indígena: De gobiernos comunitarios en busca de autonomía a la lucha por la hegemonía." In *Gobernar (en) la diversidad: Experiencias indígenas desde América Latina. Hacia la investigación de co-labor*, edited by Xochitl Leyva, Araceli Burguette, and Shannon Speed, 151–188. Mexico City: Centro de Investigaciones y Estudios Superiores en Antropología Social and Facultad Latinoamericana de Ciencias Sociales.

Sierra, María Teresa. 2009. "Las mujeres indígenas ante la justicia comunitaria: Perspectivas desde la interculturalidad y los derechos." *Desacatos* 31 (September–December): 73–96.

Sojo, Carlos. 2002. "La noción de la ciudadanía en el debate latinoamericano." *Revista de la CEPAL* 76: 25–38.

Tibán G., Lourdes, and Fernando García S. 2008. "De la oposición y el enfrentamiento al diálogo y las alianzas. La experiencia de la CONAIE y el MICC en Ecuador." In *Gobernar (en) la diversidad: Experiencias indígenas desde América Latina. Hacia la investigación de co-labor*, edited by Xochitl Leyva, Araceli Burguette, and Shannon Speed, 271–304. Mexico City: Centro de Investigaciones y Estudios Superiores en Antropología Social and Facultad Latinoamericana de Ciencias Sociales.

Velásquez, María Cristina. 2000. *El nombramiento: Elecciones por usos y costumbres en Oaxaca*. Oaxaca, Mexico: IEE.

Yescas, Isidoro. 2011. "Ixtlahuaca: El desacato del IEE." *Noticias,* January 5.

Zafra, Gloria, and Víctor Leonel Juan Martínez. 2010. "Impactos de la migración en comunidades indígenas: Ciudadanía, género y generación en San Juan Guelavía." In *Mujer y migración: Los costos emocionales de la migración*, edited by Lore Aresti de la Torre, 109–131. Mexico City: UAM-X, CSH, Depto. de Relaciones Sociales.

7 Political Subsystems in Oaxaca's *Usos y Costumbres* Municipalities

A Typology Based on the Civil-Religious Service Background of Mayors

Carlos Sorroza Polo and Michael S. Danielson
(translated by Andrew McKelvy)

Oaxaca is a multiethnic and pluricultural state, inhabited by sixteen indigenous groups, small concentrations of Afro-descendants, and a Spanish-speaking mestizo majority. If language is used to define ethnicity, one-third of the population is considered to be indigenous. In more than a third of the state's 570 municipalities, 70 percent of the population or more speaks an indigenous language. The indigenous population ranges from 40 to 70 percent in seventy municipalities. In 105 municipalities, 10 to 40 percent of the population speaks an indigenous language, and in the remaining 211 municipalities, less than 10 percent of the population speaks an indigenous language. Thus, 32 percent of the municipalities can be characterized as indigenous, 12 percent as predominantly indigenous, 18 percent as having an indigenous presence, and 37 percent as nonindigenous (INEGI 2006).

In the state of Oaxaca, there is a clear division between municipalities in terms of the method through which authorities are selected (see chapter 6, this volume). In the nearly three-fourths of municipalities (418) governed with relative autonomy in accordance with customary practice, authorities are generally chosen in public community assemblies. This system, known as *usos y costumbres* (UC), represents what a number of analysts consider to be a cultural feature of indigenous societies with a Mesoamerican style of political organization and representation. Citizens residing in the remaining 27 percent (152 municipalities) conduct elections using political parties.

Usos y costumbres communities may be viewed as entities that maintain their traditions and the unique features of their cultures and worldviews or as societies that, though they preserve some traditional features of culture and organization, are "in transition," borrowing new cultural practices, adapting, innovating, and transforming to more "modern" ways of life (García Canclini 1999). The UC system is a method of community organization in which civil life mingles with and is incorporated into religious practices. This system is rooted in a worldview according to which the individual forms a part of the community and has particular duties and rights. An individual feels compelled to offer service to the collective group, including unpaid work to benefit the community (known as *tequio*) and participation in the system of civil and religious *cargos*. Individuals gain recognition and prestige within the community through the fulfillment and completion of these *cargos*. On the basis of this acquired prestige, individuals are nominated and elected to the highest posts in communities' civil and religious hierarchies. The highest post in the religious sphere is the *mayordomía*, or hosting of a community's patron saint festival. In the civil sphere, the most important posts are in the municipal government, the very highest of which is the mayor (*presidente municipal*).[1]

A cultural system is not something static or impervious to change. It is an "open system" (or at least a relatively open system) that is influenced by the cultures that it coexists and interacts with and that exerts influence within their systems at the local, national, and transnational levels. Due to these factors, cultural systems are consolidated or modified, leading to a wide range of outcomes, ranging from relative stasis or being strengthened by the assimilation of other cultures to the disintegration of the prevailing cultural system and its eventual integration into a more powerful system or vanishing and losing its identity.

The UC system is a powerful source of indigenous identity, and signs of its vitality are seen in the consensus and disposition toward service found among the people in the municipalities where the system is in place. When asked about the likelihood of holding *cargos*, members of the local governments that were surveyed indicated that *tequio* is done in 79 percent of municipalities, religious *cargos* in 81 percent, civil *cargos* in 86 percent, and municipal government *cargos* in 94 percent.

The system of community service has been modified through migration, education, and coexistence with an external sociocultural system that generates and values individualism, rejects the collective, and practically ignores the communitarian. Even still, the communal system demonstrates its strength: it maintains or adapts itself to circumstances and influences that are, in large measure, stronger than it and contrary to it.

For this reason, it is important to verify the forms or modalities under which the UC system operates. It is likewise important to conduct research on and to highlight the presence of a communitarian system such as that which exists in Mexico's indigenous communities. In a world in which groups struggle for the recognition and acceptance of multiculturalism, it is important to make the existence of the different UC subsystems of social organization more widely known locally, nationally, and internationally, and to assert their value in society and state. It is one thing to have an academic and political discussion that values and incentivizes multiculturalism. It is quite another to understand the brutal reality of impoverishment to which indigenous communities are subjected that makes difficult or completely denies the possibility of the cultural self-determination sought by multiculturalism. Furthermore, there is a lack of material and cultural support for indigenous peoples from the state and an unwillingness of nation-states around the world to give full recognition to their rights of self-determination.

The regional vision of Mexican history has come to clash with an idea of history as centralized and of nationalist and monocultural uniformity. Enrique Florescano (2002, 549) positions himself, for example, in "rebellion against the thesis" of a uniform Mexican identity, arguing that there is not a singular collective memory. Rather, he argues, Mexico is characterized by many histories, corresponding to the multiplicity of ethnic groups and social groupings that make up the country. Rebelling against the "centralist cannon" of Mexican historiography, he laments, "We still lack a substantive essay on the development and characteristics of a regional historiography, and attention has hardly begun to be paid to groups other than creoles and mestizos, which were the only ones recognized as important figures in the nationalist historiography of the 19th and 20th centuries" (Florescano 2002, 549). We hope that the analysis presented in this chapter will improve our understanding of the unique political systems of Oaxaca's so-called UC municipalities.

On its theoretical side, multiculturalism lays out an understanding of the "other" as one that possesses rights and abilities to reproduce and reinforce his or her own culture, either individually or collectively. For this cultural reproduction and reinforcement to be possible, it is argued, cultures require recognition, respect, and the right of self-determination. This normative perspective need not be based in an essentialist primordialism that considers cultures to be rigid and slow to change (e.g., Geertz 1973). As de Sousa Santos argues, cultural systems are always incomplete and problematic, and "this incompleteness derives precisely from the fact that a plurality of cultures exist" (2010, 91). According to Adrián Scribano (1999), multiculturalism has become one of the most important fields in the social sciences, due in large part to the "ever-accelerating process of assimilation in multiethnic states." To build a social theory of the multiculturalist phenomenon, Scribano (1999) argues, "it is necessary to build a multiculturalism-sensitive social theory multiculturally. For this to happen, attention must be paid to what can be learned from local problems and the people affected by them."

This chapter takes as its unit of analysis the mayors of the UC municipalities in Oaxaca. It examines their backgrounds of civil and religious service to the community, as well as the relationship between their pathways to the mayor's office and their education and occupations. In so doing it creates a typology of municipal subsystems. This descriptive analysis improves our understanding of the internal diversity among indigenous municipalities, allowing us to move beyond such overly simplistic dichotomies as UC versus political party system or indigenous versus mestizo. The pathway mayors take to power is an important indicator of the degree to which UC communities have maintained their traditional forms—which require many years of religious and civil service in the community—or have taken on nontraditional forms in which the "ladder" (*escalafón*) of local service has ceased to be the dominant pathway to local authority.

The hypothesis here is that there is great cultural and structural diversity among the UC municipalities that results from and reflects the cultural, social, economic, and political changes that have taken place in Oaxaca. These changes have affected the local expression of culture in different ways across the state. To demonstrate this internal diversity, we examine original survey data gathered from municipal authorities in Oaxaca's UC municipalities. This chapter provides a sweeping view of the social, cultural, civil, and political pathways that mayors in UC municipalities have followed leading up to their selection for that office by their community. Specifically, we present data on the extent to which the traditional paradigm of power granted under UC, according to which mayors are expected to have fulfilled a combination of civil and religious *cargo*s and activities before reaching the highest levels of municipal authority, persists and the extent to which it has changed. By doing so, we attempt to make clear the ways in which many cultures coexist in Oaxaca's UC communities, but also how the residents of these communities often live in conditions of enormous economic, social, and educational deprivation. We thus hope to point out not so much the political surface of the Oaxacan municipalities, short-term or conflict-laden as they often are, but rather the complex cultural, economic, and social base formed by this world that is so special and, for many of us, so little understood.

Data were collected through a survey conducted in 2007 and 2008 in 417 of the 418 Oaxacan municipalities recognized as UC, the Survey of Oaxaca, Mexico Customary Law Municipalities. For the biographical data analyzed here, responses were obtained in 378 UC municipalities (90 percent of the total).

We begin by presenting basic demographic, social, and economic characteristics of Oaxaca's UC mayors, including their history of *cargo* service. Second, we discuss mayors' civil and religious *cargo* service in greater detail, outlining a preliminary typology of pathways to the mayor's office. Third, we use cluster analysis to construct a more sophisticated typology, demonstrating that there are three distinct subsystems of UC municipalities. This empirical analysis shows that the categories of "individualistic" and "communitarian" often discussed in debates about multiculturalism (see introduction, this volume) are concretely reflected within indigenous municipalities in Oaxaca. Within a single state, and even within specific municipalities (particularly those classified as semitraditional), strong communitarian dynamics are mixed with more modern, individualistic determinants of who gains local political power. Finally, we draw on the analysis of this typology of municipalities to draw conclusions about the social characteristics of the local governing elite in Oaxaca's UC communities.

MAYORS: WHO THEY ARE

Basic Characteristics

The position of mayor is dominated by men, with women holding the post in only 1 percent of municipalities. That figure changes slightly with each election, but even in the best of cases the percentage of female mayors has not exceeded 2 or

3 percent. Moreover, there is no evident trend of increased women's representation in mayors' offices.

Younger (29–44 years of age) and middle-aged (45–54) adults serve as mayor at rates of 34 percent and 38 percent respectively, while a little more than a quarter (28 percent) are older (between 55 and 75). The mean age is 48.8 years, with a median of 48, indicating to some degree that the path to becoming a mayor in Oaxaca is linked to civil and religious *cargos*, which must be undertaken before seeking and gaining election to the community's highest political position.

As for language, the largest proportion of mayors speak Spanish exclusively (50 percent), and a nearly equal proportion speak Spanish and an indigenous language (43 percent), an indispensable asset for a mayor in dealing with state and federal agencies and authorities. Even so, 6 percent of mayors responded that they could only speak an indigenous language, thus requiring the assistance of translators for their dealings with state officials and administrative duties. Four mayors (1 percent of the total) speak English, likely learned as a result of their migration experience. The fact that half of the mayors speak only Spanish, and the other half are bilingual or speak only an indigenous language, allows assemblies to operate using a very marked ethnolinguistic criterion. According to the survey, 50 percent said that the assembly for electing municipal officials was held in Spanish, while the other half reported that their assemblies communicated in an indigenous language.

Nearly one-quarter of the mayors (24 percent) reported having had a migration experience. Of these, 55 percent had had their last experience in the United States, 44 percent elsewhere in Mexico, and 1 percent in Canada.

The distribution of last jobs held before becoming mayor—or perhaps the one that some still held while in office—was as follows: almost half (45 percent) said they had been peasants, while the remainder had been manual or wage laborers, business owners, teachers, professionals, government workers, and had held other jobs. The proportions of mayors among the latter occupations were quite similar, at around 8 percent for each group.

In terms of education, one in four mayors did not complete primary school or did not even complete a single year of primary school. We can assume that these mayors are functionally illiterate. Half received basic education (primary or secondary schooling completed), and the remaining quarter received an intermediate or professional education. This variable is fundamental because, as studies have shown, education level is associated with the level of poverty that families and individuals face. For this reason, we will relate this data to various aspects of the service and social pathways of mayors in Oaxaca.[2]

The association between occupation and education is as one might expect: 41 percent of peasants did not achieve any level of formal schooling, and only 3 percent were able to obtain an intermediate or advanced level. Of the wage laborers, 19 percent had no education, while at the other extreme, 65 percent of government workers received intermediate or high education, along with 100 percent of teachers and professionals. Across age groups, there is a noticeable increase in the levels of education among younger mayors: 12 percent of those between the ages of 29 and 44 received no education, along with 25 percent of those in the 45–54 age group and

42 percent of the oldest grouping. The level of functional illiteracy, then, practically doubles between the first and the second group, and again between the second and the third.

In spite of their lack of education, mayors make up a relatively educated group in the Oaxacan context. They are also at about the national average in this respect, which increases the likelihood of their acting more diligently and capably to incorporate ideas and programs that favor the development of their communities.

The relationship between education and language is also as expected: those who speak only indigenous languages have the lowest levels of education (39 percent of those who have not completed primary education), followed by the bilingual Spanish-indigenous group (33 percent of those with no formal education). Those who speak Spanish are least likely to have minimal education (18 percent of the uneducated). Education level is a kind of social reference point, helping to explain the type of work or occupation, language usage, and skill at managing the duties involved in municipal government. One can suppose, then, that the issues and problems faced by mayors can be most advantageously met by the knowledge and skills gained in schools, and that this is an important factor to improve the UC system, or at least the administration of UC municipalities.

The *Cargo* System

Seventeen percent of mayors held no civil or religious *cargos* before taking office, while 3 percent held only religious *cargos*, 38 percent undertook only civil activities in their community, and 42 percent performed both civil and religious duties. Comparing participation in religious *cargos* to participation in civil *cargos*, we find that 45 percent of the leaders held a religious *cargo* and 80 percent held a civil one. It can thus be said that, at first glance, civil *cargo* experience is more important than religious *cargo* service in order to become mayor.

Considering the *cargos* and duties that are performed prior to becoming mayor provides an initial snapshot to help us understand the background of Oaxaca's UC mayors (see table 7.1). We might consider communities in which the mayor has not held any kind of *cargo* to be the least traditional. They have the youngest leaders (by mean age), the best-educated mayors, and the lowest proportion of peasants who reach that highest governmental position. Thus they are the communities with the highest levels of modernization and development in Oaxaca.

At the other extreme, communities where one has served in civil and religious *cargos* before being elected as mayor would be the state's most traditional. It is in these municipalities that one finds the highest mean age (perhaps due to the requirement to serve in many lower-level *cargos* to be eligible), the highest proportion of officials without formal schooling, and the highest proportion of peasants in the position of municipal power. These communities, therefore, display a highly rural economic structure and very low levels of literacy, the product of poverty and of the education system's inability, when it even exists, to serve the local population. At the same time, however, consistent with arguments made by those who defend UC recognition (e.g., Martínez Luna 2007), these data suggest that when traditional

Table 7.1 Mayors' Service in Civil and Religious *Cargos*: Socioeconomic Indicators

Cargos *Held*	Age N	Age Mean	Indigenous N	Indigenous %	No Education N	No Education %	Peasants N	Peasants %
Neither civil nor religious	45	46.8	21	46.7	3	7.7	11	17.5
Religious but not civil	141	47.6	61	45.5	2	20.0	64	36.4
Civil but not religious	11	47.9	5	42.1	31	22.8	4	43.8
Both civil and religious	154	50.4	88	56.1	50	32.9	92	57.9
All mayors	351	48.9	175	48.9	86	25.5	171	45.1

Source: Author analysis of the 2008 Survey of Oaxaca, Mexico Customary Law Municipalities, Biographical Survey of Mayors.

UC practices are respected, ordinary citizens of modest means have access to positions of power that they would rarely enjoy under other political systems.

In the middle, between these two kinds of municipalities, one finds political leaders who have fulfilled only one of the two types of functions, civil or religious, and their positions with respect to age, education, and peasant labor also lie between traditional and nontraditional municipalities.

It can be inferred, then, that there is a relationship between the *cargo* system and the level of modernization or economic diversity in each place, and that, if activities that serve as prerequisites for eligibility and election as mayor are taken into account, one can speak of three kinds of communities: traditional, which constitute 42 percent of municipalities in Oaxaca; semitraditional, making up 41 percent of the municipalities; and nontraditional, which make up only 17 percent of the total number. According to this typology, less than a fifth of the municipalities have strayed from the traditional UC system, while 83 percent continue, to a greater or lesser degree, to be tied to the dynamic of service as a foundation stone for municipal organization and government in Oaxaca.

RELIGIOUS *CARGOS*

There has been a noteworthy process of secularization in Oaxacan communities. Not even half of the mayors had performed religious duties before becoming mayor. Of the 45 percent who did so, half served as *mayordomo* (host of the community's patron saint festival), and the other half held lower-level *cargos* in the church. The position of *mayordomo* is considered the highest of the religious *cargos*, and in many municipalities service as *mayordomo* is considered to be a prerequisite to being elected mayor. More specifically, within the traditional system, children begin to undertake small tasks for the church, which continue through the child's adolescence. Then, at some point during his adult life, following a rigorous selection process, he may be designated to serve as *mayordomo*.

In this chapter, a rather general listing of religious *cargos* is used. It is in no way as detailed as the listing that Cristina Velásquez used in her work on the religious *cargos* that are held in Oaxaca (Velásquez et al. 1997). However, even with a general listing, it can be said that religious service is, little by little, ceasing to be indispensable to become mayor. Of the mayors in Oaxaca's UC municipalities, 55 percent have not gone through any religious *cargo*, 27 percent have held only one, and 18 percent have had two or more.

Of those who have held only one *cargo*, 58 percent served in a lower-level one, and 42 percent have organized a *mayordomía*. Of those who have held two or more *cargos*, 35 percent have not served as *mayordomo* while 65 percent have. Seventy percent (those who held no *cargos* or only a single minor one) have no deep connection to the church; 51 percent of *mayordomos* did not follow a path of prior *cargos*, as this is the only *cargo* that they mentioned; and only 18 percent, who said they had held two or more *cargos* in the church, can be said to have had a background of religious service.

Thirty percent of UC mayors in Oaxaca have followed a path of religious service, and 23 percent of these have served as *mayordomo* in their community. We now turn to the communities where religious *cargos* are held and the kinds of people who hold them, and the characteristics of those who have served as *mayordomo*.

Among the 170 communities where the mayor has followed a religious pathway 94 percent have both civil and religious service. In the remaining 6 percent, only religious activities were undertaken. What appears to be the distinctive feature of the religious aspect is that in both types of communities there is an equal distribution between lower-level and higher-level *cargos*, with 49 percent having served only lower-level religious *cargo*, and 51 percent serving as *mayordomos*. This suggests an intense religious life in these municipalities, a finding that is perfectly in harmony with the theory that the traditional *cargo* system appears to be shrinking only because many pass directly to the post of *mayordomo*, without first going through a series of prior activities in order to become deserving of, or to achieve, this highest religious *cargo*. I now turn to the characteristics of those who hold minor *cargos* and *mayordomías* under the system.

Table 7.2 shows the relationship between mayors' age and the type of religious *cargos* held. In the first two age groups (29–44 and 45–54 years), there is an equal distribution between lower-level *cargos* and *mayordomías*, a balance that is not present in the oldest group (55–75 years), where *mayordomos* predominate over those having held lower-level *cargos*. If one adds to this the fact that the proportion of older men is greater among *mayordomos* than among the population of mayors as a whole, it is evident that this *cargo* bears a certain relationship to age. If this is true, it is another point demonstrating that, in the traditional system, there exists a pathway of religious service to the mayor's office.

Across basic, intermediate, and higher education levels, there is a balance between lower-level *cargos* and *mayordomos*, while in the group with no education the balance tilts heavily toward *mayordomos* and away from lower-level *cargos*. If one adds to this the fact that the proportion of those without formal education is higher among *mayordomos* than it is among all mayors, it can be said that the *cargo* of *mayordomo* is inversely related to level of education, since those who obtained higher education are underrepresented relative to their position among all mayors, and those with basic education are represented at the same levels. In addition, if

Table 7.2 Religious *Cargo* Service by Age Group, Education, and Occupation

	Religious Cargo but Not Mayordomo		Religious Cargo Including Mayordomo		No Religious Cargo		All Mayors	
	N	%	N	%	N	%	N	%
Age Group								
29–44 years	25	30.5	24	27.9	73	38.8	122	34.3
45–54 years	32	39.0	30	34.9	73	38.8	135	37.9
55–75 years	25	30.5	32	37.2	42	22.3	99	27.8
Level of Education								
No education	22	25.6	30	34.9	34	39.5	86	25.5
Basic education	40	24.7	39	24.1	83	51.2	162	48.1
Intermediate and higher education	15	16.9	16	18.0	58	65.2	89	26.4
Employment								
Peasant	46	26.9	50	29.2	75	43.9	171	47.9
Wage laborer	9	29.0	10	32.3	12	38.7	31	8.7
Business owner	5	16.1	9	29.0	17	54.8	31	8.7
Teacher	3	10.3	4	13.8	22	75.9	29	8.1
Professional	5	17.9	5	17.9	18	64.3	28	7.8
Government employee	6	17.6	5	14.7	23	67.6	34	9.5
Employee of private business	1	14.3	0	0.0	6	85.7	7	2.0
Other	5	19.2	4	15.4	17	65.4	26	7.3

Source: Author analysis of the 2008 Survey of Oaxaca, Mexico Customary Law Municipalities, Biographical Survey of Mayors.

education level is an indicator for standard of living, it can be inferred that among UC mayors, those who have served as *mayordomos* are likely to be poorer than those who have not.[3] In terms of occupation, business owners are the ones who most often bear the expense of serving as *mayordomo*; next in line are the other occupational groupings: teachers, wage laborers, peasants, and professionals. Business owners obviously have the economic ability to defray the costs of a *mayordomía*. The problem is that they represent less than 9 percent of the workers in their communities. The question returns, once again, to the distribution of the workers. In that respect, the peasants and wage laborers make up a greater proportion among *mayordomos* relative to their proportion of the population at large, while teachers and professionals make up a lower proportion. This shows that there are two social groupings that assume the cost of the patron saint's festival: the business owners, who remain economically solvent, and the peasants and wage laborers, who likely must spend much of their savings and go into debt, sometimes extensively so, in order to cover the cost of the festival. In sum, it is often those who have the least who must pay an extraordinary tax to the church.

Civil *Cargos*

The civil-political path that UC mayors follow is a complex one, due to the wide variety of duties that a person must fulfill in the community and the fact that these duties unfold over the course of a lifetime in an indigenous or peasant municipality. Rural communities have a multiplicity of *cargos*, which differ significantly in their importance depending on where they fall in a tiered hierarchy. The duties are divided here into five categories:

1. High-level *cargos* in the municipal government, comprising the mayor, *síndico* (judicial alderman), *alcalde* (assists *síndico* with matters of internal security and justice), *regidor de hacienda* (municipal finance alderman), and treasurer
2. Lower-level *cargos* in the municipal government, covering *regidurías con menor manejo presupuestal* (aldermen with lesser budgetary roles) and administrative support activities
3. Social development duties, with activities connected to health, education, and rural aid
4. Economic development duties, with *cargos* for managing communal and *ejido* lands (*comisariado de bienes comunales* or *ejidales*), supervising infrastructure construction (roads, water, drainage, electricity, etc.), and organizing production activities
5. Various activities related to religious life and traditional festivals, and others

In order to measure the importance of the duties performed, we constructed an index, assigning the following values to the various activities: 50 for high-level *cargos* in the municipal government, 30 for regulatory and supervisory duties related to economic development, 20 for those related to social development, 20 for lower-level *cargos* in the municipal government, and 5 for other activities. Using the sum of activities' values, we created a composite index that reflects the weight attached to the civil and political *cargos* that UC mayors have held.

We thus show that the importance of serving in *cargos* before becoming mayor is not the same across communities, as the dominant UC paradigm suggests. These activities are more important in traditional municipalities, and more educated mayors in less traditional municipalities are, in good measure, exempt from having to take part. Overall, the results are as follows: 19 percent of mayors answered that they had not held government positions nor undertaken civil activities in support of their community, whereas 81 percent of mayors said that they had done so. The weight of community service or support plays a fundamental role in the municipalities of Oaxaca and is, in large part, a prerequisite to seeking the office of mayor.

The mean weight of the civil-political activities is 83 points for semitraditional communities, in which they were performed as part of community life to the exclusion of religious *cargos*. In very traditional communities, in which both civil and religious activities were undertaken, the mean weight is 111 points. This means that there is a relationship between weight of community work and level of traditionalism: zero in nontraditional communities, growing in semitraditional communities, and strongest in those that are traditional. In addition, there is a pathway to government that runs from civil duties and lower-level positions to the highest-level positions of the government. The weight of civil and administrative support activities had a mean of 57 points, while the mean weight of activities of those who served in higher-level positions (plus other lower-level positions) was more than twice as high, at 127 points. Furthermore, in order to better understand the civil-political pathway, we divide the weight scores into three categories, with resulting means of 46 points for low-level activities, 112 for midlevel positions, and 182 points for high-level posts.

Semitraditional and traditional communities carry nearly identical weights, 48 percent and 52 percent respectively, and they comprise 81 percent of all UC municipalities in Oaxaca. Among the types of duties performed, there is a fairly similar distribution in both types of municipality: approximately 42 percent of mayors have undertaken community support activities or lower-level positions in the government, while the rest (about 58 percent) have occupied high-level positions in the government. Thus many people who become mayor have a solid civil-political track record in their communities. We now turn to the social characteristics of these mayors.

Table 7.3 shows the relationship between mayors' levels of community activity and power and age. Age patterns make abundantly clear the civil-administrative pathway

Table 7.3 Mayors' Civil *Cargo* Service Level by Social Characteristics

	Level of Civil Cargo Service					
	Low (5–70)		Medium (75–140)		High (150+)	
	N	%	N	%	N	%
Age Group						
29–44 years	62	45.9	29	29.9	13	19.1
45–54 years	42	31.1	40	41.2	25	36.8
55–75 years	31	23.0	28	28.9	30	44.1
Level of Education						
No education	23	18.1	32	33.3	26	40.0
Basic education	60	47.2	49	51.0	34	52.3
Intermediate and higher education	44	34.6	15	15.6	5	7.7
Employment						
Peasant	58	42.3	53	54.1	45	67.2
Wage laborer	12	8.8	9	9.2	8	11.9
Business owner	13	9.5	12	12.2	3	4.5
Teacher	12	8.8	6	6.1	2	3.0
Professional	16	11.7	4	4.1	0	0.0
Government employee	15	10.9	7	7.1	2	3.0
Employee of private business	2	1.5	2	2.0	0	0.0
Other	9	6.6	5	5.1	7	10.4
All Mayors	138	45.3	99	32.5	68	22.3

Source: Author analysis of the 2008 Survey of Oaxaca, Mexico Customary Law Municipalities, Biographical Survey of Mayors.

that mayors have followed under Oaxaca's UC system. The older the mayor, the more likely it is that he has a higher level of service in government positions. These data suggest that the path to becoming mayor in the municipalities of Oaxaca is marked (or preceded) by an accumulation of commissions assigned by and performed under the eye of the community, as well as by a scale of positions within the government.

Level of education suggests how unattractive public duties are as a result of being unpaid. As table 7.3 also shows, there is an inverse relationship between education level and service in the community government, with a dramatic decline in service as one passes from no education, through basic education, and on into the intermediate and higher levels. Municipal government, which is to a large extent honorary and uncompensated, is only important to those with little formal education and, given its low to nonexistent opportunity for profitability, is looked down on with disdain by the most educated segment of the population.

Occupation points to the weakness of the municipal governments. It also shows the tendency for peasants, wage laborers, and business owners to do low-paying work or for teachers and professionals to accept positions in the municipal government that entail much greater difficulty.

A TYPOLOGY OF MUNICIPALITIES

These data suggest that there are three types of municipalities in the UC system in Oaxaca. The first subsystem is characterized by nontraditional municipalities, in which mayors have not performed civil and religious *cargos* before taking office and are more likely to be professionals and have higher education levels. The second subsystem is characterized by semitraditional communities, defined by mayors' participation in only one kind of service activity, either civil or religious. Finally, the third subsystem is traditional, consisting of municipalities where both civil and religious activities are undertaken.

These subsystems, defined by the amount and kind of service given to the community by current mayors, are correlated with the socioeconomic characteristics of mayors (such as age, education, and occupation), providing strong evidence that different subsystems are present within the UC system. Indeed, reality is not as simple as a dichotomy. There are always complex mixtures in human behavior and institutions. For this reason, we constructed an index of civil and religious activity to reflect a more nuanced typology of subsystems (nontraditional, semitraditional, and traditional). Using cluster analysis, we arrived at a schema that is more closely linked to the reality of UC in Oaxaca.[4]

The use of clusters based on the civil and religious *cargo* service of mayors creates a different picture of the system: the number of nontraditional municipalities grows dramatically; the number of semitraditional ones increases slightly; and the traditional subsystem shrinks dramatically. So whereas the earlier dichotomous classification showed 17 percent of municipalities as nontraditional and 83 percent as traditional, the cluster classification produces a rate of 52 percent for nontraditional and only 16.1 percent for traditional. We turn, then, to examining how this process works.

Table 7.4 Relationship between Weight of *Cargos* and Type of Municipality

		Nontraditional	Semitraditional	Traditional	All
Mean weight religious *cargos*		10.7	30.6	46.3	22.8
Mean weight civil *cargos*		27.1	108.9	186.1	78.8
Mean age (in years)		46.8	49.7	53.4	48.9
All municipalities	N	197	121	61	379
	%	52.0	31.9	16.1	100.0

Source: Author analysis of the 2008 Survey of Oaxaca, Mexico Customary Law Municipalities, Biographical Survey of Mayors.

Age and, above all, the mean weight of the civil and religious *cargos* increases as one moves from nontraditional to traditional municipalities, as shown in table 7.4. The differences that appear seem sufficiently strong that one can speak of three clearly defined subsystems. All of them contain a given level of UC practices, but they are, at the same time, rather different in each of their levels or subsystems.

Table 7.5 shows the relationship between type of community and the fulfillment of religious and civil *cargos*. The proportion of mayors who have no prior service in religious *cargos* is very high (75 percent) in nontraditional municipalities, moderate (41 percent) in semitraditional ones, and, as was expected, very low (20 percent) in traditional municipalities. In the nontraditional municipalities, only a quarter of the mayors have taken on a religious *cargo* in the course of their life, while in the traditional communities, religious practice is a norm of community social life.

The holding of *mayordomías* follows the same pattern of norms: only one-tenth of the leaders in nontraditional municipalities have been a *mayordomo*, while in traditional ones 42.6 percent have fulfilled this duty. The distribution of activities in each type of municipality varies by subcategory: almost all of those who are inactive with regard to the church are concentrated in nontraditional municipalities; there is a clear separation between those who undertake religious activity and those who do not in semitraditional communities; and traditional municipalities represent a society that is intensely motivated by religious life. Put another way, one sees the church as a center of socialization in the traditional municipalities, religious life under challenge in the semitraditional cases, and the church separated from civil-political life in the nontraditional cases.

The core of civil activities changes as one moves from nontraditional to traditional. In the former, the activities of the current mayors have centered on local development, since 45 percent of mayors in nontraditional communities mentioned participating in work for social and economic development, as well as in lower-level positions in the government or in the posts of commissioner of communal or *ejido* resources. In semitraditional and traditional communities, on the other hand, the focus of activity is on high-level duties in the municipal government.

These trends suggest that mayors in nontraditional municipalities perform work that is chiefly concerned with community development. However, there also

Table 7.5 Relationship between Religious *Cargos* Held and Type of Municipality

		Nontraditional	Semitraditional	Traditional
No religious *cargo*	N	147	50	12
	%	74.6	41.3	19.7
Religious *cargo* but not *mayordomo*	N	29	31	23
	%	14.7	25.6	37.7
Religious *cargo* including *mayordomo*	N	21	40	26
	%	10.7	33.1	42.6

Source: Author analysis of the 2008 Survey of Oaxaca, Mexico Customary Law Municipalities, Biographical Survey of Mayors.

exists in those municipalities an important role for political groupings or parties, which enable people to ascend to the position of mayor without having gone through prior work in support of the community. Semitraditional and traditional communities have a real political pathway for becoming mayor. Those who seek or are elected to the office of mayor must first, as a social requirement, go through high-level positions in the local government, such as judicial positions or positions that direct economic resources for community improvement. This is why 69 percent of semitraditional mayors and 97 percent of traditional mayors have already served in high-level positions in their municipal governments. I now turn to considering the kinds of persons who become mayor according to the kind of municipality they serve.

Table 7.6 shows the relationship between type of community and the social characteristics of the mayors. It is important to note where the highest percentage falls. What is evident is a movement from younger to middle-aged to older mayors as one moves from nontraditional to traditional municipalities. This in turn highlights the importance of the *cargo* system in Oaxaca. When the weight of the *cargos* held is greater, a person must be older before he can be nominated and elected as mayor. For this reason, where minimal—or nonexistent—social weight is attached to the *cargos*, as is the case in nontraditional communities, it is more feasible for younger people to become mayor. On the other hand, where carrying the weight of *cargos* is absolutely required, as is the case in traditional municipalities, one must follow the prescribed civil-religious pathway and, therefore, spend many years in lower-level *cargos* before being nominated and elected to the *cargo* of mayor. It is no coincidence that one reaches the office of mayor at a more advanced age in traditional and semitraditional municipalities in Oaxaca.

The difference between mayors who are educated and those who are uneducated is very revealing. In traditional municipalities, mayors are illiterate or have only a basic command of reading and writing. In those that are semitraditional, they know the basics of reading, writing, and arithmetic. Mayors in nontraditional municipalities have higher levels of educational attainment and can therefore likely consider more complex matters, such as allocation of expenditures, financial reports, and the design and execution of community development projects. This is the reality of

Table 7.6 Type of Municipality by Social Characteristics

	Traditional		Semitraditional		Nontraditional	
	N	%	N	%	N	%
Age Group						
29–44 years	11	18.0	37	31.1	74	42.0
45–54 years	22	36.1	48	40.3	65	36.9
55–75 years	28	45.9	34	28.6	37	21.0
Level of Education						
No education	25	43.1	39	33.3	22	13.6
Basic education	28	48.3	60	51.3	74	45.7
Intermediate and higher education	5	8.6	18	15.4	66	40.7
Employment						
Peasant	41	68.3	64	53.3	66	37.3
Wage laborer	7	11.7	13	10.8	11	6.2
Business owner	3	5.0	14	11.7	14	7.9
Teacher	2	3.3	7	5.8	20	11.3
Professional	0	0.0	5	4.2	23	13.0
Government employee	2	3.3	7	5.8	25	14.1
Employee of private business	0	0.0	2	1.7	5	2.8
Other	5	8.3	8	6.7	13	7.3

Source: Author analysis of the 2008 Survey of Oaxaca, Mexico Customary Law Municipalities, Biographical Survey of Mayors.

today's Oaxaca. There are three obvious cultural and municipal government systems and three kinds of people who are at the head of their communities.

Almost half of Oaxaca's UC mayors are peasants, while the other half consists of equivalent numbers of wage laborers, business owners, teachers, and professionals. Teachers and professionals are found, quite noticeably, as mayors of nontraditional municipalities, while peasants, wage laborers, and business owners are represented well in all three types of municipalities. However, this statement needs to be fleshed out. Teachers and professionals are overrepresented, and peasants and wage laborers are underrepresented, among nontraditional municipalities. Among semitraditional municipalities, wage laborers and business owners are overrepresented, while professionals are underrepresented. In traditional municipalities, peasants and wage laborers are overrepresented, while teachers, government employees, and professionals are almost nowhere to be found.

Is this not also a clear expression of an economic world and a political world? The diversified economy of nontraditional localities opens up a space for leadership by those who have more advanced education and who have relationships with the centers of state and national power. These are the characteristics of professionals and teachers. In semitraditional communities, where the ways of community autarchy have been closed off and new possibilities for development have been opened up

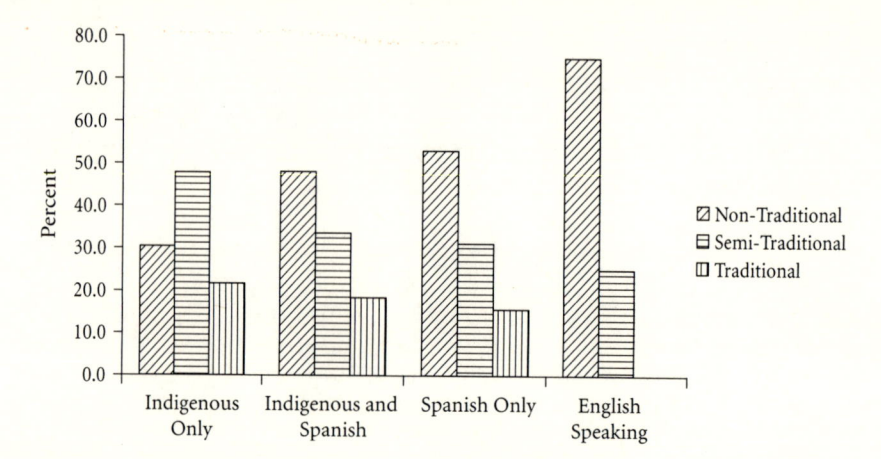

FIGURE 7.1
Relationship between Mayors' Language and Type of Municipality
Source: Author analysis of the 2008 Survey of Oaxaca, Mexico Customary Law Municipalities, Biographical Survey of Mayors.

by the phenomenon of migration and the pressures of the state, a diverse space has opened up for entrepreneurial peasants, laborers with migration experience, business owners who connect the community to the outside world, or teachers or professionals seeking to make their fortune. In the isolated and mostly closed world of traditional communities, which suffer from crushing impoverishment and find themselves with no alternatives for development, the world consists of those who stay and resist. It is thus a space for deep-rooted peasants and the few laborers who return to the community.

Figure 7.1 shows the relationship between type of municipality and the language spoken by the mayor, which stands in contrast to the tables that demonstrate large social and political differences between the three subsystems in Oaxaca. There is, to be sure, a slight cultural difference between the nontraditional and traditional worlds. In the latter, some are monolingual and the former includes migrants who can speak English. But on the whole, it is a uniform world, divided almost equally between indigenous-Spanish bilinguals and monolingual Spanish speakers. It is on this firm foundation that Oaxacan culture is built. In this area, one does not find differences between traditional and nontraditional, but rather many deep currents, which constitute the enormous multicultural variety that frames the face Oaxaca presents to the world.

THE LOCAL GOVERNING ELITE IN OAXACA'S UC COMMUNITIES

With a basis in this analysis of the pathways to power of mayors in Oaxaca's UC municipalities, I now turn to a discussion of the formation of power elites in Oaxaca's communities and the elements that form the context within which the people "who manifest exceptional qualities or eminent aptitudes" to govern their communities are selected (Valdivielso del Real n.d.).

As a working hypothesis, I propose four key factors that explain the election of each mayor:

1. The individual and his history within the social and institutional framework of each community
2. A group that selects and proposes to the assembly a list of people with the necessary prestige to be considered adequate to manage the mayorship
3. The type of community; in our case, divided into traditional, semitraditional, and nontraditional
4. The individual trajectory of those elected, which is, in the end, a type of social practice and behavior that is key for reaching positions of power as community representatives

The group in each municipality that proposes candidates is what could be referred to as a "nongoverning elite," the members of which have social recognition such that their voice is heard with interest and a level of reverence by the general population. In UC assemblies in Oaxaca, the nongoverning elite can be united or divided. In cases where there is a group that deliberates on, agrees about, and determines the people who may occupy the posts in the municipal government, this is considered to be a group of distinguished citizens that are fully recognized by their community and as such have the ability to select those who are eligible to be elected by the assembly. There are also cases in which more than one group gives opinions, proposing candidates and competing for the votes of the assembly. In these cases, the result is often a competition between different interest groups for municipal power. Those municipalities in which the distinguished citizens define the candidates are the traditional communities, while interest group competition is characteristic of the nontraditional municipalities.

On the other hand, the individuals to be elected should possess the attributes of prestige recognized by the community. Here again, the concept of prestige varies depending on the type of community. Traditional communities produce people "of prestige" and nontraditional communities produce individuals "with prestige." The former gain their prestige from carrying out civic and religious *cargos* over the course of their lives. The latter gain their prestige from two principal sources of recognition: civil and political service in the community and their relations outside of the community, including their ability to obtain resources.

It will be useful to clarify this picture by presenting empirical data. The survey analyzed in this chapter included a question about the most important attributes to be elected as mayor. The question allowed respondents to select multiple responses among the following options:

1. To have prestige and community recognition
2. Completion of civil and religious *cargos*
3. To be a professional
4. The ability to secure external public resources
5. To have good political relations outside of the municipality
6. To have the support of interest groups or political parties

In traditional municipalities, the most likely response was that mayors should have held previous civil and religious *cargos*, while in the nontraditional municipalities, it was more important to hold a professional degree, to have the ability to obtain external resources, and to be supported by interest groups or political parties. More specifically, the positive responses were distributed in the following way: in traditional communities, respondents replied that *cargo* service was most important; in semitraditional municipalities, the ability to secure external resources was most important; and in nontraditional communities, the most important prerequisites for becoming mayor were to hold a professional degree and to have the support of interest groups or political parties. In all municipalities, it was of fundamental importance that the person had prestige.

Traditional communities emphasize the importance of service to two institutions, the church and the municipality. In semitraditional municipalities, respondents see the connection between the municipality and the state government as fundamental. Finally, in the nontraditional communities, more individualistic characteristics, such as educational attainment and political relationships, are seen as most important. This division shows the different forms of acquiring prestige in each type of community. In the traditional communities, prestige is acquired by complying with the system of *cargos* in the church and the municipality. In the nontraditional municipalities, one becomes a person of prestige through academic, professional, and political achievement. We now turn to an analysis of the specific performance of mayors within each of the subsystems of the typology developed above. Table 7.7 presents a cross-tabulation of the type of community with the level of compliance with civil and religious *cargos* required to be mayor.

In traditional communities, compliance with civil and religious *cargos* is almost absolute (80 percent). In semitraditional communities, compliance is relatively broad at 59 percent, but in nontraditional communities, compliance is significantly less (20 percent). The lack of importance of both civil and religious *cargos* appears only in the nontraditional municipalities. Thus, the political elite is formed through service to the church and the municipal government in the traditional and semitraditional places. In the nontraditional municipalities, we observe more diversified elites, whose prestige seems to be based on service to the community (civil more

Table 7.7 Municipality Type by Level of *Cargo* Participation Required to Be Mayor

	Not Civil, Not Religious		Civil, Not Religious		Not Civil, Yes Religious		Civil and Religious	
	N	%	N	%	N	%	N	%
Nontraditional	63	32.0	84	42.6	11	5.6	39	19.8
Semitraditional	0	0.0	50	41.3	0	0.0	71	58.7
Traditional	0	0.0	12	19.7	0	0.0	49	80.3
All types	63	16.6	146	38.5	11	2.9	159	42.0

Source: Author analysis of the 2008 Survey of Oaxaca, Mexico Customary Law Municipalities, Biographical Survey of Mayors.

than religious) as well as individual achievement. The next survey question asked about the social origins of the authorities.

Table 7.8 shows the relationship between the social origin of mayors (as defined by their occupation before becoming mayor) and cargo service over the course of their lifetimes. Peasants, day laborers, and businesspeople are incorporated into the local political elite through the system of civil and religious *cargos*. Professionals, teachers, and government workers access local power through three pathways: (1) civil service to the community, which does not necessarily require that they hold central posts on the town council; (2) civil and religious service; and (3) individual prestige, without having completed any previous *cargos*. Those who worked in the private sector reach the local political elite in two ways: (1) civil service to the community, and (2) personal prestige, without having served in any previous *cargos*.

For peasants, wage laborers, and businesspeople, access to the power elite happens almost exclusively through *cargo* service, rather than through individual achievement. Teachers, professionals, and government and private sector workers access local power principally through service in civil *cargos*, as well as through professional and academic achievement.

In traditional communities, the obligation to fulfill civil and religious *cargo* duties has enormous importance. The governing elite in these municipalities is almost exclusively made up of peasants, with businesspeople, teachers, and government workers in the minority. Among the mayors of traditional municipalities, there were no professionals or individuals from the private sector. We would expect that this governing elite is socially homogenous, with a collectivist orientation, whose formative experience has been realized through service to the church and the municipal government.

Table 7.8 Relationship between Mayor's Occupation and *Cargo* Service

Occupation	Not Civil, Not Religious		Civil, Not Religious		Not Civil, Yes Religious		Civil and Religious		All Service Combinations	
	N	%	N	%	N	%	N	%	N	%
Peasant	11	25.0	64	43.8	4	36.4	92	59.0	171	47.9
Wage labourer	1	2.3	11	7.5	1	9.1	18	11.5	31	8.7
Business owner	3	6.8	14	9.6	0	0.0	14	9.0	31	8.7
Teacher	7	15.9	15	10.3	2	18.2	5	3.2	29	8.1
Professional	6	13.6	12	8.2	2	18.2	8	5.1	28	7.8
Government employee	9	20.5	14	9.6	1	9.1	10	6.4	34	9.5
Employee of private business	3	6.8	3	2.1	0	0.0	1	0.6	7	2.0
Other	4	9.1	13	8.9	1	9.1	8	5.1	26	7.3
All occupations	44	100.0	146	100.0	11	100.0	156	100.0	357	100.0

Source: Author analysis of the 2008 Survey of Oaxaca, Mexico Customary Law Municipalities, Biographical Survey of Mayors.

In semitraditional communities, the obligation to fulfill civil and religious *cargos* is less important than in traditional communities. The local political elite in these places represents the typical diversity present in the state of Oaxaca. Oaxaca is majority peasant and has a wide array of professionals, with wage laborers, businesspeople, teachers, professionals, and government workers all averaging 8 percent of the population. The political elite in these semitraditional cases is homogenous across five social groups (peasants, wage laborers, businesspeople, teachers, and professionals).

In nontraditional communities, participation in civic activities is most important. The religious-civic category loses all the importance it had in the traditional and semitraditional communities. The second relevant aspect has to do with the acquisition of prestige through educational or professional achievement. We have, then, a diversified society that values community service and the ability to mobilize external resources and institutional contacts, as well as educational and professional achievement. The structure of the local political elite represents the diversification of semirural communities, with a third being peasants, and an even distribution between wage laborers, businesspeople, teachers, professionals, government workers, and workers from the private sector.

In this case, the elite function principally around a bureaucratic behavior, with the fulfillment of remunerated work in civil *cargos* carried out in the community. Local elites are clearly divided into two segments: the traditional, made up of peasants, wage laborers, and businesspeople, and the nontraditional, made up of educated and specialized workers that reach the position of mayor because of the importance given to scholarly and professional merit in these communities.

Traditional communities create a cultural elite, developed within homogeneous peasant societies that require social practices that are completely tied to the church and civil *cargo* service to the municipality. Semitraditional communities create a cultural and bureaucratic elite developed in rural societies with some level of social diversification with practices that revolve around the church and the municipal government, but not quite as much as in the traditional municipalities. Finally, nontraditional communities create a diversified elite characterized by three sources of social prestige: (1) bureaucratic behavior, (2) traditional behavior, and (3) professional merit. These are semirural societies with a more narrow peasant base, social diversification, and political life characterized by competition between groups to come to power with the support of community assemblies.

To better understand the political dynamics of Oaxacan communities, it is necessary to apply three theories: Pareto's (1935) "prestigious individual," Mosca's (1939) theory of political class, and Dahl's (1961) theory of democratic pluralism.

CONCLUSION

Oaxaca is served through a system of *cargos* that allow access to municipal power. It is not, however, a uniform system, but one that exhibits many differences. First, we find a clear differentiation between three subsystems: nontraditional, semitraditional, and traditional. Each of these has a specific dynamic in its cultural, economic, social, and political order. One way of considering how municipal power is attained is to look at the pathways that mayors follow. This is the theme examined in this chapter.

The nontraditional system shows a weak combination of civil and religious activities and tends to be somewhat individualistic. Thirty-two percent of mayors in nontraditional municipalities never gave any prior service to their community, and none followed the track of combined service to the church and the municipality. Nevertheless, the system's strength rests in service to the community. Forty-five percent of current mayors undertook activities related to local social and/or economic development, land governance, or administrative support for the municipal government. Here, the way to the mayor's seat is found in the individual's connections to political parties or associations, as well as in his service in assigned work, *comisariados,* and community support activities.

In the traditional system, the road is more prolonged and demands much more effort. In these municipalities, a complex and long series of civil and religious *cargos* operates. Almost every one of the present mayors was previously named to relevant *cargos* in the local government, and 43 percent have served as *mayordomo*. In general, the mayor receives this *cargo* as the culmination of a long record of service, in which he had to make large contributions of both wealth and time toward upholding the religious beliefs and mitigating the poverty of his community.

The semitraditional system operates more in line with the traditional. The charge to religious service and government duties is not borne as faithfully as it is in the traditional system, but neither is there the level of individualism and freedom of action that one finds in the nontraditional system. Sixty-nine percent of mayors had to take on high-level government duties, and a third of them have served as *mayordomo* or have undertaken socioeconomic development activities for their communities. It is, then, an intermediate space between the unbending pyramid of the traditional systems and the more secularized, civil system of the nontraditional municipalities.

Thus, one can speak of three sociopolitical categories framed by a society that is complex and multicultural, or in which the political sphere, reflecting the womb from which it came, becomes complicated and fragmented to the point of infinity. The chief point of divergence can perhaps be found in the following: the axis or nucleus around which the system turns is the acquisition of social-community prestige, and social prestige is the indispensable basis for being nominated and elected to the position of mayor. But prestige can be worked out in two ways. In the nontraditional system, it allows a person to reach a political position through which he can obtain power in three ways: engaging in service to the community throughout his or her life, gaining public support through traditional civil and religious norms, and gaining prestige through professional careers and political connections within and outside of the community. In the traditional system, everything depends on the prestige gained from service to the municipality and the church. The mayorship, more than being a source of political power, has an ethnic-cultural significance, and is the culmination of a lifetime of service to one's community.

With respect to elites, we move from the unitary to the diversified. Those in traditional communities are selected as potential mayors by a group of distinguished people, that is, a nongoverning elite, which offers the post to the person who has ascended the full ladder of service of the *cargo* system. Selection of mayors in nontraditional communities, on the other hand, is characterized by competition between interest groups as each proposes their most prestigious candidates before the community assembly, which evaluates them and decides which person will best serve the interests of the community.

NOTES

1. Much has been written about the traditional or typical place of the communitarian UC system, which incorporates the religious, social, and political life of a community. Some of the most important texts include Aguirre Beltrán (1956), Carrasco (1979), Medina (2007a, 2007b), Korsbaek (1996), and Martínez Luna (2007).
2. A number of works have established a significant relationship between poverty and the level of education in a population. Works that use this relationship to show the historical and contemporary development of Mexico include Meyer (2007) and Zenteno (2008).
3. Data were not collected on the socioeconomic status of mayors.
4. As Salvador Figueras (2001), professor at the Universidad de Zaragoza in Spain, writes: "Cluster analysis, also known as numerical taxonomy and pattern recognition, is a multivariate statistical technique which produces the division of objects into groups (clusters) such that the profiles of objects in the same group are very similar (internal cohesion) and those of objects in different clusters are distinct from each other (external isolation)."

REFERENCES

Aguirre Beltrán, Gonzalo. 1956. *Formas de gobierno indígena*. Mexico City: Imprenta Universitaria.

Carrasco, Pedro. 1979. "La jerarquía cívico religiosa en las comunidades de Mesoamérica: Antecedentes precolombinos y desarrollo colonial." In *Antropología Política*, edited by Josep Llobera. Barcelona: Anagrama.

Dahl, R. A. 1961. *Who Governs? Democracy and Power in an American City*. New Haven, CT: Yale University Press.

de Sousa Santos, Boaventura. 2010. *Para descolonizar occidente. Más allá del pensamiento abismal*. Buenos Aires: Consejo Latinoamericano de Ciencias Sociales—CLACSO and Prometeo Libros.

Figueras, Manuel Salvador. 2001. "Análisis de conglomerados o cluster." *5campus.org, Estadística*. http://www.5campus.org/leccion/cluster.

Florescano, Enrique. 2002. *Memoria mexicana*. Mexico City: Editorial FCE.

García Canclini, Néstor. 1999. *La globalización imaginada*. Barcelona: Editorial Paidos-Ibérica.

Geertz, Clifford. 1973. *The Interpretation of Cultures*. New York: Basic Books.

INEGI (Instituto Nacional de Estadística y Geografía). 2006. *Conteo de población y vivienda de México 2005*. Mexico City: INEGI.

Korsbaek, Leif. 1996. *Introducción al sistema de cargos*. Toluca: Universidad Autónoma del Estado de México.

Martínez Luna, Jaime. 2007. "Comunalidad y autonomía." *Cuadernos y caminos* (blog). January 30. http://tallerurquiamaru.blogspot.com/2007/01/comunalidad-y-autonoma-jaime-martnez.html.

Medina, Andrés. 2007a. "Los pueblos originarios del sur del Distrito Federal: Una primera mirada etnográfica." In *La memoria negada de la ciudad de México: Sus pueblos originarios*, edited by Andrés Medina, 29–124. Mexico City: UNAM/UACM..

Medina, Andrés. 2007b. "Los sistemas de cargo en la Cuenca de México: Una primera aproximación a su trasfondo histórico." *Alteridades* 5 (9): 7–23.

Meyer, Lorenzo. 2007. *El espejismo democrático: De la euforia del cambio a la continuidad*. Mexico City: Océano.

Mosca, G. 1939. *The Ruling Class*. Westport, CT: Greenwood.

Pareto, V. 1935. *The Mind and Society*. New York: Harcourt Brace.

Scribano, Adrián. 1999. "Multiculturalismo, Teoría Social y Contexto Latinoamericano." *La factoría* 9 (June–September). http://www.revistalafactoria.eu/articulo.php?id=131.

Velásquez, María Cristina, et al. 1997. *Usos y costumbres para la renovación de los ayuntamientos de Oaxaca*. Oaxaca City, Mexico: Centro de Investigaciones y Estudios Superiores de Antropologia Social/Instituto Estatal Electoral de Oaxaca.

Valdivielso del Real, Rocío. n.d. "Teoría de las élites." In *Diccionario crítico de ciencias sociales*, edited by Román Reyes. Universidad Nacional de Educación a Distancia. http://www.ucm.es/info/eurotheo/diccionario/E/teoria_elites.htm.

Zenteno, René. 2008. Presentation at Seventh Seminario Regional de Innovación, Tijuana, Baja California, February 25.

8 Community Strength and Customary Law
Explaining Migrant Participation in Indigenous Oaxaca

Michael S. Danielson

What explains varying levels of participation by migrants in the political and social life of their hometowns? Do indigenous customary law institutions and the organizational strength of hometowns function as mechanisms through which community leaders can encourage migrants to contribute funds and return home to provide direct service to their communities of origin? To what extent are migrants making it to higher levels of authority in their hometowns, and what are the potential impacts of this for democratization?

Much of the scholarship on indigenous rights, multiculturalism, and customary law recognition has focused on ideologically charged normative debates between those who prioritize individual rights and pluralism granted by nation states (Barry 2001) and those who hold that for certain groups within societies, the unit of rights recognition should be the community or group (Kymlicka 1995; see introduction, this volume, for a summary). This normative-philosophical debate is increasingly being complemented by empirical scholarship examining the practical outcomes of real-world examples of multicultural and autonomous collective rights recognition. This has particularly been the case in Latin America, where there have been several examples of indigenous rights recognition. Perhaps the most successful example—from a proindigenous autonomy perspective, at least—was the 1995 recognition of indigenous customary law, or *usos y costumbres* (UC) in three-fourths of municipalities in the southern Mexican state of Oaxaca. UC institutions in Oaxaca have been credited and blamed for a range of outcomes. On the one hand, the recognition of the right to self-determination of long-disenfranchised and excluded indigenous communities helps to right a historical injustice and opens up a local autonomous space within which groups may participate and make decisions on their own terms. On the other hand, however, this local autonomy has been criticized for sanctioning the violation of constitutionally recognized individual rights such as the right to vote in local elections (women and other groups are often denied these rights in UC municipalities) or the protection of private property.

In this chapter, I focus on the ways in which UC communities have responded to the increasingly prevalent issue of out-migration and the continued participation of migrants after leaving and upon returning. The focus on migration sheds light on the tension between individual and collective rights that is at the crux of debates about multiculturalism in some unexpected ways. Some of the data analyzed in this chapter demonstrate that migrants can suffer sanctions and the loss of rights to their land and as community citizens (see chapter 6, this volume, for a useful discussion of the concept of community citizenship) when they fail to fulfill obligations to serve in voluntary service jobs (*cargos*) or community labor (*tequio*) or to make financial contributions to patron saint festivals or community public works. At the same time, however, the analysis shows that UC communities that engage in these punitive and arguably illiberal practices have managed to preserve a degree of communal unity that is often lost in other high-migration places. Furthermore, when considered within the context of debates about the role of migration and remittances and development (outlined below), it may be that strong UC communities are more successful in channeling migrant remittances toward development-enhancing public investments and infrastructure development. Finally, although one might argue that the individual rights of migrants are violated by UC authorities, the analysis shows that migrants are overrepresented in positions of political power locally, suggesting migrants are not merely victims of rights violations but are also empowered members of their municipalities.

Over the past several decades, levels of global migration have increased rapidly (Hatton and Williamson 2005). Mexico has sent migrants to the United States for a very long time, but the current wave of migration from Mexico consists of an increasing share from the country's southern states, including people from the rural and indigenous communities in the state of Oaxaca. Despite high levels of migration from indigenous communities in Oaxaca, however, there is significant variation in the degree and nature of migrant ties with their home communities. While many migrants send remittances to their family members back home, significant numbers organize with others from their communities residing in U.S. migrant-receiving locales to send collective remittances for public works in their hometowns. Additionally, migrants continue to participate in a number of local institutions and civic and religious customary practices, even when abroad.

Thus, on one side, traditional customary practices and institutions have shown a surprising degree of resiliency when faced with globalizing and modernizing forces such as migration. At the same time, however, scholars must be careful not to idealize or caricature indigenous communities as closed, stagnant, and pristine. To the contrary, like any community faced with rapid economic and social change, Oaxaca's UC communities have had to adjust and evolve with the times. The emigration of large numbers of young adult and working-age men from all communities places stress on the social and political systems there. Migration places particularly acute stress on the system of *cargos* and *tequios* that forms the foundation of UC political structure, due to a dearth of working-age men to fill these often unpaid positions (see chapter 6, this volume). In response, some UC communities and authorities have found ways to influence, coerce, and otherwise ensure relatively high levels of migrant public and financial engagement in home communities.

In this chapter, I consider a range of ways in which migrants continue to be engaged in public community life through continued direct participation in their communities (on extended return visits or upon resettling) or monetary contributions. First, I focus on migrant participation in customary norms and institutions in Oaxaca (UC), and their funding of public works. Second, I conduct preliminary descriptive analysis of the migration experience of members who hold positions of administrative and agrarian authority in municipalities. After outlining my theoretical orientation and situating the analysis within the body of relevant literature on migration's effects on sending communities in Oaxaca and beyond, I operationalize and test hypotheses using data from the 2008 Survey of Oaxaca, Mexico Customary Law Municipalities. This survey, which covers 417 of Oaxaca's 418 customary law municipalities, contains a wealth of information concerning municipal political structure and practices, migrant participation in community practices and contribution to public goods, and biographical information about the mayor, judicial alderman (or *síndico*), and the commissioner of communal resources (the highest level of authority in charge of administering collectively titled communal lands).

In Oaxaca's 418 customary law–governed municipalities, the actions of political leaders, community members, and engaged migrants are channeled through the unique sets of political and social institutions known as *usos y costumbres*. The way in which individual actions and UC institutions interact to create social outcomes is highly influenced by the demographic, economic, cultural, and social changes brought about by international migration. The question, then, is: how does the persistent phenomenon of mass migration interact with municipal customary institutions in Oaxaca? The recognition of municipal autonomy has arguably afforded communities and their authorities with additional leverage with which to compel and otherwise encourage the continued participation of migrants. Are the different practices employed in UC municipalities to promote the continued participation of migrants successful?

Simplified, and perhaps simplistic, arguments in favor of multiculturalism and the recognition of autonomy might emphasize that the underlying justification for multiculturalist policies such as UC in Oaxaca is that these communities follow unique customary practices that are deeply rooted in their cultural inheritance, and in some sense stable. The rejoinder to this argument would take any evidence demonstrating that practices in UC municipalities stray from their "traditional purity" as weakening the normative foundations of indigenous autonomy. More constructivist accounts (see, e.g., chapter 1, this volume), however, emphasize that indigenous communities are not, nor should they be expected to be, pure spaces separated from the conflicts, changes, and practices of the so-called outside world. The prevalence of the phenomenon of indigenous migration, plus the fact that a majority of indigenous Mexicans live in urban areas, clearly reflect that the conception of the closed indigenous peasant community is a myth. This does not necessarily mean, however, that there is no justification for the recognition of indigenous autonomy. Indeed, after moving beyond the "noble savage" myth to consider the agency of indigenous people, we are still faced with the question as to whether tensions internal to indigenous communities are best worked out within autonomous spaces or within the normative systems of the national states of which they form a part.

In the broader context of debates about the costs and benefits of international migration to sending communities, the findings presented in this chapter suggest a not-often-articulated benefit of strong customary law institutions and authorities: that they help to hold communities together despite the destabilizing impacts of international migration. This does not, however, seem to be due to cultural factors, such as that indigenous peoples have a more communal and less individualistic ethos compared to mestizos. Rather, the mechanism that seems to account for this community strength is institutional—namely, UC sending communities are able to exercise leverage over their members through threats of sanctions, loss of land rights, and the loss of community citizenship.

The chapter begins with a discussion of the theoretical orientation used to approach the questions explored. Second, I summarize some of the key findings and debates in the vast literature exploring the sending-community effects of international migration. Third, I outline some theoretical and empirical research that focuses on Oaxaca, Mexico—particularly the integrity of UC systems in the face of migration—and has attempted to transcend the contradictions of the dependency-development debate. Fourth, I specify the hypotheses to be empirically evaluated. Fifth, I discuss the data that will be analyzed, operationalize the key variables, and report the statistical results of the analysis. Finally, I discuss the implications of the statistical results presented, given the prevailing debates about the impact of migration in sending communities. I conclude by discussing some of the normative implications of the findings and fruitful directions for future research.

THEORETICAL ORIENTATION

One can interpret the dilemmas and behavioral constraints facing local political authorities in Oaxaca and elsewhere with reference to scholarship on rulers and states as theorized by North (1981) and Levi (1988). That is, North's and Levi's rulers can be read as metaphors for political actors at the subnational level. Insofar as all human interaction is fundamentally political (Foucault 1980; Lane 2004, 2007), this metaphor can be extended to understand the constraints, trade-offs, and payoffs of individuals generally. North's (1981) "neoclassical theory of the state" and Levi's (1988) "theory of predatory rule" focus on the basic constraints and determinants of the ruler and view rulers as discriminating monopolists who aim to maximize state revenue. Levi moves somewhat beyond North's theory, though, by considering the ruler's constraints "vis-à-vis agents and constituents, their transaction costs, and their discount rates" (Levi 1988, 10). The focus on the concept of the ruler's discount rate, that is, how much he values the present compared to the future, is a particularly important addition to North's theory and might prove very useful in understanding the behavior of local authorities in Oaxaca.

In addition to conceptualizing the discount rate of the ruler, Levi also moves beyond the neoclassical contract theory assumption of the equality of the parties involved. In so doing, she argues that "rulers can use the same state organization as both a productive enterprise and a protection racket" (Levi 1988, 12). Sometimes constituents are so weak that they wholly lack the capacity to enter into a contractual relationship with the state, such that we can conceptualize their relationship as an exchange of tax revenue for the service of protection. The limiting case is that in which, relatively powerless vis-à-vis the ruler, a constituent pays a tax to ensure his protection from the ruler and his agents in the state apparatus. This theoretical perspective closely parallels Charles Tilly's (1985) thesis that the state functions in the same way as a protection racket or organized crime syndicate. In some cases for Levi, though, the state does enter into contractual relationships with constituents, specifically those that have some power, or a lot of power. The logic of the theory can be carried forward to understand situations in which the tables are turned, and the ruler is the less powerful party to a contract.

Local authorities in Oaxaca—particularly among the more despotic caciques—may use their institutional and personal power to extract revenue from community residents, migrants, and others (including in some, but certainly not all *tequio* labor) for their short- and medium-term political gain. Even the most benign and democratic leaders may use their legitimate authority to "tax" the community to provide for any number of local public goods. With respect to the questions addressed in this chapter, one could hypothesize that efforts by the authorities to compel, motivate, coerce, and otherwise influence migrants to continue supporting the community (and not just their families) from abroad may solve an immediate social and political problem, while creating a long-term problem (for their continued authority). The alliances made by modernizing European kings with the bourgeoisie against the nobility solved the immediate problem of raising revenue to fend off aristocratic and external rivals. But these alliances strengthened the ascendant bourgeoisie such that it could ultimately dispense with its royal ally and take the reins of power itself (see Huntington 1968). Similarly, by extracting resources from migrants or compelling them to return from abroad to serve the community, Oaxacan migrants may be kept comparatively more bound to their hometowns than they otherwise would be. However, as Cohen (1999, 2001, 2004) and Mountz and Wright (1996) have suggested, migrant contributions increase the status of migrants and their families locally. It follows then that in compelling migrants to contribute to municipal projects and the cultural life of the community, authorities may inadvertently strengthen the potential power of the migrants, should they return to seek positions of authority. In short, every solution has a problem.

Though I reject the simple rational choice assumption of *homo economicus*, I seek to understand the collective phenomena studied in terms of the strategic and political behavior of communal authorities, migrants, and community members. Jack Knight's institutional theory, as presented in his *Institutions and Social*

Conflict, "is grounded in the relationship between rational action and institutional structure, but it centers on the distributional conflict characterizing much of the macro-level analysis of those institutions" (1992, xii). For Knight, prevailing theories of institutions and collective action place too much explanatory emphasis on collective benefits achieved. Instead, Knight emphasizes the need to focus on the distributional effects of different institutional arrangements and conflict between different individuals and groups about what institutions should be established (pp. 13–14). Previous theory that has emphasized the inherently distributive nature of institutions, such as that in the Marxist and structuralist traditions, has not considered "microfoundations, or the mechanisms by which institutions emerge and change" (p. 14). On the other hand, most theory with microfoundations has assumed, following Adam Smith's "invisible hand," that efficient social equilibria spontaneously emerge and that "inefficiency is the product of state intervention in the natural order of things" (p. 13). Although at times here I may refer to the collective needs and goals of unity, development, and sustainability, I proceed under the assumption that the relative unity or fragmentation of a community is a function of the behavior of its members. Further, the institutional and policy equilibria reached tend to be designed by the same people who most benefit from their design (Knight 1992, 1995; Moe 2006). The "community" does not act, want, or need, in a strict sense.

The fact that community leaders, faced with the loss of large portions of their working-age population, make use of their powers of sanction and influence to raise money from migrants for the public coffers and compel their participation in posts of community service cannot be explained by the fact that their actions may serve certain collective ends. Collective outcomes such as the paving of a road, the celebration of the patron saint of a town, and the social and political stability of a municipality (which these material and cultural public goods may help achieve) are best understood, rather, by looking at how members of the community interact with each other and organize themselves to achieve certain goals (Moe 2006).

By this I do not mean to argue that individuals, even very powerful individuals, have full control, knowledge, or understanding of the consequences of their actions. Social systems—even those in the small and relatively isolated communities of indigenous Oaxaca—are quite complex and unpredictable. Local elites as well as migrants necessarily act within inherited political, social, and cultural systems and are accordingly subject to choices made by their predecessors as well as endogenous institutional and cultural evolution and exogenous economic and political factors.

DEPENDENCY OR DEVELOPMENT?

Before discussing specific hypotheses, I now turn to a brief summary of the central debate among scholars who have studied the sending-community effects of international migration. The unifying concern of this vast literature is to determine if migration and remittances from migrants help to generate economic development in sending communities or if they are responsible for persistent underdevelopment, economic stagnation, and dependency.

Dependency Perspectives

During the 1970s and 1980s, scholars inspired by the *dependista* critique of modernization theory—many in anthropology—began to study the impacts of migration on small rural communities in the underdeveloped world and viewed the impacts in a decidedly negative light (see VanWey et al. 2005; Cohen 2004; Binford 2003, for summaries of this literature). Coming from a structuralist or historical structuralist theoretical perspective, scholars of the dependency school argued that migration and migrant-sending communities needed to be analyzed within the context of the global capitalist economic system.

For these scholars, the position of poor countries on the global periphery and their residents within this world system is one of dependency (Kearney 1986). By inserting traditional communities into the capitalist world system, contrary to what is argued by modernization theorists, these theorists argue that migration creates economic dependency for communities and accordingly jeopardizes the integrity of local social systems. In their widely cited study of the Mixteca region of Oaxaca, Stuart and Kearney (1981, 26) found that young working-age members of the community migrate in search of higher incomes to meet the consumption needs of their families, but that this short-term income boost is insufficient to bring about "positive changes" sufficient to "ameliorate" the causes of migration.

At a certain point, communities become dependent upon the remittances sent by migrants for their continued survival such that they cease to be organized around local social and economic processes. Accordingly, communities become dependent upon continued migration to maintain stable levels of income, without ever reaching a point where sustained development takes place. This "migration syndrome," as it is called by Reichert (1981), exacerbates inequality in communities. As migrants and their families are able to afford more newly discovered consumer goods due to their remittance income, more consumer demand is created among migrant and nonmigrant households that cannot be met but with further migration, bringing concomitant social and cultural disintegration.

In addition to the social and economic strains of increased inequality, high-migration communities are often characterized by low numbers of young, able-bodied workers due to brain and brawn drain. Accordingly, future development and investment prospects are limited. Although he is generally placed in the "development" camp in this debate, Jeffrey Cohen (2004, 102) sums up this perspective well: "A local system cannot survive if it is built around the very young and very old." What is more, as Wilson argues, the process of international labor migration from Mexico to the United States reflects the latter's dependence on the former. Mexican communities and families absorb the costs of both reproduction and maintenance of this labor source (i.e., Mexican children are raised and prepared for work at no cost to the receiving country and communities provide a social safety net for unemployed, sick, and retired migrants), while the "US market enjoys the benefits of migrant productivity" (Wilson 2000, 196).

Development Perspectives

In the 1990s, some scholars began to view the impact of migration and remittances in a much more positive light, recasting the negative light that dependency theorists had placed on consumption, and estimated both the composition of direct remittance spending and the indirect multiplier effects of these expenditures. Durand and Massey (1992) empirically confirmed the claim of dependency scholars that most remittances are used for basic household expenditures. Although he does confirm that migration and remittances tend to increase inequality at the local level, Jones (1998, 8) finds that remittances serve the necessary function of providing a social safety net for families and entire rural communities. This finding is echoed by several other scholars (see, e.g., Taylor et al. 1996; Portes et al. 2007).

Among the most influential works of these scholars is an article by Durand, Kandel, Parrado, and Massey (1996). In it, the authors argued for a reframing of the debate about migration and development, and against the tendency of other scholars to assume that remittances cannot stimulate local development unless they are invested in productive enterprises or infrastructure development. For Durand and his colleagues, the then-prevailing view that migration leads to dependency and economic stagnation was "misleading because it ignore[d] the conditions under which productive investment [was] likely to be possible and profitable" (Durand et al. 1996, 249). Following on their earlier work (Durand and Massey 1992), Durand and his colleagues estimated national and community-level multiplier effects to better account for the full stimulative impact of remittance spending, even though a great majority of these transfers are spent on allegedly unproductive consumption. Specifically, they estimated (using 1990 data) that every dollar remitted to Mexico generated $2.90 in economic activity due to indirect multiplier effects. Community-level multiplier effects were also calculated and were found to be even more significant in sending communities than in the nation as a whole.

TRANSCENDING THE DEPENDENCY-DEVELOPMENT DICHOTOMY?

In this section, I reflect on the sources of the division between dependency and development approaches and briefly outline some recent theoretical and empirical research that focuses on Oaxaca, Mexico, and has attempted to transcend this debate. The empirical and theoretical advances of scholars arguing that migration positively impacts local and national development are compelling and well rooted in empirical research. Nevertheless, these findings have not by any means ended the debate. Notwithstanding the reliably measured direct and indirect economic benefits of migrant remittances, at least part of the disagreement between these two schools of thought is a matter of interpretation. Discussing the history of this debate from a dependency perspective, Binford argues that the "revisionist [read: development] perspective on migration and remittances involves another effort to put a happy face on a dismal situation" (2003, 306). This is explainable because those who view migration as positive set the standard for evaluation at a very low level. Indeed, Stuart and Kearney (1981, 37) conclude that "the effects of migration on the socioeconomic development of the community are contradictory," as the migration-dependent community they studied would have been far worse off in the absence of migration. At the same time, though, they caution that the community has become locked into a pattern of dependency on migration similar to a narcotics addiction (p. 37). From a different perspective, and not considering caveats such as Stuart and Kearney's, Durand and his colleagues (1996) argued that the error of those who view migration pessimistically is their failure to consider the observed phenomena with reference to what would be realistic development prospects for the communities involved in the absence of migration. That is, given the relatively dire prospects for rural Mexican communities and those who make choices to migrate, migration can be interpreted as a legitimate survival strategy that has helped to sustain the very existence of communities in the face of overpopulation, underproduction in agriculture, and exogenous economic shocks such as the fall in the price of maize, coffee, or other commodities or the shutting down of a mine. For Binford, these scholars (labeled "functionalists") focus on individual choices to migrate (or not) but often fail to question these choices within broader structural and historical contexts. That is, the methodological focus on individual choice leads functionalist scholars to accept neoliberal capitalism as a given rather than examining its structural contradictions and impacts on communities (Binford 2003, 306).

Though he explicitly aims to transcend the contradictions and moralistic tone of the dependency-development debate, Cohen (2004) echoes the optimistic perspective on migration. Specifically, he develops and tests a "household model" of migration that redefines what are understood as "local cultural patterns and social processes" in Oaxaca's Central Valleys by conceiving of migration as "embedded in a series of sociocultural patterns" (Cohen 2004, 29). He continues: "The outcome, then, is a culture of migration, a system in which migration is integrated and integral to ongoing sociocultural development" (p. 29). Cohen rejects primordial conceptions of local cultural practices in Oaxaca, considers migration within a process of "ongoing sociocultural development" in sending communities, and—contrary to the structuralism of the dependency school—recasts rural Oaxacans as actors in modernity and globalization rather than as passive victims. With his household unit of analysis and his focus on the agency of rural Oaxacans and their household decisions to migrate, though, he chooses to not critically examine the broader economic structures within which migration fits. Accordingly, Binford and other structuralists and neodependency theorists would likely accuse Cohen of fallaciously assuming that what is is what ought to be. A rejoinder to this sort of criticism might seek to move the focus from the normative to the positive by asserting simply that what is is what ought to be studied.

Also studying Oaxaca's UC communities, but in the mountainous Mixteca region rather than the Central Valleys, Michael Kearney, beginning with his work with Stuart (Stuart and Kearney 1981), argues that migration and the arrival of market capitalism and wage labor to Oaxacan communities have led to a monetization of local economies and have put significant strain on the integrity of communal practices. His more recent research (Kearney 1996, 2000), similar in this respect to Cohen's, does not treat migrant populations as passive in the face of globalization. That said, as he emerges from a dependency perspective, his focus now is on the transnational nature of international migration and the structurally constrained position of Oaxacan migrants at the bottom of a deterritorialized transnational class system. Rejecting the primordial dualisms of classical anthropology (traditional-modern, peasant-proletariat, etc.), Kearney (1996) analyzes the cultural development of Oaxaca's indigenous communities as they negotiate new ethnic and political identities in the face of the structural processes of globalization of which transnational migration is an integral piece. Cohen (1999, 2004) contends that Oaxacan communities are actors in the process of globalization, and that they have found ways to use migration not only to support themselves economically but to develop new "structures of cooperation" that help preserve community unity and customary practices in the face of these forces.

At the level of empirical theory, this does not necessarily contradict the arguments of the dependency school or of Kearney's (1996) "post-peasant" perspective of transnationalism. What it seems to reflect, however, is differences in the way the same empirical phenomena are interpreted. To some extent, disagreements may be rooted in the distinct normative positions of the two authors and the two schools of thought. Whereas Cohen, as well as those of the development school, view the globalization and modernization of rural peasant and indigenous communities as either positive, neutral, or inevitable, Kearney and dependency theorists see the capitalist penetration of traditional communities and the insertion of migrants as workers in this system as exploitative and generally negative. Furthermore, dependency scholars tend to reject positivistic scholarship that uncritically explains social phenomena and, rather, hope that their work, or the actions of the communities they study, will lead to positive social change.

As a rejoinder to Cohen's point that migrants and their communities are actors in globalization, not victims of it, one need not conclude that a person lacks agency or decision to also conclude that that person or group has been victimized by a system. Similar to Moe's (2006) criticism of economics-based rational choice theory, Cohen seems wedded to the assumption that all action by individuals is voluntary. Moe (2006) argues that many decisions made by individuals and groups cannot rightly be classified as voluntary choices. That is, in many cases, decisions are made under situations of coercion and severely constrained options. In many cases the choice to leave one's community and migrate to the United States should not be considered voluntary.

VanWey and her colleagues (2005) conducted an important study that squarely focused on the role and function of UC institutions in Oaxaca in utilizing migrant remittances to achieve community goals. In attempt to move beyond the dependency-development debate, these authors suggest that the relative benefits and costs of migration to sending communities are a function of the level of "community organization" (VanWey et al. 2005, 85). Though they cite past research (Lindstrom 1996, in VanWey et al. 2005, 85) that has found that migrants remit more frequently to communities with a "complementary infrastructure," they argue that in the context of Oaxaca's UC communities, this infrastructure can be thought of endogenously. Accordingly, they argue that "more strongly organized" communities in Oaxaca "are able to encourage or coerce migrants into providing remittances for community projects, thus supporting community economic development and the economic dynamism that is often seen as a prerequisite for remittances" (VanWey et al. 2005, 85). Referencing Ostrom (1990), the high level of organization that some of Oaxaca's rural UC communities are able to achieve through the traditional *cargo* system facilitates the socially beneficial collective choices to raise revenue from migrants through voluntary and obligatory contributions (VanWey et al. 2005, 89). Communities that threaten migrants with the loss of the rights of community membership (including land rights) were able to successfully influence migrants to return for service and contribute funds to community projects and patron saint festivals (p. 94).

This study is a useful complement to Cohen's (1999) research, which finds that communities organize themselves to gather remittances and savings to cover the customary duties of public office, patron saint festivals, and other aspects of traditional community life with the support of migrants in Los Angeles and elsewhere in the United States. With a microfocus on individual and household social action, he studies how migrant community contributions and norms of reciprocity "create and/or reproduce identity and become frameworks for negotiating and coping with ongoing social, economic and political change" (Cohen 1999, 4). Because of the fact that participation in village political life in public service positions (*cargos*) and nonremunerated community labor (*tequio*) takes community members away from productive or income-generating labor, migrant remittances—even when they go to families and not directly to community projects—help to indirectly sustain levels of participation in customary public life (Cohen 2004, 22). Nevertheless, Cohen underemphasizes the importance of the increased social inequality that is associated with migration, though he empirically confirms its existence. Wealthier families with the means to send members abroad to work become wealthier, while those who cannot afford to migrate in the first place fall further behind.

A flaw in the approaches of both Cohen and VanWey and her colleagues may be that they implicitly assume that the public decisions made by community assemblies and local authorities—what they choose to do with the collective remittances—are in the collective interest of the "community." Though this might be approximated in some cases, there is no reason to think that authorities will necessarily even attempt to use monies on projects that are most collectively beneficial. Similarly, hometown associations in the United States often have influence, if not full decision-making power, over the projects and investments for which their contributions are used. Knight's (1992) theoretical logic suggests that a choice about the use of any public good (as with the design of any social institution) is not understandable in terms of the social utility that public good has, but rather in terms of its expected personal utility for the individuals with the most influence over its design.

HYPOTHESES

In this section I make more explicit the concrete hypotheses that I address by analyzing data from the 2008 Survey of Oaxaca, Mexico Customary Law Municipalities.

Hypothesis 1

More "organized" communities are expected to be able to compel higher levels of migrant hometown participation on a number of levels. The types of participation examined here include direct or monetary participation in *tequio*, religious *cargos*, civil *cargos*, and patron saint festivals as well as collective remittances in the form of migrant contributions to public works. In effect, I am proposing to use quantitative data on Oaxaca's UC municipalities to see if VanWey and her colleagues' findings hold for all of the state's UC municipalities (theirs was a comparative qualitative study of four municipalities). As VanWey and her colleagues conclude:

> There appears to be a strong relationship between community organization and remittances from migrants to community groups. In the most organized communities, however, community government accesses remittances through fees assessed on migrants for missed *tequios*, and donations received for festivals, maintenance of religious structures, or occasionally for maintenance of other infrastructure. These donations evidently allow the community to avoid or reduce fees assessed on resident households, or to spend these fees on projects. In the less organized communities, remittances only go to families and religious festivals. (2005, 97)

Below I present statistics from a comprehensive survey of UC municipalities (417 out of 418) to see if this finding holds more generally. Specifically, I operationalize the strength of community organization as defined by VanWey and her colleagues to test whether municipalities that use various means at their disposal to influence migrants to contribute monetarily in support of public goods or to return home to offer direct service are successful in raising more funds from migrants and in keeping them more engaged in the community. More directly, I test the correlation between collective remittances and whether or not municipal authorities surveyed classified such contributions from migrants as obligatory.

This hypothesis connects the specific analysis of migration and UC in Oaxaca with more general questions about the impact of migration on sending communities if one considers UC as one of a more general type of community institution. Seen within this context, Taylor's (1999, 74) argument that migration is likely to more positively affect development where local institutions are constructed so as to be able to "gather savings by migrant households and make them available to local producers," one can view UC institutions as mechanisms through which both family and collective remittances can be organized and channeled toward social goods (though there is no reason to think that these will be "good" in a normative sense). The difference is that Taylor is talking about banking, insurance, and other institutional organizations in sending countries and communities with the capacity to "soak up" many dispersed pools of savings and make them available as capital for productive investment.

This is also echoed by Hernando de Soto's (2000) well-known and controversial thesis about underdevelopment. The parallel that I see between the more formal banking, insurance, and legal institutions discussed by Taylor and de Soto and the less formal customary norms and institutions of Oaxaca's UC communities (as well as Scott's [1976] "moral economies") is that social institutions—that is, established and trusted patterns of behavior among those in a social group—serve the same function as banks and insurance companies in channeling and organizing external flows of capital from remittances to productive or socially beneficial ends. Of course, caveats are in order. I do not here take a stand that UC practices and social institutions necessarily allow for socially optimal collective outcomes. The point, rather, is simply that UC institutions in Oaxaca may increase the likelihood of migrant collective action, specifically through contributions to public works. Furthermore, unequal actors negotiate institutional arrangements—UC and otherwise—with the intention of benefiting themselves but that also can facilitate collective action, resulting in more optimal social outcomes (Knight 1992, 1995; Ostrom 1990). Optimality aside, the outcome variable of interest here is migrant participation in the public sphere, which is expected to correlate positively with community strength.

Hypothesis 2

Migration experience can serve as a pathway to greater social status, influence, and direct political power. Among other potential mechanisms, the individual contributions and collective remittances from migrants for local public works, religious festivals, and their fulfillment of *cargo* and *tequio* obligations may help migrants to increase their status. Authorities today (or yesterday) may compel migrants to return to serve in positions of unpaid community labor or to make financial contributions in order to maintain community standing and to increase their own status. Nevertheless, insofar as compelling (or incentivizing) continued migrant engagement increases the status of migrants, authorities may end up paving the way for their own demise.

> From the migrants' points of view, the support of community projects, particularly fiestas, is an avenue to increased social status. Cohen points out that the loosening of household budgets through remittances from migrants to families allows those families to support the community more and to attain more status in the community (Cohen 2001). Mountz and Wright (1996) find that remittances from migration pay for increases in the social status of families in the village largely through the sponsorship of fiestas by these families. (VanWey et al. 2005, 100)

Though it is not possible to directly test this hypothesis with the cross-sectional survey data available, a preliminary descriptive finding that migrants have relatively higher community status vis-à-vis the community at large can be indirectly tested by considering the migration experience of members of the municipal authority.

The biographical data to be used in this analysis were collected in surveys of the three most important positions of municipal authority: mayors, *síndicos* (or judicial aldermen), and the commissioners of communal resources. The last officials head the commission that is responsible for governing communal lands and is a very important position of local authority in Oaxaca's UC municipalities, given the high proportion of their territory that is made up of communally titled property.

A finding that the portion of municipalities governed by former migrants is higher than the average percentage of migrants in municipal populations would be consistent with this hypothesis. In his analysis of household survey data in Oaxaca's Central Valleys, Cohen finds that migrant households participated in *cargos* and *tequios* at rates similar to those of nonmigrants and that "over time [they] tended to serve in more *cargos* and in higher-ranking positions in those *cargos* than nonmigrants did" (2004, 71). This suggests that, in addition to comparing the migration history of members of the authority to that of the average municipality, if migration leads to increases in status and local power, we would expect mayors to be more likely to have been migrants than lower-ranking members of the civil, agrarian, and religious service.

EXPLAINING MIGRANT PARTICIPATION: DATA AND METHODS

The data used for this analysis were generated from the 2008 Survey of Oaxaca, Mexico Customary Law Municipalities, an extensive elite-level survey of authority figures in 417 of Oaxaca's 418 UC municipalities. Specifically, through six different questionnaires a wide range of information was collected, including the forms of political and social organization, the nature of local customary practices, the political behavior of different groups within the municipalities (including migrants, women, non-Catholics, and others), and the public service and migration biography of the mayor, judicial alderman, and the commissioner of communal resources.

Hypothesis 1 Variables

Dependent Variables: Types and Levels of Migrant Participation

The first set of operational indicators concerns the direct and monetary participation of migrants in different community practices and institutions. Specifically, these include *cargos* in the administrative authority (or the *ayuntamiento*), religious *cargos*, *tequio*, and patron saint festivals. The presence (yes or no) and nature (direct or monetary) of migrant participation in these practices is shown in figure 8.1. Migrants participated most—through both monetary contribution (42.1 percent) and direct participation (31.5 percent) in patron saint festivals. Monetary contribution was second most common in *tequio* (41.7 percent), but direct service was lowest for this practice (21.9 percent). Civil *cargos* had the highest nonparticipation rate (47.3 percent) and more direct service (29.3 percent) than monetary contribution (23.1 percent). To analyze the correlation between migrant participation and community strength, I conceptualize the above summarized series of variables as ordinal

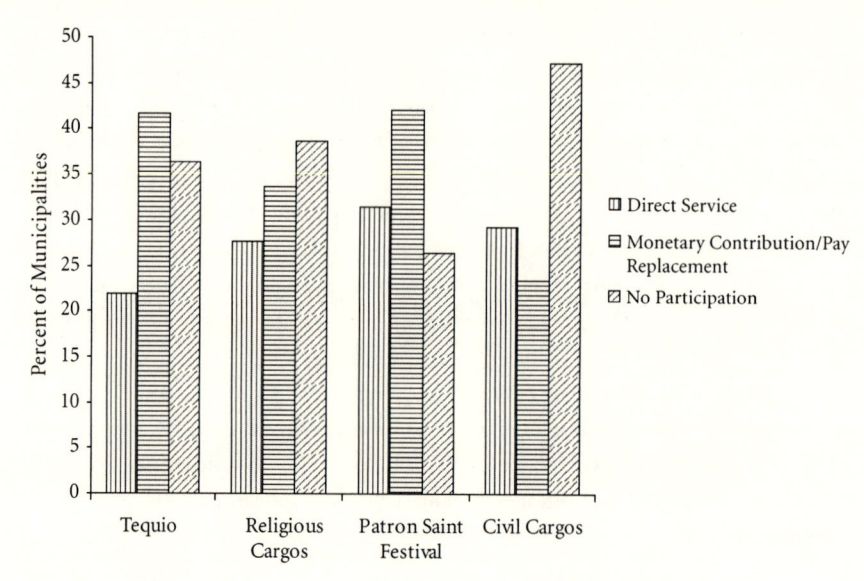

FIGURE 8.1

Migrant Participation in *Usos y Costumbres* Institutions

Note: Total $N = 417$, although the valid N varies. The above values reflect the valid percentage for each category, and accordingly represent the best estimate of the population percentage for all 418 UC municipalities.

Source: Author analysis of the 2008 Survey of Oaxaca, Mexico Customary Law Municipalities.

indicators of migrant participation. Nonparticipation is coded as 0, monetary participation as 1, and direct participation as 2.

The second type of migrant participation considered is financial support for projects to benefit the community. Municipal authority figures surveyed were asked if migrants send financial contributions for public works projects—39 percent said they did (see figure 8.2). Authorities were also asked to indicate the types of projects that had been funded by migrants during the past four years. Based on this series of questions, it was found that migrants had funded at least one public works project in 43.9 percent of municipalities (see figure 8.2). Interestingly, migrants were far more likely to have funded projects related to the church (34.6 percent of municipalities) than roads (11.7 percent), sports facilities (11.2 percent), or mausoleums (10.1 percent).

Independent Variables: Community Strength and Organization

Community strength is expected to increase the likelihood that migrants will continue to participate directly and monetarily in their communities of origin. We classify municipalities as stronger when they punish migrants for failing to serve in community public institutions—specifically the municipal council—and when they require them to make contributions for public works projects. Measures of strength so defined are gleaned from survey questions asking what sanctions are applied when migrants are named to serve in municipal *cargos*. Migrants are not named to municipal *cargos* when they are abroad in the majority of municipalities (54.4 percent), and in 18.5 percent of municipalities a replacement is found. Nevertheless,

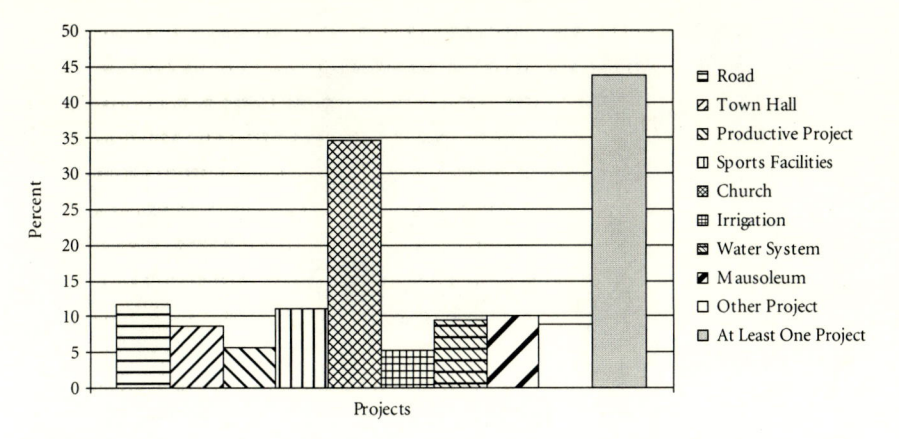

FIGURE 8.2
Migrant-Funded Public Works Projects in the Past Four Years
Source: Author analysis of the 2008 Survey of Oaxaca, Mexico Customary Law Municipalities.

in a not insignificant 35.1 percent of municipalities, migrants must return to serve when they are named to *cargos*, and if they do not they might be subject to fines or loss of land or community membership rights. As table 8.1 shows, fines for noncompliance are charged in 14.2 percent and loss of community membership rights is a consequence of failing to serve when called in 13.4 percent of municipalities. Loss of land is less than half as common (5.6 percent) as a sanction for failing to serve when named to a *cargo* in the municipal civil authority. Overall, migrants were sanctioned in at least one way for failing to serve when called in more than one in four municipalities (28.1 percent).

Table 8.1 Indicators of Community Strength

	N^1	%	Valid N
Sanctions for not returning to serve when called[2]			
Must pay a fine	51	14.2	359
Loss of community rights	48	13.4	359
Loss of land rights	20	5.6	359
Other sanction	13	3.6	359
At least one form of sanction	101	28.1	359
Migrant contributions to public works			
Migrants contribute	149	39.0	382
Contributions are voluntary	109	76.2	143
Contributions are obligatory	34	23.8	143
Migrants don't contribute	233	61.0	382
Contributions are voluntary	222	95.3	233
Contributions are obligatory	11	4.72	233

Source: Author analysis of the 2008 Survey of Oaxaca, Mexico Customary Law Municipalities.
[1]Total $N = 417$, although the valid N varies. The values reflect the number of "yes" answers. The percentages reported are the valid percentage.
[2]Categories are not mutually exclusive.

Table 8.2 Sanctions and Support for Public Works and Levels of Participation in Migrants' Hometowns Using Pearson's Pairwise Correlations

		Migrants Contribute to Public Works	Migrants Financed Public Works in the Past 4 Years	Civil Cargos[1]	Religious Cargos[1]	Tequio[1]	Patron Saint Festival[1]
Migrant financing of public works is obligatory	r	0.29***	0.17***	0.13*	0.04	0.08	−0.01
	N	376	349	329	339	354	353
What happens if migrants fail to return when they are called to serve in a cargo?							
Fined	r	0.22***	0.13*	0.24***	0.16**	0.16**	0.09
	N	333	310	306	317	330	327
Lose land	r	0.09	0.06	0.15*	0.14*	0.09	0.08
	N	333	310	306	317	330	327
Lose community rights	r	0.00	0.00	0.17**	0.13*	0.11*	0.04
	N	333	310	306	317	330	327
Another sanction	r	0.03	0.02	0.15**	−0.01	0.02	0.10
	N	333	310	306	317	330	327
At least one sanction	r	0.17**	0.11*	0.34***	0.20***	0.21***	0.13*
	N	333	310	306	317	330	327

Source: Author analysis of the 2008 Survey of Oaxaca Mexico Customary Law Municipalities.
[1] No participation = 1; monetary contribution = 2; direct participation = 3.
*Correlation is significant at the 0.05 level (two-tailed).
**Correlation is significant at the 0.01 level (two-tailed).
***Correlation is significant at the 0.001 level (two-tailed).

For the second test of hypothesis 1, I examined the level of migrant contributions to public works—collective remittances—in the community with respect to whether such contributions are obligatory or voluntary. Quite simply, it is expected that municipalities where contributions for public works are required from migrants will have a higher incidence of contribution, followed by those where contribution is voluntary. Even so, it may be that migrants are eager to make contributions to increase their status in the community even when such contributions are not required, a potential mechanism through which migrants might gain positions of power in local government, as expected by hypothesis 2. As reported in table 8.2, among those places where migrants contributed to public works, a majority contributed voluntarily (76.2 percent) rather than by obligation (23.8 percent). Even so, migrants failed to contribute despite requirements in fewer than one in twenty cases (4.7 percent).

Hypothesis 1 Findings: Correlates of Migrant Participation

According to hypothesis 1, the level of migrant participation is expected to be positively correlated with indicators of "community strength." To evaluate this hypothesis, the correlation between community strength (the independent variable) and indicators of migrant participation in community institutions or monetary contributions (the dependent variable) is estimated.

Table 8.2 presents a correlation matrix of the variables discussed above. Though all pairs of relationships are of interest, the key sets of relationships for evaluating hypothesis 1 are those that correlate different sanctions with the level of migrant participation and those that estimate the correlation between migrant contributions to public works and whether or not contributions are obligatory. As noted above, participation variables are conceptualized as ordinal, with direct participation equal to 2, monetary contribution equal to 1, and no participation equal to 0. In all but a few select cases, there is a statistically significant correlation between each of the ordinal variables for the level of migrant participation in *tequio*, religious *cargos*, patron saint festivals, and civil *cargos* (in the direction expected according to hypothesis 1) with the different sanction variables. As the different sanction variables refer only to the sanctions for nonparticipation when migrants are called to serve in *cargos* in the municipal authority, the most direct and perhaps appropriate test is of the correlation between the different sanction variables and the level of migrant participation in civil *cargos*. As table 8.2 shows, migrants are more likely to participate in civil *cargos* where they can be fined ($r = -0.24$, significant at the 0.001 level), where they can lose land ($r = -0.15$, significant at the 0.05 level), where they can lose community rights ($r = -0.17$, statistically significant at the 0.01 level), and where there are other sanctions for not serving ($r = -0.15$, significant at the 0.01 level). The strongest correlation was that between migrant participation in civil *cargos* and the dummy variable equal to 1 if at least one type of sanction was applied ($r = 0.34$, significant at the 0.001 level).

Although data on the sanctions for not participating in *tequio*, religious *cargos*, and patron saint festivals were not gathered, I take willingness to sanction migrants for nonparticipation in civil *cargos* as a good proxy of general community strength and expect it to help explain variation in migrant participation in other practices. As expected, migrant participation in these activities is greater in places where migrants are sanctioned for not participating when named to civil *cargos*.

The second set of relationships examined to evaluate hypothesis 1 includes those between migrant contributions to public works and indicators of community strength. As shown in table 8.2 concerning migrant contributions to public works (as measured by a direct survey question of current authorities and imputed from migrant-funded projects), making contributions obligatory makes them more likely ($r = 0.29$ and $r = 0.17$, both significant at the 0.001 level). Also as expected, migrant contributions were more likely in municipalities classified as strong based on the sanction indicators. Migrants were more likely to contribute to public works in places where migrants were fined for not serving in *cargos* when named ($r = 0.22$, significant at the 0.001 level) and where at least one sanction was applied ($r = 0.17$, significant at the 0.01 level).

Hence, I cannot reject hypothesis 1 as tested here, as it appears that making contributions obligatory, not surprisingly, increases the likelihood of contributions. Nevertheless, the fact that in most municipalities where migrants have contributed, their contribution was not required, suggests the need for further research to determine what other factors help explain the determinants and likelihood that migrants support public works in their hometowns. Furthermore, the increasing attractiveness of positions of municipal authority over the past fifteen years suggests that migrants may contribute to public works and otherwise continue to participate in hometown public life not only because they are forced to but because they aspire to reach higher levels of power locally.[1] Making contributions from migrants obligatory and compelling their continued participation might help current authorities to maintain power and legitimacy at the moment. However, one long-term consequence might be that migrants gain status locally, become motivated to reach higher levels of power (perhaps to reform community institutions to benefit migrants and their families), and come to be leaders of a new political class locally. I present some preliminary descriptive statistics below to begin examining this hypothesis.

MIGRANT OVERREPRESENTATION IN POSITIONS OF MUNICIPAL POWER?

To examine hypothesis 2, I make use the biographical information—particularly the recent migration history—of those in the three most important positions of authority in UC municipalities: the mayor, the *síndico* (or judicial alderman), and the commissioner of communal resources. According to hypothesis 2, migrants are expected to have higher social status in municipalities where they have contributed to public works and other collective goods (Cohen 2004; VanWey et al. 2005). It may be that an unintended consequence of past authorities' efforts to extract resources from migrants for community or personal ends is that migrants gain in social status and accordingly are well positioned to assume positions of local power.

Migration experience was notable among Oaxaca's UC authorities. More than one in four mayors (27.3 percent), 23.4 percent of judicial aldermen, and 18.7 percent of communal resources commissioners have been migrants at some point in the past. Unfortunately, the Mexican census does not collect data on whether or not individuals have ever been migrants, which would allow for a comparison between the migration history of members of the authority and the general population. Instead, to provide a preliminary answer to the question of whether former migrants are overrepresented in positions of authority, I compared the percentage of the population in the average UC municipality and the average Oaxaca municipality that lived outside of the state five years earlier with the percentage of mayors, judicial aldermen, and commissioners of communal resources who did so right before taking on the *cargo*. I also compare these percentages to the percentage of the total Oaxaca population who lived outside of the state five years earlier. These data come from the INEGI (2005) *Conteo de Población y Vivienda*. Specifically, in 2005 people were asked where they lived five years before.

As table 8.3 indicates, and consistent with expectations, municipal authority figures were significantly more likely to have been recent migrants than the municipal population in general. Specifically, 7.7 percent of mayors, 7.1 percent of judicial aldermen, and 4.6 percent of communal resources commissioners had been migrants

Table 8.3 Authorities Living Outside of Oaxaca before Occupying Their Posts in Comparative Perspective

	N	%	Valid N
Mayor	28	7.7	364
Judicial alderman (*síndico*)	27	7.1	355
Commissioner of communal resources	14	4.6	304
Average: UC munis.	n/a	1.4	418
Average: Oaxaca munis.	n/a	1.5	570
Oaxaca state (thousands of people)	53	1.7	3,104

Source: Author analysis of the 2008 Survey of Oaxaca, Mexico Customary Law Municipalities; INEGI (2005).

just before assuming their current position of authority. By comparison, in the average UC municipality only 1.4 percent of the population had lived outside of the state five years earlier. That is, when compared to the average UC resident, mayors were more than five times more likely to have been recent migrants, judicial aldermen were 5.1 times more likely, and commissioners were 3.3 times more likely.

DISCUSSION AND CONCLUSION

The findings presented above regarding the correlates of migrant participation and of their apparent overrepresentation in the highest positions of municipal authority suggest several avenues for future research. This analysis has homed in on questions of customary political and social institutions, and the ways in which these may serve as a mechanism to encourage continued social, economic, and indeed political engagement by migrants in their hometowns. It has been shown that migrants participate in civil and religious *cargos, tequios*, and patron saint festivals at higher rates when current authorities are willing to sanction them than when they do not. Furthermore, migrants provide significant resources to their communities of origin for public works and other projects in the form of collective remittances. Given that these data are exclusively from UC municipalities, it is difficult to argue, based on these findings, that UC institutions as recognized by the Oaxacan constitution provide mechanisms to improve the productive value of remittances. Nevertheless, the results do suggest that this may be the case. That is, authorities in party-based municipalities are not equally empowered to sanction migrants for failing to to support their communities, either monetarily or through direct participation. The ability of UC authorities to extract labor and resources from migrant and other community members may indeed be seen as negative on a number of levels. That said, consistent with the study by VanWey and her colleagues, this community strength may very well be serving as a mechanism through which migrant remittances are channeled to more productive and collectively valuable ends.

Gaining an understanding of whether this leads to sustainable economic development is a topic for future research. In terms of political development and potential democratization of local power structures, however, the continued engagement of migrants in their hometowns promoted by UC authorities may serve, inadvertently, as a mechanism through which migrants gain the community status and motivation to seek higher levels of municipal influence. Indeed, as this analysis has shown, former migrants are overrepresented at the highest levels of municipal authority, especially mayor. Insofar as migrant mayors enter the local political fray independently of dominant political factions or families, this may represent a step toward greater pluralism and democracy.

Among the potential explanations for the overrepresentation of migrants in the municipal authority could be that migrants who are compelled to continue to participate monetarily or directly in their communities gain status and motivation to reach higher levels of influence in their hometowns. An alternative explanation could be that recent migrants become municipal authorities at higher rates specifically because of the fact that they have been compelled to return home to serve their communities. Accordingly, this finding may not be an indicator of the power and influence of migrants. Future refinements of this analysis that gather data to compare the percentage of municipal authorities who were recent migrants with the percentage of adult men might reveal that migration is not, as it appears here, a fast track to positions of high community status and prestige. Furthermore, research that analyzes more completely the nature of the trajectories that lead people to these positions of municipal power (see chapter 7, this volume) will likely shed further light on this hypothesis, while suggesting numerous other related and interesting avenues for future research.

NOTES

1. It is evident that Oaxaca's UC communities have been undergoing a series of changes. Whereas traditionally, service in the municipal government as well as lower-level *cargos* and *tequios* were seen unequivocally as service and implied a significant financial burden, higher-level *cargos* are increasingly sought after by community members and migrants alike. Among the most important causes of this perceived change is the simple fact that those who serve now often draw a salary and have access to significant financial resources due to national policies to decentralize the distribution of federal resources.

REFERENCES

Barry, Brian. 2001. *Culture and Equality: An Egalitarian Critique of Multiculturalism.* Cambridge, MA: Harvard University Press.

Binford, Leigh. 2003. "Migrant Remittances and (Under)Development in Mexico." *Critique of Anthropology* 23 (3): 305–336.

Cohen, Jeffrey H. 1999. *Cooperation and Community: Economy and Society in Oaxaca.* Austin: University of Texas Press.

Cohen, Jeffrey H. 2001. "Transnational Migration in Rural Oaxaca, Mexico: Dependency, Development and the Household." *American Anthropologist* 103 (4): 954–967.

Cohen, Jeffrey H. 2004. *The Culture of Migration in Southern Mexico.* Austin: University of Texas Press.

de Soto, Hernando. 2000. *The Mystery of Capital: Why Capitalism Triumphs in the West and Fails Everywhere Else.* New York: Basic Books.

Durand, Jorge, William Kandel, Emilio A. Parrado, and Douglas S. Massey. 1996. "International Migration and Development in Mexican Communities." *Demography* 33 (2): 249–264.

Durand, Jorge, and Douglas S. Massey. 1992. "Mexican Migration to the United States: A Critical Review." *Latin American Research Review* 27 (2): 3–42.

Foucault, Michel. 1980. "Power, Sovereignty and Discipline." In *Power/Knowledge*, edited by Colin Gordon. New York: Pantheon.

Hatton, Timothy J., and Jeffrey G. Williamson. 2005. *Global Migration and the World Economy: Two Centuries of Policy and Performance*. Cambridge, MA: MIT Press.

Huntington, Samuel P. 1968. *Political Order in Changing Societies*. New Haven, CT: Yale University Press.

INEGI (Instituto Nacional de Estadística, Geografía e Informática). 2005. "Conteo de población y vivienda, 2005." Sistema Nacional de Información Estadística y Geografica. http://www.inegi.org.mx.

Jones, Richard C. 1998. "Remittances and Inequality: A Question of Migration Stage and Geographic Scale." *Economic Geography* 74 (1): 8–25.

Kearney, Michael. 1986. "From the Invisible Hand to Visible Feet: Anthropological Studies of Migration and Development." *Annual Review of Anthropology* 15: 331–361.

Kearney, Michael. 1996. *Reconceptualizing the Peasantry: Anthropology in Global Perspective*. Boulder, CO: Westview Press.

Kearney, Michael. 2000. "Transnational Oaxacan Indigenous Identity: The Case of Mixtecs and Zapotecs." *Indentities* 7 (2): 173–195.

Knight, Jack. 1992. *Institutions and Social Conflict*. New York: Cambridge University Press.

Knight, Jack. 1995. "Models, Interpretations, and Theories: Constructing Explanations of Institutional Emergence and Change." In *Explaining Social Institutions*, edited by Jack Knight and Itai Sened, 95–119. Ann Arbor: University of Michigan Press.

Kymlicka, Will. 1995. *Multicultural Citizenship*. New York: Oxford University Press.

Lane, Ruth. 2004. "Pitkin's Dilemma: The Wider Shores of Political Theory and Political Science." *Perspectives on Politics* 2 (3): 459–473.

Lane, Ruth. 2007. *The Game of Justice: A Theory of Individual Self-Government*. Albany: State University of New York Press.

Levi, Margaret. 1988. *Of Rule and Revenue*. Berkeley: University of California Press.

Lindstrom, David P. 1996. "Economic Opportunity in Mexico and Return Migration from the United States." *Demography* 33 (3): 357–374.

Moe, Terry M. 2006. "Power and Political Institutions." In *Rethinking Political Institutions: The Art of the State*, edited by Ian Shapiro, Stephen Skowronek, and Daniel Galvin, 32–71. New York: New York University Press.

Mountz, Alison, and Richard Wright. 1996. "Daily Life in the Transnational Migration Community of San Agustin, Oaxaca and Poughkeepsie, New York." *Diaspora* 5 (3): 403–428.

North, Douglas. 1981. *Structure and Change in Economic History*. New York: Norton.

Ostrom, Elinor. 1990. *Governing the Commons: The Evolution of Institutions for Collective Action (Political Economy of Institutions and Decisions)*. New York: Cambridge University Press.

Portes, Alejandro, Cristina Escobar, and Alexandria Walton Radford. 2007. "Immigrant Transnational Organizations and Development: A Comparative Study." *International Migration Review* 41 (1): 242–281.

Reichert, Joshua. 1981. "The Migrant Syndrome: Seasonal U.S. Wage Labor and Rural Development in Central Mexico." *Human Organization* 40 (1): 56–66.

Scott, James C. 1976. *The Moral Economy of the Peasant*. New Haven, CT: Yale University Press.

Stuart, J., and Michael Kearney. 1981. *Causes and Effects of Agricultural Labor Migration from the Mixteca of Oaxaca to California*. Working Papers in US–Mexican Studies no. 28. La Jolla: Program in United States–Mexican Studies, University of California at San Diego.

Taylor, J. Edward. 1999. "The New Economics of Labor Migration and the Role of Remittances in the Migration Process." *International Migration* 37 (1): 63–88.

Taylor, J. Edward, Joaquín Arango, Graeme Hugo, Ali Kouaouci, Douglas S. Massey, and Adela Pellegrino. 1996. "International Migration and Community Development." *Population Index* 62 (3): 397–418.

Tilly, Charles. 1985. "War Making and State Making as Organized Crime." In *Bringing the State Back In*, edited by Peter Evans, Dietrich Rueschemeyer, and Theda Skocpol, 169–191. Cambridge: Cambridge University Press.

VanWey, Leah K., Catherine M. Tucker, and Eileen Diaz McConnell. 2005. "Community Organization, Migration and Remittances in Oaxaca." *Latin American Research Review* 40 (1): 83–107.

Wilson, Tamar Diana. 2000. "Anti-immigrant Sentiment and the Problem of Reproduction/Maintenance in Mexican Immigration to the United States." *Critique of Anthropology* 20 (2): 191–213.

PART FOUR
THE STATE AND MULTICULTURAL RIGHTS: ENABLER OR MENACE?

9 Multicultural Reforms for Mexico's "Tranquil" Indians in Yucatán

Shannan Mattiace

INTRODUCTION

During the 1990s throughout Latin America, congresses passed reforms that constitutionally enshrined rights for indigenous peoples (and in some cases people of African descent) for the first time. While economic reforms passed in the wake of the 1980s debt crisis preceded the promulgation of Indian rights, both reform movements coincided in the 1990s. Both the neoliberal reforms and the multicultural policies that accompanied them have transformed the relationship between states and citizens. What that transformation consists of, however, has been a subject of debate.

Donna Lee Van Cott (2006) viewed the adoption of multicultural policies by nation-states across the Americas in the 1980s and 1990s as opening up spaces for indigenous movements to make unprecedented demands for rights. While she recognized the constrained nature of the context within which these demands were made (political elites in Colombia and Bolivia in the early 1990s, for example, opened spaces for indigenous participation in constitutional reforms largely for their own reasons), she argued that the rights attained were significant. Charles Hale (2002), in contrast, takes a more critical view of what he has dubbed "neoliberal multiculturalism," which he sees as a possible menace to more substantive Indian rights. By recognizing cultural rights, he argues, nation-states have rejected demands for land and resources. The gist of Hale's argument is that neoliberal multiculturalism precludes more radical demands from being made. Indeed, in Hale's view, radical indigenous voices have been pushed aside under neoliberal multiculturalism, while policymakers have recognized more moderate and conservative Indian leaders as the legitimate interlocutors.

Bret Gustafson's (2002) work resonates with Hale's but focuses more on the continuity between current multicultural reforms and past policies. He argues that recent reforms should be understood as the latest iteration in a long history of negotiations between the state and indigenous peoples. Gustafson argues that we should view liberal indigenism as a modernization of political identities and not as a sign of "the recent inclusion of heretofore excluded indigenous peoples" (2002, 274). Nation-states, he suggests, have long sought to forge a relationship with indigenous peoples and that relationship shifts and changes over time—in response to external and internal influences. Gustafson says that within the liberal indigenism of the 1990s, indigenous collectivities were being reimagined as localized entities and granted new arenas of participation, no longer as corporatist peasant unions but as differentiated communities engaging a uniform national template of municipal politics (276). Gustafson urges us to see these policy reforms not as empowerment but as another step in the negotiated relationship between the state and indigenous peoples. Writing about Bolivia, Postero (2004) also sees neoliberal multicultural reforms as part of an ongoing relationship between the state and indigenous peoples, but one that was based on a new kind of "governmentality." The neoliberal Bolivian state of the 1990s, she argues, reached out directly to isolated indigenous communities (circumventing regional governments and corporatist organizations), thus precluding interregional and cross-regional alliances among indigenous communities and organizations.

In chapter 1 of this volume, José Antonio Lucero synthesizes the motivations for multicultural reforms on two axes: whether reforms were initiated from the top down or the bottom up and whether pressure came predominantly from domestic or international arenas (table 9.1). In sum, the question of who has supported multicultural reforms and why has been the subject of vibrant debate among scholars of Latin America. In this essay, I apply and extend this debate to look at the case of Yucatán state.[1] Yucatán is worthy of examination, as it has one of the largest indigenous-language groups—Maya—in all of Mexico. Legislation on Indian rights, which in Yucatán was titled the Law for the Protection of the Rights of the Maya Community (Maya Community Law 2011), was passed by the state congress in April

Table 9.1 Motivation for Multiculturalism

	Domestic	*International*
From above	Democratic legitimacy; elite partisan calculations	ILO Convention 169, UN,[1] World Bank
From below	Social movement pressures	TANs[2]

Source: chapter 1, this volume.

[1.] I refer here to the International Labour Organization's Convention 169, promulgated in 1989. Convention 169 is one of the most progressive and far-reaching single documents on indigenous rights to date. After more than twenty years of negotiations between nation-states and indigenous peoples, the United Nations (UN) Permanent Forum on Indigenous Issues published its long-awaited Declaration on the Rights of Indigenous Peoples in September 2007.

[2.] Transnational Advocacy Networks. TANs link activists working on similar causes across two countries or more. Keck and Sikkink (1998) note that TANs organized around Indian rights have been among the most durable and powerful.

2011, and a Regulatory Law (2011) was approved in December 2011.² In this essay, I argue that the multicultural reforms enacted in Yucatán to date are the result of top-down, national-level factors that have pushed state legislators to move forward in the area of Indian rights. Multicultural reforms in Yucatán are not the result of grassroots pressure: there has been no Indian or Maya political movement to speak of in Yucatán, unlike other regions of Mexico, such as Chiapas, Oaxaca, Guerrero, and Michoacán, where strong regional movements exist.³

In the chapter's first section, I provide a brief political history of Yucatán, focusing on actors and events that are most relevant to understanding Maya-state relations. Next, I argue that the 2011 Maya Community legislation and the subsequent regulatory law were not the result of grassroots pressure. I lay out three principal reasons to explain the absence of an indigenous sociopolitical movement in Yucatán: (1) peasant leagues, used in other areas of Mexico and Latin America as ethnic organizing structures in the 1980s and 1990s, lacked autonomy, given the industrial character of Yucatán's agricultural sector, which has been historically tied to henequen production; (2) progressive Catholic Church networks, used in other parts of Mexico and Latin America as vehicles for indigenous transcommunity organization, were not present in Yucatán due to the conservative theological orientation of the Yucatecan bishopric; and finally (3) nongovernmental organizations (NGOs), which could have been used as building blocks for ethnic organization, are too small scale and concentrated in the capital city of Mérida to effectively link communities across the state around indigenous rights. Additionally, long-standing indigenous organizations from within Yucatecan civil society are largely focused on Maya history and culture.

Finally, in the third section, I argue that multicultural reforms in Yucatán have dovetailed with recent federal reform of the judicial system.⁴ In the period between 2007 and 2011 as Yucatecan policymakers were drawing up legislative language on Indian culture and rights, politicians at the federal level were proposing significant constitutional and legislative reforms to dramatically alter judicial procedures at the federal, state, and local levels: namely, to move Mexico from an inquisitorial (*inquisitorio*) to an adversarial (*acusatorio*) judicial system. Oral arguments would now become the norm, marking a significant break with the current system based on written judicial procedures. I suggest that Yucatecan state officials saw their multicultural legislation as an opportunity to utilize Maya *usos y costumbres* regarding the administration of local justice as a way to more effectively deliver the judicial reforms that were emerging from Mexico City. I argue in this section that state officials' recognition of "Maya justices" (*jueces mayas*), included in the 2011 legislation, may bring citizens closer to their local governments, but does not seek to strengthen Maya political autonomy.

THE CONTEXT: KEY HISTORICAL, SOCIAL, AND POLITICAL FACTORS IN MAYA-STATE RELATIONS

Based on Mexican Census Bureau (INEGI 2005) statistics, Yucatán ranks second in the number of indigenous peoples as a percentage of total state population. In

Yucatán, 33.5 percent of the population over the age of five speaks an indigenous language (538,355 individuals), second only to Oaxaca state (35.3 percent).[5] Unlike most other Mexican states whose indigenous population consists of peoples of distinct indigenous ethnicities, in Yucatán, the indigenous population is overwhelmingly Maya.

For a variety of geographical and political reasons, native community structures in Yucatán have been severely eroded and the degree of state penetration, even in the most remote Maya villages, is high. In the eighteenth and nineteenth centuries, Maya rose up against white and criollo elites in defense of land and autonomy and against onerous tribute payments and broken promises. Mayas living in the eastern part of the state were at war for most of the years between 1847 and 1901 (the Caste War), with intermittent fighting continuing until the 1930s. Losses are difficult to measure, but it is commonly asserted that between one-third and one-half of Yucatán's population of 600,000 died or were displaced in the conflict (Wells and Joseph 1996, 27). Reed (1964) argues that in the first four years alone approximately 35 percent of the population (275,000) lost their lives.[6] After the most intense fighting of the Caste War ended (after 1849), the Yucatecan state harshly repressed Maya who collaborated with the "agitators." As a result, Maya in the central and western regions of the state drew a stark line between themselves and the rebellious Indians of the east. From this point onward, the Maya of central and western Yucatán called themselves mestizos, rejecting the terms Indian or Maya. It was also in these central and western regions of Yucatán where large haciendas broke up ethnic communities in the last quarter of the nineteenth century, forcing indigenous peoples to work as peons on their former lands.

In the wake of the Mexican Revolution in the 1920s, the national government aggressively pushed forward indigenist policies in states with large native populations such as Yucatán.[7] These policies were focused largely on education and health, with the express purpose of Mexicanizing Indians and assimilating them into the "revolutionary family" as mestizos.[8] Beginning in the 1930s, the PRM (Party of the Mexican Revolution) dominated political life.[9] While the later PRI (Party of the Institutional Revolution) did not govern democratically—Mexico was a one-party state during this time—its governing style in Yucatán hewed more to "inclusionary corporatism" than to outright repression. PRI leaders in Yucatán, in particular the powerful Víctor Cervera Pacheco, who served as interim governor from 1984 to 1988 and was elected to a six-year term in 1995, governed through patronage and "soft" authoritarianism, mobilizing citizens in official labor and peasant unions.

As a counterpoint to the PRI, the Catholic Church has been a powerful actor in Yucatán, particularly in terms of social policy and in its influence on the attitudes and persuasions of rank-and-file Catholics. Compared to other archdioceses throughout Mexico—particularly its neighbor to the south, the Archdiocese of San Cristóbal de las Casas, Chiapas, under Samuel Ruíz (1960–1998)—the Yucatecan Catholic Church has long been a conservative force to be reckoned with. During the twenty-six-year tenure of Archbishop Manuel Castro Ruíz (1969–1995), the church did not support ethnic consciousness raising and had no program similar to the diaconate training promoted by Samuel Ruíz in Chiapas.[10] After Castro Ruíz retired in 1995, Emilio Berlie Belaunzarán continued the conservative course set by his predecessor. While a small group of progressive priests in southeastern Yucatán have drawn inspiration from Ruíz's work in Chiapas, specifically the Indian-centered theology he promoted (*teología india*), they face a hostile bishop who actively discourages the promotion of Christian base communities or anything that smacks of liberation or Indian theology.

As is well known, 1994 was a key year for indigenous mobilization and ethnic consciousness throughout Mexico, with the public emergence of the EZLN (Ejército Zapatista de Liberación Nacional) in Chiapas on January 1. In subsequent years, indigenous peoples in Chiapas put Indian culture and rights on the national political agenda. In an official dialogue with national governmental officials in the mid-1990s, the EZLN and governmental representatives and advisors hammered out a bill on indigenous rights and culture (San Andrés Accords) that President Fox sent to Congress in December 2000. In Yucatán, while the EZLN movement has had some impact on raising ethnic consciousness, a regional indigenous movement has not emerged in force. The appearance of the EZLN has galvanized a small group of Yucatecan activists, particularly in the area of NGOs dedicated to human and Indian rights. As I argue in this chapter, however, there is to date no cohesive and coherent advocacy network organized to pressure state legislators and to defend Indian rights and culture in Yucatán.

National-Level Constitutional Reforms and Yucatán's Response

The constitutional reform package of 2001, which was a dramatically modified version of the bill President Fox sent to Congress in late 2000, made states responsible for defining and limiting Indian autonomy. The compromise bill, approved by both houses of Congress in spring 2001 and subsequently ratified by the stipulated two-thirds of states, does not sanction or protect autonomy for indigenous peoples at the national level.[11] Even before the national-level debate in 2001, however, several Mexican states had made changes to their constitutions and to secondary laws to protect Indian rights (see Bailón 2003). The state making the most substantive changes was Oaxaca, whose 1995 constitution allowed municipal governments that registered with the state to elect local authorities based on local practices (*usos y costumbres*).[12] A second wave of constitutional modifications occurred in the wake of President Ernesto Zedillo's call in 1998 to implement state-level reforms. Changes were made to state constitutions in Veracruz, Nayarit, Michoacán, Quintana Roo, Campeche, and Chiapas (Assies et al. 2006, 45).[13] A third wave of reforms occurred after the 2001 constitutional reform (e.g., San Luis Potosí).

Of southern Mexico's indigenous states, Yucatán was the last to make substantive constitutional and legislative changes in the area of Indian rights. After a long process of deliberation, which included several *consultas* (public meetings) with varying participation of Mayas—the Yucatecan state congress made changes to its state constitution in 2007 (Constitutional Reform 2007). After more than a year elapsed without any additional reforms or relevant legislation (which the constitutional decree mandated), the state congress resumed debate in 2008 in the context of drafting such legislation. It was not, however, until April 2011 that legislation on Indian culture and rights was passed. Later that year, in December, a regulatory law was also approved.

In general terms, this legislation is largely culturalist in that it focuses on the promotion of Maya culture and language and does not substantively address issues of land or resources. While the Maya Community Law and its regulatory legislation does mention the importance of socioeconomic development in Maya communities (and the state's role in promoting it), much more attention is paid to the provision of Maya translators, to the promotion of Maya culture and language, to the use of Maya medicine, and, most importantly in terms of the space dedicated to it, to the selection of Maya justices to adjudicate cases on the local level. The law also calls for the expansion of the state's premier indigenist institution, the Institute for the Development of Maya Culture of the State of Yucatán (Instituto para el Desarrollo de la Cultura Maya del Estado de Yucatán, INDEMAYA). INDEMAYA was created in 2001, largely to foment the development of Maya culture and to coordinate the activities of many different governmental agencies active in Maya communities throughout the state. The 2011 legislation requires INDEMAYA to compile and maintain a registry of Maya communities where Maya justice can be practiced and Maya justices are selected by the community.[14]

Similar to legislation in Campeche, Chiapas, and Quintana Roo states, the Yucatecan law creates a new jurisdiction for Maya justices (*jueces mayas*) at the local level. These justices are charged with administering the law of the land at the local level in accordance with community "uses, customs, and traditions" (Maya Community Law 2011). The language of the legislation is consistently paternalistic: the state grants rights to Maya communities rather than acknowledging a set of governmental institutions and practices already there. In several different places throughout the document the state is charged with "helping" Maya communities to develop and implement internal systems of government. In this way, the state seems to assume that there are few existing mechanisms of justice and norms at the local level and that the Maya will be developing their *usos y costumbres* in collaboration with the government.[15] Indeed, the law states that local Maya justices must communicate and collaborate with INDEMAYA on the Maya community registry the institute is charged with compiling. If there are disagreements about what constitutes indigenous law at the local level, aggrieved parties may file an appeal of the ruling and/or enter the "regular" justice system to adjudicate their claims. Finally, the legislation is clear in its insistence that Maya women participate in local decision making and that no local norm or custom contradict state or national laws. While this legislation is unprecedented in acknowledging Maya norms and practices at the local level, it continues a long history of paternalistic treatment and development assistance flowing from the state down to Maya local communities. Notwithstanding the few consultations held by state officials in local communities throughout the state before changes were made to the state constitution in 2007 and the state's solicitation of proposals from civil society organizations in the long process of drafting legislation on Indian rights and culture, the 2011 legislation was a top-down initiative developed in the absence of a grassroots indigenous social movement, about which more is said below.

While the onus for legislating in the area of Indian autonomy was placed on the states as a result of the 2001 national constitutional changes, it took six years before the state constitutional changes were made and another four years for Indian rights legislation to be passed. Two significant institutional changes occurred in those six intervening years that set the foundation for the 2007 constitutional changes. The first was the creation of a state-level indigenist institution, INDEMAYA, in 2001 under the new administration of Patricio Patrón of the National Action Party (PAN), and the second was the creation of a new legislative committee to deal with indigenous affairs, called the Ethnic Affairs Committee (Comisión de Asuntos Étnicos) in 2004. (The name of the committee was changed in January 2011 to the Permanent Committee for the Respect and Preservation of the Maya Culture, or Comisión Permanente para el Respeto y Preservación de la Cultura Maya). Given both entities' significance to the ultimate passage of Indian rights legislation in Yucatán, I discuss each in more detail in what follows.

INDEMAYA

In January and February 2007 I conducted interviews with several officials at the Yucatán branch of the National Commission for the Development of Indigenous Peoples (Comisión Nacional para el Desarrollo de los Pueblos Indígenas, CDI [until 2002 the National Indigenist Institute, INI]) and at the state indigenist agency, INDEMAYA (see appendix). Structurally, Mexican indigenist institutions are headed up by the federal agency, the CDI. Most states with large indigenous populations have their own state-level agency. Yucatán's state agency is relatively new, created at the start of the 2000–2007 administration of PAN governor Patricio Patrón. In this section, I present a brief history of the CDI's activities in Yucatán and the formation of INDEMAYA in early 2001.

Similar to initiatives taking place in other Mexican states, in the 1980s, the INI in Yucatán supported the formation of several new centers and events dedicated to the promotion of Maya culture through Maya-speaking *promotores*.[16] Between 1983 and 1987 the INI sponsored annual Maya Cultural Forums (Encuentros de Cultura Maya) held in different Maya localities. In those same years, the institute ran a program for Maya writers (Rosales and Llanez 2003, 551). These programs boosted Maya cultural and literary production throughout the peninsula. During the 1980s and 1990s, several new publications and texts in the Maya language were published, sparking the formation of writer associations, some of which later joined the National Association of Writers in Indigenous Languages (Asociación Nacional de Escritores en Lengua Indígena) (Rosales and Llanez 2003, 551).[17]

Immediately before Patricio Patrón assumed office in 2001, a new state agency was formed to deal with "Maya affairs" or what would be called the "Indian question" in other parts of Mexico. Consistent with my argument that national-level pressures have been significant in explaining legislative changes in the area of Indian law in Yucatán, high-ranking officials of INDEMAYA told me in 2007 that the incoming

PAN administration created the agency in 2001 in order to take advantage of federal monies dispersed in the wake of the 2001 national constitutional changes on Indian culture and rights. The new agency was INDEMAYA, and its mission was "to promote the creation of development policies based on full respect for the cultural values of the Maya people. To guarantee the appropriate channeling and utilization of human, material, and financial resources to the ethnic group for the purposes of development through appropriate coordination among governmental institutions. To stimulate the widest possible access to public sector services and to diffuse and consolidate the Maya language" (INDEMAYA 2001).

As its mission statement implies, INDEMAYA does not dispense monies directly to communities or organizations, but coordinates with and channels Maya demands to appropriate state agencies.[18] According to Eduardo López Salcido, subdirector at INDEMAYA in 2007, the institute's Maya employees spend time in Maya communities talking to people about their needs—in the areas of health care, agriculture, and education, for example—so as to take these demands to the corresponding state agencies. INDEMAYA also promotes its own program initiatives, many of which are of a cultural nature. For example, the institute sponsors Maya language and dance competitions to encourage Maya to continue to speak and to pass on the language. INDEMAYA also works to train interpreters who serve as translators in legal cases and has initiated a program on migration and migrant communities. According to then-director Diana Canto Moreno, one of INDEMAYA's most successful initiatives has been the campaign "Aquí Estamos" (Here we are). Focused on Maya culture, this program seeks to raise Maya *auto-estima* (self-esteem) through television spots highlighting the accomplishments of Maya across the state. Canto also told me that the agency works with state officials "to sensitize them to Maya issues." The agency, for example, has worked with the Health Ministry on initiatives that combine traditional and Western medicine. Compared to the CDI, which has almost fifty years' experience in Yucatán, INDEMAYA is just beginning to establish itself as a presence in the state. So far, with a few exceptions, its programming and initiatives seem to be largely focused on language and cultural expression.

On occasion, INDEMAYA has engaged more explicitly political issues. This was the case between 2004 and 2006 when it participated—alongside the CDI and state legislators—in spearheading several *consultas* among the Maya in an attempt to take their pulse on the issue of Indian rights.[19] My interviews with officials at the two agencies revealed palpable tension between CDI and INDEMAYA in the leadership of these *consultas*. Patricia Guarneros, director of the CDI from 2004 to 2007 with almost three decades of experience within the agency, told me that one of her main goals as CDI director was to hold the state government's feet to the fire and to inform the public about the *consulta*: to make sure that "reglas mínimas [basic rules]" were followed.[20] For Guarneros, the point of these *consultas* was to lay the groundwork for state-level reform on Indian rights following the San Andrés Accords. In our interview, Guarneros referred to Yucatán as an outlier in the area of Indian rights legislation compared to other states, such as Oaxaca, San Luis Potosí, and Chiapas. Even neighboring states such as Campeche and Quintana Roo, she noted, had made greater strides in this area than Yucatán. In Guarneros's view, state government officials in Yucatán, including those at INDEMAYA, had made "no serious attempt to modify the constitution on the state level" and were uninterested in putting issues of autonomy and land ownership on the table—issues that were central, she noted, in the San Andrés Accords. Guarneros told me that governmental officials rationalized their resistance by claiming that Maya in Yucatán do not want to talk about autonomy or territory ("they have their land") and that they certainly are not like "los revoltuosos chiapanecos [the rebellious chiapanecos]."[21] In Guarneros's view, the state government, including INDEMAYA, wanted to limit conversation at the *consultas* to talk of public policy and civil rights, such as the right to education, health care, and so forth.[22] Interviews with INDEMAYA officials, as well as with Representative Juan Valencia (PAN), member of the Ethnic Affairs Committee in the Yucatán state legislature from 2004 to 2007, suggested that committee members coordinated closely with INDEMAYA officials as state legislators were drafting an Indian rights bill.[23]

In assessing the overall impact of INDEMAYA and CDI on state legislation in the area of Indian rights, INDEMAYA's vision and programming more closely reflect the mores and values of the state government.[24] Namely, there is less racial discrimination in Yucatán than in other Mexican states and the Maya are generally a peaceable people, in contrast to the *indios* in other parts of Mexico. State officials in Yucatán resist using the term "peoples" to describe the Maya, preferring terms such as "Maya community," *indígena Maya* (Maya indigenous person), or *etnia maya*. My research suggests that the work of the CDI in Yucatán is not dissimilar from that of other Mexican states. Its programming and project initiatives are set at the national level, and state-level directors, like Patricia Guarneros, often have experience in working with indigenous communities in more than one state.[25] It is not uncommon for directors to be trained as anthropologists from the National School of Anthropology and History in Mexico City, which is true in Guarneros's case, providing them with a national network of colleagues.

Ethnic Affairs Committee/Permanent Committee for the Respect and Preservation of Maya Culture

In 2004, a new permanent committee was added to the institutional structure of the Yucatecan legislature, the Comisión de Asuntos Étnicos, or the Ethnic Affairs Committee. Representative Juan Manuel Valencia (PAN), one of three original members of the committee, told me that it was created in 2004 at the behest of the leaders of the three major parties in Congress (*los coordinadores*). According to Valencia, the idea was that more attention needed to be paid to the *etnia maya* (Maya ethnic group). In Valencia's view, the PRI spearheaded the formation of this committee because the party needed to cozy up to rural voters after having lost the governorship in 2000. This loss, he said, was compounded in 2004 by additional losses in municipal elections. As the PAN began to make significant inroads into rural areas, Valencia said, the PRI got scared. In Valencia's view, the PRI acted opportunistically with regards to Indian rights; PRI deputies saw advancing Indian rights as a way of revitalizing its rural base. I asked Valencia why, in his view, the PRI focused on rural voters' ethnic identity rather than appealing to them as campesinos. According to Valencia, this was a result of the attention paid to indigenous issues at the national level in 2001, which coincided with the creation of INDEMAYA in early 2001 and whose director, Diana Canto, "put more emphasis on Maya issues" (ella dio más empujón a lo Maya).[26]

In an interview with PAN deputy José Antonio Aragón Uicab, president of the Ethnic Affairs Committee in the 2007–2010 state congress, Aragón said that like many deputies serving on the committee he was new to the topic of Indian rights.[27] For this reason, he said, committee members consulted with indigenous rights experts as they worked out the language of the 2007 changes to the state constitution. Notwithstanding his lack of formal experience, Aragón noted that all of the committee members are from the interior of the state—that is, Maya areas of Yucatán—and "understand the problems of the indigenous population." Besides that, he said, "our ancestors are Maya; they spoke Maya. I understand it, although I cannot speak it."[28]

In January 2011, the name of the Ethnic Affairs Committee was changed to the Permanent Committee for the Respect and Preservation of Maya Culture. In an interview with the president of the committee in 2012, Tito Sánchez (PAN), Sánchez said that his initial interest and experience with issues related to the Maya population was sparked by his participation in the Knights of Columbus as a youth member. Sánchez spoke of mission trips to Maya communities in rural Yucatán that he took as a young knight that opened his eyes to the poverty in these villages. Despite the change in leadership and name of this congressional committee, members, then and now, seem to view the legislation as a way to help indigenous peoples, who are viewed as being in need of state guidance.

ETHNIC MOBILIZATION IN YUCATÁN

Thus far, I have argued that changes at the national level in Mexico in the area of Indian rights incentivized governmental officials in Yucatán, motivating them to create a state indigenist institute, INDEMAYA, in 2001, and to make changes to the state constitution in 2007. Amending the state constitution paved the way for legislation on Indian culture and rights, which culminated in the 2011 Maya community legislation and its subsequent regulatory law. These state-level changes were not the result of grassroots pressure: there is no indigenous movement to speak of in Yucatán today. In her influential 2005 book, *Contesting Citizenship in Latin America*, Deborah Yashar argues that indigenous movements in the Americas have formed in places where networks—such as peasant leagues, church organizations, and NGOs—are strong.[29] In this section, I examine the relative strength of these networks in Yucatán.

Peasant Leagues

Many indigenous activists throughout Latin America used the experience they gained in peasant organizations in the 1970s and 1980s as a foundation for subsequent indigenous activism in the 1990s. While peasant organizations were typically based on class identities—often eclipsing and ignoring racial and ethnic issues—demands for land and defense of agricultural self-sufficiency were taken up by indigenous activists, even as they left official organizations to form their own independent ones. The experience Maya peasants garnered in Yucatán's National Peasant Confederation (CNC), however, was more proletarian than peasant based. As Villanueva Mukul notes, "the bulk of [henequen workers'] demands were oriented more toward proletarian issues than to peasant ones, such as higher salaries, bonuses, and credit advances" (1993, 16).[30] Maya peasants did not engage in a struggle for land rights; as Baños Ramírez (1989) argues, most of their demands centered on a higher price for the henequen they produced as well as demands for more credits and higher pensions. Thus, for Baños Ramírez (1989, 282), henequen producers in Yucatán cannot be called peasants in a strict sense of that word in that that they did not enjoy even a minimal level of control over their agricultural production. Unlike indigenous peasants in other regions of Mexico who cut their organizational teeth by mobilizing around land reform, Maya peasants had little or no interest in land; their principal interest was in obtaining credit from the state. Rosales and Llanez also argue that there was no movement for land in Yucatán as there was in other Mexican states: "The mobilizations in these years [1970s and 1980s] privileged economic demands of a working class stripe, such as those advanced by the henequen *ejidatarios* in Yucatán in relation to credit or *las carteras vencidas* of corn farmers in the center and east of the state. The latter emphasized the importance of marketing products independently of the state" (2003, 550).[31]

While the state exercised hegemonic control over henequen producers located in the northwestern region around Mérida, peasants living in eastern and southern Yucatán enjoyed more autonomy from the state. This relative autonomy, however, has not translated into ethnic-based organization. I spoke with several movement organizers and cultural promoters who have lived and worked in the southern agricultural region who asserted that Maya both in and outside the henequen zone shared what they called a "mentality of dependency." Feliciano Sánchez, who has worked for over twenty years as a cultural promoter at the Center for Popular Culture (a branch of the National Council for the Arts and Culture), underscored the impact that the state's ecology has had on community solidarity and autonomy. "Yucatán is a very flat state, a place where no one can hide," he said. "This has made it difficult for Maya communities to exercise de facto autonomy.... Our communities have been open to outside influence much more than Chiapas and Oaxaca." While peasants' level of dependence on the CNC and the state was greatest in the henequen zone, Sánchez spoke of the penetration and influence of political parties in the countryside throughout Yucatán. He said that community organizers are fighting an uphill battle against party operators and state officials to capture Mayas' attention.

In the late 1970s, economic alternatives offered by the tourist and oil industries in the neighboring states of Quintana Roo and Campeche, respectively, also attracted Mayas' attention. With the massive development of Cancún in the late 1970s, extending down the Caribbean coast in the 1980s and 1990s, a steady and increasing number of Maya peasants left their villages in search of economic opportunities on the Maya Riviera. In the 1980s, the expansion of petroleum exploration and production in Campeche also attracted thousands of rural Yucatecan migrants (Baños Ramirez 2000). Several of my informants commented on migration to the Maya Riviera and to Campeche as key factors in explaining the general weakness of Maya organization. Without the escape valve of migration to mitigate the effect of neoliberal policies on the Yucatecan countryside in the 1980s and 1990s, there may have been more organizational activity, or "voice" (see Hirschman 1970). Instead, Mayas exited to Cancún and Campeche, voting with their feet.

Catholic Church Networks

Numerous scholars have documented indigenous' peoples use of Catholic Church networks to make connections across local communities and to forge ethnic-based organizations throughout the continent (see Cleary and Steigenga 2004; Yashar 2005).[32] This has not been the case in Yucatán, however. The Yucatecan Church is widely considered to be one of the most conservative in the country. For twenty-six years it was under the helm of Archbishop Castro Ruíz, who was succeeded in 1996 by the equally conservative Emilio Berlie. Both bishops actively sought to shut down the work of progressive priests, who had been markedly influenced by the 1968 bishops' conference held in Medellín (where a "preferential option for the poor" was officially promulgated) and the work of liberation theologians more broadly. While in Yucatán this group of priests was never very large (averaging around ten clergy), they have worked for decades on issues related to social justice, human rights, and, in the last fifteen years, Maya cultural identity and autonomy. Today, the work of these priests is focused on an ecological agricultural school (Escuela de Agricultura Ecológica) in the southern town of Maní, where students study organic agricultural techniques and take courses in Maya history and culture.[33]

The priests who founded the Escuela de Agricultura Ecológica in the mid-1990s view their work and vocations through the lens of liberation theology. Padre Atilano Ceballos Loeza ("Tilo") told me that the same simple principles that guided the formation of base Christian communities throughout Latin America provided the foundation for their project, namely the idea of "seeing, thinking, and acting" (*ver, pensar, actuar*). From the start, Padre Tilo said, the bishop opposed the project and tried to close it down. While "the hierarchical church" did succeed in scaring away several of the priests initially involved in the project, a core group of four priests remained. Maní was chosen as a site, as it was geographically close to two of the priests involved in the project, and the land was good for farming. Funding for the project came from the German Catholic Church, which not only provided the initial start-up financing but was the principal donor for the first ten years of operation.

By 2007, the school had approximately seventeen students.[34] The curriculum consists of three main branches (*módulos*) of study: *agro-forestal* (forestry); *agro-pecuario* (farming); and *humana-social* (social humanism). Courses taken in the first module include instruction on diseases (*plagas*), planting, and composting. *Agro-pecuario* courses deal with animal management (*manejo de animales*), beekeeping, birds, fisheries, and animal reproduction. In the third module, *humana-social*, students take courses on fair trade, rural sustainable development, the Bible and land issues, Yucatecan history, and Maya culture, language, and spirituality. Bernardo Xiú, a graduate of the program who now works at the school, described the course he took on the history of Yucatán: "I have discovered so much more about Maya culture. It is only now that we are beginning to understand our history, our Maya history, our culture." Motivated by this course, he began a project of "rescuing" Maya stories that were passed down to him from his parents and grandparents.

While cultural revitalization is an explicit goal of the priests and graduates currently working at the school, the Escuela Agrícola is not tied to other efforts in the region to forge regional networks of Maya farmers around common goals. This has less to do with the efforts of those working at the school—who are passionate and devoted to the place and to the students—than with the lack of institutional support from those higher up in the church hierarchy. Indeed, the archbishop has actively opposed the work of these priests for years.

NGO Networks

In addition to national peasant leagues and churches, NGOs have provided resources for the creation of transcommunity networks. Across Latin America, indigenous activists have utilized human-rights NGOs for this purpose. While Yucatán has a number of NGOs working in the area of human rights, no cohesive networks around Indian rights and culture have emerged to link Maya (and their allies) across communities.

One of the most visible NGOs working in this area is Grupo Indignación, based in Chablekal, north of Mérida. Several of those working for Grupo Indignación are clergy or were heavily influenced by liberation theology and the progressive Catholic Church. The director, Father Raúl Lugo, for example, is also involved in the Ecological School at Maní. My visit to Grupo Indignación and interview with José Euán Romero suggest that while the NGO is not officially linked to the Catholic Church, the language used to talk about its work comes very much from the progressive Catholic tradition.

In January 2006, Subcomandante Marcos of the EZLN came to Yucatán with several indigenous delegates as part of his presidential "noncampaign" (*la otra campaña*). The EZLN asked Grupo Indignación to organize the three-day visit, which involved meetings with several indigenous organizations, a (not anticipated) visit to Chichén Itza, and a final public march and demonstration in the center of Mérida. For those at Grupo Indignación working on Indian rights and culture, the EZLN's visit was an opportunity to further their work in this area with the hopes of sparking awareness and activism among the Maya. Another organization stimulated by the EZLN's visit was the Maya Peninsular Forum (Foro Maya Peninsular), which was formed in the wake of the uprising to represent the Yucatán peninsula within the National Indian Congress (Congreso Nacional Indígena, or CNI), an organization closely tied to the EZLN. In 1999, members of the Maya Peninsular Forum received the Zapatista delegates who came to promote the EZLN's *consulta* and were intensely involved in national-level discussions on the 2001 legislation on Indian rights. While members of the forum have coordinated with Grupo Indignación on specific legal and political initiatives regarding changes in the state constitution with respect to Indian rights, the forum is a more explicitly political association whose main goal is the implementation of the San Andrés Accords. One of the forum's founding members and current leaders, Guillermo May Correa, told me the organization had assumed the San Andrés Accords as its own and that it would continue to fight until these accords become law.[35]

Another NGO that has established a visible public presence since its founding in 1990 is Mayaón (Somos Maya). Today, Mayaón is one of the longest-lasting and most visible Maya organizations on the peninsula. The organization was officially constituted as a civil society association in 1990 by Maya leaders in two areas: bilingual teachers from in and around Valladolid and peasants from the southern region of the state. The organization's goals center on deepening understanding of Maya culture, language, and values and fighting against all forms of discrimination (Quintal 2005, 357). In the words of Bartolomé Alonzo Caamal (1993), one of the founding members and a bilingual teacher from Valladolid, it is imperative that Maya people understand and embrace the rich history they share as Maya. According to Alonzo, Maya continue to live under a neocolonial form of subordination in that Maya do not know their own history.[36] One of Mayaón's principal demands is to promote the use of the Maya language. The organization does not typically organize public protests and marches, but attempts to reach its goals through participation in public forums—organized both by the government and by NGOs—and making their voice heard through the press (Quintal 2005, 360). Since its founding, the organization has strenuously lobbied state officials to make Maya an official language in government offices and to push for more and better bilingual education. In a 2009 interview, Alonzo underscored the cultural work of Mayaón in its focus on reinvigorating the use of the Maya language, encouraging the formation of a historical consciousness among Maya, and placing value on Maya cultural expressions.[37]

Mayaón has approximately sixty members who are organized into regional organizations, meeting once a year in a plenary session (Quintal 2005; Rosales and Llanez 2003). Most, Alonzo noted, are bilingual teachers from Yucatán state.[38] Unlike many organizations in Yucatán that focus strictly on Maya rituals, culture, and customs, Mayaón did not emerge from state and federal indigenist institutions and maintains a certain degree of autonomy from these official organizations. Its focus on Maya (neocolonial) history also sets it apart from indigenism, which tends to focus on culture—understood largely as folklore. While Mayaón is not a large organization and has not allied with other organizations to increase its potential influence, its leaders are visible in public spaces, such as newspapers, on the radio, and in public forums. Today, Alonzo Caamal continues to be active in the organization, making declarations in the press and acting as a spokesperson for the organization in public forums and meetings, as is Amadeo Cool May, radio announcer for the XPET, indigenist radio station in Peto, Yucatán (Quintal 2005, 358).

Mayaón was an active participant in the forums held by state legislators leading up to the 2011 Indian rights legislation.[39] According to an interview with José Antonio Aragón Uicab (PAN), member of the Ethnic Affairs Committee during the 2007–2010 state congress, of all Yucatecan social organizations, Mayaón was the most involved. As I have pointed out, the Maya Community Law focuses heavily on Maya language and culture, specifically, granting Maya the right to use their language in dealings with state officials and expanding bilingual and intercultural education. Alonzo sees Mayaón's culture, history, and language focus as providing the foundation that will allow Maya to make larger, more political demands in the future (2009 interview). For Alonzo, the organization's demands are means to something bigger, not ends in themselves (2009 interview). Nevertheless, Mayaón's general orientation toward culture and its concentration, within a fairly narrow professional community of bilingual teachers around Valladolid, make it an unlikely base for ethnic-based political organization.

To sum up, the networks and organizations that in other regions of Latin America have provided resources for ethnic-based organization—peasant leagues, the progressive Catholic Church, and NGOs—have not served as vehicles for ethnic-based leadership and organization in Yucatán. First, the experience that Maya garnered in peasant leagues, namely the Yucatán state branch of the CNC and its affiliates, was focused more on proletarian issues such as income and credit and less on land reform. In other regions, including Chiapas, peasants parlayed experience gained in fighting for land reform to mobilizing for demands as Indians. I argue that demands for salary increases and provision of credit transfer less well to ethnic-based organization than experience gained in fighting for land reform. The heavy hand of the CNC in Yucatán, given the high capital requirements of the henequen industry, made independent organization less likely, and when it emerged it tended to be short-lived. Second, the progressive Catholic Church has been weak in Yucatán, due largely to decades of conservative leadership at the top of the ecclesiastical hierarchy. Bishops have frowned on anything that smacks of liberation theology and have actively discouraged priests from engaging in social issues. While a small group of progressive priests have been active in the state for years and have focused their energies on cultural revitalization and leadership training, these initiatives have operated on a small scale and have not served to effectively link Maya communities translocally. Third, while NGOs based on human and indigenous rights exist in Yucatán, they also tend to be small-scale operations. One of the most visible and long-standing NGOs, Mayaón, focuses on revitalizing Maya memory and pride in Maya history, explicitly distancing itself from social and political demands.

LOCAL JUSTICE AND INDIAN LAW IN YUCATÁN

In contrast to growing literature on Indian law and local justice in states such as Oaxaca, Chiapas, and Puebla, relatively little has been written about Yucatecan Maya *usos y costumbres*.[40] Only two volumes have been published on Indian law in Yucatán, both edited by Esteban Krotz: *Aspectos de la Cultura Jurídica en Yucatán* (1997) and *Aproximaciones a la Antropología Jurídica de los Mayas Peninsulares* (2001). In large part, this paucity of literature reflects the fact that Maya communities in Yucatán are not as geographically isolated and culturally marginalized as many indigenous communities in other Mexican states. While there are very few indigenous communities in Mexico and, indeed, throughout the Americas, that have not been significantly shaped by Western legal norms and practices, relatively more remote communities have continued to practice indigenous forms of conflict resolution and administer local justice to a greater extent than less remote ones (Gabbert 2011).[41]

In personal interviews, however, several people working in the area of human rights spoke about the practice of local justice in Maya communities throughout Yucatán. While these practices have not, in themselves, led to ethnic identity formation and consciousness in Yucatán state (at least not at a macro level), they may be reinvigorated going forward as the result of the 2011 Indian rights legislation that acknowledges and builds on the work of local justices in adjudicating and resolving conflicts at the local level (*jueces mayas*). In the next section, I describe a small community north of Mérida, Chablekal, where local justice is administered through a syncretic mix of Maya and non-Maya customs.

Local Justice in Chablekal

In Chablekal, local Maya authorities have exercised de facto autonomy for years.[42] While Chablekal is administratively dependent on the municipality of Mérida, several local authorities serve the community, including a municipal and *ejidal* representative (*comisariado municipal y ejidal*) and a justice of the peace (*juez de paz*). Because Chablekal is not a municipality, the law stipulates that the mayor of Mérida has the authority to name local authorities. In practice, however, these authorities have been chosen by the community and later sanctioned by the municipal government.[43] Both the *comisariado municipal* and the *juez de paz* have historically administered justice on the local level.[44] While these officials are legally charged to exercise "Western" norms as laid out in the state constitution, José Euán Romero, a former judge from Chablekal, told me that after they are sworn in through an official ceremony at the state legislative building in Mérida, they "set aside" the code of justice to practice community norms. He also noted that local authorities tend not to use the Ministerio Público (public prosecutor), but rather, Maya "normative systems of indigenous justice."[45]

Speaking more broadly about community justice norms throughout the state, Baltazar Xool, who works at the State Human Rights Commission (Comisión de Derechos Humanos del Estado de Yucatán) and specializes in community law, told me that local justices of the peace receive training in positive law but exercise community norms in the villages.[46] In his work on local elections in dozens of municipalities across Yucatán, Professor of Anthropology Efraín Poot also observed the "large presence of older forms of organization on the community level." According to Poot, these structures are so quotidian that they seem to be part of the "subsoil" (*substrato*), and are not explicitly flagged as Maya or Indian, much less used as a basis for ethnic organization and mobilization.[47]

In 2008, Mexico introduced a series of constitutional and legislative changes that are bringing significant changes to its criminal justice system (Ingram and Shirk 2010, 1). These judicial sector reforms consist of four main elements: (1) changes to criminal procedure through the introduction of new oral adversarial procedures, as well as alternative sentencing and dispute resolution; (2) greater emphasis on the due process rights of the accused (i.e., the presumption of innocence and an adequate legal defense); (3) modifications to police agencies and their role in criminal investigations; and (4) tougher measures for combating organized crime (Ingram and Shirk 2010). The federal government has set a 2016 deadline for all states to revise their constitutions and criminal codes to achieve compliance with the 2008 reforms. Yucatán's Indian rights legislation includes the use of Maya justices, who hear oral arguments and use alternative sentencing and dispute resolution based on local uses and customs. These federal reforms, and their impact on the 2011 Indian rights legislation in Yucatán, are taken up below.

Federal Judicial Reform and Indian Law

Over the course of the last fifteen years, a significant number of Latin American countries have been engaged in a process of far-reaching judicial reform. In contrast to the case (or common) law tradition of the United States, Latin American judiciaries have historically followed a code law tradition. In this tradition, the law consists of statutes created by governments, and "judges are expected to apply relevant statutes to the facts of each case" (Blake 2008, 90; see also Finkel 2008, 7). Unlike case law systems, in which judges hear oral arguments at which the accused is present, code law countries rely heavily on written juridical procedures. In a 2003 survey conducted in three Mexican states, 80 percent of prisoners sentenced and detained had never spoken with the judge who condemned them (in Carbonell and Ochoa 2008, 51). Under the reforms approved in 2008, the Mexican federal government and, eventually, all state governments will adopt many aspects of the adversarial model over the coming years (Ingram and Shirk 2010, 10). Most relevant to our purposes here are changes that legalize alternative mechanisms to resolve conflicts, including the privileging of consensus as a chief means of conflict resolution.

Support for judicial reform throughout Latin America is based on several perceived failings of the current system. As Blake (2008) notes, the reliance on written procedures, combined with understaffing, make for an exceedingly slow and inefficient system. From a civil and human rights perspective, a system of written judicial procedures makes it difficult for uneducated citizens to participate in their own defense (Blake 2008, 90). Complaints about the failures of the country's judicial system are not unique to Mexico. Between 1990 and 2006, one-third of all Latin American countries moved toward greater reliance on oral trials (Blake 2008, 90).[48] In a 2009 interview, Tenth District Circuit judge Pablo Monroy Gómez argued that the shift toward oral arguments at the federal level was due to crisis within the federal judicial system. That crisis, he said, led to the search for alternatives to the inquisitorial system.[49]

One of the five principal sections of the 2011 Indian rights legislation is dedicated to the issue of Maya justice, highlighting the work of Maya justices. Maya justices are to be chosen by their communities and are charged with applying local uses and customs in the resolution of cases. In the regulatory law for this legislation, more information is provided about the procedure Maya justices should follow in the resolution of cases. According to the regulations, after being made aware of an accusation, the Maya justice should notify the accused party within five days of receiving the initial denunciation. The justice will then bring both parties together, in the justice's presence, to resolve the case. The regulatory law underscores the work of Maya justices in reconciling the interested parties according to community uses and customs (Regulatory Law 2011, 12). In an interview, Deputy José Antonio Aragón Uicab, president of the Ethnic Affairs Committee of the Yucatecan state congress (2007–2010), spoke about an early version of the legislation that was circulating during the 2007–2010 legislation session.[50] Aragón said that he and the committee's technical secretary, Victor Ramírez, originally put forward the idea of including *jueces de paz y conciliación maya* (later referred to as *jueces mayas*) after hearing papers presented in a series of forums held in the state legislature in June and July 2008.[51] "These *jueces* already exist in many places in the interior of the state; nevertheless, they are not recognized by law," Aragón noted. "Many people consult with them [the *jueces*], yet because they don't have legal authority, people have to go into the city to resolve administrative problems; there is a lot of paperwork involved and it's costly. With the legal recognition of the figure of the *jueces de paz*, we hope that we can eliminate some of this bureaucracy, reducing costs for the people. This law is all about making something legal that has been, up to now, de facto."

The 2011 Indian rights legislation and its regulatory law grant more local community control over the Maya justices than previous versions of the law. Originally, these justices were named (or, at the least, ratified) by the municipal authorities. Under the 2011 law, Maya justices are selected by Maya communities. The law sets out bare-bones requirements for eligibility, such as an age minimum (thirty years), not having a criminal record, knowing the uses and customs of the local community, and speaking Maya (Maya Community Law 2011, 20–21).

CONCLUSION

I have argued in this chapter that state-level reforms in the area of Indian rights in Yucatán have occurred largely as a top-down response to pressure from the federal level. Beginning in the early 1990s in a context of neoliberal economic reform, the Mexican state has offered indigenous peoples cultural recognition and some limited rights, while simultaneously ending land reform and reducing and/or eliminating a host of socioeconomic benefits and programs. While the 1994 EZLN uprising and the resulting peace negotiations between the Mexican government and the rebels resulted in the passage of a 2001 Indian rights bill, the definition of autonomy (something the rebels fought hard for in the negotiating process) was watered down significantly and became something very different from what was imagined by the EZLN and their supporters in the peace negotiations. The EZLN and their indigenous allies understood autonomy as a right already possessed by indigenous peoples. They were not asking the state to recognize them: on the contrary, they fought for an umbrella law that would legally protect what was already theirs (see Mattiace 2003; chapter 2, this volume). In the negotiation process that took place within the Mexican Senate in the spring of 2001, the definition of autonomy that emerged was focused on the municipal level. In this view, autonomy looked more like decentralization than self-determination. In addition to limiting what was meant by autonomy, federal officials threw the issue of legislating in this area to the states. The legislation on Indian rights and culture passed by Yucatán's legislature in 2011 underscores and acknowledges Maya cultural difference and is aimed at strengthening Maya culture and language. In this chapter, I have argued that in the absence of an organized indigenous movement or a more coordinated civil society organization pushing for Indian rights, Yucatecan legislators did not deviate from the largely culturalist orientation of indigenist policymaking in Yucatán (and in Mexico more generally).

In the introduction, I underscored the debate among scholars concerning the significance of multicultural reforms. A close examination of Yucatán's multicultural reforms seems to reflect Hale's (2002) view that culturalist understandings of indigenous rights have trumped more materialist ones. Hale worries that the process of enacting multicultural legislation marginalizes more radical indigenous voices, thereby privileging moderate voices. Very few interlocutors in Yucatán have made radical demands on the state, such as challenging the prevailing definition of autonomy as decentralization and linking cultural difference to questions of power and privilege. A commonly held understanding of Maya as *tranquilos* seems to pervade all sectors of Yucatecan society, including many, if not most, Maya themselves.

Will Yucatán's multicultural reforms expand the rights and strengthen the culture of Maya peoples in the state? The attention given to the use of the Maya language and the focus on bilingual education dovetails with long-standing linguistic demands made by social organizations such as Mayaón. The emphasis on using local Maya justices is also notable. However, state officials seem to assume that many Maya may not be aware of their *usos, costumbres, y tradiciones*. The 2011 legislation charges local governments to cooperate with Maya communities "in the development of their internal organization" (Maya Community Law 2011, 17). This is not to say that indigenous peoples will not be able to use the law to fight for greater rights per Van Cott (2006). Recognizing Maya justices at the local level may well bring citizens closer to their local governments and increase their legitimacy. However, it seems to me that in order for indigenous peoples to use this law to make claims for greater rights and a more expansive view of autonomy, a more cohesive and organized movement will need to form in order to keep pressure on the state. Rather than seeing these reforms as marking a new era in state-indigenous relations in Yucatán, my work suggests that, following Gustafson and Postero, we should view them as yet another iteration of an ongoing relationship between the state and indigenous peoples. The Yucatecan Maya have long been under the tutelage of a paternalistic state. While this was true in many other indigenous regions of Mexico, the hand of the state was arguably more heavy and paternalistic in Yucatán than it was elsewhere. Certainly, the state henequen industry continued to exert a high degree of control over Maya campesinos' lives until the late 1980s and early 1990s. Absent an independent peasant movement, Maya have had very little experience in making demands for autonomy vis-à-vis the state.

Yucatecans have long perceived themselves as different and distant from the rest of Mexico. Like Texans in the United States, it is not uncommon to see Yucatecans sporting T-shirts declaring the "Independent Republic of Yucatán" and "¡Yucatán es diferente!"[52] Indeed, on two occasions in the nineteenth century, the state declared itself independent of Mexico, and it was not until the mid-twentieth century that the state was connected to Mexico City via an all-weather road. In terms of ethnic discrimination and relations between Maya and non-Maya people, Yucatecans have also perceived themselves as different. With the passage of the 2011 Maya Community Law in Yucatán, the state is now more in line with other states in the area of multicultural legislation. Maybe Yucatán, going forward, will not be so different after all.

ACKNOWLEDGMENTS

The author would to thank her exceedingly capable research assistant in Mérida, Rodrigo Llanes Salazar, for help in conducting many of the interviews. Heartfelt thanks also go to all those individuals who agreed to be interviewed for this chapter. Special thanks to Professor George Ann Huck in Mérida, an intrepid fieldworker. Finally, thanks to the Allegheny College Academic Support Committee for their financial support for this project.

APPENDIX: LIST OF INTERVIEWEES

Interviews conducted by author unless stated otherwise.

>Bartolomé Alonzo Caamal, founding member of Mayaón (NGO) and bilingual teacher, Mérida, July 25 and August 26, 2009. Interviews conducted by research assistant Rodrigo Llanes Salazar.
>Deputy José Antonio Aragón Uicab (National Action Party, PAN), president of the Comisión de Asuntos Étnicos (2007–2010), Mérida, January 30, 2009. Interview conducted by research assistant Rodrigo Llanes Salazar.
>Othón Baños Ramírez, sociologist at Autonomous University of Yucatán, Mérida, June 30, 2008.
>Rev. Atilano Ceballos Loeza ("Tilo"), cofounder of Escuela de Agricultura Ecológica, Mérida and Maní, January and February 2007.
>José Anastasio "Pepe" Euán Romero, Grupo Indignación, Chablekal, January 23, 2007.
>Patricia Guarneros Marcué, director (delegada) of CDI in Yucatán, January 12, 2007 (left post in 2007).
>Esteban Krotz, anthropologist at Autonomous University of Yucatán, Mérida, February 22, 2007, and January 6, 2009.
>Eduardo López Salcido, subdirector INDEMAYA, Mérida, January 15, 2007 (left post in 2007).

Guillermo May, activist and leader of Foro Maya Peninsular, Mérida, January 31, 2007.

Magistrate Pablo Vicente Monroy Gómez, Tenth District Circuit judge, Mérida, May 28, 2009. Interview conducted by research assistant Rodrigo Llanes Salazar.

Diana Canto Moreno, director of INDEMAYA, Mérida, February 7, 2007 (left post in 2007).

Efraín Poot Capetillo, anthropologist at the Autonomous University of Yucatán, Mérida, February 13, 2007.

Margarita Rosales, anthropologist at National Institute of Anthropology and History, Mérida, February 20, 2007.

Feliciano Sánchez, cultural promoter at the Center of Popular Culture, Mérida, July 1, 2008.

Diputado Juan Manuel Valencia (PAN), Yucatán state congress and member of Comisión de Asuntos Étnicos, Mérida, January 24, 2007 (term ended in 2007).

Bernardo Xiú, administrator and graduate of Escuela de Agricultura Ecológica, Maní, February 15, 2007.

Baltazar Xool May, Comisión de Derechos Humanos del Estado de Yucatán, Mérida, February 1, 2007.

NOTES

1. Two clarifications are in order: first, this chapter examines state legislation and Indian rights in Yucatán state, not the peninsula (Campeche became independent of Yucatán in 1857; Quintana Roo became a territory in 1902). Second, the term "Maya" is used throughout to refer to the indigenous people of Yucatán. This is not a term that individuals would necessarily use to describe themselves, and the use of this term does not imply a social or political consciousness of indigeneity or Indianness. I am referring in general terms to people whose parents or grandparents spoke Maya, who have a Maya surname, who may or may not speak Maya themselves, and who may or may not participate in some Maya cultural or ritual practices.
2. The law went into effect on January 1, 2012. Reforms to the state constitution on Indian rights and culture were made in 2007, which provided both a legal and conceptual framework for the subsequent 2011 legislation. These reforms laid out, among other things, the right of Maya to be consulted on public policies and programs affecting them, the right to apply alternative justice processes on the local level, the right to language use and bilingual education, and the right to elect their own local authorities. While these constitutional changes were not insignificant, it is important to point out that Maya people continue to be viewed as "subjects of public law" and that any right to free determination or autonomy is limited to the local level and must not violate current laws (see Constitutional Reform 2007).
3. Multicultural legislation in Yucatán acknowledges cultural difference and accords indigenous peoples special rights based on that difference. As Burguete points out (chapter 2), "recognition" of difference is a far cry from autonomy, which assumes that indigenous peoples are exercising rights on land and resources to which they have a prior claim.

4. I am indebted to Dr. Esteban Krotz, at the Autonomous University of Yucatán, for sparking my initial interest in this connection (personal communication, January 2009).

5. According to estimates from the Instituto Nacional Indigenista (INI, now the Comisión Nacional para el Desarrollo de los Pueblos Indígenas [CDI]) published in 2002, Yucatán had the largest indigenous population in the country at 981,064, totaling 59.2 percent of the state's population. This figure is significantly larger than that reported by INEGI (2005; http://www.inegi.gob.mx/est/contenidos/espanol/sistemas/conteo2005). The CDI's larger number is an estimate based on household data, which are then added to the numbers of indigenous-language speakers. The INEGI numbers are based solely on indigenous-language speakers. According to 2005 INEGI statistics, Yucatán's total population is 1,818,948 and Oaxaca's is 3,506,821. Interestingly, in both 2000 and 2010, in addition to counting Indian-language speakers, INEGI asked individuals to self-report indigenous identity. In 2000, 33.5 percent of Yucatecans age five and older self-identified as indigenous; in the 2010 census, that number (measuring the age three and older population) jumped to 62.69 percent (see http://www.inegi.org.mx/prod_serv/contenidos/espanol/bvinegi/productos/censos/poblacion/poblacion_indigena/Pob_ind_Mex.pdf for 2000 figures on self-identification and http://www3.inegi.org.mx/sistemas/TabuladosBasicos/Default.aspx?c=27302&s=est for 2010 self-identification data).

6. While some authors view this conflict as primarily racial in nature (see Bricker 1981; Sullivan 2004), others argue that the Caste War was not racially based (Gabbert 2004; Reed 1964; Rugeley 1996). The latter argue that race was important in the Caste War not because the rebels shared an ethnic consciousness, but because race was used by elites to mobilize non-Indians and to justify the abuses committed.

7. In this chapter, I define indigenist policies as state policies designed for indigenous peoples by non-Indians. Favre provides a more elaborate definition of *indigenismo* as "a current of thought and of ideas that is organized and developed around the image of the Indian. It is presented as an interrogation of Indian-ness by non-Indians in function of the preoccupations and ends of the latter" (cited in Barre 1983, 30).

8. The brief gubernatorial administration of Felipe Carrillo Puerto in Yucatán (1921–1923) was an exception to this overall trend of Hispanicization through education. Carrillo Puerto was a native Yucateco, spoke fluent Maya, and encouraged the use of Maya in the classroom, not only to facilitate the learning of Spanish but because he believed that social progress and cultural revitalization were linked goals (Fallaw 1997).

9. Yucatán had one of the most progressive state socialist parties in the immediate postrevolutionary period under governors Alvarado and Carrillo Puerto. The party that in 1942 became the PRI was a successor to the PRM and the PNR (National Revolutionary Party). These name changes did not signal a significant shift in leadership or party ideology.

10. Beginning in the 1970s, the Archdiocese of San Cristóbal de las Casas began ordaining laymen as deacons to deal with the severe shortage of priests. Deacons—who total about four hundred and outnumber priests five to one in the diocese—regularly perform baptisms and weddings and hold religious services in their communities. (They do not, however, consecrate Communion or hear confession.) Unlike deacons, catechists are not ordained and do not administer the sacraments; they typically function as lay leaders in their communities, leading Bible studies and prayer sessions. In the early 2000s, there were about eight thousand catechists in the diocese (Thompson 2002).

11. In 2001, nineteen states voted in favor of the constitutional amendment to establish indigenous rights and nine voted against the amendment (among them Chiapas). No vote was held in two states, Tamaulipas and Yucatán; Morelos did not vote on the changes (López Bárcenas et al. 2001, 128–131).
12. See Anaya Muñoz (2005) on the political forces that led to legislative passage in Oaxaca.
13. Assies et al. (2006) argue that the constitutional changes made in Quintana Roo, Chiapas, and Campeche were largely culturalist and stress the preservation of customs and traditions. While all three constitutions allow local indigenous authorities, or justices, to have jurisdiction over minor civil, family, and penal affairs, the authors argue that state legislatures did not stray too far from the parameters set by existing federal legislation. That is, legislators in Quintana Roo, Chiapas, and Campeche closely followed the guidelines of the Zedillo administration (58). See González Oropeza (2004) for a more optimistic assessment of these constitutional changes.
14. In both the Maya community legislation as well as the regulatory law, the Maya community is defined as "the group of indigenous who share the traditions, uses, and customs that belong to [*propios de*] the Maya Culture" (see Maya Community Law 2011; Regulatory Law 2011). It is noteworthy that the legislators do not refer to the Maya as peoples.
15. The same seems to hold true regarding Maya culture, language, medicine, and handicrafts. The law charges state and municipal officials with "promoting and preserving" these traditional Maya practices.
16. *Promotores* are local indigenous peoples employed by INI to carry out its programs in rural areas. Beginning with President López Portillo's administration (1976–1982), the INI sought to move away from assimilation and acculturation of indigenous peoples toward a more participatory model of ethnic interaction (see Mattiace 2003, 65–69).
17. The creation of the radio station XEPET—Voice of the Mayas—at INI's Coordinating Center in Peto in 1982 has also served to promote Maya-language programs and cultural "traditions." Mayas throughout the peninsula listen to its programs, which have created a virtual community across three states. Quintal suggests that XEPET has been instrumental in making Peto the area in Yucatán where more people assume an explicit Maya identity (Quintal 2005, 343).
18. This information came from my interviews with Diana Canto Moreno and Eduardo López Salcido, then director and subdirector of INDEMAYA respectively. It should be said, however, that INDEMAYA's charge was expanded as a result of the 2011 Maya community legislation to include supervision of public agencies in the implementation of the law.
19. As I understand them, these *consultas* functioned largely as meetings, or discussions, in which Maya were invited to share their opinions about a particular topic. In the *consultas* to which I am referring here, state officials introduced issues broadly focused on language, culture, local justice, bilingual education, and basic needs, such as health care.
20. Here, Guarneros is referring to the protocol followed in terms of informing the public about the *consultas*, issuing invitations to the gathering, as well as the compilation, dissemination, and use of the resulting information.
21. When I asked Diana Canto Moreno about the absence of language on autonomy, territory, and self-determination in the Indian rights law being discussed in the state legislature, she told me, "el pueblo Maya no habla de esas cosas" (the Maya people don't talk of these things). When I asked deputy Juan Manuel Valencia, member of the Ethnic Affairs Committee in Yucatán's state legislature (2004–2007), about language of

autonomy, he told me, "We are not in agreement with autonomy." In Valencia's view, protecting indigenous autonomy would, in effect, exacerbate *caciquismo*.

22. In Guarneros's view, state-level governmental officials and members of the PAN administration (2001–2007) tended to view the Maya as folkloric. As a non-Yucatecan, Guarneros was sensitive to the charge leveled at her by state government officials that her work on the *consultas* was evidence of "outsiders" meddling in the affairs of Yucatecos.

23. So much time elapsed between the 2007 state constitutional changes and the 2011 Indian rights legislation that there were significant shifts in the leadership of the CDI, INDEMAYA, the state congress, and the governor's office. In a 2011 interview, the leader of the Permanent Committee for the Respect and Preservation of the Maya Culture in the state congress, Tito Sánchez, said that his committee worked very closely with CDI in the process of drafting the implementing decree (interview with Rodrigo Llanes, shared with author by e-mail, February 4, 2012).

24. This was particularly true in the 2004–2007 legislative period, as legislators turned to INDEMAYA to take the pulse of Maya public opinion, leading up to the 2007 constitutional changes in the area of Indian rights.

25. With the change in state government in 2007, Guarneros was replaced by Diana Canto, former head of INDEMAYA.

26. I asked Valencia how the committee grapples with the question of who is Maya, given the relative porousness of ethnic boundaries in the state. He told me that this was a difficult question and that committee members struggled with this issue. "We have Maya within *cabildos* [municipal governing boards] who may not call themselves Maya," he said, "but are Maya." Unfortunately, he told me, "there is a lot of discrimination." Over the course of my interview with Valencia he reiterated the idea that what happened in Chiapas—namely the signing of the San Andrés Accords on Indian rights and culture—does not apply to Yucatán because the Maya are "tranquil and integrated" (*integrado*). When I asked him why the Maya were so different from indigenous peoples in the rest of Mexico, he told me that agitators from outside the state are the ones who encourage restlessness and rebellion. In his view, leaders such as Andrés Manuel López Obrador (PRD candidate for president in 2006) come to rile indigenous peoples up and offer them patronage.

27. Aragón noted that it was not until he entered office on July 1, 2007, that he began to connect with the topic of indigenous rights. The interview with Aragón was conducted by research assistant Rodrigo Llanes Salazar.

28. Interview conducted by research assistant Rodrigo Llanes Salazar.

29. Additionally, Yashar (2005) argues that motive and political associational space are crucial factors. See Mattiace (2009) for a more fulsome discussion of these factors and their application to the Yucatecan case.

30. The henequen plant, *Agave fourcroydes*, is a member of the agave family that is well suited to Yucatán's climate, particularly the relatively drier, rockier northwestern region of the state (see Alston et al. [2009] for a more detailed description of the industry and its capital requirements). While henequen has been grown by Maya peasants since pre-Columbian times, large-scale production was possible only after the invention of the mechanical rasper (*desfibradora*) in the late 1850s. Exports of henequen reached their apogee in the 1910s, although the industry continued to operate, largely under state tutelage, until 1992.

31. The high capital requirements of the industrialized henequen industry tied Maya peasants to the state in ways that made it difficult for independent peasant organizations to effectively challenge CNC rule. Even the organizations that split from the CNC and were independent of the state, such as the National Union of Agricultural Workers

(Unión Nacional de Trabajadores Agrícolas) and the Democratic Peasant Union (Unión Campesina Democrática) combined industrial and peasant demands.
32. It is important to note that the networks Yashar discusses as critical to ethnic organization—emerging from peasant leagues, the Catholic Church, and NGOs—were not created for the express purpose of ethnic organization, but have been used that way, in certain circumstances, by indigenous activists within them.
33. See Mattiace (2009) for a more detailed description of this school.
34. Telephone conversation with Padre Tilo, July 3, 2007.
35. Interview with author.
36. Alonzo described the organization's goals as follows: to foment the development of Maya language, culture, historical memory, and bilingual education (interview with research assistant Rodrigo Llanes Salazar).
37. In the 2009 interview with Llanes Salazar, Alonzo demonstrated great interest in politics and in the importance of political mobilization, even as he emphasized that Mayaón was not itself a mass or popular organization seeking to mobilize Maya for political ends. My sense is that Alonzo is very careful about distinguishing Mayaón from another organization that he is close to, the Organization of Bilingual Professionals (Organización de Profesionistas Indígenas Bilingues), which is a partisan organization tied to the CNC.
38. Interview with Llanes Salazar.
39. Alonzo Caamal was a lead author (with Baltazar Xool May) of a forty-five-page letter to state representatives titled "Proposals to Consider Regarding the Law on the Rights and Culture of the Maya Ethnic Group" (Propuestas para Considerar en la Ley Sobre los Derechos y Cultura de la Etnia Maya), dated March 30, 2011.
40. See Bailón (1999) for a political history of Oaxaca that contextualizes the state's *usos y costumbres* system. See Eisenstadt (2007) for a more recent study of the effects of the *usos y costumbres* system on postelectoral conflict. On indigenous local justice in Puebla, see Sierra (1995). See Collier (1973) for a now-classic case study on local justice in Zinacantán, Chiapas.
41. In the view of Wolfgang Gabbert, who has worked extensively on legal pluralism in the Yucatán peninsula, "community structures in Yucatán state and Campeche are much weaker than in Chiapas, Oaxaca, and Quintana Roo" (e-mail communication, September 7, 2008). Gabbert explained this difference by pointing to the effects of the Caste War: government officials reacted to this war, he said, by forcing "Maya-speaking people to assimilate to 'national' culture."
42. The Mexican Census (INEGI) counted 3,626 inhabitants of Cheblekal (see http://www.citypopulation.de/php/mexico-yucatan.php?cityid=310500077). While 1995 INEGI statistics indicated that 42 percent of the population in Chablekal over five years of age spoke an indigenous language (cited in Capetillo Pasos 2001, 149), 2000 census figures listed 753 Maya speakers (INEGI 2005). Administratively, Chablekal is a commissariat (*comisaría*) of the municipality of Mérida. I use it as a case study here, mostly because I was able to talk with a former justice of the peace from Chablekal, and because several anthropologists have written about its political and legal organization (see Capetillo Pasos 2001; Muñoz Menéndez 1997).
43. This practice was corroborated by Baltazar Xool and José Euán Romero (interviews with author). See also Capetillo Pasos (2001).
44. According to Muñoz Menéndez (1997, 56), while the justice of the peace is charged with the administration of justice, in practice his faculties are limited to the writing up of *actas* (official documents or deeds). Muñoz Menéndez suggests that it is the *comisariado municipal* who exercises real juridical power. This may change with the new Indian rights legislation, which recognizes and empowers the work of *jueces mayas*.

45. Interview with author. In Mexico, the Ministerio Público is a governmental agency that operates at the federal and local levels. It is charged with investigating and persecuting crimes, both civil and criminal. Once an initial investigation has been completed within the Ministerio Público, the judicial police are called in to investigate further. Many indigenous community officials with whom I have spoken—both in Chiapas and in Yucatán—have told me that they do not use the Ministerio Público because of its perceived ineptness and corruption. In the 2008 federal constitutional reforms to the judicial system (about which more is said below), the Ministerio Público lost some of its power. Ingram and Shirk (2010, 11) point out that with the introduction of "probable cause" as a basis for criminal indictment, "the preliminary investigation is no longer as central to the process."
46. Interview with author.
47. Interview with author.
48. As a part of the 2007 state constitutional changes, the state guarantees that Maya people may apply "their own forms of regulation for the resolution of internal conflict, as an alternative medium of justice" (Constitutional Reform 2007, 25). According to Esteban Krotz, who has followed the state-level debates on judicial reform closely, the state congress has been emboldened and empowered by the reforms coming out of Mexico City. In his view, the current discussion on the use of *jueces de paz* (or *jueces mayas* as they are referred to in the 2011 legislation) to administer local justice is closely tied to these national-level reforms of the judicial system (Krotz, personal communication, January 2009). In Yucatán, the *jueces de paz* are not exclusively Maya, but are in use throughout the state in Maya as well as in mestizo (mixed-race) municipalities. The 2011 Indian rights legislation, however, refers only to *jueces mayas*.
49. Monroy does not see the shift toward orality in Yucatán as being directly affected by the federal changes (interview with research assistant Rodrigo Llanes Salazar).
50. Interview with Rodrigo Llanes Salazar.
51. Several of the people interviewed for this chapter participated in these forums, including Professor Esteban Krotz and research assistant Rodrigo Llanes Salazar.
52. The latter is an official slogan of the state's Ministry of Tourism.

REFERENCES

Alonzo Caamal, Bartolomé. 1993. "Los Mayas en la conciencia nacional." In *Movimientos indígenas contemporáneos en México*, edited by Arturo Warman and A. Argueta, 35–61. Mexico City: UNAM; Miguel Ángel Porrúa.

Alston, Lee, Shannan Mattiace, and Tomas Nonnenmacher. 2009. "Coercion, Culture, and Contracts: Labor and Debt on Henequen Haciendas in Yucatán, Mexico, 1870–1915." *Journal of Economic History* 69 (1): 104–137.

Anaya Muñoz, Alejandro. 2005. "The Emergence and Development of the Politics of Recognition of Cultural Diversity and Indigenous Peoples' Rights in Mexico: Chiapas and Oaxaca in Comparative Perspective." *Journal of Latin American Studies* 37 (3): 585–611.

Assies, Willem, L. Ramírez Sevilla, and M. C. Ventura Patiño. 2006. "Autonomy Rights and the Politics of Constitutional Reform in Mexico." *Latin American and Caribbean Ethnic Studies* 1 (1): 37–62.

Bailón Corres, Moisés Jaime, ed. 1999. *Pueblos indios, élites, y territorio: Sistemas de dominio regional en el sur de México: Una historia política de Oaxaca*. Mexico City: El Colegio de México.

Bailón Corres, Moisés Jaime, ed. 2003. *Derechos humanos y derechos indígenas en el orden jurídico federal Mexicano*. Mexico City: Comisión Nacional de Derechos Humanos.

Baños Ramírez, Othón. 1989. *Yucatán: Ejidos sin campesinos*. Mérida: Universidad Autónoma de Yucatán.

Baños Ramírez, Othón. 2000. "La Península de Yucatán: En ruta de la modernidad (1970–1995)." *Revista Mexicana del Caribe* 5 (9): 164–191.

Barre, Marie Chantal. 1983. *Ideologías indigenistas y movimientos indios*. Mexico City: Siglo XXI.

Blake, Charles H. 2008. *Politics in Latin America*, 2nd ed. Boston: Houghton Mifflin.

Bricker, Victoria R. 1981. *The Indian Christ, Indian King: The Historical Substrate of Maya Myth and Ritual*. Austin: University of Texas Press.

Capetillo Pasos, Martha. 2001. "Autoridades Mayas en el municipio de Mérida." In *Aproximaciones a la Antropología Jurídica de los Mayas Peninsulares*, edited by Esteban Krotz, 147–158. Mérida: UADY.

Carbonell, Miguel, and Enrique Ochoa Reza. 2008. "El abismo del sistema penal." *Nexos* 333 (June): 51–56.

Cleary, Edward L., and Timothy J. Steigenga, eds. 2004. *Resurgent Voices in Latin America: Indigenous Peoples, Political Mobilization, and Religious Change*. New Brunswick, NJ: Rutgers University Press.

Collier, Jane Fishburne. 1973. *Law and Social Change in Zinacantan*. Palo Alto, CA: Stanford University Press.

Constitutional Reform of 2007. 2007. *Diario Oficial del Gobierno del Estado de Yucatán*. April 11: 23–30. Mérida, Yucatán. http://www.yucatan.gob.mx/servicios/diario_oficial/diarios/2007/2007-04-11.pdf.

Eisenstadt, Todd. 2007. "*Usos y Costumbres* and Postelectoral Conflicts in Oaxaca, Mexico, 1995–2004: An Empirical and Normative Assessment." *Latin American Research Review* 42 (1): 52–78.

Fallaw, Ben. 1997. "Cárdenas and the Caste War That Wasn't: State Power and Indigenismo in Post-Revolutionary Yucatán." *Americas* 53 (4): 551–577.

Finkel, Jodi S. 2008. *Judicial Reform as Political Insurance: Argentina, Peru, and Mexico in the 1990s*. Notre Dame, IN: University of Notre Dame Press.

Gabbert, Wolfgang. 2004. *Becoming Maya: Ethnicity and Social Inequality in Yucatán since 1500*. Tucson: University of Arizona Press.

Gabbert, Wolfgang. 2011. "Indigenous Law as State Law: Recent Trends in Latin American Legal Pluralism." In *The Governance of Legal Pluralism: Empirical Studies from Africa and Beyond*, edited by Markus Weilenmann and Werner Zips. Munster: Lit Verlag.

González Oropeza, Manuel. 2004. "Ten Years after the Highlands Revolted: Justice for the Indigenous People in Mexico." Paper presented at the conference Chiapas: Ten Years Plus, University of Texas at Austin, August.

Gustafson, Bret. 2002. "The Paradoxes of Liberal Indigenism: Indigenous Movements, State Processes, and Intercultural Reform in Bolivia." In *The Politics of Ethnicity: Indigenous Peoples in Latin American States*, edited by David Maybury-Lewis, 267–306. Cambridge, MA: Harvard University Press.

Hale, Charles R. 2002. "Does Multiculturalism Menace? Governance, Cultural Rights and the Politics of Identity in Guatemala." *Journal of Latin American Studies* 34 (3): 485–524.

Hirschman, Albert O. 1970. *Exit, Voice, and Loyalty: Responses to Decline in Firms, Organizations, and States*. Cambridge, MA: Harvard University Press.

INDEMAYA (Instituto para el Desarrollo del Pueblo Maya del Estado de Yucatán). 2001. "Misión y Visión del Instituto." http://www.indemaya.gob.mx/sobre-indemaya/mision-vision.html.

INEGI (Instituto Nacional de Estadística Geográfica e Informática). 2005. *Perfil sociodemográfico de la población hablante de maya: XII Censo General de Población y Vivienda 2000.* Mexico City: Instituto Nacional de Estadística, Geografía e Informática.

Ingram, Matt, and David A. Shirk. 2010. "Judicial Reform in Mexico: Toward a New Criminal Justice System. Special Report." San Diego, CA: Trans-Border Institute, University of San Diego. http://catcher.sandiego.edu/items/peacestudies/2010-IngraShirk-JRM%20%282%29.pdf

INI (Instituto Nacional Indigenista), Sistema de Información Geográfica. 2002. *Indicadores socioeconómicos de los pueblos indígenas de México 2002.* Mexico City: Instituto Nacional Indigenista, Programa de Naciones Unidas para el Desarrollo, Consejo Nacional de Población.

Keck, Margaret E., and Kathryn Sikkink. 1998. *Activists beyond Borders: Advocacy Networks in International Politics.* Ithaca, NY: Cornell University Press.

Krotz, Esteban, ed. 1997. *Aspectos de la cultura jurídica en Yucatán.* Mérida: Consejo Nacional para la Cultura y las Artes; Maldonado editores.

Krotz, Esteban, ed. 2001. *Aproximaciones a la antropología jurídica de los Mayas Peninsulares.* Mérida: Universida Autónoma de Yucatán.

López Bárcenas, Francisco, Guadalupe Espinoza Sauceda, Yuri Escalante Betancourt, Ximena Gallegos Toussaint, and Abigail Zúñiga Balderas, eds. 2001. *Los derechos indígenas y la reforma constitucional en México.* Mexico City: Centro de Orientación y Asesoría a Pueblos Indígenas.

Mattiace, Shannan L. 2003. *To See with Two Eyes: Peasant Activism and Indian Autonomy in Chiapas, Mexico.* Albuquerque: University of New Mexico Press.

Mattiace, Shannan L. 2009. "Ethnic Mobilization among the Maya of Yucatán." *Latin American and Caribbean Ethnic Studies* 4 (2): 137–169.

Maya Community Law of 2011 (Ley para la Protección de los Derechos de la Comunidad Maya del Estado de Yucatán). 2011. *Diario Oficial del Gobierno del Estado de Yucatán.* May 3: 3–23. Mérida, Yucatán. http://www.yucatan.gob.mx/servicios/diario_oficial/diarios/2011/2011-05-03.pdf.

Muñoz Menéndez, Cristina. 1997. "Aproximación a una tipología de los delitos, las sanciones y las autoridades en un pueblo Yucateco." In *Aspectos de la cultura jurídica en Yucatán*, edited by Esteban Krotz, 49–74. Mérida: Consejo Nacional para la Cultura y las Artes; Maldonado editores.

Postero, Nancy. 2004. "Articulations and Fragmentations: Indigenous Politics in Bolivia." In *The Struggle for Indigenous Rights in Latin America*, edited by Nancy Postero and Leon Zamosc. Brighton, UK: Sussex Academic Press.

Quintal Avilés, Ella Fanny. 2005. "'Way Yano'One': La Fuerza Silenciosa de los Mayas Excluidos." In *Visiones de la diversidad: Relaciones interétnicas e identidades indígenas en el México Actual*, vol. 2, edited by Miguel Angel Bartolomé, 291–371. Mexico City: Instituto Nacional de Antropología e Historia.

Reed, Nelson. 1964. *The Caste War of Yucatán.* Palo Alto, CA: Stanford University Press.

Regulatory Law (Reglamento de la Ley para la Protección de los Derechos de la Comunidad Maya del Estado de Yucatán). 2011. *Diario Oficial del Gobierno del Estado de Yucatán.* December 30: 4–13. Mérida, Yucatán. http://www.yucatan.gob.mx/servicios/diario_oficial/diarios/2011/2011-12-30.pdf.

Rosales González, Margarita, and Genner Llanez Ortiz. 2003. "La defensa y la transformación de un legado: Organizaciones indígenas en la peninsula de Yucatán." In *Los investigadores de la cultura Maya 11*, vol. 2, 549–562. Campeche: Universidad Autónoma de Campeche; SEP; DGICSA.

Rugeley, Terry. 1996. *Yucatán's Maya Peasantry and the Origins of the Caste War*. Austin: University of Texas Press.

Sierra, María Teresa. 1995. "Indian Rights and Customary Law in Mexico: A Study of the Nahuas in the Sierra de Puebla." *Law and Society Review* 29 (2): 227–254.

Sullivan, Paul R. 2004. *Xuxub Must Die: The Lost Histories of a Murder on the Yucatán*. Pittsburgh: University of Pittsburgh Press.

Thompson, Ginger. 2002. "Vatican Seeks to Curb Mexico's Indian Deacons." *New York Times*, March 12, A10.

Van Cott, Donna L. 2006. "Multiculturalism versus Neoliberalism in Latin America." In *Multiculturalism and the Welfare State: Recognition and Redistribution in Contemporary Societies*, edited by Keith G. Banting and Will Kymlicka, 272–296. Oxford: Oxford University Press.

Villanueva Mukul, Eric. 1993. *Crisis Henequenera, reconversión económica y movimientos campesinos en Yucatán, 1983–1992*. Mérida: Maldonado editores; FCA UADY.

Wells, Alan, and Gil M. Joseph. 1996. *Summer of Discontent, Seasons of Upheaval: Elite Politics and Rural Insurgency in Yucatán, 1876–1915*. Palo Alto, CA: Stanford University Press.

Yashar, Deborah. 2005. *Contesting Citizenship in Latin America: The Rise of Indigenous Movements and the Postliberal Challenge*. Cambridge: Cambridge University Press.

Conclusion

Balancing Tensions between Communitarian and Individual Rights and the Challenges They Present for Multicultural States

Willibald Sonnleitner and Todd A. Eisenstadt

At the cusp of the new millennium, after five hundred years of oppression and domination, indigenous identities have been driven from invisibility to the forefront of Latin American public opinion and public policy agendas. However, as we have seen throughout this book, the empirical expressions of this recognition and accompanying appreciations of sociocultural diversity bring a host of normative virtues, but also some tensions and contradictions that manifest themselves both in the nation-state and in the local communities it governs.

In theory—and in the representations by many who lend symbolic meaning to this complex social process—a categorical opposition between positive rights and customary rights is frequently created. While the latter tends to idealize the association with the supposed purity and harmony of the indigenous communities, the former tends to be stigmatized for its individualistic connotations and for its well-known practical limitations. Communitarian rights advocates argue that indigenous practices guarantee mechanisms for equal participation (both horizontal and inclusive), while "Western" representative democracy is constrained to more detailed, unequal, conflictive, and delegative electoral participation. Ideally, then, societies should recognize traditional forms of government that, by exercising autonomy, would preserve the internal peace and "natural" equilibrium of the communities.

However, when looking at the strategies and conflicts produced in the environment of the indigenous communities, this abstract dichotomy collapses. It dissolves, rather, to take the shape of hybrid processes that transcend the apparent opposition between tradition and modernity, combining and altering the demand for collective and individual rights in practice, as nation-states strive to both recognize and respect the diversity of minority groups while also propelling a national agenda of citizen inclusion and human rights for all.

Similarly, the tension between authoritarianism and democracy, far from resolving this dichotomy between communal politics and individualism, instead spans this dichotomy and may even widen the breach. In practice, the demands for increased local participation, equality, and political inclusion emerge simultaneously within the communities as well as from other sectors of Latin American societies that are coping with the legacies, inertia, and resistance of dominant groups that continue using exclusionary practices to preserve their privileges and interests, outside and inside these communities. Hence the need to look at the tensions, differences, and contradictions that affect the communities, as well as the strategies and alliances that transcend the local actors, in many cases, at the community level, only to articulate themselves within a larger regional or national dynamic.

To explore this complexity and the light and dark sides of communal politics, this last chapter reports an analysis of three cases that were tried in Mexico's Tribunal Electoral del Poder Judicial de la Federación (the Federal Electoral Court, or TEPJF by its Spanish acronym) seeking to implement a more multicultural perspective on state justice. The cases all relate to the implementation of citizen rights under Oaxaca's customary law system. As pointed out by Juan Martínez (chapter 6), the state of Oaxaca recognized customary law in the 418 municipalities governed by these customary norms, known as *usos y costumbres* (UC), in municipal authority elections. After remaining on the margins of nationally afforded rights, indigenous communities benefited (at least on paper) from reforms of the federal constitution in 2001, which brought Mexico's multicultural composition and the legal existence of indigenous communities and neighborhoods to the fore, opening the possibility for the TEPJF to also adjudicate in multicultural conflicts.

Recognizing traditional norms and excluding political parties from local communal politics in much of Oaxaca has produced a growing number of electoral conflicts that have exceeded the mediating capacities of local authorities. Disgruntled groups have stormed the courts to challenge decisions made by UC leaders. In contrast with the sharp decrease in postelectoral conflicts at the federal level, postelectoral conflicts in local UC communities have not only increased in these Oaxacan municipalities but have grown more violent than in the rest of the country (Eisenstadt 2004, 2007). Similarly, these conflicts have registered a notable exclusion of peripheral communities (*agencias*), religious minorities, immigrants (see chapter 8, this volume), and women from participating in many UC communities. UC election promoters have insisted that the conflicts were exogenous in character and that the virtues of communal politics guarantee consensus, stability, and peace. However, sixteen years after these reforms legalizing long-held UC practices, many of the UC cases resolved in the TEPJF convey both advantages and limitations of how communal politics is practiced in those 418 municipalities of Oaxaca.

To better contribute to this debate, this last chapter studies the microlevel dynamics of three communitarian conflicts. Far from developing at the margins of the institutional spaces and national politics, the UC elections in San Jerónimo Sosolá, San Juan Bautista Guelache, and San Miguel Chimalapa bring to light the conflicting interests and norms faced by state authorities seeking to weigh traditional and constitutional forms of political representation and participation. These cases prompt us to reconsider the meaning of consensus and the practical implications of the communal assemblies from the perspective of those who compete and participate in them, as well as those they exclude or who abstain from participating for fear of reprisals or complications.

Without providing a representative sample of all the electoral conflicts of Oaxaca, the cases analyzed here illustrate four transverse issues related to (1) the increase in postelectoral conflicts in UC municipalities and the forms these take; (2) the hybrid character of the practices and the strategies of communal actors in UC; (3) the overlaps and gaps between both normative systems (UC and state positive law); and (4) the problem of legitimacy in the absence of shared and consensual rules applied fairly by all actors.[1]

These issues pose some central challenges to multinational states in implementing the recognition of rights awarded to ethnic and cultural minorities. In addressing the inconsistencies and consistencies between customary and state positive law (in theory and in practice), we return to a theme addressed by other authors in this volume (such as Lucero and Burguete), but from the vantage of the state, which must reconcile the rights of all its citizens, rather than those of indigenous groups or other social actors. These four themes return us to the central questions addressed in the introduction and throughout this volume, such as the need to construct institutions that reconcile collective rights with individual rights, both outside and inside the communities. We address them in relation to the relevant cases.

PLURALISM VERSUS FACTIONALISM IN UC COMMUNAL ELECTIONS

When the communal politics of ethnic enclaves are viewed from the outside, they often are seen as fostering consensus rather than differences, in the spirit of Eric Wolf's "closed corporate communities." To Wolf, in Mesoamerica and Java, peasant organizations are similar in that "in both areas they are corporate organizations, maintaining a perpetuity of rights and membership; and they are closed corporations, because they limit these privileges to insiders and discourage close participation of members in the social relations of the larger society" (2001, 148). However, from an endogenous and microlevel perspective, a community only starts to exist when a leader, self-empowered and self-designated, speaks and acts on its behalf. This leads us to consider how these leaders, in many farming communities, rural and indigenous, frame their views of factionalization and the existence of subgroups.

Far from the idyllic image of closed corporate communities, local governments are the object of constant struggles for control over limited resources, involving various factions—that is to say, powerful groups with ties based on vertical loyalties that structure the farming communities around asymmetrical dependencies, patron-agent exchanges, and/or clientelism. These factional dynamics do not always turn on formally constituted, durable organizations; rather, they manifest circumstantially, above all when some conflict or competition puts the transfer of power into play, as is usually the case in times of elections.

This concept of fluid power distributions in multicultural communities is useful for analyzing the micropolitical dynamics of these rural polities, as it places the focus on an intermediate level of analysis that is neither fully individualist nor fully communitarian. This ambiguity allows us to transcend the usual dichotomy and to distinguish between different types of intercommunal conflicts as: (1) those that occur between individuals and factions (e.g., the breaking of communal UC norms by a citizen), (2) those that occur between two or more factions (e.g., the competition for municipal posts), and (3) those that involve intersecting factions (e.g., conflicts of center versus periphery, which occur frequently between the "municipal seat" [*cabecera*] and other locations). Of course, these are ideal types, and most conflicts cannot be placed in just one category.

It is precisely these types of situations where electoral processes unravel in Oaxaca's UC communities. But the communities not only participate in regularly held assemblies and communal meetings to select and renew local authorities via UC; they also vote according to state positive law constitutional procedures in federal and local legislative elections and in elections for president and governor. Hence we can analyze the evolution of their political and electoral behavior, both via UC at the municipal level and via partisan elections and secret ballots in statewide and national electoral contests.

The contents of the vote in rural Oaxaca fall far short of the classical model and the ideal of free and competitive elections, which are pluralistic and protective of individual citizen rights. This does not mean that the vote has no meaning for peasants and indigenous people in Oaxaca. But rather than casting a vote based on ideological preferences, it seems that many cast votes based on loyalty to factions, on tactical alliances with external forces, and/or on exchanges and expectations of a symbolic or material nature. In this regard, the strife and conflict in San Jerónimo Sosolá, San Juan Bautista Guelache, and San Miguel Chimalapa provide us with illustrative examples.

THE DISPUTE OVER CANDIDATE ELIGIBILITY IN SAN JERÓNIMO SOSOLÁ

The conflict in San Jerónimo Sosolá calls into question several widespread preconceptions about UC elections. After a contested customary election in 2010, the Xalapa Regional Chamber (Sala Regional Xalapa) of the federal electoral court (TEPJF) reversed the decision of the Electoral Institute of Oaxaca and ordered new elections there because the requirement that all candidates be at least twenty-five years old had rendered one twenty-two-year-old candidate ineligible (TEPJF 2010a). However, the appeals body (Sala Superior) of the TEPJF reversed the judgment, concluding that the minimum age of eligibility was derived from a majority agreement expressed by the UC community, and was therefore subject to community approval (TEPJF 2011).

The case hinges on a clear fact: the candidate's age. But beyond being just a conflict between positive law and customary law, this case illustrates the overlap between constitutional/individual rights norms and traditional/communal norms. For starters, it is about a traditionally organized election set up autonomously to elect local authorities, whose procedures and results are contested by other sectors in the same municipality that solicit the intervention of external authorities from outside the community. It is therefore an endogenous conflict that overwhelms the capacity of community mediation and has to be resolved by higher authorities, constituted at the state level (Electoral Institute of Oaxaca) and the federal level (Regional Chamber and Superior Chamber of the TEPJF).

Second, it is a new expression of an ongoing political struggle extending back at least to the previous cycle's postelectoral conflict. Earlier controversies led to annulment by the TEPJF of the community's UC election in 2008, and the organization of a special election which was won by the faction that had contested the first election. Since then, the agreement on how to organize local elections was broken as the ruling faction promoted the same mechanism that allowed them to come to power (annulment of elections on technical grounds, followed by another election), while the losing faction promoted an alternative procedure that they believed would increase their chances of winning local offices.

But above all, questions about the legitimacy of the electoral mechanism are reflected in multiple views of postelectoral conflict management. The divergence arises from a factional dispute within the community, but transcends its origins and is reproduced in the Electoral Institute of Oaxaca, as reflected in the differing positions of the UC Directorate and the General Council even within the Electoral Institute of Oaxaca. The divergence of views is expressed, finally, at the federal level, as the Regional and Superior chambers of the TEPJF disagreed in their judgments. The Regional Chamber argued that voters were arbitrarily excluded by the candidate eligibility age criteria, while the appeals Superior Chamber argued that local citizens did have the authority to establish their own norms with respect to eligibility, and upheld the community's decisions. So the disagreement within the community was in this case echoed by the split judicial authorities.

The dynamics of the factional dispute are even more complicated than whether a candidate met the age criteria. Despite being a city of only 2,559 inhabitants, San Jerónimo Sosolá extends over a mountainous territory that is difficult to access, poorly integrated, and badly connected. This is a highly marginalized municipality, consisting of twenty-six far-flung local population *agencias*, predominantly rural and dispersed, without paved roads, making communication more frequent with neighboring municipalities than with the *cabecera* (county seat). This extreme territorial fragmentation results in a weak influence of the *cabecera* (San Jerónimo) over the affairs of most *agencia* hamlets, and in different strains with the other peripheral localities and *agencias* regarding, among other issues, the political sphere.

Since the 1995 creation of UC, the inhabitants of all twenty-seven of Sosolá's communities have ceased participating in secret-ballot municipal elections, but they have all continued voting this way in federal and state legislative elections and for the presidents and governors. Overall, the faction that consistently votes for the centrist

Party of the Institutional Revolution (PRI) retains the top spot thanks to a growing division in the other factions that create political loyalties in the community (the leftist Party of the Democratic Revolution, PRD; the rightist National Action Party, PAN; or other smaller parties). But even the PRI-supporting majority has lost its ability to mobilize voters. While in the 1994 general election the PRI main faction still received support of 40 percent of the local electorate, in the 2009 midterm congressional elections that party only received the support of 17.5 percent of those registered.

The geographical dispersion of party support is also quite uneven. The PRI faction enjoys broad support in the county seat (San Jerónimo) but faces strong opposition from rival factions supporting the PRD and/or PAN in the peripheral voting stations of Pueblo Viejo, San Mateo, and San José.

Far from revealing strong and consistent ideological preferences, these voting patterns convey the existence of differentiated factional loyalties that coalesce around particular leaders competing for local offices. However, they call attention to the relative stability of these partisan patterns over time, thereby providing a good indicator of the relative strength of each group. Far from following the imaginary lockstep consensus of UC communitarianism, the community is a sum of factions that create unequal influence in each of the municipality's local hamlets.

These divisions are also reproduced in the famous communal assemblies where the same factions mobilize followers in the competition for municipal offices. Table C.1 shows the percentage of adults who participated in each of the meetings organized by incumbent local authorities in 2010 to define whether the traditional election in Sosolá should be decided by secret ballot or by a public assembly. On average, 42 percent of the registered electorate attended the first round of the eleven meetings, whereas the follow-up meeting was attended by only 35.9 percent of the total voting-age population. In both meetings at each locale, the ruling faction was able to mobilize relative majorities, with an average of 33 percent in the first and 30.3 percent in the second, against an opposition that mobilized only 8.5 percent and 5.6 percent of the adult population on average (see table C.1).

The breakdown of these attendance and participation averages by location conveys a wide variation in local behaviors. Ten of the thirteen participating locations apparently voted "unanimously": five in favor of the ruling PRI faction's proposal, and five against it. But with the exception of Santa Lucía, participation rates were low, as absences of eligible voters rendered "community consensus" relative at the local level. In the Santa María Tejotepec meeting, the PRI faction mysteriously won 102 percent of the votes (while the other faction still managed to garner 26 percent).

Finally, the vote was divided in the three remaining localities, with varied results. In Cieneguilla, the opposition faction won the first assembly before withdrawing completely in the second communal vote. In San Juan, the ruling faction won the first vote with 27.4 percent, but it did not get a single vote in the second round, where 41.1 percent of the local population voted for the opposition. In Santa María Tejotepec, the turnout curiously included 128 percent of the voting-age population, with the ruling faction getting overwhelming support in both assemblies, by improperly mobilizing supporters who did not reside in the locality (see table C.1).

Table C.1 Turnout by Proposition in the Two Rounds of Communal Assemblies Organized in San Jerónimo Sosolá in 2010

Hamlet	Voting Station	Voting Age Pop.	First Round of Assemblies (%)			Second Round of Assemblies (%)		
			Prop. A (Vote by Secret Ballot)	Prop. B (Vote by General Assembly)	Total Turnout	Respect for the Popular Consultation	Integration of a New Communal Electoral Commission	Total Turnout
San Juan Sosolá	927	73	27.4	12.3	46.6		41.1	41.1
San Jerónimo Sosolá		59					10.2	10.2
El Progreso Sosolá		40	45.0		47.5	55.0		55.0
El Parián		10					20.0	20.0
Santa María Tejotepec	928	82	102.4	25.6	128.0	97.6		97.6
Ojo de Agua		52	40.4		40.4	80.8		80.8
Cieneguilla		44	4.5	34.1	38.6	29.5		29.5
Santa María Yolotepec		20	20.0		20.0			
San Mateo Sosolá	929	339	49.9		49.9	34.2		34.2
Santa Lucía Sosolá		205	93.7		93.7	95.1		95.1
Río Florido Sosolá		72		40.3	40.3			
San José Sosolá	930	110		35.5	38.2		40.0	40.0
Minas de Llano Verde		77		23.4	23.4		6.5	6.5
Total Turnout		1,546	33.0	8.5	42.0	30.3	5.6	35.9

In short, the ideal of communal political participation stemming from consensus can be very attractive for those seeking to embody the will of the community, but it cannot endure the factional strife that has prevailed as the stakes of municipal offices have risen with the increased electoral competition for public offices (openly expressed in the presidential, gubernatorial, and legislative races) and the increased flow of resources from the central government to the municipalities. At the most local levels, unanimity can still be achieved if there is a low turnout, but this "absolute consensus" falls apart when the election appeals to wider interests that coexist in the community. This empirical finding is fundamental to understanding traditional politics in UC elections. The observation of this trade-off between participation and consensus is not limited to the case of Sosolá, but can also be seen in San Juan Bautista Guelache and San Miguel Chimalapa.

EXCLUSIONS AND IRREGULARITIES IN SAN JUAN BAUTISTA GUELACHE AND SAN MIGUEL CHIMALAPA

Because of their similarities, the cases of San Juan Bautista Guelache and San Miguel Chimalapa can be analyzed together. Both electoral conflicts occurred in 2010 and exceeded the capacity of community mediation. As in San Jerónimo Sosolá, various factions first competed in a traditional election but later also demanded arbitration by the TEPJF. In both cases, the Xalapa Regional Circuit of the TEPJF found grave irregularities due to the restriction of universal suffrage, and ordered new elections to guarantee more inclusive and egalitarian conditions for participation (TEPJF 2010b, 2010c).

San Juan Bautista Guelache has 6,287 inhabitants (as of 2010) and an average degree of marginalization and is much better integrated into Oaxaca's transportation and economic grids than San Jerónimo Sosolá. But as in the former community, tensions between the *cabecera* and *agencias* often manifest in elections. The pro-PRI faction enjoys wide support in the *cabecera* of San Juan, while facing a growing but increasingly fragmented opposition in the outlying hamlets where at least three major factions contend.

In 2010, disgruntled groups in the San Gabriel, La Asunción, and San Miguel hamlets challenged the exclusive manner in which traditional elections were held. In particular, they complained that they had not been consulted in the integration of the municipal ballots. They sought to have voting booths set up in their localities, to avoid having to go vote in the *cabecera*, and also contested the fact that they had not been consulted or notified about the call for candidates. After confirming the complainants' allegations, the TEPJF ruled that the constitutional requirement of universal suffrage had not been met, overturned the validity of the election, and called for a new one (TEPJF 2010b).

San Miguel Chimalapa provides yet a third example of intracommunity political conflict in which opposing factions engaged in a dispute over municipal government. With 6,608 inhabitants (as of 2010), this is the most populous, geographically dispersed, and marginalized municipality of the three analyzed here. After the post-election dispute in 2007, the agreement on traditional election methods was broken and was contested openly by one of the four candidates for the office of mayor in 2010. Despite protests, a general assembly was organized on October 17, 2010, when the candidate of the PRI faction won "unanimously among those present by the system of 'show of hands'" (TEPJF 2010c, 3).

Again, significant irregularities were evident in this election: roadblocks obstructed the participation of some citizens; a sudden change of venue where the assembly occurred may have also prevented dissenters from attending; and public voting by show of hands replaced the secret ballot box system used in 2007. The meeting organizers elaborated on the presence of 2,300 people but did not specify how elections officers would identify and validate the presence of candidates nor record the number of votes each candidate received (TEPJF 2010c, 37, 43). After the assembly, the winning candidate was even formally registered under the symbol of the PRI, contradicting the independent spirit of UC elections. On November 10, 2010, the Electoral Institute of Oaxaca validated the election. But on November 27, the losing candidate filed a writ of dissent, arguing that he was prevented from voting and from receiving others' votes at the general assembly. On December 31 of the same year, the election was annulled by the Xalapa Regional Chamber of the TEPJF, which ordered a new election.

In San Miguel Chimalapa, as in the other two Oaxacan UC municipalities discussed, the lack of community consensus and the tensions between the feuding factions are also prominently reflected in local electoral results from federal legislative and presidential contests. The faction allied with the PRI retained a dominant position overall, thanks to its strong support in Rancho Viejo, El Palmar, Rio Grande, Cuauhtémoc Guadalupe, El Compuerto, Vista Hermosa, and El Porvenir (that vote in polling stations 1338, 1341, 1342, and 1344).

But this dominant group also faced a well-organized opposition from dissenting factions in the other seven outlying hamlets (that vote in polling stations 1339, 1340, and 1343). In Cieneguilla and Las Anonas (station 1339), the PRD grew considerably after 1994 and got even more votes than the PRI faction in 2006. In Benito Juarez (station 1340) and in Emiliano Zapata, Las Conchas, San Felipe, and Las Cruces (station 1343), the PRD factions even represented overwhelming majorities in 1994 and 1997, before they lost supporters in 2000 and were outnumbered by other rival factions, either that same year in station 1343 or since 2003 in station 1340.

Further research is needed to interpret the reasons of these peculiar micropolitical trends in San Miguel Chimalapa's dissenting hamlets. What is clear from our data is the growing fragmentation and the internal diversity of this traditional community that, far from a consensual political behavior, is structured by competing political factions with changing and uneven support in the *cabecera* and in the different outlying hamlets.

THE END OF UNANIMITY: DEMOBILIZATION AND FRAGMENTATION OF THE COMMUNITY

We now summarize the main findings of the three cases analyzed before placing them in the larger universe of the 570 municipalities in Oaxaca. In particular, let us stress the high and increasing electoral diversity of these three UC municipalities, as this is also a swiftly growing broader trend, reflected in the evolution of three summary indicators that require us to rethink the concept of communitarian "unanimity."

1. A sharp decline occurred in voter turnout between the federal legislative interim elections in 1997 and 2009, from 73.3 percent to 42 percent in San Jerónimo Sosolá (−31.3 percentage points), from 42.6 percent to 29.8 percent in San Juan Bautista Guelache (−12.8 points), and from 67.8 percent to 60.9 percent in San Miguel Chimalapa (−6.9 points). With the exception of San Miguel, the extent of

the drop is much greater than in the rest of the state, where the average turnout fell from 49 percent to an average of 41.4 percent (−7.7 points).
2. Consequently, the ability to mobilize major community support by the dominant factions decreased significantly between 1994 and 2009, falling from 40 percent to 17.5 percent of voters registered in San Jerónimo Sosolá and from 39.1 percent to 11 percent of those registered in San Juan Bautista Guelache, and increasing only from 29.9 percent to 39.8 percent of those registered in San Miguel Chimalapa. This change contrasts with the rest of the state, where the PRI declined from 33.7 percent to 18.1 percent of the voters registered during the same period.
3. Change was even more significant fragmentation (i.e., the number of relevant factions in each population center) among the communities analyzed. In 1994, political action centered on two local groups in the great majority of the localities of all three municipalities. By 2009 only San Miguel Chimalapa still had only two factions, while San Miguel Chimalapa and San Jerónimo Sosolá were divided among a growing number of factions, three and four, as in most of Oaxaca.

In these conditions of increasing demobilization and fragmentation, it would be illusory to view community politics as a collective and consensual will when, at least in these three cases of conflict (as in many others where factional conflicts spill into the courts), electoral competition has grown as competitive as the plural electoral politics characteristic of the rest of the state and country's party system in general.

Second, when looking at the cultural diversity of the municipalities studied, it is worthwhile to place them in the broader context of the 415 other UC municipalities as well as the 152 "constitutional" municipalities (those adhering to conventional electoral laws with secret ballots and political parties). The reforms of 1995 and 1998 were intended to benefit the indigenous people of Oaxaca. However, contrary to what one might think, more than half (54.1 percent) of the 418 municipalities currently governed by *usos y costumbres* have Spanish-speaking majorities rather than indigenous-language majorities, while a quarter (25.7 percent) of the 152 municipalities with the constitutional electoral system have a majority of indigenous-language speakers (see table C.2).

Research by Sorroza and Danielson (chapters 7 and 8, this volume) shows that while 80 percent of the mayors of the UC municipalities occupied some civil office

Table C.2 Linguistic Composition of the 570 Oaxacan Municipalities

	Percentage Indigenous Language Speakers					
	0–50%		50–100%		Total	
Type of Elections	Number	%	Number	%	Number	%
Usos y costumbres	226	54.1	192	45.9	418	73.3
Constitucionales	113	74.3	39	25.7	152	26.7
Total	339	59.5	231	40.5	570	100.0

Source: INEGI (2001).

before being elected, only 45 percent held religious positions. In a departure from the traditional system of candidate selection, in which completion of *cargos* is required to be mayor (see chapters 7 and 8), only 16 percent of elected mayors now meet that requirement, which is a relic of the past. Hence, if the categories are going to retain any empirical basis, there is a need to distinguish different categories of constitutional (which may also be indigenous and have traditional *cargo* systems) and UC (which also can be mixed and secular) municipalities, according to their linguistic composition and their effective organization in systems of civic and religious positions.

Third, the increasing number and intensity of conflicts in the UC municipalities is alarming. Unlike the federal level, where they have been declining since the 1990s, conflicts seem to be increasing in communities that are governed by the UC system (see table C.3). Furthermore, research suggests that excessive violence can be triggered by UC community postelectoral conflicts, killing some forty people—that is, 20 percent of the national total in just the state of Oaxaca—early in the decade (Eisenstadt 2011, 119).

These conflicts are associated with political exclusion, according to a study by Eisenstadt and Ríos (2012), due principally to tensions between center *cabeceras* and periphery *agencias* documented in the cases above. A previous study by Ríos

Table C.3 Oaxaca Postelectoral Conflicts, 1989–2007, by Local Election Cycle (Absolute Percentage of Conflicts in All 570 Oaxaca Municipalities)

	1989–1991	1992–1994	1995–1997 (Electoral Reform Approved)	1998–2000	2001–2003	2004–2006
Non-UC	40	56	50	29	21	25
% of 570 munis.	9.6	13.4	12.0	6.9	5.0	6.0
UC	7	20	56	62	71	44
% of 570 munis.	1.2	3.5	9.8	10.9	12.5	7.7
Overall number	47	76	106	91	92	69
Overall % Conflictive	10.8	16.9	21.8	18.8	17.5	13.7

Source: Database assembled by the authors and coded from Oaxaca Electoral Institute data and from continuous coding of national (*La Jornada, Reforma*) and local (*Noticias—Voz e Imagen de Oaxaca*) press accounts between 1989 and 2006. Coding explained in Eisenstadt (2004, 293–298).

Notes: The total number of municipalities from which percentages were extracted has changed because of constant addition and redistricting of municipalities. The total number of municipalities nationwide was 2,389 for 1989–1991; 2,395 for 1992–1994; 2,418 for 1995–1997; 2,427 for 1998–2000; and 2,435 for 2001–2003. Similarly, the total number of UC municipalities in Oaxaca in 1995 was 412, whereas in 1998, 2001, and 2004, this number increased to 418. Since the number of municipalities in Oaxaca has remained constant at 570, the increase in UC municipalities diminished the number of municipalities holding standard party-based elections from 158 in 1995 to 152 for 1998–2004. Multiple opposition party mobilizations in one municipality were rare, but when they occurred we entered only the mobilization by the higher vote getter among the runner-up parties credited with the conflict, as that party was considered to be the main postelectoral contender (and usually there was a large margin between second- and third-place finishers). Just as electoral contention was either PRI-PAN or PRI-PRD but almost never PAN-PRI-PRD (at least not until the late 1990s), postelectoral contention also followed this pattern during the period under study.

(2006) documented the prevalence of minority exclusion in the 412 UC municipalities in early 1995. At that time, some 21 percent of citizens in outlying towns were banned from participating in local elections, while in 18 percent women were precluded from participating. More recently, another study carried out in 404 UC municipalities showed low participation by women and citizens from communities outside the municipal seat in civil and religious *cargos*, and found these exclusions to be statistically correlated with higher levels of postelectoral conflict (Eisenstadt 2011, 113–114). Given this mix of causes and effects, it would be simplistic to attribute postelectoral conflicts to UC electoral systems alone. Many of them are related, in fact, to high levels of marginalization and socioeconomic exclusion, which limit opportunities for human development in these communities and restrict citizens' chances to expand liberties and political capabilities. Indeed, the rural municipalities of Oaxaca have some of the worst social indicators in all of Mexico.

Undoubtedly, *usos y costumbres* may offer important normative advantages when organized by consensus, building cohesive communities with deference to common histories and collective identities. A survey of 404 Oaxacan UC municipalities conveyed that some 65 percent of the communal assemblies sometimes or always effectively raise public discussions about the type of leaders who should serve, and some 76 percent explicitly consider the candidates in contention (Eisenstadt 2011, 109). But some of the practices commonly associated with UC restrict the freedom of voters, at least by individual or human rights norms, and contribute to sociopolitical exclusion. Since the pioneering studies of social psychology, the strength of pressures to conform with group norms has been well documented. Expressing dissent is known to create psychological stress and to carry substantial individual and social costs that inhibit public expression and create incentives to unquestioningly accept norms perceived by the majority (Lewin 1951; Asch 1955).

Thus, it is much harder to espouse unpopular personal convictions or to disagree at a community assembly where votes are calculated by physically "lining up" or via a show of hands, neither of which afford the protection of anonymity as found in secret ballot elections. In the absence of a secret ballot, people who agree with the mainstream tend to participate to a greater extent, and those who fear that their opinions are in the minority tend to be quiet or simply abstain. As we observed in the case of San Jerónimo Sosolá, it is not the same to participate in one big general assembly that simultaneously mobilizes an entire municipality, as to attend decentralized, small parallel meetings organized in various formats by local authorities, where social pressures can be readily brought to bear (see table C.1).

But regardless of the local dynamics and sociological pressures exerted by different forms of communal elections, both traditional assemblies and recorded voting trends, as depicted in the cases above, convey an increasing pluralism rooted and growing at the municipal level, although many communities continue to convey "unanimous" votes but with low and unequal participation.

In addition, the three case studies provide excellent examples of the overlap between the constitutional and customary realms, illustrating the hybrid nature of the strategies of community actors, who, despite any rhetoric to the contrary, may ultimately measure success by whether they win or lose, rather than by whether the communitarian norms of their ancestors were loyally followed. In heavily contested elections and where UC has a weaker hold, the leaders of the PRI and opposition factions resort to traditional rules, as well as to federal laws and institutions, depending on their immediate objectives.

Finally, the Oaxaca cases underscore the complex relationship between the two regulatory systems and the long-running tensions and disagreements over interpretation of *usos y costumbres*. In the absence of formal political parties, UC factions arise within the same communities but often overwhelm established arenas of contestation and move on to the state electoral institute and, sometimes, to the federal electoral courts. In this context, the role of electoral justice is crucial for regulating conflicts in UC municipalities in Oaxaca. Since the court's landmark ruling in 2000 to overturn the first UC election, in the rural town of Asunción Tlacolulita (which was actually ignored by local authorities, who did not comply with the verdict), the TEPJF has been constructing legal doctrine to require communal elections to adhere to fundamental constitutional rights, subsuming local processes of leader selection to national federal laws.

At the same time, there is an increasingly widespread awareness of the value of pluralism and inclusiveness. Groups have advocated for incorporating secret ballots and other federal voting procedures into their own local political practices, but they also seek, quite often, to retain communal assemblies and other communal voting practices. The trick is to integrate these forms of exercising civic responsibilities not from a dichotomous perspective artificially separating traditional and modern, but from a mixed perspective that is at once cross-cultural and multidimensional, taking into account dynamic expressions within localities and among communities, and their linkage to state and nation.

BALANCING NATION-STATES, SUBNATIONAL AUTONOMIES, AND LEGAL ORDERS

The internal complexity of Oaxaca's intracommunity conflicts invites comparisons to the experiences of Chiapas and Yucatán within Mexico, as well as to the Andean indigenous rights movements, such as in Bolivia and Ecuador, and to return to some of the central issues addressed throughout this book. Indeed, the problems posed by UC elections in Oaxaca highlight the tensions of communitarian identities versus equal suffrage and pluralism, and also address the broader issues of participation and community representation, inclusion and exclusion of majorities and minorities, and local community relationships with national multicultural states and societies. Against this backdrop we must consider the many meanings intertwined with the concept of multicultural autonomy.

It may be possible from a theoretical perspective to put individual rights on one side of the ledger and collective rights on the other. But one of the most basic lessons of Oaxaca's experience with UC is that these neat categories break down in practice, creating enormously messy gray areas. The electoral conflicts just analyzed, as well as the cases studied by Danielson (chapter 8) where migrants are disenfranchised from elections but must serve the community anyway, even if from abroad, offer clear examples of how difficult it can be for communities to navigate this complex terrain. While these situations constrain basic human rights of migrants and dissidents within communities, communal majorities balance these against credible collective rights claims made through processes that very often do have long histories of cultural validation. In the next section, we discuss how individual versus communitarian rights demands could be reconciled in Mexico, relating these cases to others in Bolivia, Ecuador, and Colombia.

As pointed out by Lucero (chapter 1), autonomy as a concept contains a slew of meanings, connotations, and frames. Drawing from extensive research in the Andes, he proposes a complex typology to capture the uneven strength and weakness of multicultural policies in Latin America, their origins (from above or below) and their controversial effects on indigenous populations.

In this chapter, we refer to autonomy as the degree to which groups can operate independently from the state and its dominant culture as well as the degree to which individuals are free to make conscious decisions about the institutions, parties, and practices they support. The examples given throughout this book focus on different units of autonomy (individuals, factions, interest groups, communities, regions, federated states, etc.). For example, focusing on the 2009 constitution in Bolivia, Centellas's analysis (chapter 4) shows the practical and operational limits of a mainly symbolic recognition of collective rights. And, shifting to the subnational level, Cooke (chapter 3) underscores the manipulation, seemingly unintended, of multiculturalism by Bolivian elites to legitimize their own regional autonomy claims against Evo Morales's new regime.

Martínez Novo (chapter 5) also argues that, even though it was created with strong popular support "from below," indigenous autonomy in Ecuador was quickly co-opted by the state "from above," distributing benefits to selected leaders but leaving the indigenous populations without resources to implement their autonomy on the ground. Finally, Mattiace's study of Yucatán (chapter 9) demonstrates the limits of autonomy from above and the absence of grassroots organization and mobilization in one of the most indigenous states of southern Mexico. Beyond the specificities of the contexts, all these case studies illustrate how difficult it is to translate legal recognition of indigenous autonomy into workaday institutions.

Furthermore, only a frank consideration of the trade-offs between individual and communitarian rights can yield the kind of self-aware multiculturalism that simultaneously respects the rights of groups and their individual members. Normatively, one form this could take is the adoption of "conditional multiculturalism" (Danielson and Eisenstadt 2009, 153, 156), whereby institutions of autonomy are constructed that allow groups to revere and sustain whatever cultural norms they choose, but with the stipulation that they respect citizens' constitutional rights and include an "opt out" clause so that individuals can choose not to participate without penalty or the loss of group rights.

Would experiments in self-governance by Mexico's indigenous citizens have fared better if they had included more expansive autonomy rights? As Burguete argues (chapter 2), the recent experience of Chiapas shows that despite the reforms introduced in federal and local legislation, constitutional multiculturalism has not had an impact on the lives of indigenous populations. In fact, formal and rhetorical recognition of rights without a relevant share of state resources or competent governance seems to be of limited use. As indicated by the cases of Catalonia and Quebec, which have faced strict limits in efforts to gain autonomy from Spain and Canada, such autonomy is only beneficial to communities with the means and capacities to effectively call their own shots.

Critics of greater self-governance, like the former director of the Oaxaca Electoral Institute, Cipriano Flores Cruz (advisor to the PRI, interview, Oaxaca, May 17, 2005), argue that further autonomy would have prompted the state to abandon these poor and "autonomous" areas. Ultimately, this would leave the indigenous region's interests totally unrepresented at the national level, where the overwhelming majority of Mexico's public resources are doled out. Flores Cruz argued that better representation of indigenous positions within existing government and partisan structures is called for. The broader point is that autonomy must be coupled with strong local and democratic governance to deliver communities the independence they seek from the state. Autonomy coupled with weak and authoritarian local governance will be manipulated and will disenfranchise the very groups it is intended to empower.

But how can local autonomy for communitarian practices be reconciled with effective participation and representation in a larger nation-state that is also constitutionally committed to individual rights? First, we must clarify a recurring, but largely unfounded, myth. Not all indigenous communities are isolated from national politics, and in fact many participate intensively in national politics via associations, parties, and interest groups. For example, the mobilization of the peasant indigenous communities of Chiapas has been strong and consistent since the end of the 1970s, contributing directly and decisively to the broader process of democratization (Viqueira and Sonnleitner 2000). Furthermore, there was a large-scale electoral participation of indigenous regions throughout the 1990s, with a significantly higher turnout than that registered in the mestizo regions and major cities since 2001 (Sonnleitner 2012b). Therefore, in many indigenous areas of Mexico, rather than incentivizing autonomy, the challenge may be to preserve high levels of mobilization and political-electoral participation. Activism to ensure that their interests are effectively represented may ultimately gain more strength for indigenous groups than autonomy without resources. Perhaps both autonomy and resources would be preferable, but many indigenous communities live in poor areas and may need to mobilize for resources first.

A lack of representation at the national level also contributes to the problem. While the number of indigenous legislators in the federal Congress increased significantly from one in 1991–1994 to eighteen in 2006–2009, these advances are still inadequate, given that indigenous communities comprise around 10 percent of Mexico's population, and the Congress has five hundred members. In the last Congress (2009–2012), the number of indigenous representatives declined to sixteen. Also, the composition of these indigenous seats is changing. Of the eighteen representatives elected in 2006, seventeen were elected to majoritarian seats in single-member districts, whereas three years later (2009) only ten of the sixteen were elected via district vote counts (Sonnleitner 2012a). The remaining six were appointed from the major parties' proportional representation lists (closed lists, which parties use to select two hundred of the five hundred seats).

Perhaps most importantly, these formal advances in the number of indigenous legislators do not seem to be translating into the production of new laws nor in concrete gains for indigenous peoples. Despite the creation of twenty-eight "indigenous majority" districts with the redistricting of 2004, voters still seem to prefer nonindigenous candidates in eighteen of these districts, reflecting the predominance of factors besides ethnicity in these elections. Hence the need to rethink the problem, not just in terms of increased quantitative and descriptive representation, but also in terms of substantive representation. To be legitimate and effective, policymakers must not only belong to a particular ethnic group but also should be elected in a plural and competitive manner, which is transparent, inclusive, and attentive to the group's needs. Only then will they also become responsive to the problems of their constituents once they are in Congress, having to be accountable through their terms of service (Sonnleitner 2012a). Group autonomy may be important, but autonomy should exist across programmatic areas as well as just in geographical terms.

Finally, we must not forget that empowerment requires expanding the political rights of indigenous citizens (and other citizens), rather than restricting these rights. After centuries of exclusion, segregation, and domination, indigenous movements have managed to execute their claims to greater representation within the state and to gain some of their own representatives. It is important, now, that these representatives also meet the expectations of their constituents, defend the interests of their communities, and be accountable for doing so. Far from opposing indigenous forms of political participation, representative democracy provides a space for indigenous representation and guarantees that indigenous rights can be exercised in a pluralistic form, with respect for diversity, differences, and human rights. Greater autonomy may well be part of indigenous communities' demands, but these should also be addressed in a manner that does not discriminate against nonindigenous citizens.

STATES, COMMUNITIES, AND LEGAL PLURALISM: CONSTRUCTING AUTONOMOUS INSTITUTIONS

As has also been argued throughout this book, one possible pitfall of studying collective action and communitarianism is assuming that movement leaders always speak for movement followers. Instead of taking such a simplistic approach, we have sought to integrate different levels of analysis and to disaggregate group data to the level of factions and individuals to better understand the perspective of the people whom movement leaders claim to represent. We now consider how individual attitudes and preferences are driving the development of proposals for new autonomous indigenous institutions that would support indigenous rights.

"Constitutional multiculturalism," as recognized in Latin America (Van Cott 2000), refers to a set of reforms that recognize the rights of groups and is based in part on the work of liberal rights activist Kymlicka (1995). Unlike other strong autonomists, Kymlicka attempts to solve the problems of discrimination against minorities by creating a multiculturalism paradigm that recognizes group rights as long as they do not violate the human rights of individual members. Within this perspective, some institutions have emerged in Mexico that afford a minimal degree of autonomy to indigenous peoples, and which the government formally recognizes.

But in practice, state authorities have done little more than allow weak rural municipalities to autonomously decide who governs, passively tolerating Darwinian electoral conflicts and sometimes replacing whoever survives with governor-dispatched municipal administrators. The TEPJF did enforce some rulings, starting with its landmark Yucatán verdict in 2000: the electoral judges ruled that the state had selected an illegal electoral commission and ultimately sent officials to enforce the creation of a new electoral commission after the governor refused to comply with the court's ruling (see Eisenstadt 2004, 244–252). Since then, federal electoral courts have heard many cases from Oaxaca and have even overturned some elections there. But until recently, court rulings were often ignored by local officials, and federal authorities refused to take any further action to enforce them.

The Mexican Supreme Court's official investigation of state government repression of APPO (Asamblea Popular de los Pueblos de Oaxaca) and teacher protesters in Oaxaca in 2006 was also weak. And despite regulatory changes in Chiapas and Oaxaca calling for the creation of indigenous courts to arbitrate disputes over traditional legal norms within indigenous communities, these courts have no docket, and insufficient numbers of translators have been hired to mediate for indigenous citizens. In other words, southern Mexico's indigenous citizens have received lip service, but little in the way of real change.

As for the San Andrés Accords signed in 1996, to this day they have not been applied, nor have the decentralized Zapatista administrative units managed to contribute visibly to governance in their areas of influence. The uprising's genuine achievements—raising concerns about the concentration of poverty in indigenous areas and offering an alternative frame for second-wave reformers—seem mostly to be in the past. The material benefits of increased state spending and extensive international assistance have also abated. Chiapas is no longer governed by the PRI, but the movement's goal of formal indigenous autonomy remains far out of reach. Not only have the rebels' more ambitious aims gone unrealized, a survey (Eisenstadt 2011) shows that ethnic claims are actually less central to the political beliefs of indigenous people in Chiapas and Oaxaca than histories of oppression, economic marginalization, and forms of local land tenure. Surprisingly, ethnicity does not contribute to explaining political behavior or electoral competition patterns either, which depend instead on other sociodemographic and economic variables, as well as on the agency of a wide array of social, political, and religious actors (Sonnleitner 2001, 2012b).

The empirical reality of the role of ethnic identity in Mexico, and in the Andean regions also covered in this book—and in most other places—is quite complex. In Oaxaca, UC did diminish conflicts after elections in many communities, especially where historical norms of customary law were known to exist (see Eisenstadt and Ríos 2012). Contrary to some of the juxtapositions between individual rights and communitarianism, there is substance to the argument—in many conflict-free municipalities—that individualism is "self-interested" and normatively bad, whereas communalism is "authentic," other-regarding, and normatively good. Indeed, as argued in the introduction, Oaxaca's UC was not so much an indigenous system as a new institutional framework that could be used for a variety of purposes and was readily manipulated by local elites. In that sense, it was not all that different (arguably) from the ways in which the old PRI utilized "traditional" leaders in Chiapas for their own political purposes (as Rus so artfully conveys in his 1994 work). Thus, rather than an opportunity to normatively assess the worth of communalism versus individualism, these cases may be another view of what Povinelli (2010) calls "the cunning of recognition"—that is, it is dominant power that still creates the frameworks for politics. Difference in some cases may be used to empower otherwise disempowered groups, but in other instances it is managed, channeled, or fragmented in ways that disempower, as Lucero conveys (chapter 1). State-society (or elite-subaltern) dynamics are still very much working against the relatively less powerful and, given the ways in which this system was created, this should not be all that surprising.

While the Zapatista movement had great emotional power, as an empirical matter, it could not solve the problems it so sharply diagnosed. The fact that collective rights claims dominated the debates during a decade when neoliberal globalization, deregulation, and open markets were expanding in rural Latin America had costs. Despite these large-scale socioeconomic transformations, the rebels kept their focus dogmatically on identity issues rather than on the broader issue of rural sustainable development that encompassed peasant and indigenous autonomy. Liberalization of corn commodities markets in 2005 hit Mexican rural dwellers especially hard. As stated by Otero (2007, 76) in a salient critique, this narrow "ethnic politics" focus "misses important class-structural aspects behind the fight for autonomy, such as control over land and territory." Furthermore, it equates corporatism only to ethnic-based organization (i.e., that which is "not indigenous") rather than to a system of interest articulation that can occur around class or economic interests.

President Calderón did not further Mexico's prospects for rural development when he abolished the Secretariat for Agrarian Reform in the summer of 2009, markedly weakening the future of both *ejidos* and communal lands as state-supported nonprivate forms of land tenure. While the effort to survey and title all lands during the Fox and Calderón administrations did not succeed in rural southern Mexico to the same extent as it did in the more privatized north,[2] most observers assume that Mexico's interest in using land reform as a redistributive mechanism to help bolster livelihood in the countryside has ended. Rural dwellers, now without any state supports for agricultural products, have increasingly had to sell their land and move to Mexico's cities or to the United States.

For many of those who have stayed behind in Oaxaca, UC continues to repress individuals and minorities in indigenous communities, including Protestants and other non-Catholic groups, residents of outlying towns not connected to municipal seats, and women. Oaxaca human rights activists like Sara Méndez (2005) still believe that individual and communal rights can be reconciled: "We understand that the community has to reproduce itself, but on the other hand, we want authorities to consider the position of individuals, and it is time for rights to be recognized from inside communities as well as just from the outside." It is worth noting, however that there are areas where Oaxacans have articulated a coherent vision for their practice of UC, despite the indigenous movement's history of disunity in the state's conflict areas, and UC has offered a useful model of partially autonomous institutions in Oaxaca's conflict-free UC areas (constituting over half of the state's UC municipalities) and, perhaps, for places like Bolivia and the sites of other burgeoning Latin American indigenous rights movements.

BALANCING CUSTOMS, INDIVIDUAL RIGHTS, AND AUTONOMY: ROLES FOR COURTS AND CONSTITUTIONS

While many studies grant much consideration to autonomy "from above" or "on the ground," little attention has been paid to how autonomy laws should be implemented operationally in order to reconcile and balance collective and individual rights. That is, what collective citizenship rights should a multinational state cede to regional groups to grant them autonomy, and what price for this redistribution of rights is too high, especially in terms of individual and human rights?

This question has to be considered each time that communitarian decisions tend to limit or exclude the rights of individuals or groups within their own communities, as in the case of non-Zapatista indigenous communities stuck in Zapatista-held areas where state services, like health care and education, are being refused by the EZLN or as in the case of women like Eufrosina Cruz who, after being elected mayor in a traditional election, had to renounce her personal right to political participation and leave her community so that her community could allegedly achieve a time-honored collective vision of customary law and order.

Despite all the attention to multicultural reforms, texts on the impact of the 2001 constitutional reforms of indigenous rights in Mexico (Rabasa Gamboa 2002; Bailón Corres 2003) carefully trace the genealogies of the latest reforms, but make almost no mention of any concrete cases or recent jurisprudence at all. To complete the conflicts studied in the first section of this chapter, let's now consider the experience of the Colombian Constitutional Court, which has compiled perhaps the most extensive corpus of rulings and doctrinal consistency in the hemisphere. Straddling the line between individual and communitarian rights, this court "has developed a jurisprudence that seeks to maximize the autonomy of indigenous communities and to respect their ways of doing justice without embracing an unconditional cultural relativism" (Assies n.d., 11).

The court's decisions have often been controversial, such as 1997 Case T-523, upholding an indigenous consultative verdict that a political enemy of a murder victim was to be punished for instigating the murder at the hands of guerrillas (by denouncing the deceased to guerrillas as a paramilitary fighter shortly before he was slain). The sentence was that the denouncer of the victim should be whipped sixty times, expelled from the northern Cauca community where he resided and committed the offense, and lose all political rights there (Assies n.d., 7).

The court's decision was roundly condemned by human rights groups but consistent—after a finding that the whippings and expulsion did not constitute torture—with its doctrine that judges should be guided by cultural relativism and as full a view as possible, based on extensive anthropological research, of the social context and meaning and purpose of sanctions. The Colombian Constitutional Court has elsewhere (perhaps most famously in 1998 decision U-510) further specified that conflicts are inevitable between the sphere of liberties and collective rights, and that indigenous communities are to be treated as unique and diverse pluriethnic communities, but that said diversity is limited by the rights delineated in the national constitution (Sánchez Botero 2010a, 300–307). More broadly, Sánchez Botero (2010b) summarized the court's position as accepting three universally sacrosanct individual rights: (1) the right to life, (2) the right to preserve the integrity of one's body, and (3) the right to due process (however codified in a given cultural context).

The Colombian Constitutional Court standard seems to allow violations such as the prohibition of the women's vote in Oaxaca. Furthermore, it seems to deny many external protections of minority groups and individuals, as per those mentioned in Kymlicka's (1995) effort to develop a theory of multicultural rights but which parts from the assumption of strong individual rights. But the Colombian Constitutional Court has taken a provocative and bold stand, and moved the debate from abstractions to concrete cases.

While the Zapatistas of Chiapas did an excellent job of putting on the agenda the problems of southern Mexico's rural indigenous peasants, Oaxaca seems to be the setting for the next stage of addressing these grievances in Mexico. If the national and state courts start taking responsibility for rulings rather than just letting the caciques deal "customarily" with internal conflicts, Oaxaca's many savvy indigenous rights movements with their deliberative leaders and broad arrays of options may help advance the development of legal and political institutions to protect group interests without sacrificing individual rights. If they also manage to incorporate and systematize cases from the nearby indigenous states of Guerrero, Michoacán, Puebla, Quintana Roo, Tabasco, Tlaxcala, Veracruz, Yucatán, and Chiapas, they may be able to create a new national model of multicultural conflict resolution emanating from the south, for a change.

THE OAXACA CHALLENGE BEYOND OAXACA: BROADENING AND PLURALIZING THE ACADEMIC DEBATE

In Mexican—and universal—culture and literature, "Western liberal individualism" is often associated with base instincts, selfishness, and neoliberalism, whereas "indigenous communalism" is associated with purity, heritage, stewardship of the land, and authenticity. Mexico's recent history with collective rights calls into question the accuracy of these associations. Starting with the federal government's post–World War II assimilationist policies to support a uniform "cosmic race" and running all the way to 2000 and the collapse of the PRI state and its corporatist structures like the National Indigenous Institute, communalism's good name has taken some blows. As we have seen, most recent efforts to build multicultural institutions in Chiapas, Yucatán, and Oaxaca and at the national level have led to frustrating or distasteful outcomes. The 2001 indigenous rights constitutional reforms have not been fully implemented (Bailón Corres 2009); the 1996 San Andrés Accords have languished; and the Zapatistas' communitarian rallying cries do not resonate like they used to.

Similarly, efforts by Mexico's opposition governments to dismantle the PRI's corporatist machines have been slowed down in many states, like Oaxaca, where authoritarian governance persisted to 2010, in part as an unintended consequence of UC recognition and the ease with which authoritarian governors and local bosses could manipulate UC outcomes. The absence of any legal baseline standards for resolving UC disputes in Oaxaca—or anywhere in Mexico, really—opened the system to abuse by local caciques and the governor. The failure of APPO and the teachers' union to unify and broaden their calls for change in 2006 demonstrates how successful Oaxaca's political elites have been in dismantling rural threats and narrowly channeling urban ones.

With the new context opened in 2010 by the gubernatorial victory in Oaxaca by an anti-PRI coalition for the first time ever since 1929, the Oaxaca experiment may have a more enduring legacy than the violent insurgency in Chiapas. The Zapatistas may have been among the first indigenous movements to be heralded for ushering in a more authentic and natural form of democracy in the age of globalization, and without their rebellion there probably would not have been any UC recognition in Oaxaca. Nevertheless, the new generation of Chiapas constructivists like Burguete (chapter 2), Mattiace (2003), Inclán (2008), Eisenstadt (2011), Sonnleitner (2001, 2012b), and Trejo (2012) alike have noted the difficult internal contradictions faced by the movement.

If Oaxaca's indigenous rights movements intend to move forward and rescue their weak autonomous structures from authoritarian and corporatist domination, they will need to be reconceptualized within a long-term political struggle and local differences will need to be transcended to form regional power centers. Mexico's federal government and courts will also have to make some clear choices and then enforce them, as the Colombians have. Only then will Oaxaca's indigenous people start to develop the kinds of subnational power-sharing institutions that consociationalists from Lijphart (1977) to Norris (2008) have found best represent plural societies like those in southern Mexico.

All of these challenges underscore the importance of a broad debate, critical and pluralistic, on multicultural movements in Latin America. To capture the tensions between communitarianism, autonomy, and human rights, this debate needs to be anchored in sound knowledge, founded by systematic and empirical research. The minority status of indigenous peoples and communities in Latin American nations justifies their access to mechanisms that allow them to expand their economic, social, cultural, political, and electoral rights. Consistent with this fundamental principle of justice, it is equally important to ensure respect for personal rights and universal participation, effective representation, and inclusion of all minorities within their communities.

Far from opposing peasant and indigenous forms of communal politics, pluralism is a condition and a guarantee that they can be exercised with respect for diversity, internal differences, and basic human rights. Latin America's dynamic and diverse peoples come from a range of cultural origins—pre-Hispanic European, African, Asian, and many mixes of these. The *usos y costumbres* debate in Oaxaca, and the Andean experiments in multicultural governance addressed here, are larger than just the groups of people they directly impact. Our common future, and our ability to equitably represent diverse, rich, and culturally dynamic communities everywhere, as well as national and universal objectives and aspirations, are at stake in striking a proper balance.

NOTES

1. These cases were sent out by the TEJPF for analysis by a panel of specialists during the IV Seminario Internacional del Observatorio Judicial Electoral 2011, in October 2011, at TEPJF headquarters in Mexico City, where one of the coauthors participated.
2. While recent data are harder to find because the program has officially ended, Chiapas and Oaxaca were Mexico's least cooperative states with the surveying and titling of *ejido* and communal lands, as of 2003. By that time, the program, called PROCEDE, had registered between 70 and 100 percent of publicly held lands in every other state, but just over 50 percent of these lands in Chiapas and Oaxaca (Rivera Nolasco 2004, 134).

REFERENCES

Asch, Salomon E. 1955. "Opinions and Social Pressure." *Scientific American* 193: 31–35.

Assies, Willem. n.d. "Indian Justice in the Andes: Re-rooting or Re-routing." Unpublished manuscript.

Bailón Córres, Moisés Jaime. 2003. *Derechos Humanos y Derechos Indígenas en el Orden Jurídico Federal Mexicano*. Mexico City: Comisión Nacional de los Derechos Humanos.

Bailón Córres, Moisés Jaime. 2009. "Legislación Federal y Estatal en Materia de Derechos Indigenas: Saldos al 2009." In *Derecho y sociedad en Oaxaca indígena—logros alcanzados y desafíos pendientes*, edited by Víctor Leonel Juan Martínez and Katya Salazar Luzula, 1–11. Washington, DC: Fundación para el debido proceso legal.

Danielson, Michael S., and Todd A. Eisenstadt. 2009. "Walking Together, but in Which Direction? Gender Discrimination and Multicultural Practices in Oaxaca, Mexico." *Politics and Gender* 5 (June): 153–184.

Eisenstadt, Todd A. 2004. *Courting Democracy in Mexico: Party Strategies and Electoral Institutions*. New York: Cambridge University Press.

Eisenstadt, Todd A. 2007. "*Usos y Costumbres* and Post-electoral Conflicts in Oaxaca, Mexico, 1995–2004: An Empirical and Normative Assessment." *Latin American Research Review* (February): 52–77.

Eisenstadt, Todd A. 2011. *Politics, Identity, and Mexico's Indigenous Rights Movements*. New York: Cambridge University Press.

Eisenstadt, Todd A., and Viridiana Ríos. 2012. "Ethnic Politics and Post-electoral Violence: Lessons from Mexico for Other Emerging Democracies." Unpublished manuscript.

IFE (Instituto Federal Electoral). 2010. *Sistema de Consulta de la Estadística de las Elecciones Federales. Atlas de Resultados Electorales Federales 1991–2009* (CD-ROM). Mexico: IFE.

Inclán María. 2008. "From the ¡Ya Basta! to the *Caracoles*: Zapatista Protest Mobilization under Transitional Conditions." *American Journal of Sociology* 113 (5): 1316–1350.

INEGI (Instituto Nacional de Estadística, Geografía e Informática). 2001. *XII Censo General de Población y Vivienda*. Mexico City: INEGI.

Kymlicka, Will. 1995. *Multicultural Citizenship*. New York: Oxford University Press.

Lewin, Kurt. 1951. *Field Theory in Social Science: Selected Theoretical Papers*, edited by D. Cartwright. New York: Harper and Row.

Lijphart, Arend. 1977. *Democracy in Plural Societies: A Comparative Exploration*. New Haven, CT: Yale University Press.

Mattiace, Shannan L. 2003. *To See with Two Eyes: Peasant Activism and Indian Autonomy in Chiapas, Mexico*. Albuquerque: University of New Mexico Press.

Méndez, Sara. 2005. Human rights activist at Centro Derechos Humanos Tierra del Sol in Tlaxiaco, interview in Oaxaca, May 15.

Norris, Pippa. 2008. *Driving Democracy: Do Power-Sharing Institutions Work?* New York: Cambridge University Press.

Otero, Gerardo. 2007. "Review Article: Class or Identity Politics? A False Dichotomy." *International Journal of Comparative Sociology* 48 (1): 73–80.

Povinelli, Elizabeth. 2010. *The Cunning of Recognition: Indigenous Alterities and the Making of Australian Multiculturalism*. Durham, NC: Duke University Press.

Rabasa Gamboa, Emilio. 2002. *Derecho Constitucional Indígena*. Mexico City: Universidad Nacional Autónoma de México.

Ríos Contreras, Viridiana. 2006. "Conflictividad postelectoral en los Usos y Costumbres de Oaxaca." Undergraduate thesis in political science, Instituto Tecnológico Autónomo de México (ITAM).

Rivera Nolasco, Marco A. 2004. "Reporte de Investigación: Controversias Agrarias y su Relación con el Avance del PROCEDE 1992–2003." *Estudios Agrarios* 26: 121–148.

Rus, Jan. 1994. "The 'Comunidad Revolucionaria Institutional': The Subversion of Native Government in Highland Chiapas, 1936–1968." In *Everyday Forms of State Formation: Revolution and the Negotiation of Rule in Modern Mexico*, edited by Gilbert M. Joseph and Daniel Nugent, 265–300. Durham, NC: Duke University Press.

Sánchez Botero, Ester. 2010a. *Justicia y Pueblos Indígenas de Colombia*, 3rd ed. Bogotá: Universidad Nacional de Colombia.

Sánchez Botero, Ester. 2010b. "Como entender el derecho en contextos de diversidad cultural?" Presentation at Seventh International Congress of the Latin American Network of Legal Anthropology, Lima, Peru, August 2.

Sonnleitner, Willibald. 2001. *Los indígenas y la democratización electoral: Una década de cambio político entre los tzotziles y tzeltales de Los Altos de Chiapas (1988–2000)*. Mexico City: El Colegio de México/IFE.

Sonnleitner, Willibald. 2012a. *La representación legislativa de los indígenas en México: De la representatividad descriptiva, a una representación de mejor calidad*. Mexico City: TEPJF.

Sonnleitner, Willibald. 2012b. *Elecciones chiapanecas: Del régimen posrevolucionario al desorden democrático*. Mexico City: El Colegio de México.

TEPJF (Tribunal Electoral del Poder Judicial de la Federación). 2010a. Sentencia de la Sala Regional Xalapa sobre el caso de San Jerónimo Sosolá, Ponencia: Magda. SX-JDC-398/2010 y acumulados. Yolli García Álvarez, Secretario: Víctor Manuel Rosas Leal, TEPJF.

TEPJF (Tribunal Electoral del Poder Judicial de la Federación). 2010b. Sentencia sobre el caso de San Juan Bautista Guelache, Ponencia: Magda. SX-JDC-415/2010. Claudia Pastor Bonilla, Secretario: Rodrigo Santiago Juárez, TEPJF.

TEPJF (Tribunal Electoral del Poder Judicial de la Federación). 2010c. Sentencia sobre el caso de San Miguel Chimalapa, Ponencia: Magda. SX-JDC-438/2010. Claudia Pastor Badilla, Secretario: Rodrigo Santiago Juárez, TEPJF.

TEPJF (Tribunal Electoral del Poder Judicial de la Federación). 2011. Sentencia de la Sala Superior sobre el caso de San Jerónimo Sosolá, Ponencia: Magdo. SUP-REC-2/2011. Salvador Olimpo Nava Gomar, Secretario: Juan Carlos Silva Adaya, TEPJF.

Trejo, Guillermo. 2012. *Indigenous Insurgency: The Breakdown of Religious and Political Monopolies and the Rise of Ethnic Mobilization in Mexico*. New York: Cambridge University Press.

Van Cott, Donna Lee. 2000. *The Friendly Liquidation of the Past—the Politics of Diversity in Latin America*. Pittsburgh: University of Pittsburgh Press.

Viqueira, Juan Pedro, and Sonnleitner, Willibald, eds. 2000. *Democracia en tierras indígenas: Las elecciones en Los Altos de Chiapas (1991–1998)*. Mexico City: El Colegio de México/CIESAS/IFE.

Wolf, Eric R. 2001. "Closed Corporate Peasant Communities in Mesoamerica and Central Java." In *Pathways of Power: Building an Anthropology of the Modern World*. Berkeley: University of California Press.

Index

Aboriginal Popular Movement (Bolivia), 96
Above, autonomy/multiculturalism from, 5, 8, 13, 21, 259, 264
  in Bolivia, 90
  in Ecuador, 14, 112, 124, 259
  incentives/motivations for, 22(table), 218(table)
  in Oaxaca, 8, 138
  in Yucatán, 15, 218
Abusos y costumbres, 7
"Acceptable Indian," 137
Acción Ecológica (Ecuador), 125
Accords on Indigenous Rights and Culture (Mexico). *See* San Andrés Accords
Acosta, Alberto, 121
Administrative decentralization, 12
ADN (Bolivia), 106
Adversarial judicial system, 219, 232, 233
Affirmative action, 104, 113, 118, 119, 120, 126
Afro-Bolivians, 102, 109n14
Afro-Colombians, 135
Afro-Ecuadorians, 23, 119, 120
Afro-Latin Americans, 19, 22, 31–32, 34–35
Agencias, 145, 148, 150–51, 247, 250, 253, 256
  defined, 163n15
Agrarian reform. *See* Land rights and reform
Alanís Figueroa, María del Carmen, 5, 7
ALBA. *See* Bolivarian Alliance for the Peoples of Our America
Albó, Xavier, 71, 97, 98
Alcaldes, 143, 148, 178
Alcohol distributers, 10
Aldermen. *See* Regidor
Alianza País (Ecuador), 111, 117, 118, 120–21
Alonzo Caamal, Bartolomé, 230–31
Altos, Chiapas, 51
Amazon, 28, 34, 113, 118, 122, 127

Andean nations, xv(map), 14, 32–33, 67–131, 85n3, 262. *See also* individual countries
Anderson, Mark, 34–35
Ángeles Carreño, Graciela, 7
Antidiscrimination laws, 14, 113, 118–19, 120, 126
Appadurai, Arjun, 31
APPO. *See* Asamblea Popular de los Pueblos de Oaxaca
Aproximaciones a la Antropología Jurídica de los Mayas Peninsulares (Krotz, ed.), 231
"Aquí Estamos" (INDEMAYA campaign), 224
Aragón Uicab, José Antonio, 226, 230, 234
Archdiocese of San Cristóbal de las Casas, Chiapas, 220, 238
Argentina, 19, 20(table), 25
Asamblea de Autoridades Municipales del Sector Zoogocho (Oaxaca), 142, 157
Asamblea Popular de los Pueblos de Oaxaca (APPO), 157, 262, 266
Asociación Nacional de Escritores en Lengua Indígena (Mexico), 223
Aspectos de la Cultural Jurídica en Yucatán (Krotz, ed.), 231
Assies, Willem, 44
Asunción Tlacolulita, Oaxaca, 7, 258
Asymmetrical dependencies, 248
Atlantic Charter, 41
Austerity measures, 28, 71, 74
Australia, 24
Authoritarianism
  in Bolivia, 30
  liberal, 33
  in Oaxaca, 25, 155–60, 162, 266
  tension between democracy and, 247
  in Yucatán, 220
Automatic citizenship rights, 14
Autonomistas (Bolivia), 79, 82

Autonomy, 4–5
  from above (*see* Above, autonomy/
    multiculturalism from)
  balancing customs, individual rights,
    and, 264–65
  balancing nation-states, legal orders,
    and, 258–61
  from below (*see* Below, autonomy/
    multiculturalism from)
  collective (*see* Collective rights/
    autonomy)
  conceptual boundaries in, 41–43
  constructing institutions with, 261–64
  defined, 6, 259
  heteronomous, 58
  individual (*see* Individual rights/
    autonomy)
  multiculturalism distinguished from, 40, 46
  political parties and quest for, 9–11
  preconditions of, 10, 46
  role for courts and constitutions, 264–65
Autonomy (Bolivia), 11–12, 67–87, 258, 259
  conceptions of, 72–73
  constitution on, 101, 102, 103–5, 107–8
  emergence of indigenous discourse on,
    73–76
  emergence of indigenous politics, 71–72
  in Media Luna (*see* Media Luna, Bolivia)
  transition to indigenous power, 76–78
Autonomy (Chiapas), 11, 49, 53, 54–59,
    72, 258
Autonomy (Ecuador), 14–15, 112–13,
    121–23, 258, 259
Autonomy (Oaxaca), 3, 5–6, 8–10, 136–41,
    143
  disputes over community, 150–52
  migrants and, 194–95
  municipalities as floor and ceiling of,
    139–41
  resistance/concession question, 137–39
Autonomy (Yucatán), 5, 227, 235, 258, 259
Avalos, Isaac, 36n5
Ayllus, 12, 15n6, 71, 84
Aymara, 11, 19, 24, 26, 27, 67, 68, 71, 72,
    74, 94, 97, 98(table), 102, 103
Ayo Ayo, Bolivia, 11
Ayuntamiento, 15n4, 205
Ayutla, Oaxaca, 158

Baños Ramírez, Othón, 227
Banzer, Hugo, 79, 80, 106

Barrientos, René, 91
Bastos, Santiago, 45
Bayart, Jean-François, 15n3
Bebbington, Anthony, 27, 127
Bechtel, 78
*Becker, 28, 32
Belize, 19, 20(table)
Below, autonomy/multiculturalism from,
    13, 15, 21, 218(table), 264
  in Bolivia, 5, 90, 93, 98
  in Ecuador, 14, 15, 259
  incentives for, 22(table)
  in Oaxaca, 8
  in Yucatán, 5
Beni, Bolivia, 31(table), 82, 96
Benito Juarez, Oaxaca, 254
Berlie Belaunzarán, Emilio, 221, 228
Berlin Wall, fall of, 22
Bilingual education
  in Bolivia, 26, 75
  in Chiapas, 50
  in Ecuador, 24, 27, 112, 114, 121–22
  in Mexico, 10
  recognition without redistribution in, 114
  in Yucatán, 230, 231, 235, 237n2
Binford, Leigh, 199, 200
Blair, Harry, 12
Blake, Charles H., 233
Bobrow-Strain, Aaron, 11
Bolivarian Alliance for the Peoples of Our
    America (ALBA), 111–12, 128n1
Bolivia, 4, 5, 11–12, 13, 14, 67–110, 112, 126,
    127, 135, 137, 217, 218, 258, 259, 264
  autonomy in (*see* Autonomy (Bolivia))
  constitutional multiculturalism in (*see*
    Constitutional multiculturalism
    (Bolivia))
  decentralization in, 13, 82–83, 84, 91,
    94–95
  as a distinct case, 70–71
  Ecuador compared with, 113, 117
  futility thesis on, 23–24
  indigenous population of, 71, 85n2
  jeopardy thesis on, 32
  multicultural policies in, 19, 20(table)
  perversity thesis on, 25–27, 29, 30–31
  pluri-multi period in, 26, 68, 71, 72, 77,
    80, 83, 85n1
  post-multicultural, 27
  "refounding" of, 83, 91, 101
  revolution of 1952 in, 71, 73, 74, 79, 92

usos y costumbres of, 72, 95, 101, 104, 107–8
women of, 32
Bolivian Workers Federation. *See* Central Obrera Boliviana
Bollaños Berra, Gumesildo, 8
Brazil, 19, 20(table), 21, 34
Bretón, Victor, 116
Bucarám, Abdalá, 115
Burguete Cal y Mayor, Araceli, 5, 10, 14, 15n3, 72, 248, 259, 266
Busch, Germán, 92

Cabeceras, 5, 145, 249, 250, 253, 254, 256
Cacicazgos, 156
Caciques, 9, 154, 159, 196, 265, 266
Cacuango, Dolores, 32
Calderón, Felipe, 263
Calderón, Guido, 123
Callao, Peru, 11
Cambas, 81, 84
Campeche, Mexico, 221, 222, 224, 227, 228, 237n1, 239n13
Campesinos, 19, 67–68, 71, 74, 78, 89, 226
Campesino sindicatos. See Sindicatos
Camus, Manuela, 45
Canada, 22, 43, 173, 260
Cancún, Mexico, 227, 228
Canto Moreno, Diana, 224, 226, 239n18
Capitalía movement (Bolivia), 100
Capitalization Law (Bolivia), 78
Capulapam de Méndez, Oaxaca, 148
Caracoles, 137, 163n3
Cárdenas, Victor Hugo, 26, 74, 76
Cargos (Oaxaca), 6, 7, 8, 11, 143–45, 147–50, 153, 154, 257
civil (*see* Civil *cargos*)
defined, 163n11
mayors and, 174–82, 185, 186–90, 256
migrants and, 149, 193, 194, 202, 203, 204, 205, 206–7, 209, 210, 211, 212n1
prestige offered by, 185, 186–88
religious (*see* Religious *cargos*)
Carrillo Puerto, Felipe, 238n8,9
Caste War, 220, 238n6, 241n41
Castro, Milka, 43
Castro Ruíz, Manuel, 220–21, 228
Catalonia, Spain, 260
Catholic Church
of Bolivia, 101, 128n3
of Ecuador, 114, 122
of Oaxaca, 147, 148

role in ethnic organization, 241n32
of Yucatán, 219–21, 228–29, 231
CDI. *See* Comisión Nacional para el Desarrollo de los Pueblos Indígenas
Ceballos Loeza, Atilano, 228–29
Centellas, Miguel, 5, 14, 259
Central Obrera Boliviana (COB), 93, 94
Centro, Chiapas, 51
Cervera Pacheco, Victor, 220
Chablekal, Yucatán, 229, 232–33
Chachawarmi, 32–33
Chaco War, 92
Chakras, 33
Chávez, Hugo, 29, 30, 112, 114, 127
Chiapas, Mexico, 3, 8, 11, 14, 40–41, 43, 46, 47–59, 72, 138, 221, 259–60, 262, 263, 265, 266
autonomy in, 49, 53, 54–58, 72, 258
constitutional multiculturalism in (*see* Constitutional multiculturalism (Chiapas))
jeopardy thesis on, 32
political parties in, 9
usos y costumbres of, 50, 51, 52, 53–54
women of, 32
Yucatán compared with, 219, 222, 224, 227, 231
Zapatistas in (*see* Zapatista National Liberation Army)
Chichén Itza, Mexico, 229
Chile, 71, 137
Bolivian gas export and, 27, 78, 94
multicultural policies in, 19, 20(table), 21
Chimán, 90
Chuji, Mónica, 118–19
Chuquisaca, Bolivia, 30, 31(table), 82, 103
CIDOB. *See* Confederation of Indigenous Peoples of Bolivia
CIE. *See* State Indigenous Council
Cieneguilla, Oaxaca, 251, 252(table), 254
Citizenship rights
automatic, 14
in Bolivia, 69, 71–72, 77
in Brazil, 21
in Ecuador, 114
insurgent, 21
in Oaxaca, 136, 140, 141–52, 144, 146–47, 149–50, 152, 160–62, 193, 195
Citizen's Revolution (Ecuador), 111, 113
Ciudad Ixtepec, Oaxaca, 156

Civil *cargos*, 257
　mayors and, 172, 174, 175, 178–82, 185, 186–88, 189
　migrants and, 203, 205, 206–7, 208(table), 209, 211
　by municipal type, 180–82
　percentage of municipalities with, 170
　prestige offered by, 185, 186–88
Clandestinidad, 25
Clientelism, 9–10, 115, 152, 248
Closed corporate communities, 248
CNC. *See* Confederación Nacional Campesina
CNE. *See* Corte Nacional Electoral
CNI. *See* Congreso Nacional Indígena
Coalición Obrera Estudiantil del Istmo (Mexico), 158
COB. *See* Central Obrera Boliviana
Coca farmers *(cocaleros)*, 13, 26, 27, 68, 74, 98–99
Cochabamba, Bolivia, 26, 30, 31(table), 77–78, 82–83, 94, 104
CODENPE (Ecuador), 24, 27, 29
Cohen, Jeffrey H., 196, 198, 200–202, 204–5
Cold War, 41
Collective rights/autonomy, 13–14
　balancing customs, individual rights, and, 264–65
　in Bolivia, 72–73, 89
　in Chiapas, 11
　in Ecuador, 119, 126–28
　in Oaxaca, 3, 5–6, 7–8, 11, 144, 146–47, 161, 162
Colloredo-Mansfeld, Rudi, 117
Colombia, 4, 15, 72, 135, 217, 259, 266
　constitutional reform and, 5, 6, 36, 264–65
　multicultural policies in, 19, 20(table)
　UN Declaration on Indigenous Rights and, 22
Colonialism, 41, 42, 58, 59n1, 72, 102. *See also* Decolonization
Colonos, 157
Columbus's voyage (quincentenary celebration), 4
Comisión de Asuntos Etnicos (Yucatán). *See* Ethnic Affairs Committee
Comisión Nacional para el Desarrollo de los Pueblos Indígenas (CDI) (Yucatán), 223–25, 238n5, 240n23

Comité de Padres de Familia (Oaxaca), 149
Comité Pro-Santa Cruz (CPSC) (Bolivia), 79–82
Comités de vigilancia, 95
Commissioners of communal resources (Oaxaca), 205, 210–11
Commission of Communal Resources (Oaxaca), 152
Committee of 24, 41
Communism, 22–23, 43. *See also* Socialism
Communist Party (Ecuador), 114, 115
Communities
　constructing autonomous institutions in, 261–64
　demobilization and fragmentation of, 247–58
　disputes over autonomy of, 150–52
Community citizens, 144, 150
Comunalicracia, 8
Comuneros, 141, 142, 163n8
CONAIE. *See* Confederation of Indigenous Nationalities of Ecuador
CONDEPA. *See* Conference of the Fatherland
Conditional multiculturalism, 6, 119, 126, 259
Confederación Nacional Campesina (CNC) (Mexico), 48, 152, 227, 231, 240n31, 241n37
Confederación Sindical Única de Trabajadores Campesinos de Bolivia (CSUTCB), 26, 36n5, 74
Confederation of Indigenous Nationalities of Ecuador (CONAIE), 27–30, 70, 123, 124–25, 137
　accused of racism, 122
　conflict with Correa, 111–12
　creation of, 114
　crisis of, 114–18
Confederation of Indigenous Peoples of Bolivia (CIDOB), 26, 75, 77, 90, 108n7
Conference of the Fatherland (CONDEPA), 76
Congreso Nacional Indígena (CNI) (Mexico), 229
Consejo de Administración (Oaxaca), 156
Consociationalism, 105–8
Constituent Assembly (Bolivia), 27, 29, 67, 69, 82, 83, 88, 89, 91–101
　ethnic distribution of, 97(table), 98(table)

frustration in, 98–101
historical context of, 92–95
snapshot of, 95–98
Constituent Assembly (Ecuador), 115, 118, 120
Constitutional Court (Colombia), 6, 264–65
Constitutional multiculturalism (Bolivia), 5, 11, 14, 36, 67, 69, 75, 82, 83, 88–110, 259
  advances and limitations in, 101–5
  celebration of, 88–89
  consociationalism issue, 105–8
  in historical context, 92–95
  institutional reform under, 101
  symbolic reform under, 101–5
Constitutional multiculturalism (Chiapas), 40–41, 43, 46, 47–59, 259–60
  autonomy and, 54–58
  reduced to rhetoric, 47–48
  self-determination and, 54–58
  traditional authorities under, 50–52
  traditional institutions under, 48–49
  usos y costumbres under, 50, 51, 52, 53–54
Constitutional multiculturalism (Ecuador), 112, 115
  advances and ambiguities in, 118–21
  futility thesis on, 23
  postconstitutional conflicts, 121–25
Constitutional multiculturalism (Latin America), 44–46, 135, 261–62
  defined, 261
Constitutional reforms
  Colombia and, 5, 6, 36, 264–65
  Mexico and, 23, 92
  Oaxaca and, 138–39, 221
  role for, 264–65
  Venezuela and, 5
  Yucatán and, 221–23, 225, 226, 232–33
Constitutional representation/participation (Oaxaca), 248, 250, 255, 256, 257–58
Consultas, 221–23, 224–25, 229, 239n19
Conteo de Población y Vivienda (INEGI), 210
Contesting Citizenship in Latin America (Yashar), 226
Convergence Party (Mexico), 152
Cooke, Erik, 5, 14, 259
Cool May, Amadeo, 230
Cooperaciones, 144
Corn farmers, 227, 263

Correa, Rafael, 14, 23–24, 28–30, 111–13, 116, 119, 120, 121, 123, 127–28
  CONAIE vs., 111–12
  criticism of policies, 29–30
  divisions within indigenous movements and, 117–18
Corte Nacional Electoral (CNE) (Bolivia), 98, 100, 103
Cosmetic multiculturalism, 45
Cosmovisiones, 102
Costa Rica, 19, 20(table)
Costas, Rubén, 81, 82
Cotacachi, Ecuador, 117
Cotopaxi, Ecuador, 111, 117
Council of Citizen's Participation and Social Control (Ecuador), 122, 128
Courts, role for, 264–65
CPSC. *See* Comité Pro-Santa Cruz
Criollo elites, 220
Cruceños, 79, 80
Cruz Mendoza, Eufrosina, 7, 15n1, 146–47, 161, 163n16, 264
CSUTCB. *See* Confederación Sindical Única de Trabajadores Campesinos de Bolivia
Cuauhtémoc Guadalupe, Oaxaca, 254
Cuba, 24
Cué, Gabino, 158
Cuéllar, Savina, 100
Cultural diversity, 40, 43–44, 47–50, 53, 57–59, 255
Cultural relativism, 264–65
Cunning of recognition, 24, 263
Customary law. *See Usos y costumbres*

Dahl, R. A., 188
Danielson, Michael S., 6, 7, 8, 15, 255, 258
Debt crisis, 12, 217
Decentralization, 21
  administrative, 12
  in Bolivia, 13, 82–83, 84, 91, 94–95
  defined, 12
  economic (functional), 12
  in Mexico, 12–13, 151
  political, 12
Decolonization, 41–42, 46, 59
Decree 196 (Ecuador), 122
*Deer, 33
De Juarez, Guelatao, 142
De la Cadena, Marisol, 33

De la Cruz, Pedro, 119
Del Carmen Alanís Figueroa, María, 5
Demiralp, Seda, 69
Democratic pluralism, theory of, 188
Democratization, 12, 261
   in Bolivia, 70, 73, 91
   in Chiapas, 260
   in Chile, 137
   in Ecuador, 112
   in Oaxaca, 25
   tension between authoritarianism and, 247
   Third Wave, 70, 73
Dependency perspectives. *See under* Migrants (Oaxaca)
De Soto, Hernando, 204
De Sousa Santos, Boaventura, 118, 171
Development perspectives. *See under* Migrants (Oaxaca)
Díaz-Polanco, Héctor, 45, 73
DINEIB. *See* Dirección Nacional de Educación Intercultural Bilingüe
Dirección de Asuntos Indígenas (Chiapas), 48
Dirección Nacional de Educación Intercultural Bilingüe (DINEIB) (Ecuador), 24, 27, 29, 121
Discount rate of ruler, 195–96
Durand, Jorge, 199, 200

Eastern Europe, 22–23, 43
Eaton, Kent, 79
Economic (functional) decentralization, 12
Ecuador, 4, 13, 111–31, 135, 137
   autonomy in, 14–15, 112–13, 121–23, 258, 259
   Citizen's Revolution of, 111, 113
   conflicts over institutional control, 121–25
   constitutional multiculturalism and (*see* Constitutional multiculturalism (Ecuador))
   crisis of the indigenous movement in, 114–18
   futility thesis on, 23–24
   "junta of national salvation" in, 28
   multicultural policies in, 19, 20(table)
   perversity thesis on, 25, 27–30
   women of, 32, 119
Ecuador: From Banana Republic to No Republic (Correa), 127–28
Ecuadorian Federation of Indians. *See* Federación Ecuatoriana de Indios

Ecuarunari, 112, 128n2
Education
   bilingual (*see* Bilingual education)
   in Ecuador, 114
   of Oaxaca mayors, 173–74, 175, 176–77, 179(table), 180, 182–83
Eisenstadt, Todd A., 15, 33, 119, 256, 266
Ejército Zapatista de Liberación Nacional (Mexico). *See* Zapatista National Liberation Army
Ejidatarios, 142
Ejidos, 11, 138, 147, 178, 181, 263, 267
El Alto, Bolivia, 74, 104
El Compuerto, Oaxaca, 254
Electoral Institute of Oaxaca, 249, 250, 254, 260
Electoral Tribunal of Judicial Power (Mexico), 5
Elites, 21
   of Bolivia, 14, 68, 70, 79, 81, 217
   of Chiapas, 9
   of Colombia, 217
   nongoverning, 185, 190
   of Oaxaca, 4, 25, 138, 184–88, 189–90
   of Yucatán, 220
El Palmar, Oaxaca, 254
El Porvenir, Oaxaca, 254
El Salvador, 19, 20(table)
Emiliano Zapata, Oaxaca, 254
Encuentros de Cultura Maya, 223
English language, 173, 184
Environmentalism, 21, 113, 121, 123
Escalafón, 8, 172
Escobar, Arturo, 113
Escuela de Agricultura Ecológica, 228
Esperón Angón, Cesar, 8
Esther, Comandanta, 32
Ethnic Affairs Committee (Yucatán), 223, 225–26, 230, 234, 239n21
Euán Romero, José, 229, 232
Europe, 41, 43. *See also* Eastern Europe
Executive Decree 1585 (Ecuador), 121
External protections, 45, 48, 51
EZLN. *See* Zapatista National Liberation Army

Factionalism, 248–49
Federación Ecuatoriana de Indígenas Evangélicos (FEINE), 28, 115, 124

Federación Ecuatoriana de Indios (FEI), 115, 124
Federación Nacional de Organizaciones Campesinas Indígenas y Negras (FENOCIN) (Ecuador), 116, 119, 124
Federalism, 139
FEI. *See* Federación Ecuatoriana de Indios
FEINE. *See* Federación Ecuatoriana de Indígenas Evangélicos
FENOCIN. *See* Federación Nacional de Organizaciones Campesinas Indígenas y Negras
Florescano, Enrique, 171
Flores Cruz, Cipriano, 10, 260
Forest peoples, 114
Foro Indígena Nacional (Mexico), 3
Foro Maya Peninsular, 229–30
Foucault, Michel, 24
Fox, Vicente, 221, 263
FPTP electoral system (Bolivia), 103–4, 105
French, John, 118, 127
Friendly Liquidation of the Past, The (Van Cott), 36
Functionalists, 200
Futility thesis, 18, 22–24

Gandhi, Mahatma, 33
García Linera, Alvaro, 100–101
García Meza, Luis, 79
Garifuna, 34
Garman, Christopher, 12
Gas wars (Bolivia), 67, 77, 81, 94. *See also* Natural gas
Gender complementarity, 32–33
Glorieta, La (Bolivian military academy), 100
*Goni, 26
González Garrido, Patrocinio, 48
Good Government Councils (Chiapas), 9
Gottberg, Luis Duno, 114
Gramsci, Antonio, 24
Grand bargaining, 106
Greene, Shane, 34
Grupo Indignación, 229–30
Guaraní, 70, 71, 72, 102
Guarneros, Patricia, 224–25
Guatemala, 19, 20(table), 45, 70
Guelatao de Juarez, Oaxaca, 142
Guerrero, Mexico, 219, 265

Gundermann, Hans, 44
Gustafson, Bret, 25, 35, 218, 235
Gutiérrez, Lucio, 28, 29, 30, 115, 116
Guyana, 19, 20(table)

Haggard, Stephan, 12
Hale, Charles, 5, 8, 24, 25, 35, 217–18, 235
Health Act (Chiapas), 48–49
Health care. *See* Traditional medicine
Henequen industry, 227, 231, 235, 240n30
Hernández Chávez, Rafaela, 147
Heteronomous autonomy, 58
Highway construction project (Bolivia), 27, 90
Hirschman, Albert, 18–19, 22–23, 24, 31–32, 34, 35
Holston, James, 21
Honduras, 19, 20(table), 34
Hooker, Juliet, 32, 34
Household model of migration, 200
Human rights, 15, 41, 46, 264
 in Bolivia, 11, 84, 107
 in Chiapas, 50–52
 in Ecuador, 119, 121, 126
 in Oaxaca, 141, 143
 in Peru, 11
 in Yucatán, 221
Humphreys Bebbington, Denise, 127
Hydrocarbon resources, 27, 31, 78, 80–81
Hydrocarbons Law (Bolivia), 78

IEE. *See* Instituto Estatal Electoral
Ihualtepec, Oaxaca, 153
Illiteracy, 173, 174, 182
"Imaginary Zapatista" movement, 3, 15n2
IMF. *See* International Monetary Fund
Inclán, María, 266
Inclusionary corporatism, 220
Inculturation theology, 114, 128n3
INDEMAYA. *See* Instituto para el Desarrollo de la Cultura Maya del Estado de Yucatán
Indian Congress and Constitutional Convention (Bolivia), 89, 92–93
"Indian problem," 73, 85n3
"Indian question," 223
Indigenism, 44, 230, 238n7
Indigenismo, 19
Indigenous and Peasant Movement of Cotopaxi, 117

Indigenous languages
  in Bolivia, 71, 75, 97, 102, 109n11
  in Ecuador, 120
  in Oaxaca, 8, 169, 173, 174, 184, 220
  in Yucatán, 220
Indigenous Pachakuti Movement (Bolivia).
  See Movimiento Indígena Pachakuti
Indigenous Peace and Conciliation Court
  (Chiapas), 51–53, 61n17
Indigenous population
  of Bolivia, 71, 85n2
  Mexican states with large, xiv(map)
  of Oaxaca, 13, 169
  worldwide, 43, 59n3
  of Yucatán, 219–20, 238n5
Indigenous Rights and Culture Act of the
  State of Chiapas, 51, 55
Indigenous Tupac Katari Movement
  (Bolivia), 74
Indios permitidos/permitted Indian, 35, 128
Indios rebeldes, 35
Individual rights/autonomy
  in Bolivia, 89
  in Chiapas, 11
  in Ecuador, 119
  in Oaxaca, 5–6, 7–8, 11, 144, 146–47,
    161, 162
  role for courts and constitutions,
    264–65
INI. See National Indigenist Institute
Inquisitorial judicial system, 219
Institutional theory, 196–97
Institutions and Social Conflict (Knight),
  196–97
Instituto Estatal Electoral (IEE) (Oaxaca),
  145, 150, 154, 155, 160
Instituto para el Desarrollo de la Cultura
  Maya del Estado de Yucatán
  (INDEMAYA), 222, 223–25, 226
Insurgent citizenship, 21
Inter-American Development Bank, 45
Interculturalidad/interculturality, 113,
  119–20, 126, 128n4, 136, 163n1
Interlegality, 53, 140
Internal colonialism, 42–43, 58
Internal restrictions, 45, 46
International Covenant on Civil and
  Political Rights, 41–42
International Covenant on Economic,
  Social and Cultural Rights, 41–42

International Labour Organization
  Convention 169 (ILO 169), 4, 21, 23,
    218(table)
  Bolivia and, 69, 70, 75
  Chiapas and, 47
  Mexico and, 47
  Yucatán and, 218n1
International Monetary Fund (IMF), 28
International Network of Indigenous
  Oaxacans, 152
International Work Group for Indigenous
  Affairs (IWGIA), 42
Isiboro Sécure National Park and
  Indigenous Territory (TIPNIS)
  (Bolivia), 90, 105
IWGIA. See International Work Group for
  Indigenous Affairs
Ixtlán de Juárez, Oaxaca, 143, 158

Jehovah's Witnesses, 148
Jeopardy thesis, 19, 22, 31–35
Jones, Richard C., 199
Juan Martínez, Victor Leonel, 5, 247
Juchitán, Oaxaca, 154, 156, 158
Judicial aldermen. See *Síndicos*
Judicial system (Yucatán), 219, 231–34
Jueces de paz, 232, 234, 242n48
Jueces maya, 219, 222, 232, 234
Juicio de Protección a los Derechos Políticos
  de los Ciudadanos (Mexico), 160
Juntas de Buen Gobierno (Mexico), 137
Juxtlahuaca, Mexico, 7

Kandel, William, 199
Kantuta flower, 102
Katari, Tupac, 68, 74
Katarista movement, 68, 71, 74, 89, 92
Kearney, Michael, 198, 200–201
Kichwa language, 111, 113, 120
Knight, Jack, 196–97, 202
Knights of Columbus, 226
Kollas, 81, 84
Krotz, Esteban, 231
Kymlicka, Will, 44–46, 48, 261–62, 265

La Asunción, Oaxaca, 253
Land rights and reform. See also Territory
  (indigenous)
  in Bolivia, 27, 75, 79, 95, 102
  in Chiapas, 9, 11, 47, 48

in Ecuador, 114
in Mexico, 263
in Peru, 13
in Yucatán, 227, 231
Languages
  bilingual education in (*see* Bilingual education)
  English, 173, 184
  indigenous (*see* Indigenous languages)
  Kichwa, 111, 113, 120
  Maya, 223, 224, 230, 231, 235
  Mixtec, 8
  Spanish (*see* Spanish language)
La Paz, Bolivia, 74, 78, 80, 82, 84, 90, 104, 109n13
Las Anonas, Oaxaca, 254
Las Conchas, Oaxaca, 254
Las Cruces, Oaxaca, 254
Latifundios, 79
Latifundista, 9
Law for the Protection of the Rights of the Maya Community. *See* Maya Community Law
Law of National Institution of Agrarian Reform. *See* Ley Instituto Nacional de Reforma Agraria
Law on the Rights of Indigenous Peoples and Communities (Oaxaca), 139
Lazarte, Silvia, 100
Left, 22
  in Bolivia, 92, 93–94, 95
  in Ecuador, 111, 113, 114, 116, 123, 126
  New, 118, 127
Left Revolutionary Party (Bolivia), 93
*Leon de Leal, 33
Levantamientos, 21
Levi, Margaret, 195–96
Ley de Convocatoria (Bolivia), 95, 99–100
Ley de Participación Popular (Bolivia). *See* Popular Participation law
Leyes malditas, 26
Ley Instituto Nacional de Reforma Agraria (Ley INRA) (Bolivia), 75, 77, 95
Liberation theology, 114, 228, 229, 231
Lijphart, Arend, 89–90, 105, 106, 266
Llanez Ortiz, Genner, 227
Loayza, Román, 26, 36n5
López López, Leovijildo, 9
López Obrador, Andrés Manuel, 158, 164n27, 240n26

López Salcido, Eduardo, 224
López Valencia, Alan, 7–8
Los Angeles, California, 148–49
Lucero, José Antonio, 5, 12, 14, 218, 248, 259, 263
Lugo, Raúl, 229
Lynchings, 11

Macas, Luis, 28, 29, 115, 117
Magdalena Octolán, Oaxaca, 153
Mahuad, Jamil, 28, 115
Mamani Ramírez, Pablo, 103
Maní, Yucatán, 228
March for Territory and Dignity (Bolivia), 75, 90
March toward the East (Bolivia), 80
Marcos, Subcomandante, 229
Marka, 71
Marshall, T. H., 14
Martínez Cobo, José R., 42
Martínez Luna, Jaime, 8, 10–11
Martínez Novo, Carmen, 14, 27, 259
Marxism, 21, 59n5. *See also* Communism; Socialism
MAS. *See* Movimiento al Socialismo
Massey, Douglas S., 199
Mattiace, Shannan, 5, 13, 15, 259, 266
Maya, 218–45. *See also* Yucatán, Mexico
  Caste War and, 220, 238n6
  factors in relationship with state, 219–23
  language of, 223, 224, 230, 231, 235
  traditional medicine of, 222, 224
  as *tranquilos,* 235
  usos y costumbres of, 219, 222, 231, 235
Maya Community Law, 218–19, 222, 231, 236
Maya Cultural Forums, 223
Mayaón, 230–31, 235
Maya Peninsular Forum, 229–30
May Correa, Guillermo, 230
Mayordomía, 170, 175, 176–77, 181, 189
Mayors (Oaxaca), 8, 15, 146–47, 148, 156, 157, 170, 171–90
  basic characteristics of, 172–73
  cargo service and, 174–82, 185, 186–90, 256
  formation of power elites and, 184–88, 189–90
  migrants as, 173, 205, 210–11, 212
Mazatlán Villa de Flores, Oaxaca, 151, 154

MBL (Bolivia), 109n10
MCPs. *See* Official multicultural policies
Media Luna, Bolivia, 30, 67–69, 72, 73, 76, 77, 78, 96, 99, 104, 135
    results of autonomy movement, 83–85
    rise of autonomy in, 79–82
"Menace of multiculturalism," 5, 24, 217
Menchú, Rigoberta, 70
Méndez, Sara, 263–64
Mérida, Yucatán, 219, 227, 229, 232
Mesa, Carlos, 27, 78, 81
Mestizaje, 19
Mestizos
    of Bolivia, 67, 70, 74, 76, 92, 97–98
    of Ecuador, 113, 116, 119, 120, 122
    of Oaxaca, 169, 195
    of Yucatán, 220
Mexican Revolution, 220
Mexico, 11, 15, 135, 137, 161, 260–61. *See also* individual regions of
    broadening the academic debate in, 265–67
    constitutional reforms and, 23, 92
    decentralization in, 12–13, 151
    futility thesis on, 23
    introduction of multiculturalism concept in, 44
    jeopardy thesis on, 32
    multicultural policies in, 19, 20(table)
    political parties and quest for autonomy in, 9–11
    rejection of multiculturalism in, 43
    states with large indigenous populations, xiv(map)
    women of, 32
Miahuatlán, Oaxaca, 154
MICC. *See* Movimiento Indígena y Campesino de Cotopaxi
Michoacán, Mexico, 143, 219, 221, 265
Migrants (Oaxaca), 7–8, 15, 142, 161–62, 192–212
    cargos and, 149, 193, 194, 202, 203, 204, 205, 206–7, 209, 210, 211, 212n1
    citizenship rights and, 150
    community strength and organization and, 206–8
    correlates of participation, 208–10
    dependency-development dichotomy, 199–202
    dependency perspectives, 195, 198

    development perspectives, 193, 195, 199
    explaining participation of, 205–10
    mayorality served by, 173, 205, 210–11, 212
    overrepresentation in positions of power, 210–11
    remittances and, 193, 197–98, 199, 201–2
    sanctions for participation failure, 206–7, 208(table), 209
    tequio and, 193, 194, 196, 202, 203, 204, 206(figure), 208(table), 209, 211, 212n1
    theoretical perspective on behavior, 195–97
    types and levels of participation, 205–6
    usos y costumbres and (*see under Usos y costumbres* (Oaxaca))
    voting rights and, 6, 148–50, 162, 193, 247, 258–59
Migrants (Yucatán), 227–28
Migration syndrome, 198
Mingas, 135
Mining
    in Bolivia, 13, 67–68, 74, 80, 81
    in Ecuador, 24, 29–30, 111, 112, 114, 118, 124–25
    silver, 81
    tin, 13, 67–68, 81
Ministerio Público (Yucatán), 232, 242n45
MIP. *See* Movimiento Indígena Pachakuti
MIR (Bolivia), 106, 109n10
MITKA. *See* Movimiento Indígena Tupac Katari
Mitla, Oaxaca, 159
Mixteca, Oaxaca, 198, 200
Mixtec language, 8
MNR. *See* Movimiento Nacionalista Revolucionario
Modernization theory, 198
Moe, Terry M., 201
Molina Maldonado, Norma, 7
Monroy Gómez, Pablo, 233
Montubios, 120
Moral economies, 204
Morales, Evo, 4, 5, 11, 14, 70, 76, 77, 78, 82, 84, 107, 108, 113, 117, 135, 259
    at ALBA meeting, 112
    ambition to "refound" Bolivia, 83, 91
    clashes with U.S., 30
    class solidarity sought by, 68
    constitutional multiculturalism and, 89, 91–92, 93, 94, 95, 96, 98–99, 100, 101
    futility thesis on, 23–24

highway construction and, 90
increased power of, 106
Media Luna movement and, 67, 69, 73
perversity thesis on, 26, 27, 29
vote share won by, 31(table)
Mosca, G., 188
Mosonyi, Esteban, 114
Mountz, Alison, 196, 204
Movimiento al Socialismo (MAS) (Bolivia), 4, 30, 67, 69, 72, 74, 76
big-tent alliance, 95, 106
constitutional multiculturalism and, 89, 90, 91, 93, 94, 95–98, 99, 100, 101, 104, 106, 107, 108
at the helm of state, 82–83
Media Luna movement and, 79
revolutionary tradition of, 92
Movimiento AYRA (Bolivia), 96
Movimiento Indígena Pachakuti (MIP) (Bolivia), 4, 94, 95, 96, 108n4
Movimiento Indígena Tupac Katari (MITKA) (Bolivia), 74
Movimiento Indígena y Campesino de Cotopaxi (MICC) (Ecuador), 117
Movimiento Nacionalista Revolucionario (MNR) (Bolivia), 71, 79, 91, 92, 93, 96, 106, 109n9
Movimiento Originario Popular (Bolivia), 96
Movimiento Revolucionario Tupac Katari (MRTK) (Bolivia), 74
MRTK. *See* Movimiento Revolucionario Tupac Katari
Municipalities (Oaxaca), 136, 139–41, 142, 150–52, 156–59, 161–63, 169–71
conflicts and, 143–45
as floor and ceiling of autonomy, 139–41
formation of power elites in, 184–88
nontraditional, 180–84, 185, 186–87, 188–89, 190
regional system of domination and, 157–58
semitraditional, 180–84, 185, 186, 188, 189
traditional, 180–84, 185, 186–90
Murat, José, 156–57

NAFTA. *See* North American Free Trade Agreement
National Action Party (PAN) (Mexico)
Chiapas and, 9
Oaxaca and, 9, 251
Yucatán and, 223, 224, 225–26, 230

National Association of Writers in Indigenous Languages (Mexico), 223
National Commission of Intercultural Bilingual Education (Ecuador), 122
National Indian Congress (Mexico), 229
National Indigenist Institute (INI) (Mexico), 223, 265
National Indigenous Forum (Mexico), 3
Nationalization of resources
Bolivia and, 27, 76, 78, 79, 81, 82
Mexico and, 161
National minorities, 43, 44, 51
National Peasant Confederation (Mexico). *See* Confederación Nacional Campesina
National Revolutionary Movement (Bolivia). *See* Movimiento Nacionalista Revolucionario
National School of Anthropology and History (Mexico City), 225
Natural gas, 26, 27, 76, 78, 80–81, 83, 94. *See also* Gas wars
Natural resources, 42
of Bolivia, 69, 77, 79
of Ecuador, 112, 113, 119, 120–21, 124–25, 126–27
of Oaxaca, 137, 138
Nayarit, Mexico, 221
Neoclassical theory of the state, 195, 196
Neoindigenism, 44
Neoliberal multiculturalism, 5, 12, 18, 35, 45, 217
in Bolivia, 23, 68, 70, 80, 81, 84, 94, 218
in Chiapas, 47
in Ecuador, 14, 15, 111, 115, 117, 121–22, 123, 126, 127
functionalists on, 200
in Latin America, 217
perversity thesis on, 24–31
New Left, 118, 127
Nicaragua, 19, 20(table), 72, 135
Nobel Peace Prize, 70
Noboa, Gustavo, 28
Non-Catholic minorities, 5, 143, 148, 247, 263
Nongoverning elite, 185, 190
Nongovernmental organizations (NGOs), 219, 221, 229–31
Nontraditional municipalities (Oaxaca), 180–84, 185, 186–87, 188–89, 190

Norris, Pippa, 266
Norte, Chiapas, 51
North, Douglas, 195–96
North American Free Trade Agreement (NAFTA), 47

Oaxaca, Mexico, 3–4, 5–6, 11, 135–214, 247–59, 262–64
  absent institutions of, 159–60
  authoritarianism in, 25, 155–60, 162, 266
  autonomy in (*see* Autonomy (Oaxaca))
  cargos of (*see* Cargos (Oaxaca))
  citizenship rights and, 136, 140, 141–52, 144, 146–47, 150, 160–62
  constitutional reforms and, 138–39, 221
  federalism and, 139
  indigenous population of, 13, 169
  institutionalization and, 152–55
  jeopardy thesis on, 32
  mayors of (*see* Mayors (Oaxaca))
  microlevel dynamics of conflicts in, 247–58
  migrants in (*see* Migrants (Oaxaca))
  municipalities of (*see* Municipalities (Oaxaca))
  new agreements in, 152–55
  new political map of, 159
  perversity thesis on, 25
  politics of recognition in, 138–39, 140, 141, 161
  population of, 13
  subnational institutions of, 137, 139–41
  taking the challenge beyond, 265–67
  tequio in (*see* Tequio (Oaxaca))
  usos y costumbres in (*see* Usos y costumbres (Oaxaca))
  voting/elections in (*see* Voting/electoral systems (Oaxaca))
  women of (*see* Women, of Oaxaca)
  Yucatán compared with, 219, 220, 224, 227, 231
  Zapatista uprising in, 3
Ocotlán, Oaxaca, 154
Official multicultural policies (MCPs), 18–36. *See also* Futility thesis; Jeopardy thesis; Perversity thesis
Oil
  in Bolivia, 78, 80, 83
  in Campeche, 227–28
  in Ecuador, 29–30, 118, 124
  in Mexico, 161

Okin, Susan Moller, 32
Olivera, Oscar, 78
Organic Law of Intercultural Education (Ecuador), 122
Organic Law of the State Judicial Power (Chiapas), 51
Oruro, Bolivia, 100–101
Ospina, Pablo, 116
Ostrom, Elinor, 202
Otavalo, Ecuador, 111
Otero, Gerardo, 263

Pacari, Nina, 28, 115
Pachakutik movement/party (Ecuador), 4, 115, 116, 117, 135
PAN. *See* National Action Party
Panama, 19, 20(table)
Pando, Bolivia, 82, 96
Paraguay, 19, 20(table), 92
Pareto, V., 188
Parrado, Emilio A., 199
Partido Convergencia (PC) (Mexico), 152
Partidocracia, 76, 82, 99
Partido de Izquierda Revolucionario (PIR) (Bolivia), 93
Partido de la Revolución Democrática (Mexico). *See* Party of the Democratic Revolution
Partido Socialista Unificado de México, 158
Party of the Democratic Revolution (PRD) (Mexico)
  Chiapas and, 9
  Oaxaca and, 142, 152, 154, 251, 254
Party of the Institutional Revolution (PRI) (Mexico), 265
  Chiapas and, 48, 262, 263
  Oaxaca and, 9, 138, 140, 143, 150, 152, 154, 157–59, 251, 253, 254, 255, 258, 266
  Yucatán and, 220, 225–26
Party of the Mexican Revolution (PRM), 220
Paternalism, 9, 19, 222, 235
Patrón, Patricio, 223
Patron-agent exchanges, 248
Patron saint festivals, 6. *See also* Mayordomía
  mayors and, 170, 175
  migrants and, 193, 197, 202, 205, 206(figure), 208(table), 209, 211

Patujú flower, 102
Paz Zamora, Jaime, 106
PC. *See* Partido Convergencia
Peasant leagues (Yucatán), 226–28, 231
Peasants
  of Bolivia, 67, 92
  of Chiapas, 231, 260, 265
  of Oaxaca, 173, 175(table), 177, 180, 183–84, 187, 188, 249, 265
  of Peru, 13
  of Yucatán, 227, 230
Pelucones, 118
Permanent Committee for the Respect and Preservation of Maya Culture (Yucatán), 223, 226
"Permitted Indian." *See Indios permitidos*/permitted Indian
Peru, 11–12, 13, 19, 70
  multicultural policies in, 19, 20(table), 21
  women of, 33
Perversity thesis, 18–19, 22, 24–31
Petroleum. *See* Oil
Pinochet, Augusto, 137
Pinotepa de Don Luis, Oaxaca, 153
PIR. *See* Partido de Izquierda Revolucionario
Piristas, 93
Plan de Todos (Bolivia), 26
Pluralism, 156, 158
  autonomous institutions and, 261–64
  bringing to the academic debate, 265–67
  democratic, theory of, 188
  factionalism *vs.,* 248–49
Pluri-multi period (Bolivia), 26, 68, 71, 72, 77, 80, 83, 85n1
Plurinational Electoral Organ (Bolivia), 103
Plurinationality, 14, 29, 71, 75, 102, 112, 118–21, 126
Plurinomial (PR) electoral system, 104, 105
Pochutla, Oaxaca, 159
PODEMOS. *See* Poder Democrático y Social
Poder Democrático y Social (PODEMOS) (Bolivia), 96–98, 100, 108n5
Political class, theory of, 188
Political decentralization, 12
Political parties. *See also* individual parties
  Oaxaca elections and, 9, 150, 152–55, 159, 170
  quest for autonomy and, 9–11

Politics of recognition, 43
  in Chiapas, 43, 44, 58
  in Ecuador, 117
  in Latin America, 40, 44
  in Oaxaca, 136–39, 140, 141, 160–61
Politics of the leopard, 45
Politics of the roof laminate shingle, 15n3
Ponchos dorados, 118
Pongueaje, 93
Poot, Efraín, 232
Popular Assembly (Bolivia), 89, 93
Popular Participation law (Bolivia), 79, 80, 81, 82–83, 94–95
Populist multiculturalism, 25
Positive law, 232, 248–50
Postero, Nancy, 27, 113, 218, 235
Post-peasant perspective of transnationalism, 201
Potosí, Bolivia, 103
Poverty, 71, 73, 173, 177
Povinelli, Elizabeth, 24, 263
PPB-CN (Bolivia), 104, 107
PRD. *See* Party of the Democratic Revolution
Predatory rule, theory of, 195
Presidential decree 60 (Ecuador), 120
"Prestigious individual" theory, 188
PRI. *See* Party of the Institutional Revolution
Privatization of resources
  Bolivia and, 26, 36n4, 74–75, 77–78, 94
  Ecuador and, 112, 125
  Mexico and, 47–48
PRM. *See* Party of the Mexican Revolution
PRODEPINE. *See* Programa de Desarrollo de los Pueblos Indígenas y Negros del Ecuador
Programa de Desarrollo de los Pueblos Indígenas y Negros del Ecuador (PRODEPINE), 116
Promotores, 223, 239n16
Pro-Santa Cruz Committee. *See* Comité Pro-Santa Cruz
Public works (migrant-funded, Oaxaca), 194, 206, 207(figure), 208, 209, 210
Puebla, Mexico, 231, 265
Pueblo Viejo, Oaxaca, 251

Quebec, Canada, 260
Quechua, 11, 19, 26, 70, 71, 72, 97, 98(table), 102, 103

Quilombo communities, 34
Quintana Roo, Mexico, 221, 222, 224, 227, 265
Quintero, Rafael, 123, 124
Quispe, Felipe, 26, 27, 36n5, 68, 74, 77, 78, 94

Racism, 30, 81, 114, 122, 126–27
Radical Democracy in the Andes (Van Cott), 36
Ramírez, Victor, 234
Ramón, Galo, 119
Ramona, Comandanta, 32
Rancho Viejo, Oaxaca, 254
Rational choice theory, 201
Recognition politics. *See* Politics of recognition
Recondo, David, 45
Red Internacional de Indígenas Oaxaqueños (RIIO), 152
Reed, Nelson, 220
Regidor, 57
Regidor de hacienda, 178
Regino Montes, Adelfo, 3, 4
Regional model of multiculturalism, 18, 19
Regiónes Autónomas del Atlántico Sur y Norte (Nicaragua), 72
Reichert, Joshua, 198
Reinaga, Fausto, 74
Religion, 147–48, 247. *See also* Catholic Church; Non-Catholic minorities
Religious *cargos,* 257
  mayors and, 172, 174, 175–77, 180–82, 185, 186–88, 189
  migrants and, 203, 205, 206(figure), 208(table), 209, 211
  by municipal type, 180–82
  percentage of municipalities with, 170
  prestige offered by, 185, 186–88
Remittances (from migrants), 193, 197–98, 199, 201–2
Revolutionary Tupac Katari Movement (MRTK) (Bolivia), 74
RIIO. *See* Red Internacional de Indígenas Oaxaqueños
Rio Grande, Oaxaca, 254
Ríos, Viridiana, 256–57
Rosales González, Margarita, 227
Rosario, El (Oaxaca housing development), 150

Ruís, Nicolas, 32
Ruíz, Samuel, 220
Ruiz Ortiz, Ulises, 156–57
Rus, Jan, 263

Sala Regional Xalapa (of TEPJF), 249
Salazar, Pablo, 9
Salinas de Gortari, Carlos, 9, 47–48
San Andrés Accords (Mexico), 23, 43, 46, 48–50, 53
  failure to apply, 262, 266
  on self-determination, 54
  Yucatán and, 221, 224, 225, 230
San Andrés Cabeccera Nueva, Oaxaca, 159
San Andrés Solaga, Oaxaca, 149
San Andrés y Provedencia (Colombia), 72
San Baltazar Chichicapan, Oaxaca, 153
Sánchez, Consuelo, 58
Sánchez, Feliciano, 227
Sánchez, Tito, 226
Sánchez Botero, Ester, 265
Sánchez de Lozada, Gonzalo, 25–27, 69, 76–78, 81, 106
  constitutional multiculturalism and, 89, 91
  ouster of, 67, 88, 94
  relationship with gas and oil interests, 83
Sandoval, Luis, 79
San Felipe, Oaxaca, 254
San Gabriel, Oaxaca, 253
San Jerónimo Sosolá, Oaxaca, 248, 249–53, 254–55, 257
San José Sosolá, Oaxaca, 251, 252(table)
San Juan Bautista Guelache, Oaxaca, 248, 249, 253–55
San Juan Bosco Chuxnabán, Oaxaca, 148
San Juan Cancuc, Chiapas, 52
San Juan Chamula, Mexico, 10
San Juan Guelavía, Oaxaca, 8, 147
San Juan Juquila Mixe, Oaxaca, 148
San Juan Lalana, Oaxaca, 146
San Juan Mixtepec, Oaxaca, 152, 154
San Juan Pueblo Nuevo, Michoacán, 143
San Juan Sosolá, Oaxaca, 251, 252(table)
San Luis Potosí, Mexico, 221, 224
San Mateo, Oaxaca, 251
San Miguel Chimalapa, Oaxaca, 152, 164–65n29, 248, 249, 253–55
San Miguel Quetzaltepec, Oaxaca, 145, 148, 155, 156

San Miguel Tlacotepec, Oaxaca, 8
San Pablo Güilá, Oaxaca, 151
San Pablo Macuiltianguis, Oaxaca, 148–49
San Pedro Cajonos, Oaxaca, 149
San Pedro El Alto, Oaxaca, 143
San Pedro Ixlahuaca, Oaxaca, 160
San Sebastián Tutla, Oaxaca, 149–50
Santa Ana del Valle, Oaxaca, 6, 149
Santa Catarina Ixtepeji, Oaxaca, 151
Santa Catarina Minas, Oaxaca, 7
Santa Cruz, Bolivia, 30, 76, 79–82, 84, 96
Santa Cruz Youth Union (Bolivia). *See* Unión Juvenil Cruzenista
Santa Lucía del Camino, Oaxaca, 159
Santa Lucía Sosolá, Oaxaca, 251, 252(table)
Santa María Chilchotla, Oaxaca, 154
Santa María Petapa, Oaxaca, 159
Santa María Quiegolani, Oaxaca, 7, 146–47
Santa María Tejotepec, Oaxaca, 251, 252(table)
Santa María Yohueche, Oaxaca, 148
Santi, Marlon, 30, 112, 118
Santiago Amoltepec, Oaxaca, 145, 155, 156
Santiago Laollaga, Oaxaca, 159
Santiago Yaveo, Oaxaca, 151
Santos Reyes Nopala, Oaxaca, 159
Sawyer, Suzana, 35
Scott, James C., 204
Scribano, Adrián, 171
Secretaría de Asuntos Indígenas (Oaxaca), 156
Secretariat for Agrarian Reform (Mexico), 263
Secret ballots, 4, 57, 152, 249, 250, 251, 253, 255, 257
Self-determination, 41–43
    in Bolivia, 68, 72, 73
    in Chiapas, 53, 54–58
    in Colombia, 135
    in Ecuador, 118
    internal restrictions and, 46
    in Oaxaca, 140, 146, 171
    United Nations on, 41–42, 46
Selva, Chiapas, 51
Semitraditional municipalities (Oaxaca), 180–84, 185, 186, 188, 189
Shining Path, 12, 13
Silver mining, 81
Sindicatos, 71, 73–74, 84

Síndicos, 57, 143, 148, 178
    importance of, 163n13
    migrants as, 194, 205, 210–11
Social class, 68, 71, 92, 117
Socialism, 111–14. *See also* Communism
Socialist Party (Ecuador), 116, 119
Socialist Party (Mexico), 158
Socio Basque (Ecuador), 123
Socio Páramo (Ecuador), 123
Solís, Doris, 124
Sonnleitner, Willibald, 15, 266
Sorroza Polo, Carlos, 8, 15, 255
*Sousa, 140
Spain, 260
Spanish language
    in Bolivia, 71, 97, 102, 109n11
    in Ecuador, 120
    in Oaxaca, 173, 174, 184
Speed, Shannon, 32
State Indigenous Council (CIE) (Chiapas), 48
"Structures of alterity," 34
Stuart, J., 198, 200
Sucre, Bolivia, 88, 98–99, 100, 109n13
Sumak kawsay, 113, 127
Supreme Court (Ecuador), 28
Supreme Court (Mexico), 262
Supreme Court of Justice (Chiapas), 51
Suriname, 19, 20(table)
Survey of Oaxaca Mexico Customary Law Municipalities, 5
    on mayors, 8, 172–88
    on migrants, 194, 203–11
Sylva, Erika, 123, 124
System of Intercultural Bilingual Education (Ecuador), 112, 114

Tabasco, Mexico, 265
Tanetze de Zaragoza, Oaxaca, 155
Tapia, Luis, 25
Tarija, Bolivia, 82, 96
Taylor, J. Edward, 203–4
TCO. *See* Tierra Comunitaria de Origen
TEE. *See* Tribunal Estatal Electoral
Telegrafo, El, 123
Tenesaca, Delfin, 112
Teología india, 221
TEPJF. *See* Tribunal Electoral del Poder Judicial de la Federación

Tequio (Oaxaca), 6, 7, 11, 142, 143, 144, 150, 153
   defined, 163n9
   migrants and, 193, 194, 196, 202, 203, 204, 206(figure), 208(table), 209, 211, 212n1
   percentage of municipalities with, 170
Territory (indigenous), 46. *See also Ejidos*; Land rights and reform
   in Bolivia, 73, 75, 90, 102, 104
   in Ecuador, 23, 118–19, 120, 125
   in Oaxaca, 138, 205
Textitlán, Oaxaca, 143
Third Wave of democratization, 70, 73
Tierra Comunitaria de Origen (TCO) (Bolivia), 90, 95, 103, 105
Tilly, Charles, 70, 196
Tilo, Padre, 228–29
Tin mining, 13, 67–68, 81
TIPNIS. *See* Isiboro Sécure National Park and Indigenous Territory
Tituaña, Auqui, 117
Tiwanaku Manifesto, 74
Tlacochahuaya, Oaxaca, 154
Tlacolula, Oaxaca, 149, 154, 159
Tlalixtac de Cabrera, Oaxaca, 147
Tlaxcala, Mexico, 265
Torres, Juan José, 79, 93
Tourism, 227
Traditional medicine
   in Chiapas, 48–49, 53–54
   Maya, 222, 224
Traditional municipalities (Oaxaca), 180–84, 185, 186–90
Transnational Advocacy Networks (TANs), 218n2
Trejo, Guillermo, 266
Tribunal Electoral del Poder Judicial de la Federación (TEPJF) (Mexico), 145, 155, 247, 249, 250, 253, 254, 258, 262
Tribunal Estatal Electoral (TEE) (Oaxaca), 145, 150, 155, 160
Trinitario-Mojeño, 90
Turkey, 60
Twin covenants, 41–42

UJC. *See* Unión Juvenil Cruzenista
ULA. *See* Unión Liberal de Ayuntamientos
Uninomial districts (Bolivia), 95, 97, 103–4, 107, 108n6
Unión Juvenil Cruzenista (UJC) (Bolivia), 30, 82
Unión Liberal de Ayuntamientos (ULA), 142
United Nations (UN), 14, 41–42, 43, 46, 58, 59
United Nations Charter, 41
United Nations Convention against Genocide, 41
United Nations Decade of Indigenous Peoples, 21
United Nations Declaration on the Granting of Independence to Colonial Countries and Peoples, 41
United Nations Declaration on the Rights of Indigenous Peoples, 4, 22, 60n7, 121, 125, 135
United Nations Permanent Forum on Indigenous Issues, 218n1
United Nations Special Committee on Decolonization, 41
United States, 22, 43
   Bolivia and, 27, 30, 77, 78, 94
   Ecuador and, 115, 126
   Mexican immigration to, 7, 161, 193, 198, 201, 263
Universal Declaration of Human Rights (UDHR), 41
Universal suffrage, 4, 91, 253
Usos y costumbres, 23
Usos y costumbres (Bolivia), 72, 95, 101, 104, 107–8
Usos y costumbres (Chiapas), 50, 51, 52, 53–54
Usos y costumbres (Maya), 219, 222, 231, 235
Usos y costumbres (Oaxaca), 4, 5–6, 7–8, 9, 15, 45, 57, 136, 138, 141, 142, 143, 159, 160–61, 169–91, 221, 247–58, 266, 267
   annulment of elections, 145
   characteristics of system, 170
   conflicts diminished by, 262–64
   eligibility dispute in elections, 249–53
   ethnicization of, 144
   exclusions under, 146, 253–54
   federalism and, 139
   hypothesis on recognition of, 157–58
   migrants and, 149–50, 192–212 (*see also* Migrants (Oaxaca))
   party-based system compared with, 153–55

perversity thesis on, 25
pluralism *vs.* factionalism in, 248–49
positive law *vs.*, 248, 249, 250
survey of (*see* Survey of Oaxaca Mexico Customary Law Municipalities)
typology of mayors in, 171–90 (*see also* Mayors (Oaxaca))

Valencia, Juan Manuel, 225–26
Valladolid, Yucatán, 230, 231
Van Cott, Donna Lee, 5, 8, 18, 19, 25, 35, 36, 113, 116, 127, 217, 235
VanWey, Leah K., 201–2, 203, 204, 211
Vargas, Antonio, 28
Vatican Council, Second, 114
Vázquez Garcia, Verónica, 7
Velasco Alvarado, Juan, 19
Velásquez, Cristina, 175
Venezuela, 24, 29, 30, 112, 113, 114
 constitutional reforms in, 5
 multicultural policies in, 19, 20(table)
 racism in, 126–27
Veracruz, Mexico, 221, 265
Villa Díaz Ordaz, Oaxaca, 148, 149
Villarroel, Gualberto, 92–93
Villnueva Mukul, Eric, 227
Vista Hermosa, Oaxaca, 254
Viteri, Carlos, 118
Vote buying, 10, 152
Voting/electoral systems (Bolivia), 71, 81, 91–92, 95–98, 103–4, 105, 107–8
Voting/electoral systems (Mexico), 10, 260–61
Voting/electoral systems (Oaxaca), 4, 142–43, 145, 151, 152–55, 158, 159, 169–70, 247–59, 262–64
 eligibility dispute, 249–53
 end of unanimity in, 254–58
 exclusions in, 146, 253–54
 migrants and, 6, 148–50, 162, 193, 247, 258–59
 pluralism *vs.* factionalism in, 248–49
 political-party system, 9, 150, 152–55, 159, 170
 women and, 5, 7, 146–47, 193, 247, 257, 263, 265

Wade, Peter, 25, 34, 35
Walsh, Catherine, 119
Warisata, Bolivia, 78

Warren, Jonathan, 34
Washington consensus, 23, 80
Water wars
 in Bolivia, 26, 67, 77–78, 94
 in Ecuador, 111, 112, 118, 124, 125
Weisbrot, Mark, 79
Welfare system (Ecuador), 123–24
Weyland, Kurt, 126
Whites, 113, 114, 220
Willis, Eliza, 12
Wilson, Tamar Diana, 198
Wiphalas, 76, 101, 102
Wolf, Eric, 248
Women
 of Bolivia, 32
 of Chiapas, 32
 of Ecuador, 32, 119
 gender complementarity and, 32–33
 jeopardy thesis on, 19, 32–34
 Maya, 222
 of Oaxaca, 5, 7, 32, 146–47, 162, 172–73, 193, 247, 257, 263, 265
 of Peru, 33
World Bank, 21, 30, 45, 77–78, 116
World Social Forums, 118
Wright, Richard, 196, 204

Xalapa Regional Chamber of TEPJF, 249
XEPET (radio station), 230, 239n17
Xiú, Bernardo, 229
Xool, Baltazar, 232

Yanomami, 114
Yashar, Deborah, 33, 70, 226
Yucatán, Mexico, 13, 15, 217–45, 258, 259, 262, 265. *See also* Maya
 autonomy in, 5, 227, 235, 258, 259
 constitutional reforms and, 221–23, 225, 226, 232–33
 ethnic mobilization in, 226–31
 federal judicial reform and Indian law in, 233–34
 indigenous population of, 219–20, 238n5
 local justice in, 231–33
Yuracaré, 90

Zafra, Gloria, 7
Zambo, 114
Zamosc, León, 116

Zapatista National Liberation Army
(EZLN) (Mexico), 3, 4, 8, 10, 14, 23,
43, 135, 137, 138, 262, 263, 264, 265
constitutional multiculturalism and, 46,
48, 49, 53, 54, 56, 59
"imaginary" movement, 3, 15n2
internal contradictions in, 266
land reforms and, 9
Oaxaca and, 3
women leaders in, 32
Yucatán and, 221, 229, 234
Zapotecs, 146, 147, 161
Zedillo, Ernesto, 221
Zizek, Slavoj, 24